Democracy and Development

Is economic development conducive to political democracy? Does democracy foster or hinder material welfare? These two questions are examined by looking at the experiences of 135 countries between 1950 and 1990. Descriptive information, statistical analyses, and historical narratives are interwoven to gain an understanding of the dynamics of political regimes and their impact on economic development and other aspects of material welfare. The findings, several of them quite surprising, dispel any notion of a trade-off between democracy and development. Economic development does not tend to generate democracies, but democracies are much more likely to survive in wealthy societies. The type of political regime has no impact on the growth of total national income, and political instability affects growth only in dictatorships. Per capita incomes rise more rapidly in democracies because populations increase faster under dictatorships. In general, political regimes have greater effects on demography than on economics.

Adam Przeworski is Carroll and Milton Petrie Professor in the Department of Politics at New York University.

Michael E. Alvarez is Assistant Professor of Political Science at DePaul University.

José Antonio Cheibub is Assistant Professor of Political Science at Yale University.

Fernando Limongi is Associate Professor of Political Science at the University of São Paulo.

CAMBRIDGE STUDIES IN THE THEORY OF
DEMOCRACY

General Editor

ADAM PRZEWORSKI   New York University

OTHER BOOKS IN THE SERIES

Democracy and Development

Political Institutions and Well-Being in the World, 1950–1990

Adam Przeworski
New York University

Michael E. Alvarez
DePaul University

José Antonio Cheibub
Yale University

Fernando Limongi
University of São Paulo

CAMBRIDGE
UNIVERSITY PRESS

CAMBRIDGE UNIVERSITY PRESS

Cambridge, New York, Melbourne, Madrid, Cape Town, Singapore, São Paulo, Delhi

Cambridge University Press
32 Avenue of the Americas, New York, NY 10013-2473, USA

www.cambridge.org
Information on this title: www.cambridge.org/9780521793797

First published 2000
7th printing 2008

Printed in the United States of America

A catalog record for this publication is available from the British Library.

ISBN 978-0-521-79032-1 hardback
ISBN 978-0-521-79379-7 paperback

Contents

Contents

Tables and Figures

Figures

Acknowledgments

Because several of these chapters were circulated independently and were presented as papers at various conferences, they accumulated numerous comments. As a result, our intellectual debts are so extensive that we can no longer be sure to whom we owe which inspiration and which criticism. Hence, with a profound apology to all those who generously taught us economics, suggested questions to be studied, offered alternative explanations, or pointed out silly mistakes, we are unable to list them.

Much of the work on this project was done when we were all at the University of Chicago.

This project was supported in part by grants from the National Science Foundation (SES-9022605 and SES-9311793). Fernando Limongi was supported by a fellowship from the Fundacão de Amparo à Pesquisa do Estado de São Paulo (FAPESP).

Introduction

Questions

Is economic development conducive to political democracy? Does democracy foster or hinder material welfare? These have been central questions on intellectual and political agendas over the past fifty years, ever since the Atlantic Charter, signed by Churchill and Roosevelt in 1941, offered the "assurance that all men in all the lands might live out their lives in freedom from fear and want." For the first time in history, democracy and development, freedom from fear and from want, were conceived as the future of all the people in the world, not as the privilege of the "civilized" nations.

In some ways, these questions are badly formulated. Political regimes, however one thinks about them, are complex. They combine many institutional features that can have emergent effects and that may work at cross-purposes. They may, at the same time, encourage economic rationality but hinder economic initiative, grant governments the authority necessary to promote development but also allow them to evade popular control, and foster long-term thinking at the cost of short-term disasters, or vice versa. Development, in turn, is a multifaceted process of structural transformations, not only economic, that becomes manifest in the growth of income, productivity, consumption, investment, education, life expectancy, and employment – all that makes for a better life. But again, these good things do not necessarily go together, and they certainly do not go together for all. Average income and even consumption can grow at the cost of increasing unemployment, of growing inequality, of immiseration for large segments of the population, of degradation of the environment. Hence, the question of the relationship between democracy and development encompasses more specific issues concerning the impacts of particular features of political regimes on various aspects of economic performance.

Nevertheless, asking these questions in their general form is inescapable. Following World War II, various dictatorial regimes appealed to the masses of the poor by presenting themselves as forces for progress, as agents of development, as shortcuts to modernity. Their claims to legitimacy, their appeals to loyalty, were that they were uniquely capable of mobilizing resources and energies to break the chains of poverty, to build a better future, to lead their respective countries to affluence, power, and prestige. Whatever their particular ideological stripes, such regimes plastered walls and minds with images that pictured how everything – homes, schools, hospitals, armies – would grow in the radiant future. They were to eradicate poverty, generate affluence, enable their countries to assume their rightful places among the powers of the world, and by the example of their own success convert others to the righteousness of their dictatorial ways. They were always the "tigers": The most rapidly growing country in the world in the 1950s, at least if we are to believe its own statistics, was communist Romania. The economic miracle of the early 1970s was the military-ruled Brazil. The economic tigers of the 1980s were the dictatorships of Singapore, South Korea, and Taiwan. In the 1990s the leader was China. And those spectacular successes repeatedly sowed doubt in the minds of even committed democrats: whether or not development did indeed require order and discipline, whether or not rationality would flow from authority, whether or not democrats could continue to trust that their own ways would be capable of lifting the masses of the world's poor from their plight.

Around 1960, when decolonialization was giving birth to many "new nations," in an international context in which communist regimes still appeared to be developing impressively, many scholars and politicians concluded that the perceived economic effectiveness of dictatorships was simply a fact of life, one that should be confronted courageously by admitting that democracy was a luxury that could be afforded only after the hard task of development had been accomplished. To cite just a few typical voices of the time, Galenson (1959: 3) claimed that "the more democratic a government is, . . . the greater the diversion of resources from investment to consumption." De Schweinitz (1959) argued that if the less-developed countries "are to grow economically, they must limit democratic participation in political affairs." La Palombara (1963: 57) thought that "if economic development is the all-embracing goal, the logic of experience dictates that not too much attention can be paid to the trappings of democracy." Dictatorships were needed to generate development: As Huntington and Nelson (1976: 23) put it, "political participation must be held down, at least temporarily, in order to promote economic development."[1]

The world thus faced, it seemed, a trade-off between democracy and development. Yet the future was not so bleak for democracy. Whereas dictatorships, even though despicable, were needed to generate development, they would self-destroy as a result of their own success. According to the dominant canon of the time, democracy would naturally emerge after a society had undergone necessary economic and social transformations. The basic assumption of modernization theory was that societies undergo one general process, of which democratization is but the final facet. Hence, the emergence of democracy would be an inexorable consequence of development. Because in that view dictatorships would generate development, and development would lead to democracy, the best route to democracy was seen as a circuitous one. The policy prescriptions that resulted from that mode of thinking rationalized support for dictatorships, at least those that were "capable of change," that is, anti-communist ones.

Communism now appears dead, and the idea that it ever portended the future seems ludicrous, albeit in omniscient retrospect. And democracy has been discovered to have many economic virtues. It is claimed that democracy encourages investment by safeguarding property rights, promotes allocational efficiency by allowing a free flow of ideas, and prompts governments to choose good policies by imposing the threat of electoral sanctions. Yet doubts remain. For many, Pinochet's Chile was the paradigm of successful economic reforms, and the economic success of authoritarian China is the model for the new Russia. Even though democratic ideals are nourishing political forces from Argentina to Mongolia, the allure of a "strong government," "insulated from pressures," guided by technical rationality, capable of imposing order and discipline, continues to seduce. Whether in the case of the Tiananmen Square massacre or the *autogolpe* of President Alberto

---

[1] Still in 1975, impressed by the growth of the communist countries, Huntington and Dominguez (1975: 60) observed that "the interest of the voters generally [leads] parties to give the expansion of personal consumption a higher priority vis-à-vis investment than it would receive in a non-democratic system. In the Soviet Union, for instance, the percentage of GDP devoted to consumption was driven down from 65% in 1928 to 52% in 1937. It is most unlikely that a competitive party system would have sustained a revolution from above like this."

Fujimori in Peru, international financial institutions, as well as governments in the developed countries, are still willing to close their eyes to violations of democratic rights and even human rights in deference to the purported economic effectiveness of dictatorships. A myopic public has to be protected from itself; economic reforms must be carried out before the people have time to react. This is still a popular belief.

Thus, whether well formulated or not, the question of the relative merits of political regimes continues to evoke intellectual analysis as well as political passion. Much of the appeal of dictatorships stems from the fact that at various moments they have seemed to offer "the best practice." The "tigers" have tended to be dictatorships. But are dictatorships necessarily tigers? The list of disasters generated by authoritarianism is long and tragic. Even the economic collapse of communism pales in comparison with the destruction caused by dictatorships in many African countries, the squandering of resources in the Middle East, or the havoc spawned by military governments in Central America. For every developmental miracle, there have been several dictatorships that have engaged in grandiose projects that have ended in ruin, or else dictatorships that have simply stolen and squandered. In turn, the record of performance among the democracies, which has featured examples of spectacular growth (notably in Western Europe until the mid-1970s) as well as of rapid deterioration (as in Latin America in the 1980s), has not reached the extremes seen among the dictatorships. Hence, to assess the impacts of political regimes, we must examine their full record, not just the best performances.

We want to know the effects of political regimes on the material well-being of the people who live under them. But well-being, like its cognates, such as welfare, utility, ophelimity, or simply happiness, is an elusive concept. It combines objective and subjective elements: the resources and capabilities that enable people to lead the lives they choose, the choices they actually make, what Sen (1988) calls "functionings," as well as their evaluations of their lives. Well-being entails being able to work and to consume, being sufficiently educated to know what choices one can make in life, being able to choose the number of children one wants, being able to live a healthy life. But whereas the conditions that people face independently of their actions can be measured objectively, well-being is difficult to assess in interpersonal terms when these conditions do afford people the opportunity to make choices. To borrow an example from Sen (1988: 18), one may starve because one does not have enough to eat or because one is fasting. Conditions per se are often difficult to distinguish from the consequences of the choices that people make under those conditions.

Nevertheless, though well-being is difficult to evaluate, destitution is manifest (Dasgupta 1993). Even such a rough measure as income can tell us whether or not people are materially deprived. A life without adequate food and shelter, threatened by disease, condemned to ignorance, is a life of destitution: The most subjectivist economist needs but a few hours to determine that what a poor village needs is clean water and a school.

We are willing to make judgments about the degrees of well-being that people experience under different political regimes because we do not believe that preferences about those aspects we study are endogenous to regimes. Whether living under dictatorship or democracy, people do not want to consume less, live shorter lives, get less education, or see their children die. Yet even if preferences were endogenous (e.g., suppose that mothers would happily offer their sons as cannon fodder for dictators), such preferences could not justify normative judgments unless they were informed by the actual experience of the alternatives.

What, then, are the observable indications of well-being? We do not neglect the intrinsic value of political and civic liberties inherent in democracy. As Dasgupta (1993: 47) argues, the view that the poor do not care about the freedoms associated with democracy "is a piece of insolence that only those who don't suffer from their lack seem to entertain" (see also Sen 1994a). Yet our question is whether or not these liberties, those necessary for people to freely choose their rulers, affect well-being in other realms. This is why we refer to "material" well-being. We are interested in the material consequences of political regimes.

Dasgupta (1993: 76) proposes that, besides political liberties, one can think of well-being along three dimensions: income and all it affords, health, and education. With all the innumerable caveats, income is simply the best overall indicator of the choices people enjoy in their lives. It is in many ways far from perfect: Even if its components were weighted at competitive market prices, those prices would necessarily ignore the capacitating effects of certain forms of consumption, as well as the very capacity to make choices that income affords.[2] Yet, at least when it is accurately computed, more income is better than less: Although income is only a means to well-being, it determines what bundles of consumption a person can choose.

One way, therefore, to assess the effects of regimes on well-being is to examine their impacts on economic growth, something about which people all around the world care.[3] The monetary value of consumption, as distinct from total income (which also includes savings), is an alternative measure. We shall ask under which regime economies develop faster, which is more likely to generate miracles and which disasters, which is more likely to ensure that development will be sustained, which is more apt to exploit advantageous conditions, and which is more adept at coping with adversities. We shall examine the impacts of political regimes on the growth of per capita income and per capita consumption, on productivity, on investment, and on the growth of employment. We shall also attempt to say something about income distribution, about poverty, and about the material security that these regimes generate, but given the paucity and poor quality of the data, there is little we can report with certainty.

Yet people's lives under democracy and dictatorship need not be the same even if those people have the same incomes. As Sen (1993: 40) put it, if "the economic success of a nation is judged only by income and by other traditional indicators of opulence and financial soundness, as it so often is, the important goal of well-being is missed." Birth rates, death rates, fertility, infant mortality, life expectancy, and school enrollment rates conjure an image of what one can expect of life under either regime. Several of these indicators focus specifically on the conditions of women.

These are, then, the aspects of material well-being we examine. Our approach is largely inductive: We consider almost all of the countries that existed at any time between 1950 and 1990 and classify their political regimes. We then examine why so many rich countries enjoy

[2] For a discussion of income as an indicator of well-being, see Dasgupta (1993: chap. 7). The UNDP *Human Development Report* provides an index that aggregates several indicators into a single measure of "human development" (HDI). Although that may be a useful summary measure, we prefer to study its components separately.

[3] Average satisfaction with life rises steeply as the per capita incomes of countries increase from low levels. The same is true of the relationship between income and life satisfaction observed among individuals within a given country. In turn, it appears that the average satisfaction level does not increase as the average per capita income of a country increases over time, but this latter observation is based on countries that already have high incomes. For a recent summary of these findings and an interpretation, see Frank (1997).

democracy and so very few poor countries do. Armed with knowledge of how political regimes rise and fall, we compare their performances in different realms.

Many of the patterns we have discovered are surprising. Indeed, our findings contradict so many preconceived notions that at times we have a feeling that we are digging a cemetery for old theories. Some findings are so puzzling that they leave us speechless. Others lend themselves to rival explanations that cannot be evaluated with the available data. All these findings do call for explanations, and we hope that others will try to understand them. But our own posture is largely minimalist: We simply try to establish what one should reasonably believe about the experience of the forty years we examine, the "facts."

Methods

Democracy and dictatorship constitute different ways of organizing political lives: of selecting rulers, processing conflicts, making and implementing public decisions. We want to know if these ways make a difference for people's lives. And this means that we need to observe democracies and dictatorships wherever they are, under the full range of conditions under which they have existed. To speak of "democracy," one must reach beyond the experience of the industrialized countries. Democracies breathe also in countries where it does not snow: Brazil, Mauritius, Jamaica. Indeed, when we look for democratic regimes that existed during any time between 1950 and 1990, we find two-thirds of them in the less-developed countries. So if we want to know about the impact of "democracy," rather than of snow, we must study all democracies we can find, wherever they are.

Yet knowledge of all the democracies that ever existed is not enough to ascertain the impact of democracy. Because this methodological point is crucial for all that follows, we need to explain the logic of our analysis. We are not the first to study the impact of regimes on economic performance. Indeed, there have been at least forty empirical studies of this subject, the first dating as far back as 1966. Yet if we think that we have something new to say, it is because we believe that all of those studies employed a faulty methodology and drew invalid conclusions.

Our aim is to assess the effects of political regimes on material well-being. How can we go about it? Take the growth of per capita income. We observe Chile in 1985 and discover that its regime was authoritarian and that its per capita income grew at the rate of 2.87 percent.

But what we want to know is whether Chile would have grown faster or slower had its regime been a democracy in 1985. And the information we have does not suffice to answer this question. Unless we know what would have been the growth of Chile in 1985 had it been democratic, how can we tell if it would have grown faster or slower than it did under dictatorship?

Had we observed in 1985 a Chile that was simultaneously a dictatorship and a democracy, we would have the answer. But that is not possible. Still, there seems to be a way out: We could look for some case that was exactly like 1985 Chile in all respects other than its regime and, perhaps, its rate of growth, and we could match this country with Chile. We could then compare the growth of dictatorial Chile in 1985 with the performance of its democratic match and draw a conclusion.

But if the fact that Chile was a dictatorship in 1985 had some causes in common with the fact that it grew at the rate observed, then a case that matches Chile in all respects other than the regimes and the rate of growth may not be found. Among all the observed cases, there will be observations without a match, or, stated differently, we will not be able to observe dictatorships under the same conditions as democracies. And this means that we will not be able to distinguish whether the observed differences in economic performance are due to regimes or to the circumstances under which they found themselves. Conclusions based on observed cases, even on all that can be observed, will be then invalid.

Imagine the following thought (or computer) experiment. Assume that the expected rate of growth is the same for all countries regardless of their regimes and that the growth of each country during each year differs from the mean only by a random error. Assume further that democracies are more likely to die, that is, to become dictatorships, when economic conditions are bad. Then it will turn out that, on the average, countries observed as democracies will grow faster than dictatorships. Regression, a conditional mean, will show the same: The coefficient on regimes will show a difference in favor of democracies. And because we have just assumed that the rate of growth does not vary across regimes, the observed difference will be due purely to the bias caused by the non-random selection of regimes. The inference that democracy promotes growth will be thus fallacious: We will observe this difference because democracies disappeared whenever they faced economic crises while dictatorships survived them, not because regimes made a difference for growth. Under these conditions, relying exclusively on the observed values will lead us astray. Our inferences will suffer from "selection bias."

The lesson is that appearances can be misleading. Comparing means of the observed cases or performing standard regression on these observations may lead to invalid conclusions. In the presence of non-random selection, the observed differences are due at least in part to the conditions under which the observations were generated and not to effects of regimes. Whenever observations are not selected randomly, inferences based on observed cases may yield inconsistent and biased estimates of the effect of being in particular states (institutions, policies) on outcomes (performance). This much is now standard statistical wisdom. Yet the implications of this failure are profound: We can no longer use the standard model of induction to make valid inferences from the observed to the unobserved cases.

There are several ways in which such a bias may arise. To take one example, democracies may be more likely to be found in countries that are already wealthy, and, in turn, such countries may systematically develop slower. This is a case of an exogenous selection on observables: Some observable factor, say per capita income, affects both the selection of regimes and the economic growth of countries. We have already provided an example in which selection is observable but endogenous: Say that democracies are more likely than dictatorships to fall when they face adverse economic conditions. Yet there may be also common causes of regime selection and economic development that we are unable to observe: Imagine that if a country happens to have an enlightened leadership, it is more likely both to have a democratic regime and to develop.

The world around us is not generated randomly. The world we observe is a result of actions of people pursuing their ends. It nurtures successes and eliminates failures. These processes are systematic, and so are their effects. The search for randomness is futile; we must proceed differently. The question is how.

To cope with the non-random nature of our observations, we revert to counterfactuals. To evaluate institutions, to assess their impact, we must ask what the outcomes would have been if other institutions had been observed under the same conditions. And if their selection is not random, these institutions are not observable under the same conditions. Hence, a recourse to counterfactuals is unavoidable. To cite Tetlock and Belkin (1996), "counterfactual reasoning is a prerequisite for any learning from history."

To correct for non-random selection, we use the observations we have to generate the counterfactuals we lack. To make such inferences, we study the process by which observations are selected into particular states, that is, the rise and fall of the particular regimes. Then we revert to an artifice: a distribution from which the observed and the unobserved cases were generated. Having assumed the population distribution and having identified the rule by which regimes are selected, we can do the rest: use the actual observations to make inferences about their counterfactual pairs, compare the outcomes, and arrive at a conclusion about the impact of regimes. And this is what we do.

Plan

This methodology underlies the organization of the book. Even though our primary question concerns the impact of democracy on development, more precisely of political regimes on material well-being, in order to study this question we must first learn how countries happen to be living under particular regimes – the impact of development on democracy.

Obviously, our preliminary task is to define "democracy" and "dictatorship" and to classify the observed regimes into these categories. Although several classifications of regimes, covering different periods and sets of countries, are now available, they can be improved by (1) a better grounding in political theory, (2) exclusive reliance on observables rather than on subjective judgments, (3) an explicit distinction between systematic and random errors, and (4) more extensive coverage. In Chapter 1, we develop a classification of political regimes guided by these objectives. This may appear to be the crucial step, because everything that follows hinges upon it. But even if regime classification has been the subject of some controversies, alternative definitions of "democracy" give rise to almost identical classifications of the actual observations. Our own classification, though more extensive than most, is no exception. It differs little from all others with which we could compare it. Hence, it turns out that in the end little depends on the way we classify regimes. If they were available for the same sample, other classifications would have generated the same results.

Once the regimes have been classified, we need to understand their dynamic. In particular, we must examine whether or not the rise and fall of political regimes have something to do with factors that also affect economic performance. We already know that if the same factors, whether or not we can observe them, affect both the selection of regimes and their performance, we must take this fact into account when studying the impact of regimes on performance.

We are thus led to reopen the problematic inaugurated by Lipset (1959, 1960) and subjected to innumerable empirical analyses since then. In Chapter 2, we ask first whether or not the incidence of democratic regimes is related to the level of development in those countries. Then we distinguish whether this relation is due to the fact that democracies are more likely to emerge as a result of economic development or only are more likely to survive when a country is already affluent. Having examined the impact of economic factors, we bring into the analysis a whole host of other considerations, such as the international political climate, the political histories of the particular countries, and their social conditions. Our purpose is to predict as well as we can which regime a country has had at a particular time, that is, to identify what we earlier called the "selection rule."

Once we know this rule, we proceed to the analysis of the impact of political regimes on material well-being. In Chapter 3, we study the impact of regimes on the growth of total income, total consumption, per worker output, investment, labor force, and the functional distribution of income. Armed with knowledge of the selection rule, we isolate the effect of regimes from the effects of the conditions under which these regimes find themselves. Because we discover that regimes have different effects in poorer and in wealthier countries, we then analyze these groups of countries separately.

Whereas the question whether or not regimes affect economic growth is controversial, the assertion that political instability thwarts economic growth seems to be almost consensual. But "instability" turns out to be a muddled notion; distinctions are needed. In Chapter 4, we examine the impacts of past, current, and expected instability on economic growth, separately under democracy and dictatorship.

In Chapter 5, we extend the analysis to demographic aspects of well-being. This is not a topic we intended to treat when we planned the book; we were driven to it serendipitously by the logic of analysis. Many, perhaps most, students of economic growth take as the dependent variable the rate of growth of income per capita. Yet whereas per capita rather than the aggregate income is what matters for individual welfare, per capita income is a result of two distinct processes: the growth of total output and the growth of population. Hence, we reasoned, we should examine them separately. To understand population growth, we study the effects of regimes on birth rates and death rates, fertility, and life expectancy. Once we assess the impact of regimes on

11

population, we return to study their effect on the growth of per capita incomes.

Because technical, typically statistical issues are entailed in many of the analyses, all the chapters include appendixes in which our methods are explained and additional tests are offered. Two general appendixes follow the text. Appendix I presents a general model of selection that organizes the entire analysis. Appendix II is a listing of variables and the sources from which they were derived.

We will not reveal our conclusions here; an impatient reader can flip the pages. We will disclose only this: Whenever regimes do make a difference, lives under dictatorships are miserable. The Churchillian view may be not enough, but it is accurate. Democracies are far from perfect, but they are better than all the alternatives.

Chapter One
Democracies and Dictatorships

Introduction

To study systematically the origins and the consequences of political regimes, we need first to determine what regime each country has had during each period of its history. This is a complicated and irredeemably controversial undertaking. Although "democracy" and "dictatorship" are concepts of everyday usage, the intuitions we associate with them are not always sufficient to determine that a particular country operated according to one or the other at a given time. Thus we must formalize these concepts in terms of rules that can be decisively and reliably applied to the observable aspects of national histories. And once we have such rules, we must apply them. Any such procedure necessitates going back and forth between conceptual analysis and historical observation. Closure is difficult to reach: In some cases, history simply has not generated the information called for by the rules, and we must accept the fact that there will be systematic errors. Other cases are so idiosyncratic that we must accept the fact that they have to be treated as random errors. Nevertheless, although no classification can be free of errors, the encouraging lesson is that independent endeavors by different researchers have led to very similar results.

Although several classifications of regimes, covering different periods and sets of countries, are now available, they can, in our view, be improved by (1) a better grounding in political theory, (2) exclusive reliance on observables, rather than on subjective judgments, (3) an explicit distinction between systematic and random errors, and (4) more extensive coverage. Thus, the purpose of this chapter is to develop a classification of political regimes guided by these objectives.

This chapter is organized as follows: The first section covers conceptual issues. The second section spells out the three basic rules we use to classify regimes. The third section focuses on the treatment of systematic errors and offers an additional rule that applies to a particular class of cases. The fourth section summarizes these rules and shows their effects on regime classification. The fifth section considers distinctions among democratic regimes and among authoritarian regimes. The sixth section enumerates some criteria we did not include. The seventh and eighth sections describe the results of applying our rules to historical observations of 141 countries between 1950 (or the year of independence) and 1990. Appendix 1.1 compares our approach with alternative measures. Appendix 1.2 lists the regimes by country and period. Appendix 1.3 provides some background information on regime transitions. Finally, Appendix 1.4 describes a somewhat smaller data set, our "short" data set, which is used in the remaining part of this book.

Democracy and Dictatorship

Our purpose is to classify the political regime observed in each country during each year either as a democracy or as a dictatorship, a term we use interchangeably with "authoritarian regime." Although we later distinguish different types of democracies and dictatorships, our basic classification is dichotomous.

Our general stance is minimalist. Perusing the innumerable definitions, one discovers that "democracy" has become an altar on which everyone hangs his or her favorite *ex voto*.[1] Almost all normatively desirable aspects of political life, and sometimes even of social and economic life, are credited as definitional features of democracy: representation, accountability, equality, participation, dignity, rationality, security, freedom – the list goes on. Indeed, according to many definitions, the set of true democracies is an empty set. And from an analytical point of view, lumping all good things together is of little use. The typical research problem is to examine the relationships among them. We want to know if holding repeated elections induces govern-

---

[1] To cite Macpherson (1966: 1): "Democracy used to be a bad word. Everybody who was anybody knew that democracy, in its original sense of rule by the people or government in accordance with the will of the bulk of the people, would be a bad thing – fatal to individual freedom and to all graces of civilized living. That was the position taken by pretty nearly all men of intelligence from the earliest historical times down to about a hundred years ago. Then, within fifty years, democracy became a good thing."

mental accountability, if participation generates equality, if freedom imbues political systems with rationality. Hence, we want to define "democracy" narrowly.

Three major distinctions dominate modern political thought concerning forms of government.[2] Montesquieu's legacy (1995 [1748]) is the distinction between limited regimes and despotic regimes. Kelsen's contribution (1945), going back to Rousseau and Kant, was to distinguish between "autonomy" (systems in which norms are determined by those to whom they apply) and "heteronomy" (systems in which the legislators are distinct from those who are subject to the laws). Finally, Schumpeter's innovation (1942) was to emphasize competition, or, to borrow Dahl's term (1971), which we prefer, "contestation," as the essential feature of democracy.

We focus on contestation. Our purpose is to distinguish between (1) regimes that allow some, even if limited, regularized competition among conflicting visions and interests and (2) regimes in which some values or interests enjoy a monopoly buttressed by the threat or the actual use of force. Thus "democracy," for us, is a regime in which those who govern are selected through contested elections. This definition has two parts: "government" and "contestation."

In no regime are all governmental offices filled by elections. Outside of classical Greece, generals, who are public officials, have never been elected. Judges rarely are. What is essential in order to consider a regime as democratic is that two kinds of offices be filled, directly or indirectly, by elections: the chief executive office and the seats in the effective legislative body.

Moreover, in a democracy, the offices that are being filled by contested elections grant their occupants the authority to exercise governance free of the legal constraint of having to respond to a power not constituted as a result of the electoral process. Thus, governmental responsibility either directly to voters or to a parliament elected by them is a defining feature of democracy. If we were to use only contested elections as the criterion, we would date the beginnings of democracy in many Western European countries to the period in which governments still were not autonomous, not independent of the crown, well before World War I. Yet, whenever that was the last step in the process of democratization, and in Western Europe most often it was, we date the advent of democracy to the time of transfer of governmental responsibility from the crown (or a non-elected upper chamber)

---

[2] See Bobbio (1989: 100–25, and chap. 4).

to the parliament. Thus we date democracy in Great Britain to 1911 (Dahl 1990), and in Germany to 1919.

Until the early years of this century, the struggle for democracy concerned primarily suffrage. In most countries, democracy emerged only gradually, in a sequence of steps. Typically, what happened first was that legislatures, elected on a nonpartisan basis and under highly restricted suffrage, divided along partisan lines and began to contest elections on a partisan basis. Then there followed extensions of political rights, which were sometimes very gradual, as in Norway or Chile, and at times instantaneous, as in Finland in 1906. In contrast, in those countries that have only recently confronted the eventuality of having to establish democratic institutions, suffrage is not an issue: It is taken for granted that it will be "universal."[3] Neither is governmental responsibility an issue.[4] In the recent cases, the only focus of conflicts has been contestation: whether or not divergent political forces would be able to compete for governmental offices and to assume office if they won elections.

Contestation occurs when there exists an opposition that has some chance of winning office as a consequence of elections. We take Przeworski's dictum that "democracy is a system in which parties lose elections" (1991: 10) quite literally: Whenever in doubt, we classify as democracies only those systems in which incumbent parties actually did lose elections. Alternation in office constitutes prima facie evidence of contestation. In most nineteenth-century Latin American countries, the incumbent presidents, even if they could not be reelected, controlled their succession. We consider such regimes democratic only when that system no longer functioned, when the opposition won an election and assumed office.

Contestation entails three features: (1) ex-ante uncertainty, (2) ex-post irreversibility, and (3) repeatability.

By "ex-ante uncertainty" we mean that there is some positive probability that at least one member of the incumbent coalition will lose in a particular round of elections. Uncertainty is not synonymous with

---

[3] The quotation marks are needed because the very notion of "universal" suffrage is a matter of convention. Suffrage was "universal" in Europe before the voting qualification was lowered from 21 to 18 years of age, and it is now "universal" at 18, rather than 16, 14, or 12. And "universal" is in turn defined relative to "citizen," itself a legally regulated notion. Immigrants often do not have the right to vote in national elections even if they have lived in a country for a long time, and in several Western European countries they constitute more than 8% of the adult population.

[4] Except in Western Samoa.

unpredictability: The probability distribution of electoral chances is typically known. All that is necessary for outcomes to be uncertain is that it be possible for some incumbent party to lose.[5] The best illustration of such uncertainty is the surprise expressed by an editorial in the Chilean right-wing newspaper, *El Mercurio*, in the aftermath of Salvador Allende's victory in the first round of the presidential elections of 1970: "No one expected that a marxist candidate could win elections through a universal, secret, bourgeois franchise." The franchise may have been "bourgeois," the chances skewed, and the victory of a Marxist candidate may have been known to be unlikely. But it was possible. The eventual outcome was not certain ex ante.

This feature of democracies has practical consequences. Most people think that Argentina under President Arturo Illia (1963–66) was democratic, even though the largest party in the country was prohibited from competing in the elections of July 1963. In turn, most agree that Mexico is not democratic, even though no party is legally banned from contesting elections. The reason is that Illia won narrowly, with 26.2 percent of votes cast, and he could have lost. In contrast, in Mexico it was certain that the Partido Revolucionario Institucional (PRI) would win.

By "ex-post irreversibility" we mean the assurance that whoever wins election will be allowed to assume office. The outcomes of elections must be irreversible under democracy even if the opposition wins. In 1929, the dictator of El Salvador, General Romero, announced that his country was about to join the family of civilized nations by celebrating the first free and honest election. He issued a *decreto-ley* that specified when the elections would take place, who would be qualified to vote, what the ballots would look like, when the polling places would be open, and so forth. The last point declared that "Army contingents will be stationed in the polling places in case the Opposition wins." That was not a democratic election.

---

[5] A strong notion of uncertainty would require that there be some chance that the major member of a coalition might find itself out of office as the result of the next election; a weak notion would extend to any member of the incumbent coalition. Under some conditions, changes of minor partners may be considered inconsequential: Italy under Christian Democratic domination may be a case in point. But in other cases, the electoral fates of minor parties can affect the orientation of a government: Israel and Germany are the relevant cases here. We have opted for the weak version: We consider any change of the governing coalition as alternation. Moreover, we do not want to imply that all alternations result directly from elections. In several countries – Poland between 1919 and 1926 is an example – a government has changed between opposing parties without an election intervening and the new government has remained in office as a result of the subsequent election.

The practical consequence of this feature is to exclude sham elections as well as periods of liberalization. Liberalization is typically intended by dictatorial regimes to be a controlled opening of the political space. When it fails, that is, when the opposition does win, a clampdown sometimes follows. Hence, there is no certainty that the opposition will be able to celebrate its victory.

The final feature of contestation is that elections must be repeated. Whoever wins the current round of elections cannot use office to make it impossible for the competing political forces to win next time. Democracy, as Linz (1984) put it, is government *pro tempore*. All political outcomes must be temporary: Losers do not forfeit the right to compete in the future, to negotiate again, to influence legislation, to pressure the bureaucracy, or to seek recourse to courts. Even constitutional provisions are not immutable; rules, too, can be changed according to rules.

The practical consequence of this last feature is that we should reserve judgment about elections, since an electoral victory may serve only to establish an authoritarian rule. This has been true in several African countries following independence. Unless the losers are given political guarantees that their ability to contest future elections will be protected, the mere fact that elections have been held does not suffice to qualify the regime as democratic. Only if the losers are allowed to compete, win, and assume office is a regime democratic.

Throughout this discussion, we have focused on democracy. We treat dictatorship simply as a residual category, perhaps better denominated as "not democracy." Our procedure is to establish rules that will disqualify a particular regime as democratic, without worrying about the nature of the regimes eliminated in this manner. Only then do we introduce some features that distinguish among different non-democratic regimes.

Operational Rules: Filling Offices by Contested Elections

Following Cardoso (1979: 38), as well as O'Donnell and Schmitter (1986: 73), by "regime" we mean the system of relations between the civil society and the state. A regime is a system of rules and practices that determine who has political rights, how they can be exercised, and with what effects for the control over the state. Hence, even if dictators succeed one another, the regime, in our sense of the term, remains the same as long as it remains a dictatorship. Thus, when General Viola overthrows General Videla, we consider the entire period as one dictatorship, rather than as "Videla" and "Viola" regimes. And even in those rare cases when the basic democratic institutions are transformed without a break in legality, as in France in 1958, we still consider each of them as a single "democratic regime."

Democracy is a regime in which government offices are filled by contested elections. The first part of this definition is easy to operationalize: it is relatively simple to observe which offices, if any, are filled as a result of elections. But whether or not these elections are contested, in the sense defined earlier, is not always apparent. The existence of more than one independent party is a sine qua non of contestation, but it may not be sufficient.

We next specify the rules we use to classify regimes: first those that are applied to assess whether or not the relevant offices were filled via elections, then those that are used to assess whether or not elections were contested.[6] Our rules are the following:

Rule 1: The chief executive must be elected.

The "chief executive" may be the president, the prime minister, or, in rare cases, a collegial body. Following Banks (1996), we define as the "chief executive" the occupant of the office formally designated as that of the head of government, thus excluding *éminences grises*: strongmen who effectively rule their countries but do not occupy a formal position.[7]

For a regime to be qualified as democratic, the executive must be directly or indirectly elected in popular elections and must be responsible only directly to voters or to a legislature elected by them. Indirect elections qualify as popular only if the electors are themselves elected. Elections by bodies that are themselves nominated do not qualify as popular elections.

Rule 2: The legislature must be elected.

The legislature can be a congress, an assembly, or a parliament. Only the lower house is considered. A constituent assembly that does not have ordinary legislative powers is not considered a legislature.

---

[6] The information about elections is based on Banks (1996), revised and updated.

[7] Such as Deng Tsao Ping, whose only formal position for many years was president of the Chinese Bridge Association. Banks sometimes considers first secretaries of the Communist Party as chief executives, while at other times he takes presidents and prime ministers as chief executives in communist regimes. We could not discover what rules he used, and we took occupants of the formal office as chief executives.

Our rule is that the legislature must be elected for a regime to qualify as democratic.

Rule 3: There must be more than one party.

In some cases, there were no parties: Either there were no elections or elections were conducted but all political parties were banned. In other cases, there was only one party. We consider such regimes authoritarian.[8]

By "party" we mean an independent list of candidates presented to voters in elections. In communist Poland, for example, three parties and a number of Catholic groups were represented in the Sejm, but until June 1989 voters were offered only one list: a National Front or Patriotic Front or whatever front it was called at the moment. Hence, in cases where the share of seats held by the major party in the legislature was less than 100 percent we checked to see if there was more than one list in legislative elections. For example, although the ruling Vanguard of the Malagasy Revolution (Arema) did not control all the seats in the parliament in Madagascar after 1976, according to Freedom House (1992: 318), "Until March of 1990, when a High Constitutional Court decree permitted multi-partyism, political associations had to operate within the FNDR as the nation's sole legal political entity." The FNDR (National Front of the Malagasy Revolution) was thus the only list offered to voters – one party by our definition.

Applying this rule, we classified as dictatorships all regime-years during which legislatures were elected but parties were banned or during which a single party held 100 percent of the seats in the legislature (except for Jamaica and Trinidad and Tobago, as discussed later) or in which only one list was offered to voters in elections.

We also extended this rule to disqualify as democratic those regimes in which incumbents used an electoral victory to establish (1) non-party rule or (2) one-party rule or (3) a permanent electoral domination. This is called the "consolidation" rule.

Consolidation of non-party or one-party rule occurred whenever incumbents either banned all parties, or all opposition parties, or forced all parties to merge with the ruling one. If an incumbent party consolidated during its tenure in office a one-party rule or a non-party rule, then the regime is considered to have been authoritarian from

---

[8] Note that we do not assume that the existence of political parties is a necessary condition for contestation; after all, most pre-1900 elections were non-partisan. We exclude from the democracies only those regimes in which all or all but one political parties were banned. Bernard Manin made us sensitive to this point.

the moment at which the incumbent party assumed office. Note that we are not examining intentions: If they tried and failed, the regime is democratic.

We say that consolidation of incumbent rule also occurred whenever there was more than one party but at some time the incumbents unconstitutionally closed the legislature and rewrote electoral rules to their own advantage.[9] The entire period preceding the closing of the legislature during which the same party was in office is then considered authoritarian. In some analyses later in this book, we relax this rule in order to identify cases in which incumbents perpetuated an *autogolpe*. In these instances, regimes are classified as democracies until the year in which the *autogolpe* occurred, allowing us to separate the cases of transition to authoritarianism caused by the incumbent chief executive.[10] These cases are listed in Appendix 1.3.

To understand how the consolidation rule was applied, consider Malaysia, a country where three elections were held between independence in 1957 and 1969. The incumbents won absolute majorities of votes in the first two elections, but not in the third. They then declared a state of emergency, closed the congress, and changed the rules in such a way as to make this unpleasant experience unrepeatable. According to Ahmad (1988: 357), "the better showing by the opposition caused a temporary loss of confidence and even the conclusion by some in the ruling party that it had lost its mandate." The parliament was dissolved in 1969, a state of emergency was proclaimed, and a tough internal-security law, still in effect, was adopted. The constitution was rewritten to ensure that no more electoral defeats would occur. Ahmad (1988: 358) comments on this event: "What is more interesting about the conduct of elections as part of the democratic process, however, was probably the unstated notion that losing an election meant virtually total political defeat. Therefore 1969 served notice to the Alliance leadership that it might have to one day face the prospect of an electoral defeat. . . . The rules of the game of Malaysian democracy were therefore set for modification after 1969 because the

---

[9] The mere act of dissolving the legislature is not sufficient to qualify as consolidation. In many cases legislatures are dissolved or suspended according to extant constitutional provisions: The 1975 Indian state of emergency was duly approved by the two houses of the legislature. In some cases, notably Australia in 1975, the constitutionality of the dissolution has been dubious. Our rule is that if elections were immediately proclaimed and took place within the immediate future under the same rules, we did not treat such a dissolution as a breakdown of democracy.

[10] Note that what we observe are the outcomes of conflicts, rather than their initiation; hence, an inference is entailed in interpreting these results.

prospect of a zero-sum electoral result would be unacceptable if Malay political supremacy was not to be assured." As a result, "the fear of an electoral defeat has been diminished under the Barisan Nasional coalition concept. The parties that have not succumbed to the taste of power by joining the BN cannot pretend to be able to form the national government at any time in the foreseeable future."

In South Korea, President Chung-Hee Park held elections once and won enough votes; then he held them again and became dissatisfied with the result, closed the congress, and assumed dictatorial powers. Five years later, he reopened the congress under new rules. President Ferdinand Marcos in the Philippines won election twice and assumed dictatorial power when he could not amend the constitution to enjoy more terms.

Because in these cases we have prima facie evidence that incumbents were not prepared to yield office as a result of elections (although one could argue that although the Malays were not willing to do it in 1969, they might have been willing to accept defeat earlier), we classify these regimes as dictatorships.

Note that this part of the consolidation rule applies only up to the moment of the unlawful change of electoral rules. If a regime unconstitutionally changed the rules in its favor but subsequently yielded office under these new rules, then the regime is considered authoritarian up to the time of the openly dictatorial interregnum, and democratic subsequently. This is why we have classified the João Batista Figueiredo term in Brazil as democratic: Although his predecessor temporarily closed the congress and made it more difficult for the opposition to win, Figueiredo's successor, Tancredo Neves, won election against the candidate supported by the military under the same rules as Figueiredo.

Thus the "party" rule is that *if (1) there were no parties or (2) there was only one party or (3) the incumbents' term in office ended in the establishment of non-party or one-party rule or (4) the incumbents unconstitutionally closed the legislature and rewrote the rules in their favor, then the regime was a dictatorship.* As shown later, the absence of legal opposition is the most frequent reason for classifying regimes as dictatorships.

These three rules appear to us to be non-controversial, and they are easy to apply. The first thing we learned from applying them is that the great majority of cases, 91.8 percent of country-years, are unambiguously classified by these three rules. There is, however, one particular class of regimes that cannot be classified one way or another.

"Botswana" and the Alternation Rule

Thus far we have classified as democracies those regimes in which the chief executive and the legislature are elected in multi-party elections. But we do not know that all regimes that satisfy these criteria are in fact democracies.

Consider Botswana. Government offices in Botswana are filled by elections, more than one party competes, there is little repression, and there are no exceptional allegations of fraud. Hence, by the rules introduced thus far, Botswana should be considered a democracy, and indeed it is generally considered to be one. Yet the same party has ruled Botswana since independence, always controlling an overwhelming majority in the legislature. Thus, the question arises whether or not elections are held in Botswana only because the ruling party is certain to win them and whether or not the ruling party would yield office if it ever lost. These are not moot questions: Looking into the future, a specialist on this country speculates that "the resulting conflict could well force the BDP [Botswana Democratic Party] to choose between losing in parliamentary elections and abandoning elections as a method of leadership selection. Given the paternalistic attitude of the BDP from President Masire down, the latter choice would not be surprising" (Holm 1988: 208). Hence, if democracy is a system in which elections are held even if the opposition has a chance to win and in which the winners can assume office, then the observable evidence is not sufficient to classify Botswana one way or another.

Botswana is an ideal type: no constraints on the opposition, little visible repression, no apparent fraud. But the issue is more general. If the same party or coalition of parties had won every single election from some time in the past until it was deposed by force or until now, we cannot know if it would have held elections when facing the prospect of losing or if it would have yielded office had it in fact lost. We must thus decide which way to err: whether we prefer to commit the error of excluding from the democracies some systems that are in fact democracies (type I) or the error of including as democracies some systems that are not in fact democratic (type II). Err we must; the question is which way.

In some cases, either antecedent or subsequent events have provided additional information. In the United Kingdom, we knew even before Blair's victory that the Conservatives had lost elections and allowed their opponents to assume office. In Japan, after a long tenure in office, the incumbent party finally lost elections and allowed the opposition to assume office. Because this is the only information we have, we use it – not without a leap of inference – to conclude that these regimes are or were democratic. The same is true when we know that incumbents unconstitutionally prevented the opposition from winning elections or assuming office. In all these cases, we use this information retroactively. This clearly is not a very satisfactory solution: One might easily imagine that even if certain incumbents were willing to allow a peaceful alternation in office later on, they might not have been willing to tolerate it earlier; conversely, even if they suppressed the opposition later on, they might not have done so earlier. But this is the only information we have; we cannot observe what might have happened. The only alternative would be to attempt to assess the degree of repression, intimidation, or fraud for each election, but, in our view, such assessments cannot be made in a reliable way.

Japan is a paradigmatic case of a long tenure in office that ended with a lawful alternation. The LDP (Liberal Democratic Party) was in office continually until the 1993 election. Yet when the incumbents finally lost, they allowed the opposition to assume office. The same was true in Mauritius, the Bahamas, Barbados, Trinidad and Tobago, the Dominican Republic, Grenada, Jamaica, St. Lucia, and the Solomon Islands. In each of these countries the same party stayed in power for at least two terms, either following independence or the birth of democracy; yet eventually it lost an election and gave up office peacefully. We use this information retroactively: Whenever a ruling party eventually suffered an electoral defeat and allowed the opposition to assume office, the regime is classified as democratic for the entire period this party was in power under the same rules. Alternation thus overrides the party rule: In Jamaica, as well as in Trinidad and Tobago, at one point, one party controlled all the seats in the legislature. Yet it lost the subsequent election and relinquished office. We therefore consider these regimes to have been democratic even during the period of one-party rule.

We have already discussed cases in which incumbents, facing the prospect of an electoral defeat or having actually been defeated, unconstitutionally closed the legislature, introduced a state of emergency, and rewrote the rules in their own favor. In such cases, we evoke the rule about the consolidation of incumbent advantage and classify the regime as authoritarian during the entire period before the openly dictatorial interregnum. In South Korea, President Park won the 1963 elections, and had he not instituted dictatorial rule nine years later, we would never have known whether or not he would ever have been ready to relinquish office. A Korean student of military politics (Se Jin Kim, cited by Han 1988: 275) commented with regard to the 1963 elections that "Park's victory was in fact a blessing for the future of democracy in Korea. Had the military lost, it can be safely assumed that the military would have ignored the electoral outcome and continued to rule even though such rule would have meant a total destruction of constitutionalism." But subsequently Park did close the congress and change the rules, and we use this information to infer that he would not have been ready to yield office during the preceding nine years.

Even when incumbents hold elections only because they expect to win, they sometimes make mistakes: They hold elections and lose. Then they have to decide whether to accept the popular verdict or override it. They can revert to post-election fraud: Anastasio Somoza is purported to have said to his electoral opponent, "You poor s.o.b., perhaps you won the voting, but I won the counting," a recipe apparently applied by the Mexican PRI in 1988. Blatant fraud constitutes prima facie evidence that the incumbents were not predisposed to permit a lawful alternation in office. Or they can publish voting results and still not allow the opposition to assume office.

Yet, to return to Botswana, in some cases history has not been kind enough to provide even the information that we have for Japan or Malaysia: All we know is that the incumbents always win. Presumably, we would want to think that if Botswana is like Japan, it should be considered democratic, but if it is like Malaysia, it should be considered authoritarian. But we do not know if Botswana is like Japan or like Malaysia. Elections may be held in Botswana only because the ruling party is sure to win, but how are we to know what would happen if they expected to lose or in fact lost?

To provide more intuition, consider Turkey between 1950 and 1960, another period generally considered democratic. The Democratic Party (DP) came to power in 1950, holding 83.8 percent of the seats. It won in 1954 with 93.0 percent of the seats, and in 1957 with 69.5 percent, until it was ousted by the military in 1960. After the 1957 elections "the DP responded to its declining support by resorting to increasingly authoritarian measures against the opposition. . . . The last straw in the long chain of authoritarian measures was the establishment by the government party in April 1960 of a parliamentary committee of inquiry to investigate the 'subversive' activities of the RPP [main opposition party]" (Ozbudun 1988: 200). Would the DP ever have yielded power peacefully had it not been deposed by force?

We choose to take a cautious stance, that is, to avoid type-II errors. While examining the histories of particular countries, we were impressed that the dream of many political elites is to rule perpetually and to rule with consent: Politicians are just PRIstas by nature. The Mexican system has been the ideal for many politicians in Latin America and, until the defeat of the LDP, the Japanese system in Asia. Attempts at creating a hegemonic system, in which some or even all opposition would be allowed but the ruling party would not be threatened with losing office, have been made at various moments in Botswana, Gambia, Senegal,[11] Argentina, Bolivia, Colombia,[12] Ecuador, El Salvador, Guatemala, Honduras,[13] Guyana, Bangladesh, Egypt, Malaysia, Pakistan,[14] the Philippines,[15] South Korea,[16]

---

[11] Coulon (1988: 154) writes about Senegal: "In 1978, a constitutional reform was adopted which put into place a system of 'controlled democracy.' The number of parties was limited to three. . . . The legislative and presidential elections of 1978 were a great success for the Socialist Party [former UPS, the ruling party] (which received 81.7 percent of the ballots cast and 82 of the 100 seats in the Assembly) and for President Senghor personally (who won 82.5 percent of the vote). . . . It must be emphasized, however, that the elections were held in a tense climate and organized in a way that threatened the secrecy of the ballot."

[12] In Colombia, Laureano Gómez was elected president with 83.8% of the vote and took office in August 1950. He continued tight censorship and increased repression against labor and violence against liberals and Protestants. He attempted to reform the constitution in order to impose a falangist-corporatist framework, freeing the presidency from most congressional constraints, centralizing power, and converting the senate into a corporatist body.

[13] In Honduras between 1965 and 1970, "the conservative, authoritarian civil-military government suppressed popular organizations and rigged the electoral machinery to assure National party victories in the 1965 and 1968 elections" (McDonald and Ruhl 1989: 113).

[14] In Pakistan, according to Rose (1988: 114–15), "Ayub's intention initially had been to establish a nonparty system but it quickly became clear that this would be counter-productive. Ayub then moved to the opposite extreme, legalized virtually all parties that applied, and formed his own party. . . . What was rather astonishing was [that] the 1962 constitution, Ayub Khan's rather cleverly disguised authoritarian system, went along from 1961 to 1969 with no serious political challenges."

[15] In the Philippines, according to Jackson (1988: 246), "the final structure created by Marcos was the Kilusang Bagong Lipuna (New Society Movement) or KBL. The KBL initially was not referred to as a political party, but was designed to select and elect candidates to local, provincial, and national offices. KBL candidates, in an atmosphere of restricted press and speech, triumphed in the 1978 interim assembly elections as well as in the 1980 local elections. The degree of limited participation is indicated by the fact that the 1978 opposition was led from a jail cell by former Senator Benigno Aquino. The interim assembly contained only fourteen non-KBL members out of 200 members. . . . President Marcos ran for reelection in June 1981 but his logical opponent, former Senator Aquino, was excluded by the constitution, which required all nominees to be at least fifty years of age (Aquino was forty-eight.) With virtually no opposition, President Marcos was reelected."

[16] In South Korea, according to Han (1988: 268–9), "the new government was born with a democratic constitution and with the expectation that it would usher in democratic

Singapore, Turkey, Taiwan, and most likely other countries where the evidence is not that direct. Indeed, it seems that many dictatorships and some democracies are just failed attempts at creating a Mexico or a Japan: Sometimes the ruling party overdoes it, and the result is a naked dictatorship; sometimes the ruling party is forced to compromise, and the result is democracy.

Suppose that politicians want power but also want to be admired and adored. Ideally, they would hold office as a result of elections. Yet the hunger for power overwhelms other motivations: They prefer to remain in office by force rather than lose power. Incumbents have some notion of how likely it is that they will win the next election. If they think they will win, they hold elections. If they think they will lose, they do not. If these assumptions are correct, then the observed sample of regimes that hold regular elections is biased in favor of "democracies," that is, regimes that look like democracies, in the sense that they permit contestation and fill offices by elections, yet are not democracies in the sense that the opposition has a chance to assume office as a result of elections. Among the observed democracies, there are some that hold elections only because the opposition cannot win and some in which the opposition would not be allowed to assume office if it won. Hence, holding elections is not sufficient to classify a regime as democratic.

We thus need one more rule: *alternation*. This rule is applicable only to cases that qualify under the preceding three rules and in which in the immediate past the incumbents either held office by virtue of elections for more than two terms or initially held office without being elected. *If all these conditions are satisfied and if the incumbents subsequently held but never lost elections, we consider such regimes authoritarian.*

In making this decision, we are buttressed by an empirical observation. Among those cases in which alternation in office via elections did occur, except for some Caribbean islands, the share of seats of the incumbents was almost always smaller than two-thirds. Hence, the conditional probability that the seat share will be larger than two-thirds given that alternation occurs is very small. Because alternations via elections are generally less frequent than seat shares in excess of two-thirds, Bayes's rule implies that the conditional probability that an

politics for South Korea. But the Rhee government was determined to remain in power – for life – which required several constitutional changes, election rigging, and repression of the opposition. Rhee was able to establish his personal dictatorship by making use of the state power as exemplified by the national police."

alternation will occur given that seat share is larger than two-thirds is also very small: 8.8 percent.[17] Countries in which one party wins an overwhelming share of seats are not likely to be democracies; this rule should classify regimes accurately about seven-eighths of the time.

Although there are some countries where a ruling party had been winning by very large margins and yet subsequently left office via elections, the striking finding is that we could have used this ex-post criterion to eliminate almost all the cases in which the same party continually held office. If we were to decide that a regime in which the ruling party always won more than two-thirds of seats was not democratic, Malaysia (where the share of seats after 1971 was always larger than 68.1) would fail by this criterion, as would Botswana (seats > 77.8), Egypt after 1976 (seats > 75), Gambia (seats > 69.7), Senegal after 1978 (seats > 83.0), South Africa (seats > 66.6), Mexico (seats > 72.2, or fraud in 1988), Guyana (seats started at 56.6, went to 83.1), and Singapore (seats = 74.5 in 1965, and all or all but one after 1968). In South Korea, the share of seats fell from 74.3 in 1967 to 55.4 in 1971, sufficient to prompt President Park to dissolve the congress, and when the legislature was opened again in 1973, the ruling party controlled 66.7 percent.

The cases distinguished by the alternation rule constitute systematic error. Those readers who prefer to err in the other direction can reclassify them (they are marked with asterisks in Appendix 1.2). But an error is unavoidable.

Summary of Rules

For convenience, we restate our rules. A regime is classified as a dictatorship during a particular year if at least one of these conditions holds:

Rule 1: "Executive selection." The chief executive is not elected (EXSELEC).

Rule 2: "Legislative selection." The legislature is not elected (LEGSELEC).

---

[17] Our prior, the probability that during a random country-year the regime will be democratic, is 0.40. The probability that any election will end with more than two-thirds of seats going to one party is 0.38. The likelihood, the conditional probability that seats will be more than two-thirds given that a regime is democratic, is 0.126. Hence, by the Bayes rule, the posterior, the probability that a country will be democratic given that seats will be more than two-thirds, is 0.0877.

Rule 3: "Party." There is no more than one party. Specifically, this rule applies if (1) there are no parties or (2) there is only one party or (3) the current term in office ends in the establishment of non-party or one-party rule or (4) the incumbents unconstitutionally close the legislature and rewrite the rules in their favor (PARTY, INCUMB).

Rule 4: "Alternation" (applies only to regimes that have passed the previous three rules). The incumbents will have or already have held office continuously by virtue of elections for more than two terms or have held office without being elected for any duration of their current tenure in office, and until today or until the time when they were overthrown they had not lost an election (TYPEII).

At the risk of repetition, we restate the relation between the "party" and the "alternation" rules. If at any time there are fewer than two parties, the regime is classified as a dictatorship. If there is more than one party, the question becomes whether or not there is a real possibility for the opposition to win and assume office. If incumbents lose elections at any time in the future, the regime is considered to have been democratic during their entire tenure in office. If incumbents repress the opposition at any time in the future, the regime is classified as a dictatorship during their entire tenure in office up to this moment. If we observe neither consolidation nor alternation, we avoid type-II error and classify the regime as a dictatorship.

Finally, a word is needed about our timing rules. In all cases of regime transitions, we code the regime that prevailed at the end of the year, even if it came to power on December 31, as, for example, did Nigeria in 1983. Transitions to authoritarianism are signaled by a coup d'état. Transitions to democracy are dated by the time of the inauguration of the newly elected government, not the time of the election. In the few cases, like that of the Dominican Republic in 1963, in which a democratic regime lasted six months (or in Bolivia in 1979, where the situation changed several times), the information about regimes that began and ended within the same year is lost.

Our data set covers 141 countries between 1950 (or the year of independence) and 1990. Altogether, during this period we found 238 regimes: 105 democracies and 133 dictatorships. They are listed, by country and period, in Appendix 1.2. Of the total 4,730 years, countries lived 1,723 (36 percent) years under democracy and 3,007 (64 percent) under dictatorship (REG).

Table 1.1 shows the numbers of cases in the sample that were

Table 1.1. Distribution of observations by
criteria used for classification as dictatorships

Executive selection: non-elected executive	1,513
Legislative selection:	940
No legislature	789
Non-elected legislature	151
Political party	2,250
No political party	651
One political party	1,599
Consolidation of incumbent rule	93
Alternation	389
Executive selection and political party	1,244
Executive selection and legislative selection	89
Legislative selection and political party	767
Executive selection, legislative selection, and political party	731
Total dictatorships	3,007
Total democracies	1,723
Total regime years	4,730

disqualified as democracies by each of the rules alone and by their combinations.

Distinguishing among Democracies and Dictatorships

Obviously, neither democracies nor dictatorships are all the same. Thus, further distinctions are required.

Given the recent popularity of this issue, we classified democracies as parliamentary, mixed, or presidential (INST). These types are defined as follows. Systems in which the government must enjoy the confidence of the legislature are "parliamentary"; systems in which the government serves at the pleasure of the elected president are "presidential"; systems in which the government must respond both to a legislative assembly and to an elected president are "mixed."[18]

In a parliamentary system the legislative assembly can dismiss the

---

[18] This criterion coincides almost perfectly with the mode of selection of the government: by legislatures in parliamentary systems, by voters (directly or indirectly) in presidential systems. For a review of the differences, see Lijphart (1992).

government, whereas under a presidential system it cannot.[19] Some institutional arrangements, however, do not fit either pure type; they are "premier-presidential," "semi-presidential," or "mixed," according to different terminologies. In such systems, the president is elected for a fixed term and has some executive powers, but the government serves at the discretion of the parliament. These "mixed" systems are not homogeneous: Most lean closer to parliamentarism insofar as the government is responsible to the legislature; others (notably Portugal between 1976 and 1981) grant the president the power to appoint and dismiss governments (Shugart and Carey 1992).

Whereas we observed 105 democratic regimes, two countries changed institutional arrangements without breaking the continuity of democracy: Brazil twice and France once. Hence, altogether there were 108 democracies, as distinguished by institutional framework. Of these, 55 were parliamentary, 9 were mixed, and 44 were presidential. Of the total 1,723 years of democracy, countries spent 1,085 (63 percent) years under parliamentarism, 150 (9 percent) under mixed systems, and 488 (28 percent) under presidentialism.

To distinguish among dictatorships, we developed three alternative typologies and examined the relationships among them.

First, some dictatorships are "mobilizing," whereas others are "exclusionary." The former organize permanent political participation through a single or dominant party and regularly hold acts of popular mobilization that they call "elections." They require individuals to manifest loyalty to the regime by participating. The latter form, exclusionary dictatorships, may or may not hold elections, but they do not promote any kind of political participation by the masses. They only require that individuals not engage in acts oriented against the regime.

Operationally, we define as "mobilizing" those dictatorships that had at least one political party, and as "exclusionary" those that did not have parties (MOBILIZE). Altogether we observed 147 mobilizing and 127 exclusionary dictatorships. Of the 3,007 dictatorial years, 1,991 (66 percent) were spent under mobilizing dictatorships, and 1,016 (34 percent) under exclusionary ones.

---

[19] The Chilean 1891–1925 democracy does not fit this classification. Although it was popularly called "parliamentary," that was a misnomer. The Chilean lower house frequently censured individual ministers, but could not and did not remove the government or the chief executive, the president. In parliamentary systems, except for some early rare cases, the responsibility of the government is collective.

Second, we distinguish authoritarian regimes according to the number of *formal* powers: executives, legislatures, and parties (DIVIDED). Our intuition is derived from Machiavelli: Whenever decision-making is collective, there must exist some rules organizing the functioning of the government (Bobbio 1989). Hence, even if the legislature is a rubber stamp or the chief executive obeys dictates of the single party, the mere existence of such bodies means that there must exist some formal rules allocating functions and specifying procedures. We are not claiming, as Kavka (1986) would, that divided governments are necessarily limited: Under dictatorship, some of these bodies may have no autonomous power and do not provide checks and balances. But the existence of rules distinguishes such regimes from those dictatorships in which the operation of government need not be organized by any formal rules.

The "powers" are always the chief executive and, if they exist, legislatures or parties. Hence, a "divided" dictatorship is one that in addition to the chief executive has a legislature or a party. "Monolithic" dictatorships have no legislatures and no parties. We observed 167 divided and 91 monolithic dictatorships, with 2,407 (80 percent) years spent under the former, and 600 (20 percent) under the latter.

Finally, another distinction, in the spirit of Montesquieu, is whether the dictatorship codifies and announces the rules it intends to apply to its subjects or governs without such rules (AUT). In the first case, rule is exercised "by fixed and established laws," whereas in the second case "a single person directs everything by his own will and caprice." "Bureaucracies" are dictatorships that have some internal rules for operating the government, at least rules regulating the competence of the chief executive vis-à-vis the legislature, and some external rules, namely, laws. To put it differently, bureaucracies are institutionalized dictatorships. Operationally, bureaucracies are dictatorships that have legislatures: Because all regimes have chief executives, the existence of a legislature implies that they must have some rules for regulating relations among different organs of government. It also indicates that rule is exercised by law, that is, that people can know the rules that dictators at least intend to enforce at a particular moment and, moreover, that these rules are universalistic in intent. In turn, "autocracies" are despotic or, in the language of Linz (1975), "sultanistic" regimes, which have neither internal rules of operation nor publicly announced universalistic intentions. Operationally, autocracies are systems in which there is a chief executive, and perhaps a single party, but no legislature. Yet some of the autocracies and bureaucracies that result from the application of these rules are, in fact, transitional regimes. We corrected for these regimes in the list presented in Appendix 1.2. Altogether, we observed 146 bureaucracies, which lasted 2,117 (70 percent) years, and 116 autocracies, during 890 (30 percent) years.

What We Did Not Include

This conception of democracy in terms of contested elections for executive and legislative offices is clearly minimalist. Hence, it may be useful to make explicit at least some of the features that we did not consider when classifying regimes as democracies or dictatorships.

First, we do not include in our conception of democracy any social or economic aspects of a society. Many scholars (Weffort 1992) and, as surveys from many countries demonstrate, most citizens perceive social or economic equality as an essential feature of democracy. Yet the questions whether or not, on the one hand, contested elections tend to generate equality in the social or economic realm (Jackman 1974; Muller 1988) and, on the other hand, whether or not economic equality makes democracy more durable (Muller 1988) are just too interesting to be resolved by a definitional fiat. We prefer to define democracy narrowly and to study its causes and consequences.

Second, we do not think that "accountability," "responsibility," "responsiveness," or "representation" should be treated as definitional features of democracy. When Dahl (1971: 1) says that "a key characteristic of a democracy is the continued responsiveness of the government to the preferences of its citizens," or when Riker (1965: 31) asserts that "democracy is a form of government in which the rulers are fully responsible to the ruled," they mean either (1) that when and only when the government is responsive, the regime is democratic regardless of anything else, or (2) that if a system is democratic by some other criteria, then the government will behave responsibly. The standard way of thinking follows Dahl, who lists several conditions that are necessary and sufficient for governments to be responsive. And it is the presence of these conditions, not responsiveness, that defines a regime as democratic: The statement that "if these conditions hold, then governments will be responsive" is a theorem, not a definition. Moreover, this theorem is most likely false unless additional conditions are specified: First, the very notion of "responsiveness" or "accountability" is muddled, and second, probably only some otherwise democratic governments are "accountable" in any intuitive sense of this term (Przeworski, Manin, and Stokes 1999). Hence, the question whether or

33

not regimes characterized by freedom of opinion, widespread participation, and repeated elections are in fact responsive is best left open
for investigation, rather than resolved by definition.

Third, whereas some degree of political freedom is a sine qua non
condition for contestation, democracy cannot be sufficiently defined in
terms of "liberties" or "freedom," or human rights, which underlie the
Gastil (1980, 1990) or the Freedom House scales. The American conception of "freedom" perceives it as a condition, not as a predicate of
actions: People *are* free, even if they never *exercise* their freedom. Thus
U.S. citizens are free to form political parties; yet they almost never
form them. They are certainly free to vote, yet about half do not. From
our point of view, to paraphrase Rosa Luxemburg, the point is not to
be free but to act freely. And acting freely in the political realm entails
enabling conditions, institutional as well as social. Whereas democracy
is a system of political rights – these are definitional – it is not a system
that necessarily furnishes the conditions for effective exercise of these
rights.[20] Thus, assessing "freedom" or "liberty" without determining
the conditions that enable its exercise can easily lead to ideologically
motivated labels that measure only similarities to the United States,
rather than the actual exercise of political rights.

Fourth, we do not include participation as a definitional feature of
democracy. In Dahl's conception of "polyarchy," both contestation and
participation are necessary to classify a regime as democratic. Indeed,
Dahl sets the participation threshold so high that by his criterion
the United States would not qualify as a democracy until the 1950s.
Vanhanen (1992) sets it lower, but still disqualifies as democracies
those regimes in which elections are contested but participation is
very limited. Yet we want to distinguish regimes in which at least some,
but not necessarily all, conflicting interests contest elections. And
empirical evidence from Western Europe (Przeworski 1975) as well as
from Latin America (Coppedge 1992) indicates that the distribution of
votes among parties changes only slowly after each extension of
suffrage, implying that even when suffrage is highly restricted, divergent interests are being represented. Moreover, we want to be able to
test theories about the effects of participation on the performance
and the durability of democracy (Huntington 1968; O'Donnell 1973;

---

[20] Mueller's libertarian view, "political equality is something that evolves without much
further ado when people are free" (1992: 988), should thus be contrasted with J. S.
Mill's insistence that "high wages and universal reading are the two elements of democracy" (quoted in Burns 1969: 290).

Huntington and Nelson 1976). Using any threshold would produce a censored sample and a bias we prefer to avoid.[21]

Fifth, as long the chief executive and the legislature were elected in contested elections, we did not delve further into civil–military relations. Several distinctions could be made here. In some regimes that we classified as democracies, civilian institutions do not control the military, who in turn do not intervene in politics. In other democracies, civilian politicians use the threat of military intervention in strategic interactions among themselves ("praetorian politics"). Finally, in some democracies (Honduras and Thailand are prototypes), civilian rule is but a thin veneer over military power, exercised by defrocked generals. Yet as long as officeholders are elected in elections that someone else has some chance of winning, and as long as they do not use the incumbency to eliminate the opposition, the fact that the chief executive is a general or a lackey of generals does not add any relevant information. Most generals who get elected only because they are generals are eliminated from consideration on the basis of other rules. Some probably sneak through; there is no measurement without error.

Finally, several countries have been ravaged by civil wars: El Salvador, Guatemala, Uganda, and Sudan are obvious cases. If a regime is a set of institutions that regulate the relationship between the civil society and the state, then there can be no regime where there is no state. To varying degrees, the very question whether a regime is or is not democratic turns out to be irrelevant. Voting typically occurs in only some parts of such countries, and legislatures frequently turn out to be ineffective.[22] We considered excluding such periods altogether. Yet the degree to which a civil war disrupts the normal functioning of the political system is difficult to assess.

Thus, to repeat, our approach is minimalist. We want to be able to examine empirically, rather than decide by definition, whether or not the repeated holding of contested elections is associated with economic performance. Democracy, to repeat, is a regime in which some governmental offices are filled by contested elections. Whether or not

---

[21] Note that if we were to use Dahl's participation threshold of 50% of adults to qualify countries as democratic, we would date Western European democracies quite late: in the case of Belgium or France, after World War II. The proportion of the population age 20 years or older who could vote in the 1946 election, the last one before women got the right to vote, in Belgium was 45.5%, of whom 90.3% voted, which yields a participation rate of 41.1%. In France in 1936, 40.1% of those age 20 and over could vote, and the turnout was 84.4%, implying a participation rate of 33.7%.

[22] Most of Banks's coding for "ineffective legislature" was due to civil wars.

regimes in which the rulers are elected tend to generate social and economic equality, control by citizens over politicians, effective exercise of political rights, widespread participation, or freedom from arbitrary violence, as well as economic growth, high employment, low inflation, and public services, should be studied empirically rather than decided definitionally.

Stability and Change of Political Regimes

Of the 141 countries that we observed for at least some time between 1950 and 1990,[23] 73 were already independent in 1950, and 68 gained sovereignty after 1950 (Table 1.2).

Independence, as we know, came in waves. From 1950 through 1959, eight new countries entered the world of sovereign states: Oman, Laos, Morocco, Sudan, Tunisia, Ghana, Malaysia, and Guinea. The largest wave occurred between 1960 and 1968, when forty-one new countries appeared in the world (with the single largest expansion having occurred in 1960, when seventeen African countries gained independence). The remaining nineteen countries became independent between 1969 and 1981, with the largest additions occurring in 1971, when Bangladesh and some of the Persian Gulf states were created (Bahrain, Qatar, and the United Arab Emirates), and in 1975, with the independence of the last Portuguese colonies in Africa (Angola, Cape Verde Islands, and Mozambique) and of the Comoro Islands, Suriname, and Papua New Guinea. The last country to become independent prior to 1990 was Belize, in 1981.

Because our observations begin with 1950, and about half of the countries became independent only later, the aggregate distribution of regimes over the years depends on two factors: changes of regimes in the already existing countries and the entrance of new countries into the world (Table 1.3).

Given that the number of countries changed over time, one should

[23] Because our observations end with 1990, the data set does not include any of the countries that resulted from the breakup of the Soviet Union (Armenia, Azerbaijan, Belarus, Estonia, Georgia, Kazakhstan, Kyrgyzstan, Latvia, Lithuania, Moldova, Tajikstan, Turkmenistan, Ukraine, and Uzbekistan), Yugoslavia (Bosnia and Herzegovina, Croatia, Macedonia, Slovenia), Czechoslovakia (Czech Republic and Slovakia), Ethiopia (Eritrea), and Somalia (Somaliland). The Soviet Union, Yugoslavia, Czechoslovakia, Ethiopia, and Somalia, however, are part of our data set. Moreover, because no economic data were available, the data set does not include Albania, Antigua and Barbuda, Bhutan, Brunei, Cuba, Cyprus, the Democratic People's Republic of Korea (North Korea), Dominica, Kiribati, Lebanon, Libya, Maldives, Namibia, St. Kitts and Nevis, St. Lucia, St. Vincent and the Grenadines, and São Tomé and Príncipe.

Table 1.2. Number of countries, old and new, by year

	Large data base: 141 countries				Short data base: 135 countries				
Year	Total	Old	New	Entering	Total	Old	Entering/ exiting	New	Entering/exiting
1950	73	73	0		0	0		0	—
1951	74	73	1	138[a]	50	50		0	
1952	74	73	1		52	52	85, 98	0	
1953	74	73	1		52	52		0	
1954	75	73	2	88	55	55	83, 84, 87	0	
1955	75	73	2		56	56	86	0	
1956	78	73	5	30, 40, 44	58	57	82	1	30
1957	80	73	7	18, 89	60	57		3	18, 89
1958	81	73	8	19	60	57		3	
1959	81	73	8		60	57		3	
1960	98	73	25	3, 5, 7, 9, 10, 12, 16, 21, 25, 27, 28, 32, 33, 35, 38, 43, 46	65	57		8	3, 5, 19, 33, 46
1961	101	73	28	37, 42, 137	90	67	24, 58, 79, 81, 92, 97, 104, 121, 127, 128	23	7, 9, 10, 12, 16, 21, 25, 27, 28, 32, 35, 38, 42, 43, 44
1962	108	73	35	1, 6, 34, 45, 60, 64, 135	97	67		30	1, 6, 34, 37, 45, 60, 64
1963	109	73	36	22	98	67		31	22
1964	112	73	39	26, 47, 116	101	67		34	26, 47, 116
1965	115	73	42	17, 48, 95	104	67		37	17, 48, 95
1966	119	73	46	4, 23, 50, 72	108	67		41	4, 23, 50, 72
1967	120	73	47	100	108	67		41	
1968	122	73	49	29, 41	110	67		43	29, 41

(continued)

Table 1.2 (continued)

	Large data base: 141 countries				Short data base: 135 countries				
Year	Total	Old	New	Entering	Total	Old	Entering/ exiting	New	Entering/exiting
1969	122	73	49		110	67		43	
1970	123	73	50	130	112	67		45	100, 130
1971	127	73	54	78, 136, 139, 141	117	70	109, 111, 119	47	40, 78
1972	127	73	54		117	70		47	
1973	128	73	55	49	117	70		47	
1974	130	73	57	20, 56	118	70		48	20
1975	136	73	63	2, 8, 11, 31, 75, 132	124	70		54	2, 8, 11, 31, 75, 132
1976	137	73	64	36	125	70		55	36
1977	138	73	65	13	126	70		56	13
1978	139	73	66	133	127	70		57	49
1979	139	73	66		127	70		57	
1980	140	73	67	134	128	70		58	135
1981	141	73	68	51	131	71	103	60	51, 133
1982	141	73	68		131	71		60	
1983	141	73	68		131	71		60	
1984	141	73	68		132	71		61	134
1985	141	73	68		135	72	90	63	56, 88
1986	141	73	68		135	72		63	
1987	141	73	68		132	69	15, 24, 92	63	13, 49
1988	141	73	68		129	68	83	61	13, 49
1989	141	73	68		126	67	109	59	42, 133
1990	141	73	68		112	63	58, 91, 121, 127	49	2, 4, 32, 38, 41, 46, 50, 75, 100, 116

[a] See Appendix 1.2 for country codes.

Table 1.3. Democracies and dictatorships in old and new countries

	All	Old countries			New countries			Entering sample		
Year	Total	Total	Dem	Dic	Total	Dem	Dic	Total	Dem	Dic
1950	73	73	35	38	0	0	0	0	0	0
1951	74	73	34	39	1	0	1	1	0	1
1952	74	73	35	38	1	0	1	0	0	0
1953	74	73	35	38	1	0	1	0	0	0
1954	75	73	34	39	2	1	1	1	1	0
1955	75	73	34	39	2	1	1	0	0	0
1956	78	73	34	39	5	2	3	3	1	2
1957	80	73	34	39	7	2	5	2	0	2
1958	81	73	36	37	8	1	7	1	0	1
1959	81	73	37	36	8	0	8	0	0	0
1960	98	73	39	34	25	3	22	17	3	14
1961	101	73	39	34	28	4	24	3	1	2
1962	108	73	36	37	35	6	29	7	2	5
1963	109	73	35	38	36	5	31	1	0	1
1964	112	73	34	39	39	6	33	3	1	2
1965	115	73	33	40	42	7	35	3	0	3
1966	119	73	34	39	46	7	39	4	1	3
1967	120	73	33	40	47	6	41	1	0	1
1968	122	73	31	42	49	7	42	2	1	1
1969	122	73	31	42	49	5	44	0	0	0
1970	123	73	31	42	50	6	44	1	0	1
1971	127	73	32	41	54	6	48	4	0	4
1972	127	73	32	41	54	5	49	0	0	0
1973	128	73	31	42	55	6	49	1	1	0
1974	130	73	32	41	57	7	50	2	1	1
1975	136	73	33	40	63	9	54	6	2	4
1976	137	73	32	41	64	9	55	1	0	1
1977	138	73	31	42	65	9	56	1	0	1
1978	139	73	31	42	66	10	56	1	1	0
1979	139	73	34	39	66	11	55	0	0	0
1980	140	73	33	40	67	12	55	1	1	0
1981	141	73	33	40	68	12	56	1	1	0
1982	141	73	34	39	68	12	56	0	0	0
1983	141	73	37	36	68	11	57	0	0	0
1984	141	73	39	34	68	12	56	0	0	0
1985	141	73	40	33	68	11	57	0	0	0
1986	141	73	42	31	68	13	55	0	0	0
1987	141	73	42	31	68	13	55	0	0	0
1988	141	73	44	29	68	14	54	0	0	0
1989	141	73	45	28	68	13	55	0	0	0
1990	141	73	48	25	68	12	56	0	0	0

Note: See Appendix 1.2 for country codes.

expect that the number of regime transitions would vary as well. As a null hypothesis, suppose that the probability of any democracy or dictatorship dying during a particular year is constant over time and is equal to the average rate over the entire period: 0.0261 for democracies and 0.0173 for dictatorships. The expected number of transitions from a given type of regime is then the product of the number of such regimes and their probability of dying. Comparison of the expected and the observed numbers of transitions suggests that until 1961 there were more transitions to democracy and fewer transitions to dictatorship than one would expect to happen by chance. The period from 1958 to 1973 was hostile to democracies; more of them died and fewer were born than one would expect. Finally, the post-1974 period was again favorable to democracies and hostile to dictatorships.

This periodization is due to Huntington (1991), according to whom (1) the "second wave" of democratization began in 1943 and ended in 1962, (2) the "second reverse wave" started in 1958 and ended in 1975, and (3) the "third wave" of democratization began in 1974. Note that Huntington refers to these patterns as "waves." If all he means is that the frequency of regime transitions was not the same during the entire period, then his observation stands. But were these "waves" in the sense that each transition made it more likely that another transition in the same direction would follow?

Consider first the seventy-three countries in our sample that were independent in 1950, when thirty-five of them (48 percent) were democratic. By 1960 the number of democracies among these countries increased to thirty-nine, only to fall to thirty-one by 1968. It was still thirty-one in 1978, after which it climbed back to thirty-nine in 1984 and to forty-eight in 1990. Hence, with regard to the "old" countries, those countries that were independent in 1950, our count roughly agrees with Huntington's analysis. But even among "old" countries, the waves depicted by Huntington are less general than they first appear. Fluctuations in the distribution of democracies among the countries that were independent in 1950 can be observed only in Latin America. In 1950, eight of the eighteen Latin American countries were democratic; that number went down to six in 1955, up to twelve in 1959, where it remained until 1961, and down again to five in 1976. The number of democracies went up again after that, to reach fourteen in 1986, where it remained until 1990. Outside Latin America, the proportion of democracies remained relatively constant, around 48 percent, from 1950 through 1985 (Figure 1.1). Only after that year, as

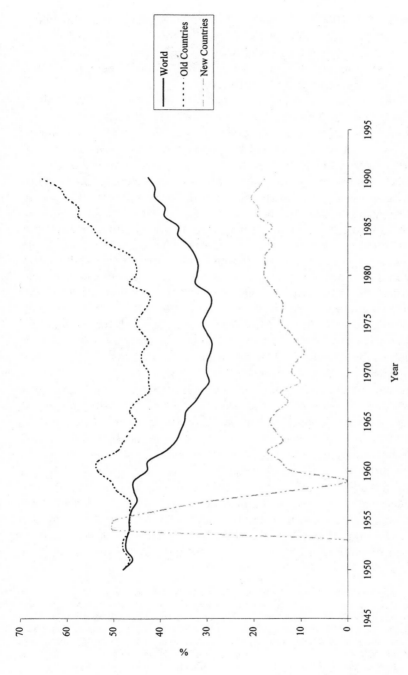

Figure 1.1. Proportions of democracies in the world, in old countries, and in new countries

a result of the democratization of Bangladesh, Pakistan, the Philippines, South Korea, Poland, Bulgaria, Czechoslovakia, and Hungary, did the number of democracies in the "old" countries outside Latin America start to increase: to 51 percent in 1985, to 55 percent in 1986, and to 62 percent in 1990 (Figure 1.2).

The story for countries that became independent after 1950 is entirely different. Three out of twenty-five (12 percent) newly independent countries were democratic in 1960; subsequently the numbers were seven out of forty-nine (14.3 percent) in 1968, ten out of sixty-six (15.1 percent) in 1978, and twelve out of sixty-eight (17.6 percent) in 1990. Hence, the proportion of democracies among these "new" countries grew slightly but steadily over the period. In turn, the decline of the aggregate proportion of democracies in the world during the 1960s was largely due to the emergence of new countries rather than to transformations of old ones. The "reverse wave" covering the 1960s was mostly due to the fact the number of countries increased dramatically in the 1960s, and a large proportion of the new countries entered the world as dictatorships. Thirty-two of the forty-one countries that became independent between 1960 and 1968 did so under authoritarian regimes.[24] With a few exceptions, most of them remained authoritarian for the rest of the period. Hence, the waves of democratization and authoritarianism are at most limited to "old" countries, and particularly to Latin America.

Another way to examine whether or not regimes come and go in waves is simply to observe transitions by year. If transitions come in waves, we would expect that in each successive year more countries would transit in one direction, cresting at some peak, and then initiating the same pattern going in the other direction.

The annual frequency of transitions presented in Figure 1.3 does not show such a pattern. Between 1950 and 1961 (the tail end of Huntington's second wave of democratization) there were eleven transitions to democracy, but also nine to dictatorship (Table 1.4). Between 1958 and 1973 (during the "reverse wave") there were twenty-five transitions to dictatorship, but also sixteen to democracy. Finally, between

---

[24] The countries that emerged as dictatorships after independence are Algeria, Benin, Botswana, Burkina Faso, Burundi, Cameroon, Central African Republic, Chad, Gabon, Gambia, Ivory Coast, Kenya, Lesotho, Madagascar, Malawi, Mali, Mauritania, Niger, Rwanda, Senegal, Swaziland, Tanzania, Togo, Uganda, Zaire, Zambia, Zimbabwe, Guyana, Singapore, Yemen Arab Republic, Western Samoa, and Kuwait. The countries that emerged as democracies are Congo, Mauritius, Nigeria, Sierra Leone, Somalia, Barbados, Jamaica, Trinidad and Tobago, and Malta.

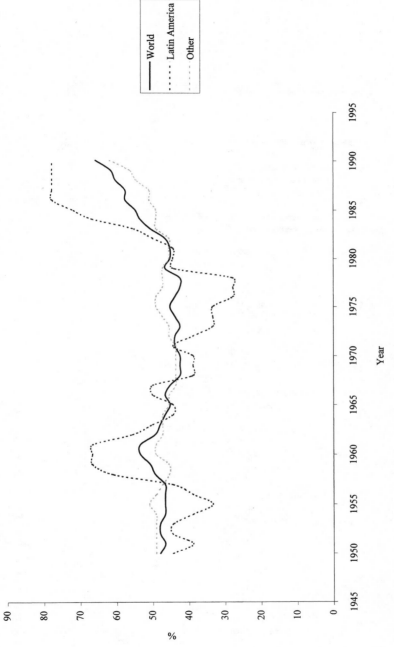

Figure 1.2. Proportions of democracies in old countries: world, Latin America, and other regions

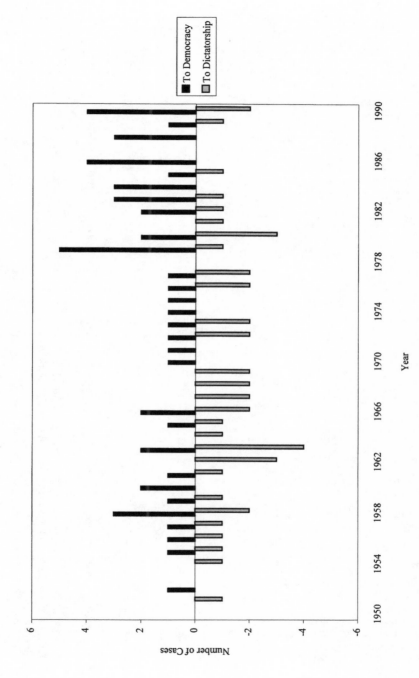

Figure 1.3. Transitions to democracy and to dictatorship by year

Table 1.4. Expected and observed numbers of transitions, by period

Periods	Transitions to democracy		Transitions to dictatorship	
	Expected	Observed	Expected	Observed
1950–1961	8.68	11	11.43	9
1958–1973	19.98	16	16.29	25
1974–1990	26.75	32	21.40	15

1974 and 1990 there were many more transitions to democracy, thrity-two, but still fifteen in the other direction. A simple statistical test is to correlate the annual numbers of transitions to democracy and to dictatorship. If regimes come in waves, then this correlation should be highly negative: During the years when there are many transitions in one direction, there should be few in the other, and vice versa. Yet the correlation is almost zero: −0.01. Moreover, the numbers of transitions in the two directions are not even autocorrelated: The annual auto-correlation of the number of transitions to democracy is −0.011, and to dictatorship −0.010.[25] Hence, however the waves roll, there is always an undertow pushing in the reverse direction. Huntington's oceanic metaphor is only that.

Dictatorships, on average, lasted longer than democracies. But because some regimes already existed in 1950 and some lasted beyond 1990, these averages could reflect the timing of their emergence as much as their ability to survive (Table 1.5).

Democracy is a phenomenon of the twentieth century. For that reason, in 1950 the democracies tended to be younger than the dictatorships. The average age of the thirty-four democratic regimes that existed then was 25.8 years. Only six of them – the United States,

[25] A more complicated way of testing whether or not regime transitions come in waves is to analyze the autoregressive structure of the series using ARIMA identification methods. If the series are indeed cyclical, they should be at least of order 2, with a pair of imaginary roots. Because the series are short, these tests are not highly reliable. Nevertheless, for all the three series – transitions to democracy, transitions to dictatorship, and the difference between them – the tests indicate that they are of order 1. The seasonal component is negligible, and all the series pass the runs test. Hence, there is no evidence for cycles.

Table 1.5. Regime duration: average age in years at end of regime spell or last year of observation

All regimes	All		Democracy		Dictatorship	
Spells completed between 1950 and 1990	18.6	(97)[a]	8.5	(45)	27.4	(52)
Spells in course by 1990	38.2	(141)	36.6	(60)	39.4	(81)
Age of regime as of 1950	34.7	(70)	26.2	(34)	42.7	(36)
Spells initiated in or after 1950	15.7	(168)	9.4	(71)	20.3	(97)
and completed by 1990	7.3	(67)	5.1	(33)	9.4	(34)
and in course by 1990	21.3	(101)	13.0	(38)	26.2	(63)

Democracies	Parliamentary		Mixed		Presidential	
Spells completed between 1950 and 1990	11.2	(19)	4.5	(4)	9.4	(25)
Spells in course by 1990	41.9	(36)	28.8	(5)	24.4	(19)
Age of regime as of 1950	31.2	(21)	7.0	(2)	20.2	(11)
Spells initiated in or after 1950	10.7	(34)	9.7	(7)	8.2	(33)
and completed by 1990	4.5	(14)	4.5	(4)	5.3	(17)
and in course by 1990	15.0	(20)	16.7	(3)	11.2	(16)

Dictatorships	Bureaucracy		Autocracy	
Spells completed between 1950 and 1990	20.9	(59)	9.3	(22)
Spells in course in 1990	26.0	(87)	13.9	(94)
Age of regime as of 1950	42.1	(28)	37.7	(8)
Spells initiated in or after 1950	12.7	(118)	7.3	(108)
and completed by 1990	7.7	(67)	6.3	(87)
and in course by 1990	19.3	(51)	11.7	(21)

[a] Number of spells in parentheses.

France, Luxembourg, the Netherlands, Norway, and Switzerland[26] – had been established before 1900. In turn, the thirty-six dictatorships that existed in 1950 had an average age of 43.8 years. Seventeen of them had been established prior to or in 1870: Ethiopia, Liberia, the

---

[26] We extended the age of a regime back as far as 1870. All regimes, democratic or authoritarian, established before that date were recorded as having been established in 1870. In Chile, democracy was first established in 1891, but there was a reversal in 1925.

Dominican Republic, El Salvador, Haiti, Honduras, Mexico, Nicaragua, Bolivia, Paraguay, China, Iran, Nepal, Thailand, Romania, Turkey, and the USSR (Russia).

However, democracies also lasted for shorter periods than dictatorships among the countries that did not exist prior to 1950. Of the 168 regimes that were established in or after 1950, 67 had died by 1990. Thirty-three were democratic, and they lasted, on average, 5.1 years; 34 were authoritarian and lasted 9.4 years. Of the 101 remaining regimes, that is, the regimes that lasted beyond 1990, 38 were democracies, and 63 were dictatorships. The former, by 1990, had lasted 13 years, and the latter 26.2 years. Dictatorships, thus, tended to last longer than democracies, regardless of when they were observed.

During the 1950–1990 period, most countries each lived under a single regime. Of the 141 countries we observed, only 41 experienced transitions between dictatorship and democracy. The remaining 100 countries never experienced regime transitions, and thus each ended the period with the same regime with which it was first observed (among these, 67 were dictatorships, and 33 were democracies). Seventeen countries had just one transition each, of which twelve were to democracy. The five countries where democracy gave way to dictatorships that lasted past 1990 are Laos, where democracy fell in 1959, Congo in 1963, Sierra Leone in 1967, Somalia in 1969, and Sri Lanka in 1977. Countries that started the period of observation as dictatorships and then established democracies that lasted beyond 1990 are Colombia in 1958, Venezuela in 1959, the Dominican Republic in 1966, Portugal in 1976, Spain in 1977, El Salvador and Nicaragua in 1984, Bangladesh in 1986, Poland in 1989, and Bulgaria, Czechoslovakia, and Hungary in 1990.[27]

Two countries began the period of observation as dictatorships, experienced brief democratic interludes, and became dictatorships again: Uganda (where democracy lasted for five years, from 1980 to 1984) and Indonesia (where democracy lasted for only two years, from 1955 to 1956). More typically, seven countries were democracies when we first observed them, went through often long periods of dictatorship, and returned to democracy. These are Grenada, Brazil, Chile, Ecuador, Uruguay, the Philippines, and Greece. Eight countries experienced three regime transitions: Nigeria, Panama, Suriname, and

---

[27] We do not count East Germany, which we treat as having dropped from the sample in 1990.

Myanmar started the period as democracies, became dictatorships, returned to democracy, and ended as dictatorships, whereas Bolivia, South Korea, Thailand, and Turkey began as dictatorships, experimented with democracy, returned to dictatorships, and became democracies again. Two countries had four transitions: Ghana and Pakistan. Sudan and Honduras had five, Guatemala and Peru had six, and Argentina, by far the record holder, had eight transitions between democracy and dictatorship.[28]

Thus, the regime histories of particular countries are highly heterogeneous. Most regimes, as we saw, lasted for a long time, with a majority of countries not experiencing any transition between democracy and dictatorship during the 1950–1990 period. Some countries alternated between dictatorship and democracy every few years: There would be a coup d'état, and a dictatorship would be established; then, often following another coup d'état, an election would be held and the democratically elected government would assume office, only to be overturned by yet another coup. In some countries this entire cycle occurred once during the period; in others it occurred twice, and in Argentina three times.

Moreover, systematic regional differences can be seen: Western Europe was predominantly democratic, and Eastern Europe was communist; in Africa, only Mauritius was democratic during its entire history; except for Israel, Middle Eastern countries were dictatorships; most of the Far Eastern countries, except Japan, were dictatorships; South Asian countries experienced some transitions; and many, but not all, Latin American regimes were highly unstable. Indeed, of the 97 transitions that occurred in the 141 countries between 1950 and 1990, 44 were in Latin America, which comprises eighteen countries[29] (Table 1.6).

The fact that most countries each lived under the same regime for most of the time between 1950 and 1990 does not mean that their rulers or their political orientations or even their institutional frameworks remained the same. The democratic regimes

---

[28] Appendix 1.3 lists countries by the number of transitions they have experienced between democracy and dictatorship.

[29] The rate of transitions per country was highest in Latin America: 2.4. Latin America was followed by Southeast Asia, where the rate was 1.57 transitions per country, and South Asia, where the rate was 1.2 transitions per country. In all other regions (including the countries of the Organization for Economic Cooperation and Development, the OECD), the rate of transitions per country was well below 1.

Table 1.6. Regimes and regime transitions by region

Region	Years of democracy	Transitions to democracy	Years of dictatorship	Transitions to dictatorship
Sub-Saharan Africa	69	6	1,170	11
South Asia	87	3	97	3
East Asia	4	2	160	1
Southeast Asia	46	5	215	6
Pacific Islands	40	0	50	0
Middle East and North Africa	68	2	513	2
Latin America	366	25	372	19
Caribbean	130	2	80	3
Eastern Europe and Soviet Union	5	4	290	0
Industrialized countries	908	3	60	1
Total	1,723	52	3,007	45

might be parliamentary, mixed, or presidential. Dictatorships, in turn, might be "bureaucracies," institutionalized regimes that promulgated laws, or "autocracies," regimes without any proclaimed rules. Using these distinctions, we observed 55 parliamentary, 9 mixed, and 44 presidential democracies, 146 bureaucracies, and 116 autocracies.

The staying power of democratic institutions was seen to be strong. During the entire period studied, democratic institutional frameworks were altered in only three instances: France in 1958, when the parliamentary system of the Fourth Republic gave way to the mixed system of the Fifth; Brazil in 1961, when presidentialism was replaced by a mixed system; and Brazil again in 1963, when presidentialism was restored after its overwhelming victory in a plebiscite held in January of that year. A few countries did change the institutional framework in their democracies after an authoritarian interregnum: Ghana, Nigeria, and South Korea replaced the parliamentary systems that had existed prior to their periods of dictatorship with presidential systems once democracy was restored. In Suriname the change was from parliamentarism to a mixed system. Pakistan was the only country that went back and forth: from parliamentarism in 1950–1955 to a mixed system in 1972–1976 and back to parliamentarism again after 1988. All of the other seventeen countries that experienced at least one authoritarian

49

interlude went back to the type of democratic institutions that had existed before the authoritarian regime.[30]

Authoritarian institutions, on the other hand, proved highly unstable. When we classify dictatorships according to the presence or absence of legislatures, we count 262 regimes, as opposed to 133 when we do not make any distinctions among them. There are, thus, 129 instances of openings and closings of legislatures (65 cases of closing, and 64 cases of opening). Again, a few countries account for a large proportion of the transitions from one type of authoritarianism to the other. Of the sixty-seven countries that remained under authoritarian regimes from 1950 through 1990, thirty-two experienced only one type of dictatorship: twenty-seven as bureaucracies and five as autocracies. The remaining thirty-five countries experienced seventy-six transitions, an average of 2.2 changes per country, from one type of authoritarianism to the other.[31]

Autocracies often emerge when democracy is overthrown and the legislature is temporarily or permanently closed: Of the forty-five cases of democratic breakdown, thirty-one resulted in this type of dictatorship. But autocracies can also emerge as a result of abortive attempts to liberalize bureaucratic dictatorships. Indeed, the cases in which an autocracy followed a bureaucracy were most frequent, suggesting that attempts at liberalization often fail: Of the eighty-seven instances in which bureaucratic regimes died, twenty-two ended in democracy, but sixty-five in autocracy.

Autocracy is not an easily sustainable form of authoritarianism. Only the four Persian Gulf monarchies (Oman, Qatar, Saudi Arabia, and the United Arab Emirates) were autocracies during the entire period. In general, autocracies do not last very long: As Table 1.5 indicates, the average duration of autocratic spells completed by 1990 was 9.3 years, and of those still in course in 1990 the duration was 13.9 years, compared with 20.9 and 26 years, respectively, for bureaucracies. Moreover, of all the regimes, democratic and authoritarian, autocracies are the ones at highest risk: During any year, an autocracy has a 10.56 percent chance of experiencing a transition to a different regime, which compares with 5.12 percent for presidential democracies, 4.11 percent

---

[30] These countries are Sudan, Grenada, Guatemala, Honduras, Panama, Argentina, Bolivia, Brazil, Chile, Ecuador, Peru, Uruguay, Myanmar, the Philippines, Thailand, Greece, and Turkey.

[31] Benin, Burkina Faso, Morocco, Kuwait, and Jordan were the most unstable authoritarian regimes according to this measure: They changed between bureaucracy and autocracy four, five, five, six, and six times, respectively.

Table 1.7. Transitions between political regimes: parliamentarism, mixed, presidentialism, bureaucracies, and autocracies

Transition from:	Transition to:					Total	Number of years	Probability
	Parl	Mix	Pres	Bur	Aut			
Parl	—	1	0	6	12	19	1,085	0.0175
Mix	0	—	1	1	2	4	150	0.0267
Pres	0	1	—	7	17	25	488	0.0513
Bur	8	4	10	—	65	87	2,117	0.0411
Aut	9	0	21	64	—	94	890	0.1056
Total	17	6	32	78	96	223	4,730	0.0471

for bureaucracies, 2.66 percent for mixed democracies, and 1.75 percent for parliamentary democracies (Table 1.7).

Stability and Change of Political Leadership

Rulers changed within each regime. By "rulers" we mean the chief executives, to whom we refer as "heads" of government, or simply "heads." These are presidents in presidential democracies, prime ministers in the parliamentary and mixed democracies, and whoever is the effective ruler in dictatorships. The latter sometimes can be designated explicitly as dictators, or they may opt for a variety of other titles: heads of military juntas, presidents, leaders of their ruling parties, executors of the state of emergency, or kings.

No changes of heads occurred during 3,927 years, one change occurred in 615 years, two changes in 101 years, three in 14, four in 3, and five in 2 years.[32] Thus, altogether there were 881 changes of heads during the period we observed, once every 5.29 years (Table 1.8). Changes were more frequent in democracies than in dictatorships. Chief executives in democratic regimes were changed once every 3.48 years, with no significant difference between prime ministers (3.41 years when we combine parliamentary and mixed regimes)[33] and

---

[32] This adds to 4,662 years. The difference from the total of 4,730 is due to the exclusion of Switzerland, Uruguay up to 1966, and Yugoslavia after 1980, each of which had a collective executive.

[33] Separately, the average is 3.77 for prime ministers in parliamentary regimes and 2.03 for prime ministers in mixed regimes.

Table 1.8. Distribution of changes of chief executives (HEADS) by regime[a]

Number of changes of heads by year	Dem	Parl	Mix	Pres	Dict	Bur	Aut	Total
0	1,254	838	89	327	2,673	1,935	738	3,927
1	354	212	50	92	261	146	115	615
2	49	31	9	9	52	23	29	101
3	6	2	2	2	8	1	7	14
4	2	2	0	0	1	0	1	3
5	0	0	0	0	2	2	0	2
Total	1,665	1,085	150	430	2,997	2,107	890	4,662
No. of changes	478	288	74	116	403	205	198	881
Average duration	3.48	3.77	2.03	3.71	7.44	10.28	4.49	5.29

[a] Excludes Switzerland, Uruguay until 1966, and Yugoslavia after 1981 because they had collective executives.

presidents (3.71 years). The difference, however, was large across types of dictatorships: Whereas in autocracies we observed one change of chief executive every 4.49 years, in bureaucracies we observed one change every 10.28 years, with an average for all dictatorships equal to 7.44 years.

Some incumbents experienced changes in their political regimes while in office. This happened during the tenure of sixty-eight chief executives; fifty-four of them survived one change of regime, nine survived two changes, three survived three changes, and one each survived five and six changes. Most of these changes were between different types of dictatorships and were due to the opening and closing of legislatures.[34] A few, however, were from democracy to dictatorship or vice versa: for example, from presidentialism to autocracy in Uruguay under Juan Bordaberry in 1973, and from autocracy to pres-

[34] The most extreme case is Jordan, where the legislature was closed for one year in 1966, as well as during 1974–1984 and again during 1985–1989, representing six regime changes from bureaucracy to autocracy. Other cases of frequent changes of regimes without a change of chief executive are as follows: Morocco, where the legislature was closed during 1963–1965, 1970–1972, and in 1978; Burkina Faso, where Sangoulé Lamizana allowed an elective legislature to convene in 1970 only to close it in 1974 and reopen it in 1978; Laos, where Souvanna Phouma closed the legislature two times, in 1966 and 1974; and Nepal, where King Mahendra experimented with legislative bodies in 1959 and 1963.

Table 1.9. Average duration (in years) of chief executives' spells[a] by regime

Type of spell	Average	Maximum	N
All	5.8	44	858
Censored[b]	8.1	39	138
Not censored	5.4	44	720
Regime change[c]	13.3	39	68
No regime change	5.2	44	790
No regime change and not censored	4.9	44	671
Democracies	3.7	23	395
Parliamentary	3.9	23	242
Mixed	2.3	7	57
Parliamentary and mixed	3.6	23	295
Presidential	4.2	12	96
Dictatorships	6.6	44	276
Bureaucracies	8.0	36	167
Autocracies	4.5	44	109
Regime change and not censored	11.8	38	49
Regime change and censored	17.2	39	19
No regime change and censored	6.6	31	119

[a] Continuous years of ruling by the same person.
[b] Spells in course by 1990.
[c] A spell with regime change is one during which the incumbent changed the type of political regime.

identialism in Nicaragua under Daniel Ortega Saavedra in 1984. Once we take those two facts into consideration, we find that prime ministers in both parliamentary and mixed regimes had the shortest average tenure (3.6 years), that the durations of democratic presidents and autocratic rulers were about the same (4.2 and 4.5 years, respectively), and that the chief executives in bureaucracies were the ones who lasted the longest (8 years) (Table 1.9).

A similar conclusion follows when we examine the rates of leadership turnover, defined as the annual number of changes in chief executive accumulated over the life span of a regime. As a benchmark, consider that the average turnover rate for all the countries we

Table 1.10. Leadership turnover
rates by regime type[a]

Regime	Turnover rate
Democracy	0.164
Parliamentary	0.140
Mixed	0.271
Presidential	0.186
Dictatorship	0.073
Bureaucracy	0.047
Autocracy	0.190
All	0.103

[a] Excluding spells in course in 1990.

observed was 0.17, somewhat less frequently than once every five years. Because, on the average, we observed each country for about thirty-three years, this turnover rate corresponds to an average of about six changes of chief executive per country.[35] When we consider leadership turnover rates across political regimes, we find a similar rate only in democracies, where it is 0.16 (Table 1.10). The turnover rate is higher in autocracies and in mixed presidential democracies. These rates imply that an average democratic spell experiences about eighteen changes of leadership, whereas an average authoritarian spell experiences nine changes. Among democracies, the number of changes of heads is thirteen in the average parliamentary regime, and six in the average presidential regime.

Conclusion

These are, then, the basic facts about political regimes in the world between 1950 and 1990. Democracy is a system in which incumbents lose elections and leave office when the rules so dictate. Dictatorships are a residual category: If a political regime is not democratic, we consider it to be a dictatorship of one stripe or another. Moreover, we do not distinguish between dictatorships that succeed one another.

---

[35] In this case, changes in chief executives were accumulated over the entire period during which we observed each country, regardless of political regime.

In most cases it is simple to apply this conception of democracy to classify the regimes that existed in the particular countries at the particular moments. All one needs to do is to observe whether or not the chief executive was elected, whether or not the legislature was elected, and whether or not there was political opposition. In some cases, however, history did not provide the necessary evidence: There was an opposition, officials were elected, but the same party always won. All one can do in such instances is to decide which error to avoid.

The resulting classification of regimes is not idiosyncratic. Whereas we were concerned to justify our approach theoretically and to ground the classification on observations, rather than judgments, our classification is almost identical with those produced by several alternative scales of democracy (see Appendix 1.1). Indeed, it seems that in spite of all their conceptual and observational differences, the various approaches yield highly similar classifications of regimes. Hence, there is no reason to think that the results that follow depend on the particular way regimes were classified.

In the chapters that follow, we first explain some of the patterns described here and then explore their consequences for economic performance and material well-being.

Appendix 1.1: Alternative Approaches

Conceptually, our scale is close to that of Bollen (1980), as well as that of Coppedge and Reinicke (1990). Bollen used four indicators: (1) whether or not elections were fair, (2) whether or not the chief executive was elected, (3) whether or not the legislature was elected, and (4) whether or not the legislature was effective. Coppedge and Reinicke coded answers to three questions: (1) whether or not elections presented voters with a meaningful choice, (2) whether or not the outcome was affected by significant fraud, and (3) whether all or some or no political organizations were banned. We used Bollen's second and third dimensions and Coppedge and Reinicke's third dimension. We did experiment with Banks's measure of legislative effectiveness, but found his assessments too unreliable. It is clear that allegations of fraud are even more frequent than its actual occurrence, and by all indications some fraud is a ubiquitous phenomenon in democracies. Screaming "Fraud!" is just part of the standard repertoire of democratic competition. Indeed, there are cases in which the opposition has withdrawn from the competition, claiming that the elections would not be conducted fairly. We conclude that there is no way to assess the validity of such allegations in a standardized way. For example, the opposition decided not to contest the 1984 Nicaraguan elections, but some of its leaders later expressed regret about 1984 once they discovered that they had won the subsequent elections in 1990. Hence, although our approach is theoretically akin to those of Bollen and Coppedge and Reinicke, we have tried to the extent possible to avoid subjective judgments by relying only on observables. The Gurr (1990) measure in *Polity II* is conceptually somewhat different, because it considers the limited character of the government by coding "constraints on the chief executive." His assessments, however, are not easy to reproduce.

Although we have been careful to specify our understanding of democracy and to distinguish it from some rival conceptions, it appears that from a practical point of view alternative measures of democracy generate highly similar results. The dimensions used to assess whether or not and to what extent a particular regime is democratic seem to make little difference.[36] To cite Inkeles (1990: 5–6), "the indicators most commonly selected to measure democratic systems generally form a notably coherent syndrome, achieving high reliability as measurement scales. . . . A testimonial to the robustness of the underlying common form and structure of the democratic systems is found in the high degree of agreement produced by the classification of nations as democratic or not, even when democracy is measured in somewhat different ways by different analysts. . . . Thus Coppedge and Reinicke, following a quite independent theoretical model, end up with a scale of polyarchy which correlates .94 with Gastil's civil liberties measure for some 170 countries in 1985. Gurr's measure performs similarly in relation to Bollen's [and] his ratings of 118 countries circa 1965 correlate .83 with Bollen's measure and .89 with a score combining Gastil's separate measures of political and civil liberties for 113 countries in 1985."

Our measure is no exception. The Coppedge-Reinicke scale for 1978 predicts 92 percent of our dichotomous regimes, the Bollen 1965 scale predicts 85 percent, and the Gurr scales of Autocracy and Democracy for 1950–1986 jointly predict 91 percent. The Gastil scale of political liberties, covering the period from 1972 to 1990, predicts 93.2 percent

---

[36] Note, however, that different measures appear to be biased in somewhat different directions. See Bollen (1993).

of our classification; his scale of civil liberties predicts 91.5 percent; and the two scales jointly predict 94.2 percent of our regimes.[37] Hence, our classification is by no means idiosyncratic. Different views of democracy, including those that entail highly subjective judgments, yield a robust classification.

The main difference between our approach and the alternatives is that we use a nominal classification, rather than a ratio scale. We believe that although some regimes are more democratic than others, unless the offices are contested, they should not be considered democratic. The analogy with the proverbial pregnancy is thus that whereas democracy can be more or less advanced, one cannot be half-democratic: There is a natural zero point. Note that Bollen and Jackman (1989) are confused: It is one thing to argue that some democracies are more democratic than others, but it is another to argue that democracy is a continuous feature over all regimes, that is, that one can distinguish the degrees of "democracy" for any pair of regimes.[38]

Bollen and Jackman (1989: 612) argue that difficulties in classifying some cases speak in favor of using continuous scales: "Dichotomizing democracy," in their view, "blurs distinctions between borderline cases." Yet why are there "borderline cases"? Suppose that we have defined democracy and not-democracy, established operational rules, and found that some cases cannot be unambiguously classified by these rules. Does this mean that there are borderline cases and that democracy is thus "inherently continuous"? And should we stick the cases that cannot be unambiguously classified, given our rules, into an "intermediate" category, halfway between democracy and dictatorship? That view strikes us as ludicrous. If we cannot classify some cases given our rules, all this means is that we either have unclear rules or have insufficient information to apply them.

We have already seen that some "borderline cases" constitute sys-

---

[37] Because other scales are ordinal (and pretend to be cardinal), whereas ours is nominal, we use probit maximum likelihood to predict our classification on the basis of these scales.

[38] They also argue by assertion, referring to "the inherently continuous nature of the concept of political democracy" (1989: 612), claiming that "since democracy is conceptually continuous, it is best measured in continuous terms" (p. 612), and that "democracy is always a matter of degree" (p. 618). Hence, in their view, the "degrees of democracy" in Mexico, in Salazar's Portugal, and in Franco's Spain were different. How they decide that "democracy is conceptually continuous," whatever that means, remains mysterious, but we are admonished that "it is important that the measurement history of this construct not repeat itself" (p. 612).

tematic error, whereas others bring random error. Systematic errors can be treated by explicit rules, such as our "alternation" rule, and their consequences can be examined statistically. There are some regimes that cannot be unambiguously classified on the basis of all the evidence produced by history. Because history produces a biased sample of democracies – sampling is endogenous (Pudney 1989) – we must revert to counterfactual judgments. In such cases we must decide which error we prefer to avoid: classifying as democracies regimes that may not be democracies, or rejecting as democracies regimes that may in fact qualify. Yet, once this decision is made, the classification is unambiguous. Mexico is not a regime intermediate between democracy and dictatorship, not a "borderline case." It is a regime in which the ruling party allows some contestation but always wins: either a democracy or a dictatorship, depending in which direction one wants to err systematically.

In turn, some errors that are random with regard to the rules will remain, and we will have to live with them. But errors are errors, not "intermediate" categories. And there are no grounds to think that a finer classification would be more precise. A finer scale would generate smaller errors, but more of them, and a rougher scale would generate larger errors, but fewer of them. And if errors of larger magnitude are less likely, the dichotomous scale will have a lower expected error.

Suppose that the true nature of democracy lies on a J-point scale, $j = 1, \ldots, J$, but its measurement is subject to error. Let the unobserved true score be D_T and the assigned value D, and let the probability of a j-point error be $P(j) = \Pr\{|D - D_T| = j\} = \alpha^j$. The reliability of the scale is then $\Pr\{|D - D_T| = 0\} = 1 - \Sigma_{j=1} \Pr(j)$. Assume that the distribution of the true observations is uniform. Then the expected value of the error will be

$$E(|D - D_T|) = \sum_{j=1} \Pr(j) * j * 2(J - j),$$

where the first factor is the probability of an error of a given magnitude, the second factor is the magnitude, and the third is the number of such errors. Assume, as an illustration, that the probability of making an error of magnitude 1 is $\alpha = 0.2$, so that $\Pr(j = 0) \approx 0.75$. Suppose that this is a Gastil scale, with seven points. Then the expected error for seven observations will be about 3.5.

Now dichotomize this seven-point scale in such a way that if $D \le 4$, then the assigned score is $D = 2.5$ (which is the midpoint value for one regime), and if $D > 4$, then the assigned score is $D = 5.5$ (midpoint for the other regime), so that each error costs three points on the seven-point scale. Let the probabilities of errors and the distributions of the true scores on the seven-point scale be the same. Then the expected value of the error is

$$E(|D - D_\mathrm{T}|) = \sum_{j=1} \Pr(j) * 3 * 2[d * j + (1 - d)(J - j)],$$

where the last factor in each expression is the number of relevant errors (e.g., the only relevant one-point error is between 4 and 5, and there are two of them, misclassifying 4 as 5 or 5 as 4), and $d = 1$ if $j \leq 4$, and $d = 0$ otherwise. At $\alpha = 0.2$, the expected error for seven observations of a dichotomous scale will be about 2.

Hence, there is less measurement error when a dichotomous scale is used. If the distribution of true observations is unimodal and close to symmetric, a more refined classification will have a smaller error, but in fact observations on all the polychotomous scales tend to be U-shaped, which advantages a dichotomous classification even more than our example with the uniform distribution.

In sum, we think that our classification has some advantages. First, it is grounded in theory. Second, it is based exclusively on observed facts. Third, it separates cases subject to systematic error. Fourth, it contains less random error than polychotomous scales. Finally, it covers every year for 141 countries during forty-one years.

Appendix 1.2: Classification of Political Regimes, 1950–1990

At least some of the years for regimes marked with asterisks have been classified as bureaucracies on the basis of our "alternation" rule.

Country	Regime	Entry	Exit
1. Algeria	Bureaucracy	1962	1964
	Autocracy	1965	1976
	Bureaucracy	1977	1990
2. Angola	Autocracy	1975	1979
	Bureaucracy	1980	1990
3. Benin	Bureaucracy	1960	1964

(continued)

Country	Regime	Entry	Exit
	Autocracy	1965	1978
	Bureaucracy	1979	1989
	Autocracy	1990	1990
4. Botswana	Bureaucracy*	1966	1990
5. Burkina Faso	Bureaucracy	1960	1965
	Autocracy	1966	1969
	Bureaucracy	1970	1973
	Autocracy	1974	1977
	Bureaucracy*	1978	1979
	Autocracy	1980	1990
6. Burundi	Bureaucracy	1962	1965
	Autocracy	1966	1981
	Bureaucracy	1982	1986
	Autocracy	1987	1990
7. Cameroon	Bureaucracy	1960	1970
	Autocracy	1971	1972
	Bureaucracy	1973	1990
8. Cape Verde	Bureaucracy	1975	1990
9. Central African Republic	Bureaucracy	1960	1965
	Autocracy	1966	1986
	Bureaucracy	1987	1990
10. Chad	Bureaucracy	1960	1974
	Autocracy	1975	1990
11. Comoros	Autocracy	1975	1977
	Bureaucracy	1978	1990
12. Congo	Presidentialism	1960	1962
	Bureaucracy	1963	1976
	Autocracy	1977	1978
	Bureaucracy	1979	1990
13. Djibouti	Bureaucracy	1977	1990
14. Egypt	Bureaucracy*	1950	1990
15. Ethiopia	Autocracy	1950	1956
	Bureaucracy	1957	1973
	Autocracy	1974	1986
	Bureaucracy	1987	1990
16. Gabon	Bureaucracy*	1960	1990
17. Gambia	Bureaucracy*	1965	1990
18. Ghana	Bureaucracy	1957	1964
	Autocracy	1965	1969

(continued)

Country	Regime	Entry	Exit
	Parliamentarism	1970	1971
	Autocracy	1972	1978
	Presidentialism	1979	1980
	Autocracy	1981	1990
19. Guinea	Bureaucracy	1958	1983
	Autocracy	1984	1990
20. Guinea-Bissau	Bureaucracy	1974	1990
21. Ivory Coast	Bureaucracy*	1960	1990
22. Kenya	Bureaucracy	1963	1990
23. Lesotho	Bureaucracy	1966	1969
	Autocracy	1970	1990
24. Liberia	Bureaucracy	1950	1979
	Autocracy	1980	1984
	Bureaucracy	1985	1989
	Autocracy	1990	1990
25. Madagascar	Bureaucracy*	1960	1971
	Autocracy	1972	1976
	Bureaucracy	1977	1990
26. Malawi	Bureaucracy	1964	1990
27. Mali	Bureaucracy	1960	1967
	Autocracy	1968	1981
	Bureaucracy	1982	1990
28. Mauritania	Bureaucracy	1960	1977
	Autocracy	1978	1990
29. Mauritius	Parliamentarism	1968	1990
30. Morocco	Autocracy	1956	1962
	Bureaucracy	1963	1964
	Autocracy	1965	1969
	Bureaucracy	1970	1971
	Autocracy	1972	1976
	Bureaucracy	1977	1990
31. Mozambique	Bureaucracy	1975	1990
32. Niger	Bureaucracy	1960	1973
	Autocracy	1974	1990
33. Nigeria	Parliamentarism	1960	1965
	Autocracy	1966	1978
	Presidentialism	1979	1982
	Autocracy	1983	1990
34. Rwanda	Bureaucracy	1962	1972

(continued)

Country	Regime	Entry	Exit
	Autocracy	1973	1980
	Bureaucracy	1981	1990
35. Senegal	Bureaucracy*	1960	1990
36. Seychelles	Bureaucracy	1976	1990
37. Sierra Leone	Parliamentarism	1961	1966
	Autocracy	1967	1967
	Bureaucracy	1968	1990
38. Somalia	Mixed	1960	1968
	Autocracy	1969	1978
	Bureaucracy	1979	1990
39. South Africa	Bureaucracy*	1950	1990
40. Sudan	Parliamentarism	1956	1957
	Autocracy	1958	1964
	Parliamentarism	1965	1968
	Bureaucracy	1969	1984
	Autocracy	1985	1985
	Parliamentarism	1986	1988
	Autocracy	1989	1990
41. Swaziland	Bureaucracy	1968	1972
	Autocracy	1973	1977
	Bureaucracy	1978	1990
42. Tanzania	Bureaucracy	1961	1990
43. Togo	Bureaucracy	1960	1966
	Autocracy	1967	1978
	Bureaucracy	1979	1990
44. Tunisia	Bureaucracy	1956	1990
45. Uganda	Bureaucracy	1962	1970
	Autocracy	1971	1979
	Presidentialism	1980	1984
	Autocracy	1985	1990
46. Zaire	Autocracy	1960	1960
	Bureaucracy	1961	1962
	Autocracy	1963	1969
	Bureaucracy	1970	1990
47. Zambia	Bureaucracy	1964	1990
48. Zimbabwe	Bureaucracy	1965	1990
49. Bahamas	Parliamentarism	1973	1990
50. Barbados	Parliamentarism	1966	1990
51. Belize	Parliamentarism	1981	1990

(continued)

Appendix 1.2: Classification of Regimes

Country	Regime	Entry	Exit
52. Canada	Parliamentarism	1950	1990
53. Costa Rica	Presidentialism	1950	1990
54. Dominican Republic	Bureaucracy	1950	1961
	Autocracy	1962	1965
	Presidentialism	1966	1990
55. El Salvador	Bureaucracy	1950	1959
	Autocracy	1960	1960
	Bureaucracy*	1961	1983
	Presidentialism	1984	1990
56. Grenada	Parliamentarism	1974	1978
	Autocracy	1979	1983
	Parliamentarism	1984	1990
57. Guatemala	Presidentialism	1950	1953
	Bureaucracy	1954	1957
	Presidentialism	1958	1962
	Autocracy	1963	1965
	Presidentialism	1966	1981
	Bureaucracy	1982	1985
	Presidentialism	1986	1990
58. Haiti	Bureaucracy	1950	1985
	Autocracy	1986	1989
	Bureaucracy	1990	1990
59. Honduras	Bureaucracy	1950	1955
	Autocracy	1956	1956
	Presidentialism	1957	1962
	Autocracy	1963	1964
	Bureaucracy*	1965	1970
	Presidentialism	1971	1971
	Autocracy	1972	1981
	Presidentialism	1982	1990
60. Jamaica	Parliamentarism	1962	1990
61. Mexico	Bureaucracy*	1950	1990
62. Nicaragua	Bureaucracy*	1950	1970
	Autocracy	1971	1971
	Bureaucracy*	1972	1978
	Autocracy	1979	1983
	Presidentialism	1984	1990
63. Panama	Presidentialism	1950	1950
	Bureaucracy	1951	1951

(continued)

Country	Regime	Entry	Exit
	Presidentialism	1952	1967
	Autocracy	1968	1977
	Bureaucracy	1978	1990
64. Trinidad & Tobago	Parliamentarism	1962	1990
65. United States	Presidentialism	1950	1990
66. Argentina	Presidentialism	1950	1954
	Autocracy	1955	1957
	Presidentialism	1958	1961
	Autocracy	1962	1962
	Presidentialism	1963	1965
	Autocracy	1966	1972
	Presidentialism	1973	1975
	Autocracy	1976	1982
	Presidentialism	1983	1990
67. Bolivia	Bureaucracy	1950	1950
	Autocracy	1951	1955
	Bureaucracy*	1956	1963
	Autocracy	1964	1978
	Presidentialism	1979	1979
	Autocracy	1980	1981
	Presidentialism	1982	1990
68. Brazil	Presidentialism	1950	1960
	Mixed	1961	1962
	Presidentialism	1963	1963
	Bureaucracy	1964	1967
	Autocracy	1968	1969
	Bureaucracy	1970	1978
	Presidentialism	1979	1990
69. Chile	Presidentialism	1950	1972
	Autocracy	1973	1989
	Presidentialism	1990	1990
70. Colombia	Bureaucracy	1950	1953
	Autocracy	1954	1957
	Presidentialism	1958	1990
71. Ecuador	Presidentialism	1950	1962
	Autocracy	1963	1967
	Bureaucracy	1968	1969
	Autocracy	1970	1978
	Presidentialism	1979	1990

(continued)

Country	Regime	Entry	Exit
72. Guyana	Bureaucracy*	1966	1990
73. Paraguay	Bureaucracy*	1950	1990
74. Peru	Bureaucracy	1950	1955
	Presidentialism	1956	1961
	Autocracy	1962	1962
	Presidentialism	1963	1967
	Autocracy	1968	1979
	Presidentialism	1980	1989
	Bureaucracy	1990	1990
75. Suriname	Parliamentarism	1975	1979
	Autocracy	1980	1986
	Bureaucracy	1987	1987
	Mixed	1988	1989
	Bureaucracy	1990	1990
76. Uruguay	Presidentialism	1950	1972
	Autocracy	1973	1984
	Presidentialism	1985	1990
77. Venezuela	Autocracy	1950	1951
	Bureaucracy	1952	1958
	Presidentialism	1959	1990
78. Bangladesh	Autocracy	1971	1971
	Bureaucracy	1972	1974
	Autocracy	1975	1978
	Bureaucracy*	1979	1981
	Autocracy	1982	1985
	Presidentialism	1986	1990
79. China, People's Republic (PR)	Autocracy	1950	1953
	Bureaucracy	1954	1990
80. India	Parliamentarism	1950	1990
81. Indonesia	Autocracy	1950	1954
	Parliamentarism	1955	1956
	Bureaucracy	1957	1959
	Autocracy	1960	1970
	Bureaucracy	1971	1990
82. Iran	Bureaucracy	1950	1960
	Autocracy	1961	1962
	Bureaucracy	1963	1983
	Autocracy	1984	1990
83. Iraq	Autocracy	1950	1950

(continued)

Country	Regime	Entry	Exit
	Bureaucracy	1951	1957
	Autocracy	1958	1979
	Bureaucracy	1980	1990
84. Israel	Parliamentarism	1950	1990
85. Japan	Parliamentarism	1952	1990
86. Jordan	Bureaucracy	1950	1965
	Autocracy	1966	1966
	Bureaucracy	1967	1973
	Autocracy	1974	1983
	Bureaucracy	1984	1984
	Autocracy	1985	1988
	Bureaucracy	1989	1990
87. South Korea	Bureaucracy*	1950	1959
	Parliamentarism	1960	1960
	Bureaucracy	1961	1971
	Autocracy	1972	1972
	Bureaucracy	1973	1987
	Presidentialism	1988	1990
88. Laos	Parliamentarism	1954	1958
	Bureaucracy	1959	1965
	Autocracy	1966	1966
	Bureaucracy	1967	1973
	Autocracy	1974	1990
89. Malaysia	Bureaucracy	1957	1968
	Autocracy	1969	1970
	Bureaucracy	1971	1990
90. Mongolia	Bureaucracy*	1950	1990
91. Myanmar	Parliamentarism	1950	1957
	Autocracy	1958	1959
	Parliamentarism	1960	1961
	Autocracy	1962	1973
	Bureaucracy	1974	1987
	Autocracy	1988	1989
	Bureaucracy	1990	1990
92. Nepal	Autocracy	1950	1958
	Bureaucracy	1959	1959
	Autocracy	1960	1962
	Bureaucracy	1963	1990
93. Pakistan	Parliamentarism	1950	1955

(continued)

Country	Regime	Entry	Exit
	Bureaucracy	1956	1957
	Autocracy	1958	1961
	Bureaucracy*	1962	1971
	Mixed	1972	1976
	Autocracy	1977	1984
	Bureaucracy	1985	1987
	Parliamentarism	1988	1990
94. Philippines	Presidentialism	1950	1964
	Bureaucracy	1965	1971
	Autocracy	1972	1977
	Bureaucracy	1978	1985
	Presidentialism	1986	1990
95. Singapore	Bureaucracy*	1965	1990
96. Sri Lanka	Parliamentarism	1950	1976
	Bureaucracy*	1977	1990
97. Syria	Bureaucracy	1950	1960
	Autocracy	1961	1969
	Bureaucracy	1970	1990
98. Taiwan	Bureaucracy*	1950	1990
99. Thailand	Bureaucracy	1950	1956
	Autocracy	1957	1968
	Bureaucracy	1969	1970
	Autocracy	1971	1974
	Parliamentarism	1975	1975
	Autocracy	1976	1976
	Bureaucracy	1977	1982
	Parliamentarism	1983	1990
100. Yemen Arab Republic	Autocracy	1967	1977
	Bureaucracy	1978	1990
101. Austria	Parliamentarism	1950	1990
102. Belgium	Parliamentarism	1950	1990
103. Bulgaria	Bureaucracy	1950	1989
	Parliamentarism	1990	1990
104. Czechoslovakia	Bureaucracy	1950	1989
	Parliamentarism	1990	1990
105. Denmark	Parliamentarism	1950	1990
106. Finland	Mixed	1950	1990
107. France	Parliamentarism	1950	1957
	Mixed	1958	1990

(continued)

Country	Regime	Entry	Exit
108. East Germany	Bureaucracy	1950	1990
109. West Germany	Parliamentarism	1950	1990
110. Greece	Parliamentarism	1950	1966
	Autocracy	1967	1970
	Bureaucracy	1971	1973
	Parliamentarism	1974	1990
111. Hungary	Bureaucracy	1950	1989
	Parliamentarism	1990	1990
112. Iceland	Mixed	1950	1990
113. Ireland	Parliamentarism	1950	1990
114. Italy	Parliamentarism	1950	1990
115. Luxembourg	Parliamentarism	1950	1990
116. Malta	Parliamentarism	1964	1990
117. Netherlands	Parliamentarism	1950	1990
118. Norway	Parliamentarism	1950	1990
119. Poland	Bureaucracy	1950	1988
	Mixed	1989	1990
120. Portugal	Bureaucracy	1950	1975
	Mixed	1976	1990
121. Romania	Bureaucracy	1950	1990
122. Spain	Autocracy	1950	1976
	Parliamentarism	1977	1990
123. Sweden	Parliamentarism	1950	1990
124. Switzerland	Presidentialism	1950	1990
125. Turkey	Bureaucracy*	1950	1960
	Parliamentarism	1961	1979
	Autocracy	1980	1982
	Parliamentarism	1983	1990
126. United Kingdom	Parliamentarism	1950	1990
127. Soviet Union	Bureaucracy	1950	1990
128. Yugoslavia	Bureaucracy	1950	1990
129. Australia	Parliamentarism	1950	1990
130. Fiji	Bureaucracy	1970	1986
	Autocracy	1987	1990
131. New Zealand	Parliamentarism	1950	1990
132. Papua New Guinea	Parliamentarism	1975	1990
133. Solomon Islands	Parliamentarism	1978	1990
134. Vanuatu	Parliamentarism	1980	1990

(continued)

Country	Regime	Entry	Exit
135. Western Samoa	Autocracy	1962	1978
	Bureaucracy*	1979	1990
136. Bahrain	Autocracy	1971	1972
	Bureaucracy	1973	1974
	Autocracy	1975	1990
137. Kuwait	Autocracy	1961	1962
	Bureaucracy	1963	1975
	Autocracy	1976	1980
	Bureaucracy	1981	1985
	Autocracy	1986	1990
138. Oman	Autocracy	1951	1990
139. Qatar	Autocracy	1971	1990
140. Saudi Arabia	Autocracy	1950	1990
141. United Arab Emirates	Autocracy	1971	1990

Appendix 1.3: Basic Data about Regime Dynamics

Asterisks indicate cases classified as regime transitions according to the regular coding rules.

(A) Transitions to Dictatorships by Incumbents

Country	Year
Cameroon	1963
Central African Republic	1962
Chad	1962
Djibouti	1982
Gabon	1967
Ghana	1972*
Kenya	1969
Lesotho	1970
Malawi	1966
Rwanda	1965
Sierra Leone	1967*
Uganda	1970
Zambia	1973

(continued)

Country	Year
Zimbabwe	1980
Ecuador	1970
Uruguay	1973*
Bangladesh	1975
South Korea	1972
Malaysia	1969
Pakistan	1956*
Philippines	1972
Turkey	1980*

(B) Countries by Regime Type and the Number of Transitions to Authoritarianism Experienced by 1950

Democracies in 1950 that had experienced no transition to authoritarianism by then:

Canada
Guatemala
Panama
United States
Brazil
Ecuador
Uruguay
India
Israel
Myanmar
Pakistan
Philippines
Sri Lanka
Belgium
Denmark
France
Iceland
Ireland
Luxembourg
Netherlands
Norway
Sweden
Switzerland
United Kingdom

Australia
New Zealand

Dictatorships in 1950 that had experienced no transition to authoritarianism by then:

Egypt
Ethiopia
Liberia
South Africa
Dominican Republic
El Salvador
Haiti
Honduras
Mexico
Nicaragua
Bolivia
Paraguay
China (PR)
Indonesia
Iran
Iraq
Jordan
South Korea
Mongolia
Nepal
Syria
Taiwan
Thailand
Hungary
Romania
Turkey
Soviet Union
Saudi Arabia

Democracies in 1950 that had experienced at least one transition to authoritarianism by then:

Costa Rica
Argentina
Chile
Austria
Finland

West Germany
Greece
Italy

Dictatorships in 1950 that had experienced at least one transition to authoritarianism by then:

Colombia
Peru
Venezuela
Bulgaria
Czechoslovakia
East Germany
Poland
Portugal
Spain
Yugoslavia

(C) Regime Transitions, by Country

NO TRANSITIONS (100 cases)

Dictatorships (67 cases)

Algeria	1962–1990
Angola	1975–1990
Benin	1960–1990
Botswana	1966–1990
Burkina Faso	1960–1990
Burundi	1962–1990
Cameroon	1960–1990
Cape Verde	1975–1990
Central African Republic	1960–1990
Chad	1960–1990
Comoros	1975–1990
Djibouti	1977–1990
Egypt	1950–1990
Ethiopia	1950–1990
Gabon	1960–1990
Gambia	1965–1990
Guinea	1958–1990
Guinea-Bissau	1974–1990

(continued)

Dictatorships (67 cases, cont.)

Ivory Coast	1960–1990
Kenya	1963–1990
Lesotho	1966–1990
Liberia	1950–1990
Madagascar	1950–1990
Malawi	1964–1990
Mali	1960–1990
Mauritania	1960–1990
Morocco	1956–1990
Mozambique	1975–1990
Niger	1960–1990

Democracies (33 cases)

Rwanda	1962–1990
Senegal	1960–1990
Seychelles	1976–1990
South Africa	1950–1990
Swaziland	1968–1990
Tanzania	1961–1990
Togo	1960–1990
Tunisia	1956–1990
Zaire	1960–1990
Zambia	1964–1990
Zimbabwe	1965–1990
Haiti	1950–1990
Mexico	1950–1990
Guyana	1966–1990
Paraguay	1950–1990
Bahrain	1971–1990
China (PR)	1950–1990
Iran	1950–1990
Iraq	1950–1990
Jordan	1950–1990
Kuwait	1961–1990
Malaysia	1957–1990
Mongolia	1950–1990
Nepal	1950–1990
Oman	1951–1990

(continued)

Democracies (33 cases, cont.)

Qatar	1971–1990
Saudi Arabia	1950–1990
Singapore	1965–1990
Syria	1950–1990
Taiwan	1950–1990
United Arab Emirates	1971–1990
Yemen	1967–1990
East Germany	1970–1988
Romania	1961–1989
Soviet Union	1950–1990
Yugoslavia	1950–1990
Fiji	1970–1990
Western Samoa	1962–1990
Mauritius	1968–1990
Bahamas	1973–1990
Barbados	1966–1990
Belize	1980–1990
Canada	1950–1990
Costa Rica	1950–1990
Jamaica	1962–1990
Trinidad & Tobago	1962–1990
United States	1950–1990
India	1950–1990
Israel	1950–1990
Japan	1952–1990
Austria	1950–1990
Belgium	1950–1990
Denmark	1950–1990
Finland	1950–1990
France	1950–1990
West Germany	1950–1990
Iceland	1950–1990
Ireland	1950–1990
Italy	1950–1990
Luxembourg	1950–1990
Malta	1964–1990
Netherlands	1950–1990
Norway	1950–1990

(continued)

Democracies (33 cases, cont.)

Sweden	1950–1990
Switzerland	1950–1990
United Kingdom	1950–1990
Australia	1950–1990
New Zealand	1950–1990
Papua New Guinea	1975–1990
Solomon Islands	1978–1990
Vanuatu	1980–1990

ONE TRANSITION (17 cases)

To Dictatorship (5 cases)

Congo	1963
Sierra Leone	1967
Somalia	1968
Sri Lanka	1977

To Democracy (12 cases)

Laos	1958
Dominican Republic	1966
El Salvador	1984
Nicaragua	1984
Colombia	1958
Bangladesh	1985
Venezuela	1959
Bulgaria	1989
Czechoslovakia	1989
Hungary	1989
Poland	1989
Portugal	1975
Spain	1976

TWO TRANSITIONS (9 cases)

Dic → Dem → Dic (2 cases)

Uganda
Indonesia

Dem → Dic → Dem (7 cases)

Grenada
Brazil
Chile
Ecuador
Uruguay
Philippines
Greece

THREE TRANSITIONS (8 cases)

Dem → Dic → Dem → Dic (5 cases)

Nigeria
Panama
Suriname
Myanmar
Thailand

Dic → Dem → Dic → Dem (3 cases)

Bolivia
South Korea
Turkey

FOUR TRANSITIONS (2 cases)

Ghana
Pakistan

FIVE TRANSITIONS (2 cases)

Sudan
Honduras

SIX TRANSITIONS (2 cases)

Guatemala
Peru

EIGHT TRANSITIONS (1 case)

Argentina

Appendix 1.4: The "Short" Data Base

Because the economic data are not available for all the countries and years described earlier, we shall be working with a somewhat smaller data set. As the earliest year for which we have data on per capita income is 1950, our observations on the rate of economic growth begin in 1951. Moreover, because the patterns of economic development for countries that rely for most of their income on oil are *sui generis*, we excluded six countries in which the ratio of fuel exports to total exports in 1984–1986 exceeded 50 percent.[39] These limitations delineate what we call our "short" data base.

The basic patterns that have been described remain unchanged as we move to the smaller data set. Overall, we lose 604 observations, 171 in the six excluded oil-producing countries, and the rest where the economic data are not available. The most significant losses are concentrated in East Asia (31.7 percent), the Pacific islands (30 percent), and Eastern Europe (36.9 percent). Because of data unavailability, we lose 78 years of democracy (4.5 percent) and 355 years of dictatorship (11.8 percent).

In the end, thus, the data set with which we work in the rest of this book contains observations for 1,645 years of democracy (1,022 of parliamentary democracies, 147 of mixed democracies, and 476 of presidential democracies) and 2,481 years of dictatorship (1,812 of bureaucracies and 669 of autocracies), for a total of 4,126 observations. They compose 99 spells of democracies (or 50 of parliamentarism, 9 of mixed systems, and 43 of presidentialism) and 123 spells of dictatorships (or 133 of bureaucracy and 98 of autocracy). This yields thirty-nine transitions from democracy to dictatorship, and forty-nine from dictatorship, to democracy.

---

[39] These countries are Bahrain, Kuwait, Oman, Qatar, Saudi Arabia, and the United Arab Emirates.

Chapter Two

Economic Development and Political Regimes

Introduction

Any casual glance at the world will show that poor countries tend to have authoritarian regimes, and wealthy countries democratic ones. The question is why. What are the conditions that determine whether democracy or dictatorship prevails? What causes political regimes to rise, endure, and fall? Can their transformations be explained generally, or are they caused by circumstances idiosyncratic to each country or period? Are they driven by economic development or by other factors, such as the preceding political history, cultural traditions, political institutions, or the international political climate?

We begin with the observation that the incidence of democracy is undoubtedly related to the level of economic development. Having established the central importance of development, we distinguish two causal mechanisms that may generate this relationship, asking whether democracies are more likely to *emerge* as countries develop economically under dictatorships or, having emerged for reasons other than economic development, are only more likely to *survive* in countries that are already developed. This analysis is extended first to the impact of economic performance and then to a panoply of social and political factors. A separate section is devoted to the impacts of different types of democratic institutions. A summary closes the chapter. The statistical models on which the analysis is based are presented in the appendixes.

Development and Democracy

First advanced in 1959, S. M. Lipset's observation that democracy is related to economic development has generated the largest body of research on any topic in comparative politics. It has been supported and contested, revised and extended, buried and resuscitated. And yet, though several articles in the *Festschrift* honoring Lipset (Marks and Diamond 1992) proclaim conclusions, neither the theory nor the facts are clear.

Aggregate patterns, such as that in Figure 2.1, show that the relationship between the level of economic development and the incidence of democratic regimes is strong and tight. Indeed, one can correctly predict 77.5 percent of the 4,126 annual observations of regimes just by looking at per capita income.[1] What remains controversial, however, is the relative importance of the level of development as compared with other factors, such as the political legacy of a country, its past history, its social structure, its cultural traditions, the specific institutional framework, and, last but not least, the international political climate.

To compare the impacts of different factors, we proceed as follows: (1) We estimate the probability that the regime in a given country during a particular year will have been a dictatorship or a democracy, conditional on the value of each independent variable and their various combinations. (2) We take as the predicted regime the one for which this probability is higher, more than 0.50, and (3) We compare these predictions with the observations. Such predictions obviously are quite rough, because they do not distinguish whether the probability that a regime is, say, a dictatorship is 0.99 or 0.51. But because all we need is a yardstick with which to compare the influences of different factors, this simple procedure is sufficient. Hence, our criterion in comparing the effects of different variables is simply the number of correct predictions. Given the controversies about comparing the fit of non-linear models, we also provide, however, an alternative measure, the Zavoina-McKelvey (1975) pseudo-R^2.

---

[1] These predictions are derived from probit, a form of non-linear regression, in which the probability that a country i will have had a dictatorial (as opposed to democratic) regime at time t is modeled as $\Pr(\text{REG}_{it} = \text{Dictatorship}) = F(X_{it}\beta)$, where $F(\cdot)$ is the cumulative distribution function (c.d.f.) of the normal distribution. A fair amount of ink has been spilled over the issue whether or not the relationship between development and democracy is linear (Jackman 1973; Arat 1988). We now know better. Democracy, however it is measured, is a qualitative or limited variable (it assumes the value of 0 or 1 under our measurement, it ranges from 2 to 14 on the Freedom House scale, from 0 to 100 on the Bollen scale, and so on). Hence, no predicted index of democracy can become negative as the level of development tends to zero, and no predicted index of democracy can exceed whatever is the maximum value of a particular scale as the level gets very large. Only a non-linear function, such as the normal or logistic (as suggested by Dahl 1971), can satisfy these constraints. This is why we use probit throughout.

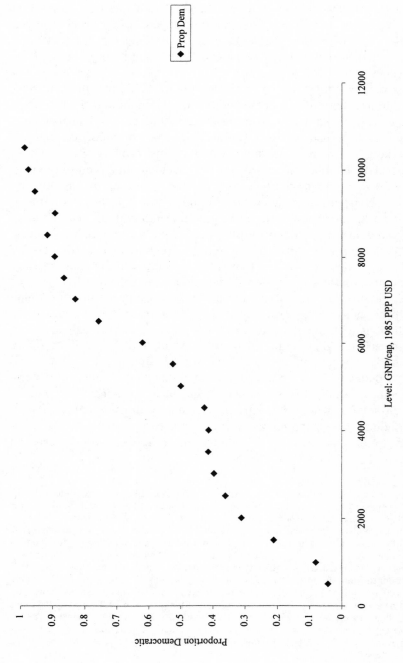

Figure 2.1. Probability that a regime will be democratic, by per capita income

Following the lead of extensive work reported by others, the factors we consider include the following:

1. The level of development (LEVEL), as measured by per capita income.[2]
2. The political legacies of a country, as summarized by two dummy variables that indicate whether or not the country became independent after 1945 (NEWC) and whether or not it was a British colony in 1919 (BRITCOL).
3. The political history of the country, as indicated by the number of past transitions to authoritarianism (STRA).[3]
4. The religious structure of the country, as indicated by proportions of Catholics (CATH), Protestants (PROT), and Moslems (MOSLEM) in the population.
5. The ethnolinguistic (ELF60) and religious (RELDIF) fractionalization of the country, measured as the probability that two randomly chosen individuals will not belong to the same group.
6. The international political environment, as measured by the proportion of other democracies in the world (ODWP) during the particular year. By "other" we mean in countries other than the one under consideration.

Table 2.1 shows the predictions based on different combinations of these variables. How one evaluates these results depends on the null model. If one knows absolutely nothing and is forced to think that a randomly chosen country has a fifty-fifty chance of having either regime, then correctly predicting more than half, 2,063 cases, is already an improvement. Because we do know, however, that there were more dictatorial years than democratic years, 60 versus 40 percent, one could correctly predict 2,481 country-years by guessing that all countries were dictatorships at all times. Except for ODWP, we list in Table 2.1 only those variables that considered alone or in thematic combinations at least match the random guess conditioned on the relative frequencies.

---

[2] All income figures are expressed in 1985 constant purchasing power parity (PPP) dollars, from the Penn World Tables (PWT 5.6). One might question that per capita income is an adequate indicator of the level of development. In some countries it clearly is not. That is why we excluded from our analysis six countries that derive most of their income from oil revenues. Even with this exclusion, income may not correspond perfectly to whatever one means by "development." Yet in our view it is the best indicator – better than energy consumption, literacy, industrialization, and other alternative measures.

[3] But to discount somewhat the distant past, we assign the value of 1 for all the transitions that occurred before 1950.

Table 2.1. Predictions of probit models of regimes

Variables	Number of correct predictions of			Proportion correct	ZM[a]
	Democracies $N = 1,645$ (40.0%)	Dictatorships $N = 2,481$ (60.0%)	Total $N = 4,126$ (100.0%)		
LEVEL	973	2,226	3,199	77.5	0.63
Legacies: NEWC + BRITCOL	1,264	1,501	2,765	67.0	0.47
Religion: CATH + PROT + MOSLEM	1,074	1,697	2,771	67.2	0.49
ELF60	0	2,481	2,481	60.0	0.40
RELDIF	0	2,481	2,481	60.0	0.39
History: STRA	19	2,459	2,478	60.0	0.39
ODWP	68	2,376	2,444	59.2	0.39
LEVEL + legacies	1,003	2,201	3,204	77.7	0.63
LEVEL + religion	1,028	2,216	3,244	78.6	0.65
LEVEL + ELF60	1,020	2,279	3,299	80.0	0.66
LEVEL + RELDIF	969	2,225	3,194	77.4	0.63
LEVEL + history	974	2,227	3,201	77.6	0.63
LEVEL + ODWP	1,005	2,233	3,238	78.5	0.64
Everything	1,136	2,241	3,377	81.4	0.70

[a] ZM stands for the Zavoina and McKelvey (1975) pseudo-R^2.

Per capita income (LEVEL) clearly outperforms a random guess. "Legacies," the colonial experience, can improve on a random guess by 7 percent, as can the distribution of religions. Ethnic and religious heterogeneity, as well as the number of past transitions to dictatorship, can correctly predict only as many cases as one would guess by knowing the marginal distribution. The proportion of other democracies in the world (ODWP) predicts poorly when considered alone.[4]

When considered along with LEVEL, no other variables, alone or in their thematic combinations, can contribute much to the prediction. Adding to LEVEL all the other variables can improve the guess by only 4 percent.[5] Hence, all the evidence indicates that it is the level of development that can best predict the incidences of various political regimes.

Whereas these variables accurately predicted 81.4 percent of the regimes that countries had at any given time, there were 749 cases in which the regime expected was not the observed one. Can we learn anything from these mistakes? Table 2.2 lists the incorrect predictions by country and period and also shows the predicted probability that the regime would be a dictatorship. Several features of this list merit comment:

1. In many countries, democracy was a colonial legacy, left to fend for itself against all odds. That was true for the Congo, Nigeria, Sierra Leone, Somalia, Suriname, Burma (Myanmar), Pakistan, the Philippines, and Ceylon (Sri Lanka), where democracy did not survive. Yet democracies that emerged from decolonialization survived in Mauritius (which by our prediction should have become a democracy only 14 years after independence, in 1982), in India (which was

---

[4] We also examined another variable not reported in the table, namely, the proportion of other democracies in the region (ODRP). This variable generates the best overall prediction, which would seem to indicate that international factors operate through a process of geographically based contagion, rather than via a worldwide political climate. We rush to emphasize, however, that this results should be interpreted with skepticism, because we estimated the model as if all the observations were independent or at least as if the number of countries in each region were large, and in some regions it was not. Although international determinants of regimes have been subjects of some speculation (Whitehead 1991; Schmitter 1991), as well as of statistical analysis (Starr 1991), a model that can distinguish different mechanisms through which international influences operate has yet to be constructed and tested. Our findings suggest, at best, that the topic merits further study, and we decided not to include the regional variable in our final analysis.

[5] One could reasonably ask why we take LEVEL as the benchmark, asking by how much other variables improve the prediction with regard to LEVEL, rather than vice versa. The reason is the asymmetry: When "legacies" are added to LEVEL, the prediction improves by 0.2 percent, but when LEVEL is added to "legacies", the prediction improves by 10.7 percent. Similarly for other variables.

Table 2.2. Incorrect predictions, by country and period, and the probability that a regime is a dictatorship during the period

Democracies predicted as dictatorships				Dictatorships predicted as democracies			
Country	Period	Pr(REG = Dic) highest	Democracy	Country	Period	Pr(REG = Dic) lowest	Dictatorship
Congo	1961–62	0.89	Fell 1963	Botswona	1986–89	0.42	Survived
Ghana	1970–71	0.86	Fell 1972	Gabon	1976–77	0.37	Survived
	1979–80	0.82	Fell 1981		1990	0.49	Survived
Mauritius	1968–82	0.73	Survived	Seychelles	1976–90	0.31	Fell 1993
Nigeria	1960–65	0.91	Fell 1966	South Africa	1950–61	0.40	Fell 1995
	1979–82	0.87	Fell 1983		1974–76	0.48	Fell 1995
Sierra Leone	1962–66	0.86	Fell 1967	El Salvador	1979–90	0.31	Fell 1995
Somalia	1961–68	0.98	Fell 1969		1953	0.50	Fell 1984
Sudan	1986–88	0.87	Fell 1989	Mexico	1950–90	0.11	Survived
Belize	1981–90	0.75	Survived	Panama	1980–90	0.34	Fell 1994
Costa Rica	1950–90	0.65	Survived	Argentina	1955–57	0.19	Fell 1958
Dominican R.	1966–87	0.76	Survived		1962	0.26	Fell 1963
El Salvador	1984–89	0.61	Survived		1966–72	0.24	Fell 1973
Grenada	1985–90	0.80	Survived		1976–82	0.14	Fell 1983
Guatemala	1951–53	0.66	Fell 1954	Bolivia	1952	0.48	Fell 1979
	1958–62	0.71	Fell 1963	Chile	1981	0.48	Fell 1990
	1966–81	0.78	Fell 1982		1985–89	0.32	Fell 1990
	1986–90	0.63	Survived	Colombia	1950–57	0.44	Fell 1958

Country	Years	Value	Outcome
Honduras	1957–62	0.75	Fell 1963
	1971	0.82	Fell 1972
	1982–90	0.75	Survived
Jamaica	1962–83	0.58	Survived
Nicaragua	1984–90	0.65	Survived
Panama	1952–67	0.65	Fell 1968
Bolivia	1979	0.63	Fell 1964
	1982–89	0.63	Survived
Brazil	1950–63	0.67	Fell 1964
Chile	1951	0.52	Fell 1973
	1960	0.50	Fell 1973
	1962–72	0.63	Fell 1973
Colombia	1960–82	0.69	Survived
Ecuador	1950–62	0.64	Fell 1963
	1979–83	0.51	Survived
Peru	1960	0.51	Fell 1962
	1963–67	0.58	Fell 1968
	1980–83	0.53	Fell 1990
Suriname	1975–89	0.99	Fell 1990
Uruguay	1962–72	0.69	Fell 1973
	1985	0.54	Survived
Bangladesh	1986–90	0.99	Survived
India	1950–83	0.83	Survived
Japan	1952–65	0.66	Survived
South Korea	1960	0.81	Fell 1961
Myanmar	1950–57	0.65	Fell 1958
	1960–61	0.66	Fell 1962
Pakistan	1950–55	0.79	Fell 1956

Country	Years	Value	Outcome
Paraguay	1952	0.50	Fell 1991
	1955	0.50	Fell 1991
	1988–90	0.43	Fell 1991
Peru	1950–55	0.45	Fell 1956
	1990	0.41	Survived
Uruguay	1979–81	0.45	Fell 1985
Venezuela	1951–58	0.05	Fell 1959
Iraq	1979–80	0.28	Survived
South Korea	1986–87	0.37	Fell 1988
Malaysia	1988–90	0.31	Survived
Singapore	1973–90	0.02	Survived
Taiwan	1984–90	0.11	Fell 1995
Bulgaria	1988–89	0.48	Fell 1990
East Germany	1979–88	0.10	Collapsed
Greece	1967–73	0.29	Fell 1974
Poland	1988	0.49	Fell 1989
Portugal	1952–75	0.37	Fell 1976
Spain	1951–76	0.11	Fell 1977
Soviet Union	1988–89	0.45	Collapsed
Fiji	1990	0.47	Survived

(continued)

Table 2.2 (continued)

	Democracies predicted as dictatorships				Dictatorships predicted as democracies		
Country	Period	Pr(REG = Dic) highest	Democracy	Country	Period	Pr(REG = Dic) lowest	Dictatorship
	1972–76	0.91	Fell 1977				
	1988–90	0.74	Survived				
Philippines	1950–64	0.84	Fell 1965				
	1986–90	0.75	Survived				
Sri Lanka	1950–76	0.94	Fell 1977				
Thailand	1975	0.86	Fell 1976				
	1983–89	0.75	Survived				
Bulgaria	1990	0.52	Survived				
Czechoslovakia	1990	0.75	Survived				
West Germany	1951	0.52	Survived				
Greece	1963	0.50	Fell 1967				
Hungary	1990	0.57	Survived				
Poland	1989–90	0.54	Survived				
Turkey	1961–79	0.95	Fell 1980				
	1983–90	0.87	Survived				
Papua New Guinea	1975–85	0.64	Survived				
Solomon Islands	1981–88	0.78	Survived				
Vanuatu	1984–90	0.96	Survived				

predicted as a dictatorship during the entire period), in Belize, in Jamaica (which was predicted as a dictatorship until 1983), in Papua New Guinea (until 1985), in the Solomon Islands (until 1988), and in Vanuatu (not by 1990). The odds against democracy in India were extremely high.

2. Some countries succeeded in living under democracy when all the observable conditions conspired against it. These attempts succeeded in Bangladesh after 1986, Thailand after 1983, and Turkey after 1983. They failed in Ghana (twice), in Sudan, and in South Korea in 1960.

3. In some countries democracy was imposed by the Allies in the aftermath of World War II. These countries include West Germany, which by our prediction should have become a democracy only by 1952, and Japan, which should have become democratic only by 1965.

4. Some countries experienced dictatorships that should not have been warranted by their observed conditions. That was true notably of the four military dictatorships in Argentina, the Fujimori *autogolpe* in Peru, the Perez Jimenez dictatorship in Venezuela between 1948 and 1958, and the military rule in Greece between 1967 and 1973.

5. Several countries have waited much longer to make the transit to democracy than their conditions would predict. They include Seychelles, South Africa, Taiwan, Chile, Portugal, and Spain. Other countries have remained in the grip of authoritarianism even though all the observable factors indicate that they should have had democratic regimes: Mexico, which we would have predicted as a democracy already by 1951 and which had a probability of 0.11 of being a dictatorship in 1990; Singapore, which had a 0.02 probability of being a dictatorship in 1990, and Malaysia. Communist countries are a topic apart, and we shall return to it.

6. Finally, these results cast a new light on the instability of political regimes in many Latin American countries. It is often observed that democracy is particularly unstable in Latin America. Yet that may be a wrong conclusion: What is unstable in Latin America is dictatorship. If we take all countries in the world that fall in the Latin American income range per capita, from $971 to $8,233, we discover that democracies are more likely in Latin America than in other regions: Being in Latin America makes democracy 12 percent more likely (t value of the dummy is 3.470) than elsewhere. It thus appears that several Latin American countries experimented with democracy in the face of adverse conditions under which countries elsewhere in the world tended to remain in the grip of dictatorships, and under those conditions, democracies had little chance for survival.

To summarize, the level of economic development, as measured by per capita income, is by far the best predictor of political regimes. Yet there are countries in which dictatorships persist when all the observable conditions indicate they should not; there are others in which democracies flourish in spite of all the odds. Thus some factors influencing the incidence of the different kinds of regimes are not identified by this analysis.

Regime Dynamics

There are two distinct reasons that the incidence of democracy may be related to the level of economic development: Democracies may be more likely to emerge as countries develop economically, or, having been established for whatever reasons, democracies may be more likely to survive in developed countries. We call the first explanation "endogenous" and the second "exogenous."

Because we are dealing with only two kinds of regimes, democracies emerge whenever dictatorships die.[6] Hence, to assert that democracies emerge as a result of economic development is the same as saying that dictatorships die as countries ruled by them become economically developed. Democracy thus is said to be secreted out of dictatorships by economic development. A story told about country after country is that as a country develops, its social structure becomes complex, new groups emerge and organize, labor processes require the active cooperation of employees, and, as a result, the system can no longer be effectively run by command: The society is too complex, technological change endows the direct producers with autonomy and private information, civil society emerges, and dictatorial forms of control lose their effectiveness. Various groups, whether the bourgeoisie, workers, or just the amorphous "civil society," rise against the dictatorial regime, and it falls.

The endogenous explanation is a "modernization" theory. The basic assumption of this theory is that there is one general process, of which democratization is but the final facet. Modernization consists of a gradual differentiation and specialization of social structures culminating in a separation of the political from other structures, and making democracy possible. The specific causal chains consist in sequences of

---

[6] This is not quite true of our data set, because different countries enter and exit the sample at different moments. For the moment, we consider the population of countries as fixed.

industrialization, urbanization, education, communication, mobilization, political incorporation, and innumerable other "-ations": a pro-
gressive accumulation of social changes that make a society ready to
proceed to the final one, democratization.

Modernization may be one reason that the incidence of democracy
is related to economic development, and this is the reading imputed
to Lipset by most commentators (Diamond 1992: 125; Huber,
Rueschemeyer, and Stephens 1993: 711). His most influential critic,
O'Donnell (1973: 3), paraphrases Lipset's thesis as saying that "if other
countries become as rich as the economically advanced nations, it is
highly probable that they will become political democracies." Democracy is endogenous, because it results from economic development
under authoritarianism. The hypothesis is that if authoritarian countries develop, they become democratic. The sequence of events we
would thus expect to observe is one of poor authoritarian countries
developing and becoming democratic once they reach some level of
development, a "threshold."

Yet suppose, just suppose, that dictatorships are equally likely to die,
and democracies to emerge, at any level of development. They may die
for so many different reasons that development, with all its modernizing consequences, plays no privileged role. After all, as Therborn
(1977) emphasized, many European countries became democratized
because of wars, not because of "modernization," a story repeated by
the Argentine defeat in the Malvinas and elsewhere. Some dictatorships have fallen in the aftermath of the death of the founding
dictator, such as a Franco, uniquely capable of maintaining the authoritarian order. Some have collapsed because of economic crises, some
because of foreign pressures, and perhaps some for purely idiosyncratic reasons.

If dictatorships die and democracies emerge randomly with regard
to economic development, is it still possible that there should be more
democracies among wealthy countries than among poor countries? If
one is to judge Lipset (1959: 56) by his own words – "The more well-
to-do a nation, the greater the chances it will sustain democracy" –
then even if the emergence of a democracy is independent of the level
of development, the chance that this regime will survive will be greater
if it is established in an affluent country. We would thus expect democracies to appear randomly with regard to levels of development, and
then to die in the poorer countries and to survive in the wealthier countries. And because every time a dictatorship happened to die in an
affluent country democracy would be there to stay, history should grad-

ually accumulate wealthy democracies. This is no longer a modernization theory, because the emergence of democracy is not brought about by development. Democracy appears exogenously, deus ex machina. It tends to survive if a country is "modern," but it is not a product of "modernization."

Some algebra may help elucidate what is entailed. Let the probability that a country, $i = 1, \ldots, N$, will have an authoritarian regime during a particular year, $t = 1, \ldots, T$, be $p_A(it)$, where the subscript "A" stands for "authoritarian," and let the probability that it will have a democratic regime be $p_D(it) = 1 - p_A(it)$. Let the probability that a dictatorship will die from one year to another be $p_{AD}(it)$, so that the probability that it will survive is $p_{AA}(it) = 1 - p_{AD}(it)$. Similarly, let the probability that a democracy will die be $p_{DA}(it) = 1 - p_{DD}(it)$. If we assume for the time being that these "transition probabilities," $p_{jk}, j = A, D, k = A, D$, are constant each year and are the same for all countries, then we can describe the evolution of regimes by

$$p_D(t) = p_{DD}p_D(t-1) + p_{AD}p_A(t-1)$$

$$p_A(t) = p_{DA}p_D(t-1) + p_{AA}p_A(t-1).$$

Therefore the proportion of regimes that will be democracies next year will depend on the proportion of democracies that survive from the current year, p_{DD}, and the proportion of dictatorships that will die, that is, become democracies, p_{AD}. Similarly for dictatorships. In matrix form,

$$\begin{bmatrix} p_D(t) \\ p_A(t) \end{bmatrix} = \begin{bmatrix} p_{DD} & p_{AD} \\ p_{DA} & p_{AA} \end{bmatrix} \begin{bmatrix} p_D(t-1) \\ p_A(t-1) \end{bmatrix}.$$

Given the transition rates, there exists a distribution of regimes that, if reached, will remain stable in the absence of exogenous disturbances. These equilibrium probabilities are

$$p_D^* = \frac{p_{AD}}{p_{DA} + p_{AD}} \quad \text{and} \quad p_A^* = \frac{p_{DA}}{p_{DA} + p_{AD}}.$$

This long-run distribution of regimes depends only on the relative rates at which they die each year, not on their initial distribution. If $p_{AD} > p_{DA}$, then in the long run there will be more democracies than dictatorships in the world. Moreover, whatever the initial distribution of regimes, their proportions will over time tend to these equilibrium values. And because the probabilities that regimes will die during any particular year are likely to be low – in fact they are low – this convergence will be monotonic, that is, the proportion of one regime will continue to increase, and that of the other to decline.[7] If at the beginning the proportion of democracies was lower than $p_D{}^*$, this proportion will continually increase over time, and the proportion of dictatorships will decline.

Suppose now that whereas dictatorships die at some constant annual rate, democracies never die, so that $p_{DA} = 0$. Then in the long run all countries will be democracies. Every time a dictatorship dies, a democracy is established, and, once it is established, it survives forever. The speed of this process will depend on the rate at which dictatorships die, but the accumulation of democracies is inexorable.

Now, to return to the issue at stake, imagine that these transition probabilities are not constant, but depend on the level of development. To keep matters simple, suppose that there are only two levels: low (L) and high (H). At the low level, both regimes have some probability of dying that is more than zero and less than one. Now consider two possibilities: One is that while $p_{AD}(L) < 1$, once dictatorships pass the threshold that defines the high level, they are certain to die, so that $p_{AD}(H) = 1$, whereas democracies die at the same rate, $p_{DA} = p_{DA}(L) = p_{DA}(H)$, at either level. The transition probabilities are thus

Level = low   Level = high

$$\begin{bmatrix} p_{DD} & p_{AD} \\ p_{DA} & p_{AA} \end{bmatrix} \qquad \begin{bmatrix} p_{DD} & 1.00 \\ p_{DA} & 0.00 \end{bmatrix}$$

Whereas the long-run proportion of democracies at the low level will be $p_D{}^*(L) = p_{AD}/(p_{AD} + p_{DA})$, at the high level it will be $p_D{}^*(H) = 1/(1 + p_{DA})$, so that the equilibrium proportion of democracies will be higher at the higher level, $p_D{}^*(L) < p_D{}^*(H)$. Thus, the proportion of democracies will be higher at the high level of development because democracies are more likely to emerge as a result of development. This is the "endogenous" (modernization) version of the explanation.

But suppose, alternatively, that authoritarian regimes die at exactly the same rate whether in poor countries or developed ones, so that $p_{AD}(L) = p_{AD}(H) = p_{AD}$, and in turn democratic regimes never die once they are established in affluent countries, so that $p_{DA}(H) = 0.00$. The transition probabilities are then

---

[7] Convergence will be monotonic if $p_{AD} + p_{DA} < 1$; otherwise, the proportions of regimes will oscillate around the equilibrium.

Level = low   Level = high

$$\begin{bmatrix} p_{DD} & p_{AD} \\ p_{DA} & p_{AA} \end{bmatrix} \qquad \begin{bmatrix} 1.00 & p_{AD} \\ 0.00 & p_{AA} \end{bmatrix}$$

and we already know that whereas the long-run proportion of democracies at the low level will be $p_D*(L) < 1$, at the high level all countries will become democracies in the long run. Hence, we will observe an aggregate relationship between the level of development and the incidence of democracies even though democracies are equally likely to emerge at any level, that is, even if development under authoritarianism does not increase the probability that a country will become democratic. This is then the "exogenous" version.

Thus, to decide which mechanism generates the relationship between development and democracy, we need to determine how the respective transition probabilities change with the level of development. Appendix 2.1 describes how we do it.

Level of Economic Development and Regime Dynamics

Examine first some descriptive patterns, presented in column 5 of Table 2.3. If the theory according to which the emergence of democracy is a result of economic development is true, transitions to democracy should be more likely when authoritarian regimes reach higher levels of development. In fact, dictatorships survive almost invariably in the very poor countries, those whose per capita incomes are under $1,000, or at least they succeed one another and the regime remains the same.[8] They are less stable in countries with incomes between $1,001 and $4,000, and even less so between $4,001 and $7,000. But if income reaches the level of $7,000, the trend reverses and they become more likely to survive. As the lower panel of Table 2.3 shows, transitions to democracy are less likely in poor countries and in rich ones, but they are more likely at the intermediate income levels. If we take all the dictatorships, their probability of dying during any year is 0.0198; for those with incomes over $1,000, this probability is 0.0280, over $5,000 it is 0.0526, over $6,000 it is 0.0441, and over $7,000 it is 0.0286; the two very wealthy dictatorships with incomes above $8,000 still survived in 1990. Hence, it appears that Huntington was correct, albeit only with regard to authoritarian regimes, when he argued that one should expect to observe "a bell-shaped pattern of instability" (1968: 43). Economic development seems to destabilize dictatorships in countries at interme-

---

[8] Remember that we treat dictatorships that succeed one another as a single spell.

Table 2.3. Transitions, by lagged per capita income (LEVLAG)

Low-high	PJK	TJK	TOT	PAD	TAD	TA	PDA	TDA	TD
0–1,000	0.0147	15	1,019	0.0063	6	945	0.1216	9	74
1,001–2,000	0.0321	32	997	0.0242	18	745	0.0556	14	252
2,001–3,000	0.0325	16	493	0.0261	8	306	0.0428	8	187
3,001–4,000	0.0201	7	349	0.0146	3	205	0.0278	4	144
4,001–5,000	0.0339	8	236	0.0469	6	128	0.0185	2	108
5,001–6,000	0.0308	6	195	0.0595	5	84	0.0090	1	111
6,001–7,000	0.0190	3	158	0.0606	2	33	0.0080	1	125
7,001–	0.0015	1	679	0.0286	1	35	0.0000	0	644
Total	0.0213	88	4,126	0.0198	49	2,481	0.0237	39	1,645

Above	PJK	TJK	TOT	PAD	TAD	TA	PDA	TDA	TD
0	0.0213	88	4,126	0.0198	49	2,481	0.0237	39	1,645
1,000	0.0235	73	3,105	0.0280	43	1,535	0.0191	30	1,570
2,000	0.0194	41	2,110	0.0316	25	791	0.0121	16	1,319
3,000	0.0155	25	1,616	0.0351	17	484	0.0071	8	1,132
4,000	0.0142	18	1,268	0.0500	14	280	0.0040	4	988
5,000	0.0097	10	1,032	0.0526	8	152	0.0023	2	880
6,000	0.0048	4	837	0.0441	3	68	0.0013	1	769
7,000	0.0015	1	679	0.0286	1	35	0.0000	0	644

Notes: PJK stands for the probability of any regime transition; TJK is their number. TOT is the total number of annual observations. PAD stands for the probability of transition from authoritarianism to democracy; TAD is their number. TA is the total number of annual observations of authoritarianism. PDA stands for the probability of transition from democracy to authoritarianism; TDA is their number. TD is the total number of annual observations of democracy.

diate levels of income, but not in those that are poor nor in those that are wealthy.

Indeed, dictatorships survived for years in countries that were wealthy by comparative standards. Whatever the threshold at which development is supposed to dig the grave for an authoritarian regime, it is clear that many dictatorships must have passed it in good health. Note that we have already excluded six wealthy countries that derive large proportions of their revenues from oil. Yet dictatorships flourished also in Singapore, East Germany, Taiwan, the Soviet Union, Spain, and Mexico for many years after those countries rose to incomes well above $5,000, an income that Austria, Belgium, France, West Germany, Iceland, Ireland, Italy, the Netherlands, and Norway did not have by 1951. Table 2.4 lists the dictatorships that survived even though the probability that they should be democracies, as predicted by the level of development alone, was above 0.50, which corresponds to per capita income of $4,115.

Conversely, many dictatorships fell in countries with low income levels. Six fell in countries with incomes below $1,000, and eighteen in countries between $1,000 and $2,000, and altogether thirty-six collapsed when the probability that the regime should be democratic, as predicted by per capita income alone, was less than 0.50. Hence, with twenty-five dictatorships surviving in wealthy countries and thirty-six falling in poor ones, the causal power of development in generating democracies cannot be very strong. The distribution of levels at which transitions to democracy occur is highly scattered.

Yet this may not be a fair test of modernization theory. After all, this theory supposes that countries develop over a longer period, so that all the modernizing consequences have time to accumulate. Let us therefore examine more closely those countries that did develop under authoritarian regimes and that at some time became "modern," which we will take somewhat arbitrarily to mean that they had a per capita income of $4,115 (Table 2.5).

Twenty dictatorships (to remind, out of 123) did develop over longer periods of time and reached "modernity." Gabon, Mexico, Syria, and Yugoslavia developed continuously for at least a decade, reached the level at which democracy would be expected to be the more likely regime, and, having remained under dictatorships, experienced a series of economic crises. Singapore and Malaysia developed over a long period, became wealthy, and remained dictatorships. In East Germany, Taiwan, the Soviet Union, Spain, Bulgaria, and Hungary competitive elections eventually took place, but at very different levels of income.

Table 2.4. Highest levels of per capita income (LEVEL) under which dictatorships survived in different countries

Country	Year	Highest level	Pr(REG = Dem)[a]
Singapore	1990	11,698	0.992
East Germany	1988	10,433	0.977
Iraq	1979	8,598	0.923
Taiwan	1990	8,067	0.895
Soviet Union	1989	7,744	0.875
Spain	1976	7,390	0.851
Gabon	1976	6,969	0.818
Venezuela	1957	6,939	0.815
Bulgaria	1988	6,866	0.809
Argentina	1980	6,505	0.776
Mexico	1981	6,463	0.772
Iran	1976	6,434	0.769
Argentina	1972	5,815	0.705
Yugoslavia	1979	5,674	0.690
Hungary	1987	5,650	0.687
Greece	1973	5,218	0.637
Uruguay	1981	5,162	0.630
Malaysia	1990	5,117	0.625
Poland	1978	5,102	0.623
South Korea	1987	5,080	0.620
Syria	1981	4,668	0.569
Portugal	1974	4,657	0.568
Argentina	1962	4,541	0.553
Argentina	1957	4,355	0.530
Suriname	1981	4,220	0.513

[a] Pr(REG = Dem) is the probability that a regime will be democratic given the level of income. It is calculated as $1 - F(\alpha + \beta * \text{LEVEL})$, where $F(\cdot)$ is the c.d.f. of the normal distribution.

Given its 1974 income level, Uruguay should have never been a dictatorship. The economic history of the Chilean dictatorship is convoluted: Its income in 1974 was $3,561; it climbed with downs and ups to $4,130 by 1981, collapsed to $3,199 by 1983, recovered to surpass the 1974 level only by 1986, and passed the threshold of $4,115 in 1989, exactly

95

Table 2.5. Countries that developed over long periods under dictatorships and reached incomes above $4,115

	Entry		Passes	Peak			Transition
Country	Year	LEVEL	Pr = 0.50	Year	LEVEL	Pr	year at Pr
Gabon	1961	1,969	1973	1976	6,969	0.82	Never
Mexico	1951	2,317	1971	1981	6,463	0.77	Never
Brazil	1965	1,864	1980	1978	3,881	0.47	1978 0.47
Chile	1974	3,561	1981	1981	4,130	0.50	No
			1989	1989	4,355	0.53	1989 0.53
Uruguay	1974	4,148	1974	1981	5,162	0.63	1985 0.48
South Korea	1961	911	1985	1988	5,606	0.68	1988 0.68
Malaysia	1957	1,282	1982	1990	5,117	0.63	Never
Singapore	1965	1,845	1972	1990	11,698	0.99	Never
Syria	1961	1,607	1978	1981	4,668	0.57	Never
Taiwan	1952	968	1979	1990	8,067	0.90	Post-1990
Bulgaria	1981	4,216	????	1989	6,739	0.80	1990 0.80
Czechoslovakia	1961	1,709	1989	1990	4,094	0.49	1990 0.49
East Germany	1971	4,995	????	1988	10,433	0.98	1990 ????
Greece	1967	3,308	1970	1974	4,966	0.61	1974 0.61
Hungary	1971	3,657	1974	1987	5,650	0.69	1989 0.68
Poland	1971	3,109	1974	1978	5,102	0.62	No
			1985	1988	4,529	0.55	1989 0.55
Portugal	1951	1,314	1973	1974	4,657	0.57	1975 0.52
Spain	1951	2,205	1964	1976	7,390	0.85	1976 0.85
Soviet Union	1961	2,536	1971	1989	7,744	0.88	Collapsed
Yugoslavia	1961	2,073	1974	1979	5,674	0.69	Collapsed

Note: This table lists countries that grew over a period of at least seven years and at some time reached a per capita income of $4,115. "Entry" is the first year of the dictatorship or 1951 or the year after the country became independent or the year after economic data became available. "Passes Pr = 0.50" is the year when the country reached a per capita income of $4,115. "Peak" gives the time when the country reached the highest income level under the particular dictatorship and the probability, as predicted by per capita income, that it would be a democracy. Finally, "Transition" gives the year the dictatorship fell, if ever, and the probability of democracy at that time.

the year of transition. The history of Poland is similar: By our criteria, it reached the threshold of democracy in 1974; it experienced an economic crisis in 1979 and a mass movement for democracy in 1980, passed the threshold again in 1985, and became a democracy in 1989. In turn, Brazil, Czechoslovakia, Portugal, and perhaps even South Korea and Greece are the dream cases for a modernization theorist. Those countries developed under dictatorships, became wealthy, and threw off their dictatorships more or less when their levels of development would have predicted. But they are few.

This is not to say that democracy did not emerge in some countries when they became modern. Indeed, perhaps in those countries that did develop over a long period, the very thought of democracy appeared on the political agenda because they were too modern – not only in those countries that became democratic just when our model predicts but also those that waited much longer: Taiwan, the Soviet Union, Spain, and Bulgaria. Modernization may create the "prerequisites" for political conflict over the form of regime. But the manner in which these conflicts will develop remains unpredictable. When conflicts over regimes are examined at a micro level, by looking at the political actors involved, their motives and their beliefs, it becomes apparent that these are situations laden with uncertainty (O'Donnell and Schmitter 1986; Przeworski 1991). Game-theoretic analyses of transitions to democracy make it apparent that the actors involved often do not know each other's preferences, the relationships of physical forces, or the outcomes of eventual conflicts (Wantchekon 1996; Zielinski 1997). And under such conditions, various equilibria can prevail: Whereas transition to democracy is one feasible outcome, so is the perpetuation of the dictatorial status quo, or even a solidification of dictatorship. Hence, even if modernization may generate conflicts over democracy, the outcomes of such conflicts are open-ended.

But if modernization theory is to have any predictive power, there must be some level of income at which one can be relatively sure that the country will throw off its dictatorship. And one is hard put to find this level: Even among the countries that satisfy the premise of the modernization theory, those listed in Table 2.5, the range of incomes at which dictatorships survived is very wide. Few authoritarian regimes have developed over a long period, and even if most of them should eventually become democracies, no level of income can predict when that should occur.

Moreover, even if to predict is not the same as to explain, "explaining" can easily entail an ex-post fallacy. Take Taiwan, which in 1952 had a per capita income of $968. It developed rapidly, passing by 1979 our threshold of $4,115; it had a probability of 0.10 of being a dictatorship in 1990, and in 1995, for the first time, elected its president in contested elections. Suppose that during all that time the Taiwanese dictatorship had faced each year a probability of 0.02 of dying, for reasons not related to development. It thus would have had a cumulative chance of about 50 percent of not being around by 1995 even if it

97

had not developed at all. Thus we might erroneously attribute to development what may have been just a cumulation of random hazards.[9] And, indeed, the Taiwanese dictatorship most likely democratized to mobilize international support against the threat from China: for geopolitical reasons, not for economic reasons.

In sum, the causal power of economic development in bringing down dictatorships appears paltry. The level of development, at least as measured by per capita income, gives little information about the chances of transition to democracy.

On the other hand, per capita income has a strong impact on the survival of democracies. As column 8 of Table 2.3 shows, in countries with per capita incomes under $1,000, the probability that a democracy would die during a particular year was 0.1216, which implies that their expected life was about eight years. Between $1,001 and $2,000, this probability was 0.0556, for an expected duration of about eighteen years, and the probability that a democracy would die in a country with an income above $4,000 was almost zero. Indeed, no democracy has ever been subverted, not during the period we studied nor ever before nor after, regardless of everything else, in a country with a per capita income higher than that of Argentina in 1975: $6,055. There is no doubt that democracy is stable in affluent countries: The probability of it collapsing is almost zero; the coefficient on LEVEL in statistical analyses of survival (see Appendix 2.2) is positive and significant, and the stark fact is that up until 1990 thirty-one democracies had lived 742 years with incomes above that of Argentina in 1975, and not one had ever fallen.

A question that has been extensively debated is whether or not the stability of democracy is monotonic with regard to the level of development. Although there are important theoretical differences and even sharper political differences between Huntington (1968; Huntington and Nelson 1976) and O'Donnell (1973), both have claimed that there is a level beyond which further development decreases the probability that democracy will survive. Huntington has argued that both regime types become unstable when a country undergoes modernization, which occurs at some intermediate level of development. O'Donnell, in turn, has claimed that democracies tend to die when a country exhausts "the easy stage of import substitution," again at some intermediate level of economic development.

---

[9] An analogy may be useful. Suppose that a woman runs a risk of 0.01 of dying from accidental causes during each year of her life, and then at the age of 78 she gets hit by a falling brick. To attribute her death to development would be to conclude that she died of old age.

Huntington (1968: 1) was concerned with stability and did not care whether regimes were democratic or authoritarian. "The most important political distinction among countries," he thought, "concerns not their form of government but their degree of government." Hence, the United States, the United Kingdom, and the Soviet Union were all systems in which "the government governs." Whether it was the Politburo, the cabinet, or the president mattered little. "The problem," he insisted, "was not to hold elections but to create organizations." Indeed, we were told, "the primary problem is not liberty but the creation of a legitimate public order" (1968: 7). Though never explicitly referring to Lipset, Huntington (1968: 35–6) observed that "in actuality, only some of the tendencies encompassed in the concept of 'political modernization' characterized the 'modernizing' areas. Instead of a trend toward competitiveness and democracy, there was an 'erosion of democracy' and a tendency to autocratic military regimes and one-party regimes. Instead of stability, there were repeated coups and revolts." We should expect "a bell-shaped pattern of political instability" (p. 43) among democratic as well as authoritarian regimes.

O'Donnell dragged Lipset over the coals for various methodological transgressions. Reflecting on his criticisms in retrospect, he observed that "Chapter I is now an archeological remnant – testimony of a debate that in 1971 had recently begun and today is finished: it is no longer necessary to lead the reader through tedious series of data to demonstrate that 'socio-economic development' does not foster 'democracy and/or political stability'" (1979: 204). What the data show, O'Donnell asserted, is that "in contemporary South America, the higher and the lower levels of modernization are associated with non-democratic political systems, while political democracies are found at intermediate levels of modernization." Hence, at least within the range observed by O'Donnell, we should observe that democracies fall as economies develop.

Is there some level of development beyond which democracies are more likely to die than they were earlier? We have already seen in Table 2.3 that the probability of a democracy dying declines monotonically with per capita income. Although O'Donnell did cite a countercase against Lipset, his account of the rise of bureaucratic authoritarianism does not undermine Lipset's theory.[10] O'Donnell studied a country that turns out to be a distant outlier: As Table 2.6 shows, three of the four

---

[10] O'Donnell was careful not to make general claims: His purpose was to explain the downfall of democracies in the Southern Cone. But his theory of "bureaucratic authoritarianism" captured the imaginations of scholars all around the world, who treated it as applicable almost everywhere.

Table 2.6. Transitions to dictatorship, 1951–1990, by last full year of democracy, per capita income, and type of democracy

Country	Year	LEVEL	Type
Argentina	1975	6,055	Presidential
Argentina	1965	5,011	Presidential
Argentina	1965	4,790	Presidential
Uruguay	1972	4,034	Presidential
Argentina	1954	3,989	Presidential
Suriname	1979	3,923	Parliamentary
Chile	1972	3,857	Presidential
Greece	1966	3,176	Parliamentary
Turkey	1979	2,957	Parliamentary
Peru	1967	2,694	Presidential
Guatemala	1981	2,534	Presidential
Suriname	1989	2,491	Mixed
Peru	1989	2,247	Presidential
Panama	1967	2,227	Presidential
Peru	1961	2,148	Presidential
Bolivia	1979	2,037	Presidential
Brazil	1963	1,889	Presidential
Guatemala	1962	1,693	Presidential
Thailand	1975	1,686	Parliamentary
Guatemala	1953	1,509	Presidential
Ecuador	1962	1,451	Presidential
Nigeria	1982	1,419	Presidential
Sri Lanka	1976	1,336	Parliamentary
Honduras	1971	1,236	Presidential
Philippines	1964	1,217	Presidential
Congo	1962	1,120	Presidential
Sierra Leone	1966	1,097	Parliamentary
Ghana	1971	1,042	Parliamentary
Honduras	1962	1,042	Presidential
Somalia	1968	1,015	Mixed
Ghana	1980	978	Presidential
Pakistan	1976	943	Presidential
South Korea	1960	898	Parliamentary
Sudan	1988	765	Parliamentary
Nigeria	1965	621	Parliamentary
Pakistan	1955	577	Parliamentary
Uganda	1984	576	Presidential
Myanmar	1961	312	Parliamentary
Myanmar	1957	267	Parliamentary

transitions to authoritarianism at per capita incomes above $4,000 occurred in Argentina, and the fourth in Uruguay. Thus, Lipset was right in thinking that the richer the country, the more likely it is to sustain democracy.

Clearly, this fact cries for an explanation. One possible account for the durability of democracies in wealthy countries, proposed already by Lipset, is that, through various sociological mechanisms, wealth lowers the intensity of distributional conflicts. An alternative explanation is that income is just a proxy for education, and more highly educated people are more likely to embrace democratic values. Education, specifically accumulated years of education for an average member of the labor force, does increase the probability of survival of democracy at each level of income.[11] The probability that a democracy will die in a country where the average member of the labor force has fewer than three years of formal education is 0.1154; it is 0.0620 when the level of education is between three and six years, 0.0080 when it is six to nine years, and zero when the average worker has more than nine years of education. The highest level of education under which a country experienced a transition to dictatorship was 8.36 years in Sri Lanka in 1977, but that was an outlier. The next highest level of education when democracy fell was 6.85 years in Uruguay.

But income is not a proxy for education. Even though these two variables are highly correlated (0.78), their effects are to a large measure independent. As Table 2.7 shows, whereas at each income level the probability of democracy falling decreases with increasing education, the converse is also true: At each level of education, the probability of democracy dying decreases with income. Hence, for reasons that are not easy to identify, wealth does make democracies more stable, independently of education.

Finally, we find no evidence of "consolidation." Democracies become "consolidated" if the conditional probability that a democratic regime will die during a particular year given that it has survived thus far (the "hazard rate") declines with its age, so that, as Dahl (1990) has argued, democracies are more likely to survive if they have lasted for some time. Examining the ages at which democracies die indicates that this

---

[11] We have data only for 2,900 country-years of education. The mean is 4.85 years, and the standard deviation is 3.12, with a minimum of 0.03 (Guinea in 1966) and a maximum of 12.81 (United States in 1985); 27.6% of the sample had educational levels lower than three years, 64.4% lower than six years, and 90.8% lower than nine years. Only 13.0% of the sample had education levels higher than Sri Lanka in 1977, and 26.1% higher than Uruguay in 1973.

Table 2.7. Regime transitions, by lagged per capita income and average education

Income	Education (in years)				
	0–3	3–6	6–9	9–	Total
0–4,000					
All	0.0208 20 961	0.0393 27 687	0.0198 5 252	0.0000 0 35	0.0269 52 1,936
Dic	0.0098 15 511	0.0294 15 511	0.0194 3 155	0.0000 0 28	0.0167 26 1,557
Dem	0.1212 12 99	0.0681 12 176	0.0206 2 97	0.0000 0 7	0.0686 26 379
4,001–8,000					
All	0.0000 0 36	0.0458 6 131	0.0172 4 233	0.0000 0 68	0.0214 10 468
Dic	0.0000 0 31	0.0434 3 69	0.0390 3 77	0.0000 0 7	0.0326 6 184
Dem	0.0000 0 5	0.0484 3 62	0.0064 1 156	0.0000 0 61	0.0141 4 284
8,001–					
All	0.0000 0 1	0.0000 0 3	0.0000 0 129	0.0000 0 251	0.0000 0 384
Dic	0.0000 0 1	0.0000 0 0	0.0000 0 4	0.0000 0 0	0.0000 0 5
Dem	0.0000 0 0	0.0000 0 3	0.0000 0 125	0.0000 0 251	0.0000 0 379
Total					
All	0.0200 20 998	0.0401 33 822	0.0147 9 614	0.0000 0 353	0.0222 62 2,788
Dic	0.0089 8 894	0.0310 18 580	0.0253 6 237	0.0000 0 34	0.0183 32 1,746
Dem	0.1154 12 104	0.0620 15 242	0.0080 3 377	0.0000 0 319	0.0288 30 1,042

Note: The first number under each level of education is the probability of transition away from a given regime; the second number is the number of such transitions, and the third is the total number of annual observations of this regime at that level of education.

is true, but once the level of development is taken into account, the hazard rates become independent of age, meaning that for a given level of development, democracies are about equally likely to die at any age (see Appendix 2.2 for details). These findings indicate that the hazard rates uncorrected for the level of development decline because countries develop, not because a democracy that has long been around is more likely to continue.

The conclusion reached thus far is that whereas economic development under dictatorship has at most a non-linear relationship to the emergence of democracies, once they are established, democracies are much more likely to endure in more highly developed countries. Yet because our systematic observations begin in 1950, the question arises whether or not these patterns also characterize the earlier period. Studies in the Lipset tradition have assumed that they do: They have inferred the historical process from cross-sectional observations. Yet the validity of such inferences is contested by followers of Moore (1966), who claimed that the Western European route to democracy was unique, not to be repeated. Note that when Rustow (1970) pointed out that the levels of development at which different countries permanently established democratic institutions varied widely, Lipset's rejoinder (1981) was that the thresholds at which democracy was established were lower for the early democracies. Is that true?

Although economic data for the pre-war period are not comparable to those at our disposal after 1950, Maddison (1995) reconstructed per capita income series for several countries going back to the nineteenth century. Table 2.8 portrays the pre-1950 experiences with democracy. The levels at which democracies were established before 1950 vary as widely as they do for the later period; indeed, they cover almost the entire range of incomes observed. The poorest countries in which democracy was experimented with before 1950 were Pakistan, which became independent in 1947 when it had per capita income of 631 (1990 G-K dollars), and India, which in 1947 had income of 641. Yugoslavia had income of 1,064 in 1921; Bulgaria had income of 1,169 in 1926; Portugal had income around 1,354 in 1910 (1913 figure); Brazil had income of 1,460 in 1946. The United States in 1830 (interpolated from 1820 to 1850) and Norway in 1884 must have had about the same income as Brazil in 1946. In turn, New Zealand had an income of 5,367 when it became independent in 1907, Venezuela had 5,102 when it first experimented with democracy in 1945, and the United Kingdom had 5,052 in 1911. Hence, the levels at which transitions to democracy occurred before 1950 were highly dispersed. Again, there was no clear threshold.

103

Table 2.8. Countries (in our sample) that experienced democracy before 1950

Country	First democracy		Pre-1950 reversal		Last pre-1950 democracy		Situation in 1950	
	Date	LEVEL	Date	LEVEL	Date	LEVEL	LEVEL	Regime
Canada (1920)	1920	3,659	None		1920		7,047	Dem
Costa Rica	1919		1948		1948			Dem
Guatemala	1945		None		1945			Dem
United States	1830	1,464^a	None		1830		9,573	Dem
Argentina	1912	3,904	1930	4,080	1946	4,665	4,987	Dem
Brazil	1946	1,460	None		1946	1,460	1,673	Dem
Chile	1891	1,949(1900)	1925	2,876	1932	2,274	3,827	Dem
Colombia	1910	1,236(1913)	1949	2,107			2,089	Dic
Ecuador	1947		None		1947			Dem
Peru	1939	1,884	1948	2,094			2,263	Dic
Uruguay	1942		None		1942			Dem
Venezuela	1945	5,102	1948	7,394			7,424	Dic
Israel (1948)	1948		None		1948			Dem
India (1947)	1947	641	None		1947		597	Dem
Myanmar (1948)	1948		None		1948		393	Dem
Pakistan (1947)	1947	631	None		1947		650	Dem
Philippines (1946)	1946		None		1946		1,293	Dem
Sri Lanka (1948)	1948		None		1948			Dem
Austria	1918	2,572	1934	2,871	1945		3,731	Dem
Belgium	1919	3,318	None		1919		5,346	Dem
Bulgaria (1908)	1926	1,169	1934	1,309			1,651	Dic
Czechoslovakia (1918)	1920	1,933	1948	3,088			3,501	Dic

Country								
Denmark	1901	2,986	None		1901		6,683	Dem
Finland (1917)	1919	1,610	1930	2,589	1944		4,131	Dem
France[b]	1875	2,198	None(?)		1875		5,221	Dem
Germany	1919	2,763	1933	3,591	1949		4,281	Dem
Greece	1926	2,368(1929)	1936	2,501	1946	1,412	1,951	Dem
Iceland (1918)	1920		None		1920			Dem
Ireland (1921)	1923	2,625(1926)	None		1923		3,518	Dem
Italy	1919	2,783	1922	2,574	1946		3,425	Dem
Luxembourg	1868		None				1,868	Dem
Netherlands	1868	2,640(1870)	None		1868		5,850	Dem
Norway (1905)	1884	1,466	None		1884		4,969	Dem
Poland (1918)	1919		1926	2,117(1929)			2,447	Dic
Portugal	1910	1,354(1913)	1926	1,536(1929)			2,132	Dic
Spain	1931	2,713	1936	2,304			2,397	Dic
Sweden	1918	2,533	None		1918		6,738	Dem
Switzerland	1870	2,172	None		1870		8,939	Dem
United Kingdom	1911	5,052	None		1911		6,847	Dem
Yugoslavia (1918)	1921	1,064	1929	1,376			1,546	Dic
Australia (1901)	1901	4,112	None		1901		7,218	Dem
New Zealand (1907)	1907	5,367	None		1907		8,495	Dem

Notes: Income figures are not the same as in the rest of the text. They are expressed in 1990 Geary-Khamis dollars, as reported by Maddison (1995). Blanks indicate that income data are not available. Democratization is dated by (1) the occurrence of contested elections organized on a partisan basis and (2) legislative sovereignty of the lower house elected by broadest suffrage (rather than responsibility to the crown or a non-elected upper chamber), whichever came later, but not by the extent of franchise or participation, and (3) when relevant, the first victory of the opposition candidate in presidential elections. For countries that became independent after 1871, dates in parentheses are for the year of independence.

[a] Interpolated, based on 1820 and 1850.

[b] The question mark refers to the Vichy regime.

Reversals occurred in four out of ten countries. And, again, they were more likely to occur in countries where democracy was established when they were poor. Among the countries for which income data are available, eight democracies subsequently fell and four survived until 1950 (but in Pakistan democracy did fall soon after) where democracy was established with incomes under $2,000. In turn, six fell and twelve survived until 1950 (indeed, until today) in countries that had incomes above $2,000 when democracy was first established. The collapse of democracy in Chile, Colombia, Peru, Austria, Bulgaria, Germany, Greece, Finland, Italy, Poland, Portugal, Spain, and Yugoslavia occurred when these countries had incomes below 3,000 1990 G-K dollars, which means well below 3,000 1985 dollars, which we have been using. The highest level at which democracy collapsed was in Venezuela in 1948, but note that the 7,394 1990 G-K dollars corresponds to roughly 4,880 1985 PPP dollars, which we have been using throughout. Hence, the Argentine 1975 income of 6,055 still stands as the highest at which democracy was ever subverted.

To conclude, there is no doubt that democracies are more likely to be found in the more highly developed countries. Yet the reason is not that democracies are more likely to emerge when countries develop under authoritarianism, but that, however they do emerge, they are more likely to survive in countries that are already developed.

Economic Growth and Regime Dynamics

The conditions that countries inherit are not sufficient to explain why regimes survive or die. Dictatorships lasted in many countries that not only were wealthy but also enjoyed other conditions that should have predisposed them toward democracy. And, conversely, some democracies were established in countries that were poor and yet endured the passage of time.

Table 2.9 presents a list of democracies that lasted at least twenty years, organized by ascending levels of per capita income at the time when they were established or, when we could not determine their initial income, when data were first available. The income figures for the pre-1950 period are based on extrapolations and are at best approximative.[12] But the range of incomes at which lasting democracies were established is so large that all the inaccuracies do not change

---

[12] To compare the pre- and post-1950 incomes, in Table 2.9 we are extrapolating incomes expressed in 1985 PPP USD, rather than the 1990 G-K dollars used in Table 2.8.

Table 2.9. Democracies that lasted at least 20 years, by per capita income and by income distribution

Country	Established (year)	First observed Year	First observed LEVEL	Lasted until	Income distribution Year	INEQ	GINI	Income distribution Year	INEQ	GINI
India	1947	1947	556	Now	1951	6.14	35.56	1990	4.30	29.69
Philippines	1946	1946	697	1965	1957	7.42	46.14	1965	16.00	51.32
Brazil	1946	1946	917	1964	1960	18.72	53.00	1970	19.28	57.61
Netherlands	1868	1868	1,050	Now	1975	4.43	28.60	1989	5.11	29.60
Austria	1945	1945	1,093	Now						
Sri Lanka	1948	1951	1,107	1977	1953	10.35	47.80	1979	8.70	43.50
United States	1830	1830	1,119	Now	1947	8.20	34.28	1990	9.60	37.80
Norway	1884	1884	1,228	Now	1962	8.08	37.52	1991	7.69	33.31
Malta	1964	1964	1,377	Now						
Dominican R.	1966	1966	1,413	Now	1976		45.00	1989	13.26	50.46
Costa Rica	1948	1951	1,449	Now	1961	8.87	50.00	1989	12.67	46.07
Colombia	1958	1958	1,613	Now	1970	8.63	52.02	1988	15.11	51.20
Chile	1932	1932	1650	1973	1968	11.42	45.64	1971	12.16	46.00
Italy	1946	1946	1,708	Now	1974		41.00	1989	4.56	32.74
France	1875	1875	1,748	Now	1956		49.00	1984	6.38	34.91
Japan	1952	1952	1,768	Now	1962	7.71	37.20	1990		35.00
Jamaica	1962	1962	1,802	Now	1958		47.71	1990	8.09	41.79
Papua NG	1975	1975	1,870	Now						
Sweden	1918	1918	1,919	Now	1967	8.92	33.41	1990	5.16	32.52
Denmark	1901	1901	2,213	Now	1976	5.44	31.00	1992	6.90	33.20

(continued)

Table 2.9 (continued)

Country	Established (year)	First observed Year	First observed LEVEL	Lasted until	Income distribution Year	Income distribution INEQ	Income distribution GINI	Income distribution Year	Income distribution INEQ	Income distribution GINI
Switzerland	1870	1870	2,226	Now				1984	5.90	32.19
West Germany	1949	1949	2,567	Now	1963	3.58	28.13			
Israel	1947	1954	2,585	Now						
Finland	1944	1944	2,636	Now	1966	5.08	31.80	1991	4.34	26.11
Ireland	1922	1951	2,816	Now	1973	8.79	38.69	1987	9.05	34.60
Belgium	1919	1919	2,960	Now	1979	4.57	28.25	1992	4.31	26.92
United Kingdom	1911	1911	3,016	Now	1961	3.95	25.30	1990	5.27	32.30
Mauritius	1968	1968	3,074	Now	1980		39.10	1991	6.48	36.69
Barbados	1966	1966	3,353	Now	1951	12.45	45.49	1979	22.67	48.86
Uruguay	1937	1937	3,492	1973						
Iceland	1922	1951	3,675	Now						
Canada	1920	1920	3,838	Now	1951	5.72	32.56	1990	4.49	27.56
Portugal	1976	1976	4,471	Now	1973	4.61	30.63	1990	7.44	36.76
Greece	1974	1974	4,966	Now	1974	6.52	35.11	1988	6.65	35.19
Luxembourg	1868	1951	5,964	Now				1985	4.11	27.13
Trinidad & Tobago	1962	1962	6,006	Now	1958	14.29	46.02	1981	13.08	41.72
New Zealand	1907	1951	6,264	Now	1973	5.43	30.05	1990	9.77	40.21
Venezuela	1959	1959	6,718	Now	1971	14.44	47.65	1990	16.18	53.84
Spain	1977	1977	7,446	Now				1989	4.20	25.91
Bahamas	1972	1978	8,740	Now	1973		30.51			

Note: All the pre-1951-level figures are based on extrapolations and are expressed in 1985 PPP USD. INEQ is the ratio of incomes of the top quintile to the bottom quintile, GINI is the Gini index.

the picture. The fact is that some democracies survived for long periods even in very poor countries, including notably the United States, which in 1830 must have had the same per capita income as many contemporary African nations, about the same as today's Nigeria.

Hence, though we already know that in affluent countries democracy is impregnable, wealth is not necessary for democracies to survive. Some democracies, like some dictatorships, appear to survive even when they face adverse conditions. The hypothesis to investigate is that the survival of regimes is due to their economic performance, that is, that they are subject to endogenous attrition.

Let us again examine some descriptive patterns. In Table 2.10, the hazard rates (the probability that a regime will die in a particular year) are calculated separately for different bands of the rates of growth of per capita income, lagged one year, at each income level. When we look at the entire sample, it is apparent that growth matters for regime survival: When per capita income has declined during the preceding year, the probability that either type of regime will die is 0.0324, but when income has grown, that probability is 0.0164, one-half. And if this difference appears small, think in terms of frequencies: One in thirty-one regimes will die when the economies are shrinking, and one in sixty-one when they are expanding.

Democracies appear to be more sensitive to growth performance. When they face a decline in income, they die at the rate of 0.0512, so that about one in twenty of them dies, but when incomes are growing, they die at the rate of 0.0152, one in sixty-six. Moreover, democracies that grow slowly, at rates of less than 5 percent per annum, die at the rate of 0.0173, whereas those that grow at rates faster than 5 percent die at the rate of 0.0132. Thus, Olson (1963) and Huntington (1968) could not have been more wrong when they thought that rapid growth destabilizes democracies.

Dictatorships are less sensitive to economic crises: Their respective probabilities of dying are 0.0240, one in forty-two, when the economy decays, and 0.0174, one in fifty-seven, when it grows.

The difference between the two regimes becomes even more pronounced when we examine the longer-term dynamics of growth. With some exceptions, the longer the economic crisis, the more likely it is that democracy will fall: The chance that a democracy will die is 1 in 135 when incomes grow during any three or more consecutive years, and 1 in 13 when incomes fall during any two consecutive years. Conversely, most deaths of democracy are accompanied by some economic crisis: In twenty-eight out of thirty-nine instances, deaths of democracies were

Table 2.10. Observed rates of transition, by lagged per capita income (LEVLAG) and lagged rate of economic growth (GLAG)

LEVLAG GLAG	All			Dictatorships			Democracies		
	PJK	TJK	TOT	PAD	TAD	TA	PDA	TDA	TD
0–1,000	0.0147	15	1,019	0.0063	6	945	0.1216	9	74
G ≤ 0	0.0193	9	467	0.0091	4	440	0.1852	5	27
G > 0	0.0109	6	552	0.0040	2	505	0.0851	4	47
1,001–2,000	0.0321	32	997	0.0242	18	745	0.0556	14	252
G ≤ 0	0.0447	14	313	0.0313	7	224	0.0787	7	89
G > 0	0.0263	18	684	0.0211	11	521	0.0429	7	163
2,001–3,000	0.0325	16	493	0.0261	8	306	0.0428	8	187
G ≤ 0	0.0522	7	134	0.0341	3	88	0.0870	4	46
G > 0	0.0251	9	359	0.0229	5	218	0.0284	4	141
3,001–4,000	0.0201	7	349	0.0146	3	205	0.0278	4	144
G ≤ 0	0.0303	3	99	0.0172	1	58	0.0488	2	41
G > 0	0.0160	4	250	0.0136	2	147	0.0194	2	103
4,001–5,000	0.0339	8	236	0.0469	6	128	0.0185	2	108
G ≤ 0	0.0500	3	60	0.0588	2	34	0.0385	1	26
G > 0	0.0284	5	176	0.0426	4	94	0.0122	1	82
5,001–6,000	0.0308	6	195	0.0595	5	84	0.0090	1	111
G ≤ 0	0.0541	2	37	0.0952	2	21	0.0000	0	16
G > 0	0.0253	4	158	0.0476	3	63	0.0105	1	95
6,001–7,000	0.0190	3	158	0.0606	2	33	0.0080	1	125
G ≤ 0	0.0857	3	35	0.3333	2	6	0.0345	1	29
G > 0	0.0000	0	123	0.0000	0	27	0.0000	0	96
7,001–	0.0015	1	679	0.0286	1	35	0.0000	0	644
G ≤ 0	0.0000	0	120	0.0000	0	3	0.0000	0	117
G > 0	0.0018	1	559	0.0313	1	32	0.0000	0	527
Total	0.0213	88	4,126	0.0198	49	2,481	0.0237	39	1,645
G ≤ 0	0.0324	41	1,265	0.0240	21	874	0.0512	20	391
G > 0	0.0164	47	2,861	0.0174	28	1,607	0.0152	19	1,254
Moving average (2)									
Total	0.0218	87	3,991	0.0200	48	2,396	0.0245	39	1,595
G ≤ 0	0.0293	31	1,059	0.0241	18	748	0.0418	13	311
G > 0	0.0191	56	2,932	0.0182	30	1,648	0.0202	26	1,284
Moving average (3)									
Total	0.0223	86	3,856	0.0208	48	2,312	0.0246	38	1,544
G ≤ 0	0.0286	26	910	0.0226	15	665	0.0449	11	245
G > 0	0.0204	60	2,946	0.0200	33	1,647	0.0208	27	1,299

Notes: G ≤ 0 means that per capita income declined or remained the same; G > 0 means that per capita income increased. PJK stands for the probability of any regime transition; TJK is their number. TOT is the total number of annual observations. PAD stands for the probability of transition from authoritarianism to democracy; TAD is their number. TA is the total number of annual observations of authoritarianism. PDA stands for the probability of transition from democracy to authoritarianism; TDA is their number. TD is the total number of annual observations of democracy.

Table 2.11. Regime transitions, by longer-term dynamics of per capita income

Incomes increased or decreased during these consecutive years	Dictatorships			Democracies		
	PAD	TAD	TA	PDA	TDA	TD
Increased						
3 or more years	0.0170	14	824	0.0074	6	807
2 years	0.0139	4	288	0.0265	5	189
1 year	0.0205	10	488	0.0315	8	254
Decreased						
1 year	0.0220	10	455	0.0549	13	237
2 years	0.0181	4	221	0.0778	7	90
3 years	0.0455	4	88	0.0000	0	31
4 or more years	0.0230	2	87	0.0000	0	27
Total		48	2,471		39	1,635

accompanied by a fall in income during at least one of the two preceding years. Dictatorships, in turn, die under all kinds of economic conditions. The probabilities of dictatorships falling are almost the same regardless whether the economy grew or declined during any number of consecutive years. And, conversely, whereas fourteen out of forty-eight transitions to democracy followed at least three years of consecutive growth, ten dictatorships fell after their countries experienced at least two consecutive years of economic decline, six after declines of three years, and two after declines of four or more years. Thus, albeit not without exceptions, deaths of democracies follow a clear pattern: They are more likely when a country experiences an economic crisis, and in most cases they are accompanied by one. But dictatorships die under the entire range of economic conditions (Table 2.11).

We know already that democracies never die in wealthy countries. Yet it is still striking how fragile poor democracies are. In countries with incomes under $2,000, of the 116 years during which declines in incomes occurred, twelve democracies fell the following year: about one in ten. Even among countries with incomes between $2,001 and

$5,000, declining incomes resulted in the fall of seven democracies in 113 years during which this happened: one in sixteen. And then, above $6,055 the miracle occurs. Longer-term patterns are the same: Among democracies with per capita incomes of less than $3,000, one in thirty-five died when incomes had grown during two or more consecutive years, but one in ten when incomes had declined during one or more consecutive years. Poor dictatorships, in turn, are impervious to economic crises, but wealthy dictatorships are more vulnerable when incomes decline. One in forty-two of them died when incomes increased during at least two consecutive years, but one in sixteen when incomes declined for at least one year.

These descriptive patterns are confirmed by statistical analyses. In Table 2.12 we show the effects of growth rates on the probabilities of regime transitions during the single preceding year, and of moving averages over two and three preceding years. Democracies turn out to be most sensitive to their growth performance during one single year; the average over two years matters less, and over three years not at all. Dictatorships as well are most sensitive to last year's growth, but longer crises still matter.

Is it then true that, to put it in the words of Diamond and Linz (1989: 17), "economic crisis represents one of the most common threats to democratic stability"? Do economic crises threaten regime stability, or does regime instability cause economic crises?

The question of what causes what is difficult, perhaps impossible, to answer. One can think of rival stories. Take democracies: It may happen that for some exogenous reason, say a jump in energy prices or international interest rates, an economy suffers a shock. No longer able to satisfy popular demands, democracy becomes vulnerable to political forces that put the blame on the "anarchy" of democratic competition; such forces promise to establish "order" and to sanitize the economy. But it is equally plausible that the shock could be political, say an electoral victory by a left-wing party: That party pursues a redistributive policy, investors are thrown into a panic, and the economy grinds to a halt. Similar stories can be told about dictatorships: Facing an economic shock, the regime can no longer legitimize itself by its economic performance, and forced to liberalize, it unleashes the forces for transition. But again, the shock might be political, say the imminent death of a founding dictator or a power struggle within the authoritarian bloc. Facing the imminent death of the regime, investors run away, and workers openly press their demands, causing economic decline. In either case, one has to be able to tell a rather

Table 2.12. Dynamic probit analysis of the impact of growth on regime survival

Lagged rate of growth

Log-likelihood	−372.9192
Restricted (slope = 0) log-likelihood	−2,685.421
Chi-squared (7)	4,625.003
Significance level	0.0000000

	Transitions to dictatorship			Transitions to democracy		
Variable	Coefficient	t ratio	Pr $|t| \geq x$	Coefficient	t ratio	Pr $|t| \geq x$
Constant	−1.1444	−5.288	0.00000	−2.5238	−13.704	0.00000
LEVLAG	−0.20098E-03	−1.399	0.16195	0.32883E-03	0.699	0.48446
LEVSQR	−0.29429E-05	−0.158	0.87411	−0.29161E-04	−1.309	0.19050
GLAG	−0.42345E-01	−2.988	0.00281	−0.21067E-01	−3.823	0.00013

Lagged moving average of growth over two years

Log-likelihood	−368.7513
Restricted (slope = 0) log-likelihood	−2,595.780
Chi-squared (7)	4,454.058
Significance level	0.0000000

	Transitions to dictatorship			Transitions to democracy		
Variable	Coefficient	t ratio	Pr $|t| \geq x$	Coefficient	t ratio	Pr $|t| \geq x$
Constant	−1.0673	−4.993	0.00000	−2.4135	−13.442	0.00000
LEVLAG	−0.22871E-03	−1.633	0.10249	0.33118E-03	0.569	0.56911
LEVSQR	−0.39442E-06	−0.022	0.98215	−0.28839E-04	−1.231	0.21821
MA2GL	−0.31652E-01	−1.675	0.09402	−0.26569E-01	−2.642	0.00823

Lagged moving average of growth over three years

Log-likelihood	−364.1207
Restricted (slope = 0) log-likelihood	−2,506.529
Chi-squared (7)	4,284.818
Significance level	0.0000000

	Transitions to dictatorship			Transitions to democracy		
Variable	Coefficient	t ratio	Pr $|t| \geq x$	Coefficient	t ratio	Pr $|t| \geq x$
Constant	−1.0418	−4.800	0.00000	−2.4894	−13.117	0.00000
LEVLAG	−0.24784E-03	−1.773	0.07627	0.33155E-03	0.466	0.64152
LEVSQR	0.10868E-05	0.063	0.95015	−0.28881E-04	−1.182	0.23730
MA3GL	−0.14568E-01	−0.648	0.51677	−0.30060E-01	−1.697	0.08977

Notes: LEVLAG, lagged per capita income; LEVSQR, lagged squared per capita income; GLAG, lagged rate of growth; MA2GL, lagged moving average of growth over two years; MA3GL, lagged moving average of growth over three years. The t ratios under "Transitions to democracy" refer to shift coefficients (α in Appendix I), not to the total coefficients ($\alpha + \beta$).

complex story in which political and economic events feed on each other in turn.

Ideally, we would like to be able to observe something like "pressures toward transition" and relate them to economic dynamics. But we cannot observe them. All we can see are visible manifestations of political mobilization: strikes (STRIKES), anti-government demonstrations (AGDEMONS), or riots (RIOTS). To draw inferences from these observations, we can reason as follows: If regimes fall when incomes decline and mobilization is not any higher than when they do not fall ("low"), then we can attribute the causal effect to economic crises. If regimes fall when incomes grow but mobilization is high, we can suspect that it is political mobilization that brings them down. If they fall when incomes decline and mobilization is high, we cannot tell which is the cause. Finally, if they fall when incomes are growing and mobilization is low, neither is the cause.

Before we follow this reasoning, note in Table 2.13 that the incidence of mobilization – the sum of the preceding three events (MOBILIZATION) – is independent of economic growth in democracies, but in dictatorships it is higher during economic crises.[13] Moreover, the incidence of mobilization is more or less the same whether or not a democracy is to fall next year, 2.47 as opposed to 1.87 during other years, but it is much higher in the years preceding deaths of dictatorships, 4.37 versus 1.01 (Table 2.14).

Given that in dictatorships political mobilization and economic crises coincide, there were only three dictatorships that fell following a year during which incomes declined but mobilization was not any higher than during other years. In turn, in eleven instances incomes were growing but mobilization was high. Hence, following our reasoning, we can attribute three deaths of dictatorships to economic crises alone and eleven to political mobilization alone. But in eighteen cases economic crises and political mobilization coincided, so that we cannot identify the cause. And in seventeen instances, dictatorships fell even though the economy was growing and political mobilization was low, and we have no way of telling what caused those dictatorships to die.

The number of cases in which democracies died while incomes fell and mobilization remained low is larger: twelve out of thirty-eight. In turn, eight democracies died while their economies were growing

---

[13] In addition to the analysis in Table 2.13, we conducted statistical analyses, which showed that the coefficient of growth on mobilization was negative and significant under dictatorships and almost zero under democracies.

Table 2.13. Incidence of political mobilization, by longer-term dynamics of per capita income

Incomes increased or decreased during these consecutive years	Dictatorships		Democracies	
	Surviving	Dying	Surviving	Dying
Increased				
3 or more years	1.05	5.79	1.97	2.00
2 years	0.94	1.25	1.83	2.60
1 year	0.71	2.30	1.65	1.13
Decreased				
1 year	1.09	5.60	1.79	2.00
2 years	1.34	5.50	1.91	5.14
3 years	1.56	5.50	1.77	—
4 or more years	0.77	1.00	1.78	—
Actions experienced				
STRIKES	0.08	0.53	0.24	0.34
AGDEMONS	0.46	2.18	0.77	0.71
RIOTS	0.46	1.65	0.86	1.42
MOBILIZATION	1.01	4.36	1.87	2.47
Total	2,354	49	1,548	38

Note: The cell entries measure average incidences of the respective variables.

yet mobilization was high. Yet again, seven deaths of democracies occurred when incomes declined while mobilization was high, and eleven when incomes grew while mobilization was low.

Because we can think of no other way to tell what causes what, all we can do is to conclude from what we can see. It is obvious that regime transitions, events that are quite rare, occur under a wide variety of circumstances. Economic crises are not sufficient to bring regimes down. Neither are waves of political mobilization. Indeed, eleven democracies and seventeen dictatorships fell when incomes were growing and mobilization was low. There are obviously other causes:

Table 2.14. Growth and mobilization during the
year preceding regime transition

Regime and income trend	Mobilization		
	Low	High	Total
Dictatorships			
Income growth			
Negative	3	18	21
Positive	17	11	28
Total	20	29	49
Democracies			
Income growth			
Negative	12	7	19
Positive	11	8	19
Total	23	15	38

Note: "Low" mobilization is an incidence below the average
for years other than that preceding a regime transition;
"high" mobilization is above that average.

deaths of the founding dictator, institutional stalemates, external wars,
foreign pressures – the list goes on.

Just consider the fall of communism. Most communist countries
experienced a sharp economic downturn between 1978 and 1980.
Czechoslovakia, Hungary, and Yugoslavia never recuperated from that
crisis. Poland, Romania, and the Soviet Union recovered from that
downturn by the early 1980s, but their growth slowed down again after
1985. Given that dictatorships are more vulnerable at income levels
at which those countries found themselves, and given their economic
slowdown, the chances that those regimes would die increased. But
they were never large: We calculated them (using the model presented
in Table 2.12) to be about one in twenty. It took an economic crisis,
a wave of popular mobilization in Poland, the Soviet defeat in
Afghanistan, a massive United States armament, and probably several
strategic miscalculations (Kaminski 1997; Przeworski 1997) for one of
them to fall. And then Henry Kissinger's dominoes tumbled, although
in the direction opposite to the one he had so eloquently predicted.

We are thus not claiming that the economic factors are sufficient to account for the different fates of regimes. The chances of regimes surviving appear to depend somewhat on these conditions, but the chances are only the odds according to which dice are thrown. Obviously, other conditions matter, as do the actions of the people living under these conditions and, perhaps, sheer luck. Thus, regime selection is in part due to observable factors, such as level of income and its growth, but in part to factors that we cannot or at least did not systematically observe.

Yet there are some things we do know. Foremost among them is that democracies never die in wealthy countries. But all the evidence we have examined also indicates that democracies in poorer countries are more likely to die when they experience economic crises than when their economies grow. In turn, dictatorships die under much more varied economic circumstances: Indeed, it appears that economic circumstances have little to do with the deaths of dictatorships.

Income Inequality

The entire analysis thus far has concerned only average or total indicators for each country. But there are good reasons to think that a factor that matters for regime stability is also the distribution of income among different groups. Under dictatorships, high income inequality may stimulate movements attracted by the egalitarian promise of democracy. Under democracy, dominant social groups may seek recourse to authoritarianism when the exercise of political rights by the poor – whether in the form of suffrage or freedom of association – results in egalitarian pressures.

Unfortunately, these hypotheses are almost impossible to test. The best available data set on income distribution (Deininger and Squire 1996) is still far from complete and combines numbers collected by different methods. For many countries, information is not available at all, and for many others it is available only for irregularly scattered years. In the end, we thus have only 542 annual observations that match our period. Moreover, some of the numbers are on an income basis, and others on an expenditure basis; some are pre- and others post-fisc. Hence, there is little to go on.

An additional complication is that the data show somewhat of a Kuznets effect, that is, the degree of inequality, as measured by the Gini index, increases and then falls with per capita income. The top panel of Table 2.15 shows Gini indices by per capita income and by regime.

Table 2.15. Income inequality and regime dynamics

A: Inequality (Gini indices) by per capita income

	Average Gini indices					
LEVEL	All		Dictatorships		Democracies	
0–1,000	34.2806	(47)	35.7348	(23)	32.8871	(24)
1,001–2,000	38.6957	(74)	37.6443	(53)	41.3490	(21)
2,001–3,000	45.5331	(52)	43.1266	(29)	48.5674	(23)
3,001–4,000	39.0088	(49)	34.7779	(29)	45.1435	(20)
4,001–5,000	36.1776	(45)	32.4200	(33)	46.5108	(12)
5,001–6,000	35.0812	(24)	33.7861	(18)	38.9667	(6)
6001–	33.0105	(251)	32.2900	(18)	33.0662	(233)
Total	35.9952	(542)	36.1355	(203)	35.9112	(339)

B1: Regime transitions by Gini indices

	PJK	TJK	TOT	PAD	TAD	TA	PDA	TDA	TD
All	0.0188	25	1,327	0.0322	19	590	0.0081	6	737
<35	0.0167	10	597	0.0376	9	239	0.0028	1	358
≥35	0.0205	15	730	0.0285	10	351	0.0132	5	379

B2: Regime transitions by ratios of top 20% to bottom 20%

	PJK	TJK	TOT	PAD	TAD	TA	PDA	TDA	TD
All	0.0192	22	1,133	0.0364	17	467	0.0075	5	666
<9	0.0146	10	685	0.0347	10	288	0.0000	0	397
≥9	0.0268	12	448	0.0391	7	179	0.0187	5	269

C1: Regime transitions by changes of Gini indices

	PJK	TJK	TOT	PAD	TAD	TA	PDA	TDA	TD
All	0.0240	29	1,209	0.0371	19	512	0.0143	10	697
<0	0.0272	17	626	0.0542	13	240	0.0104	4	386
>0	0.0206	12	583	0.0221	6	272	0.0193	6	311

C2: Regime transitions by changes in ratios of top 20% to bottom 20%

	PJK	TJK	TOT	PAD	TAD	TA	PDA	TDA	TD
All	0.0224	23	1,027	0.0361	15	416	0.0131	8	611
<0	0.0208	11	528	0.0323	7	217	0.0129	4	311
>0	0.0240	12	499	0.0402	8	199	0.0133	4	300

(continued)

Table 2.15 (continued)

C3: Regime transitions by changes in the share of the bottom 40%

	PJK	TJK	TOT	PAD	TAD	TA	PDA	TDA	TD
All	0.0222	23	1,036	0.0356	15	421	0.0130	8	615
<0	0.0246	14	568	0.0352	8	227	0.0176	6	341
>0	0.0192	9	468	0.0361	7	194	0.0073	2	274

C4: Regime transitions by changes in the share of the top 20%

	PJK	TJK	TOT	PAD	TAD	TA	PDA	TDA	TD
All	0.0222	23	1,036	0.0356	15	421	0.0130	8	615
<0	0.0163	9	551	0.0287	6	209	0.0088	3	342
>0	0.0289	14	485	0.0424	9	212	0.0183	5	273

D1: Regime transitions by changes in the income of the bottom 40%

	PJK	TJK	TOT	PAD	TAD	TA	PDA	TDA	TD
All	0.0224	23	1,027	0.0361	15	416	0.0131	8	611
<0	0.0367	11	300	0.0636	7	110	0.0211	4	190
>0	0.0165	12	727	0.0261	8	306	0.0095	4	421

D2: Regime transitions by changes in the income of the top 20%

	PJK	TJK	TOT	PAD	TAD	TA	PDA	TDA	TD
All	0.0224	23	1,027	0.0361	15	416	0.0131	8	611
<0	0.0412	10	243	0.0761	7	92	0.0199	3	151
>0	0.0166	13	784	0.0247	8	324	0.0109	5	460

E1: Regime transitions by changes in average welfare

	PJK	TJK	TOT	PAD	TAD	TA	PDA	TDA	TD
All	0.0224	23	1,027	0.0361	15	416	0.0131	8	611
<0	0.0494	12	243	0.0745	7	94	0.0336	5	149
>0	0.0140	11	784	0.0248	8	322	0.0065	3	462

Notes: PJK stands for the probability of any regime transition; TJK is their number. TOT is the total number of annual observations. PAD stands for the probability of transition from authoritarianism to democracy; TAD is their number. TA is the total number of annual observations of authoritarianism. PDA stands for the probability of transition from democracy to authoritarianism; TDA is their number. TD is the total number of annual observations of democracy.

As we see, the average index increases from 34.28 for all countries with incomes under $1,000 to 45.53 for all countries between $2,001 and $3,000 and then falls to 33.01 for all countries with incomes above $6,000. Dictatorships and democracies show similar patterns and have the same average income inequality, as measured by the Gini index.

Yet with all these caveats, some suggestive patterns do emerge. To test whether or not the level of income inequality destabilizes regimes, we considered five years (two before and two after, unless another observation was available during these years or the regime changed) around each observation of income distribution, thus obtaining 1,327 years for Gini indices and 1,133 for ratios of incomes of top and bottom quintiles. This data set still contains only six (for Gini) and five (for the ratio) transitions to dictatorship; hence the caveats should be kept in mind. Nevertheless, dichotomizing the Gini index approximately at the observed mean, that is, 35 (the actual mean is 38.3), shows that only one democracy fell during the 358 years when the Gini index was below this threshold, whereas five fell during the 379 years when inequality was higher (panel B1 of Table 2.15). The effect of inequality on dictatorships, for which we observe 19 transitions, was less pronounced. The ratio of top to bottom incomes shows the same: When this ratio was less than nine, no democracy fell during 397 years, but when it was higher, five fell during 269 years (panel B2). And, again, the effect on dictatorships was negligible. Hence, whatever these numbers are worth, they do suggest that democracy is more stable in more egalitarian societies, and the durability of dictatorships is unaffected by income distribution.

To test whether or not increasing or decreasing inequality has an effect on the stability of regimes, we took all cases in which more than one observation was available for a country, observed how income distribution changed, and calculated the rates of transition during these periods.[14] The numbers are again small, and they tend to be disproportionately drawn from the more developed countries. Not much can be learned from them. Changes in absolute income levels (see panels D of Table 2.15) matter more for the stability of both regimes than do

---

[14] Note that some of these data were presented in Table 2.9, which lists democracies that lasted at least twenty years. If we consider only poorer countries, we see that democracy survived in the Dominican Republic even though income inequality increased, but it fell in the three other poor countries where inequality increased: the Philippines, Brazil, and Chile. In turn, among countries where income inequality was reduced, democracy survived in India, Japan, Finland, and Mauritius, and fell only in Sri Lanka.

changes in the overall distribution or the income shares of particular groups (panels C). Both regimes are less stable when absolute incomes, whether of the top 20 percent or the bottom 40 percent of earners, decline.

In turn, changes in the overall distribution, whether measured by the Gini index or by the ratio, have no clear effect on the stability of regimes. Yet both regimes are slightly less stable when the share of the top 20 percent increases. Democracies, and only democracies, are somewhat less stable when the income share of the bottom 40 percent declines. Thus, with all the caveats, it appears that both regimes are threatened when the rich get relatively richer, but only democracy is vulnerable when the poor get relatively poorer.

We also calculated changes in average welfare, attaching lower weights to increases of incomes that were already higher (Atkinson 1970; logarithmic utility function). This transformation allows us to distinguish the effect of growth of the average income from the effect of changes in its distribution: There are some cases in which the average income grows but inequality increases to such an extent that the average welfare declines. Both regimes appear to be more likely to die when the average welfare falls. Moreover, comparison with Table 2.10 shows that both regimes are more sensitive to changes of welfare than of income alone, implying that when the average income declines and inequality increases – income declines at the cost of the poor – both regimes are much more vulnerable than when the average income increases and inequality is reduced.

The functional distribution of income, for which data are more extensive, shows a much stronger impact of inequality for both regimes. The data for labor share of value added in manufacturing (LS) include 2,061 annual observations, as always drawn disproportionately from poor dictatorships and rich democracies. The overall effect of the functional distribution of income is very strong: Both regimes are several times more likely to fall when labor receives less than 25 percent of value added in manufacturing. Dictatorships in countries with incomes below $4,000 are particularly vulnerable when inequality is high, but dictatorships in wealthier countries survive at somewhat higher rates when the labor share is smaller. Democracies in poor countries are less likely to survive when labor gets a lower share, whereas in wealthier countries labor almost always gets more than 25 percent, and they almost always survive (Table 2.16).

Thus, at the very least, there is no evidence that egalitarian pressures threaten the survival of democracy. Indeed, it appears that

Table 2.16. Regime transitions, by level and labor share

LEVLAG LSLAG	PJK	TJK	TOT	PAD	TAD	TA	PDA	TDA	TD
0–1,000	0.0162	5	308	0.0072	2	277	0.0967	3	31
LS ≤ 25	0.0470	4	85	0.0259	2	77	0.2500	2	8
LS > 25	0.0044	1	223	0.0000	0	200	0.0434	1	23
1,001–2,000	0.0373	16	429	0.0271	9	332	0.0721	7	97
LS ≤ 25	0.0847	10	118	0.0752	7	93	0.1200	3	25
LS > 25	0.0192	6	311	0.0083	2	239	0.0555	4	72
2,001–3,000	0.0390	11	282	0.0379	6	158	0.0403	5	124
LS ≤ 25	0.0792	8	101	0.1154	6	52	0.0408	2	49
LS > 25	0.0165	3	181	0.0000	0	106	0.0400	3	75
3,001–4,000	0.0229	5	218	0.0217	3	138	0.0250	2	80
LS ≤ 25	0.0468	3	64	0.0882	3	34	0.0000	0	30
LS > 25	0.0129	2	154	0.0000	0	104	0.0400	2	50
4,001–5,000	0.0229	3	131	0.0370	3	81	0.0000	0	50
LS ≤ 25	0.0555	2	36	0.0909	2	22	0.0000	0	14
LS > 25	0.0105	1	95	0.0169	1	59	0.0000	0	36
5,001–	0.0101	7	693	0.0779	6	77	0.0016	1	616
LS ≤ 25	0.0385	1	26	0.0588	1	17	0.0000	0	9
LS > 25	0.0090	6	667	0.0833	5	60	0.0016	1	609
Total	0.0228	47	2,061	0.0272	29	1,063	0.0180	18	998
LS ≤ 25	0.0651	28	430	0.0711	21	295	0.0518	7	135
LS > 25	0.0116	19	1,631	0.0104	8	768	0.0127	11	863

Notes: LEVLAG is lagged per capita income; LSLAG is lagged labor share of output in manufacturing.

democracies are less stable in societies that are more unequal to begin with, in societies in which household income inequality increases, and in societies in which labor receives a lower share of value added in manufacturing. Dictatorships, in turn, particularly in poorer countries, are much more vulnerable when the functional distribution of income is more unequal.

Economic Factors in Context

Two questions still remain open. Are the economic factors still important when one takes into account the cultural, social, and politi-

cal context in which they operate? And even if they do remain important, do cultural, social, and political conditions affect the rise and
decline of political regimes independently of the economy?

To move beyond economic factors, we examine the impact of an entire
panoply of variables considered simultaneously. How do the political,
social, and cultural conditions in which regimes find themselves affect
the probability of transitions from democracy to dictatorship and from
dictatorship to democracy? The data show the following (Table 2.17):

1. The impact of per capita income (lagged, LEVLAG), treated linearly,
   is apparent for both regimes, but it is orders of magnitude larger for
   democracies.
2. The rate of economic growth (lagged, GLAG) matters for the stability of both regimes, but less so for democracies. Both are less likely
   to die when growth is faster.
3. Intra-regime instability, accumulated turnover of chief executives
   (lagged, TLAG), has an important impact on the stability of both
   regimes when it is introduced linearly into the analysis. Both regimes
   are more likely to die when they experience frequent changes of
   heads of government.

There is, however, a fundamental difference between democracies
and dictatorships. A moderate frequency of alternation in office
increases the stability of democracies, but any changes of the heads of
dictatorships shorten their lives. Table 2.18 shows the observed probabilities of both regimes dying in a year that follows a particular frequency of accumulated turnover. Democracies that change their chief
executives less frequently than once in five years die at the rate of
0.0249, with an expected life of forty years. But democracies that
change their heads of governments once between five and four years,
or even more frequently, down to once in two years, have a lower probability of dying. Only very frequent changes, more frequent that once
in two years, constitute "instability" in the sense of increasing the
chances of democracies dying. Dictatorships, in turn, are most durable
when changes are very infrequent: Their expected life when changes
occur less frequently than once in every five years is seventy-four years.
But when changes occur only somewhat more frequently, once between
five and four years, their expected duration is reduced to thirty years.
As turnover becomes higher, the expected life of dictatorship dwindles,
all the way down to eight years.

Hence, a moderate frequency of alternation in office increases the
stability of democratic regimes. After all, this is the essence of democ-

Table 2.17. Dynamic probit analysis of regime transitions

Number of observations	3,942
Log-likelihood function	−291.0939
Restricted log-likelihood	−2,644.349
Chi-squared	4,706.511
Degrees of freedom	23
Significance level	0.0000000

Variable	Transitions to dictatorship			Transitions to democracy		
	Coefficient	t ratio	Pr $|t| \geq x$	Coefficient	t ratio	Pr $|t| \geq x$
Constant	0.12535	0.139	0.88954	−3.407	−3.119	0.00182
LEVLAG	−0.54617E-03	−4.467	0.00001	0.3356E-04	3.953	0.00008
GLAG	−0.23844E-01	−1.410	0.15858	−0.1997E-01	−2.215	0.02678
TLAG	0.97218	3.459	0.00054	0.5415	4.437	0.00001
RELDIF	2.5568	2.581	0.00984	0.1096	2.442	0.01459
CATH	−1.1295	−2.089	0.03672	0.1535	1.624	0.10427
PROT	−2.4463	−1.506	0.13213	−0.2615	−1.565	0.11765
MOSLEM	0.22024E-01	0.044	0.96497	−0.7248E-01	−0.085	0.93196
NEWC	−0.16120E-01	−0.036	0.97151	−0.4348	−0.906	0.36489
BRITCOL	−0.83942	−1.974	0.04837	0.1645	1.430	0.15260
STRA	0.89495	7.403	0.00000	0.3612	8.992	0.00000
ODWP	−3.7446	−1.992	0.04633	3.033	−0.319	0.74958

Frequencies of actual and predicted outcomes; predicted outcome has maximum probability

	Predicted		
Actual	0	1	Total
0	1,503	53	1,556
1	32	2,354	2,386
Total	1,535	2,407	3,942

Note: LEVLAG, lagged per capita income; GLAG, lagged rate of growth; TLAG, lagged cumulative rate of leadership turnover; RELDIF, religious fractionalization; CATH, proportion of Catholics in the population; PROT, proportion of Protestants in the population; MOSLEM, proportion of Moslems in the population; NEWC, dummy variable indicating that the country did not exist in 1945; BRITCOL, dummy variable indicating a former British colony; STRA, cumulative number of past transitions to authoritarianism; ODWP, proportion of other democracies in the world. The standard errors and the t ratios (including their signs) under "Transitions to democracy" refer to shift coefficients (α in Appendix I), not to the total coefficients ($\alpha + \beta$).

Table 2.18. Impact of intra-regime instability (turnover of heads of governments) on regime transition rates

Frequency: one change in:	PJK	TJK	TOT	PAD	TAD	TA	PDA	TDA	TD
>5 years	0.0162	45	2,777	0.0129	26	2,014	0.0249	19	763
5–4 years	0.0222	10	450	0.0292	5	171	0.0179	5	279
4–2 years	0.0351	21	597	0.0619	13	210	0.0206	8	387
2–1 years	0.0442	10	226	0.0588	4	68	0.0379	6	158
<1 year	0.0769	2	26	0.1250	1	8	0.0555	1	18
Total	0.0215	88	4,076	0.0198	49	2,471	0.0243	39	1,605

Notes: PJK stands for the probability of any regime transition; TJK is their number. TOT is the total number of annual observations. PAD stands for the probability of transition from authoritarianism to democracy; TAD is their number. TA is the total number of annual observations of authoritarianism. PDA stands for the probability of transition from democracy to authoritarianism; TDA is their number. TD is the total number of annual observations of democracy.

racy: alternating in office as a result of application of rules. Dictatorship, however, is a system whose stability depends on personal rule. Any change in the head of government is a threat to its survival.

4. As is frequently claimed, democracies are less stable in countries that are religiously heterogeneous (RELDIF). We have also experimented with another variable, "ethnolinguistic fractionalization," which measures ethnic, rather than religious, heterogeneity. This variable is statistically significant when considered alone, but plays no role once religious fractionalization is introduced.

What is striking, however, is that dictatorships are also less stable in religiously or ethnolinguistically heterogeneous societies. Note that the standard explanation for the instability of democracies in heterogeneous societies, one that goes back to J. S. Mill (1991 [1861]), is that for democracy to endure there must be some shared values, a "consensus." Yet because dictatorships are also less likely to endure in heterogeneous societies, the claim that common values are needed to support democracy reduces to the observation that regime transitions are more frequent in heterogeneous countries. Religious or ethnolinguistic heterogeneity simply makes all political regimes less stable.

5. Since Montesquieu (1995 [1748]), much has been said about the importance of culture for the emergence and durability of democracies. Recent discussions of this topic have revolved mainly around cultures identified by dominant religions. Even if Weber (1958 [1904]) himself said almost nothing about political institutions (Przeworski, Cheibub, and Limongi 1997), the idea that he saw in Protestantism the wellspring of modern democracy is widespread among contemporary political scientists. Lipset (1959: 165) claimed that "it has been argued by Max Weber among others that the factors making for democracy in this area [north-west Europe and their English-speaking offsprings in America and Australasia] are a historically unique concatenation of elements, part of the complex which also produced capitalism in this area," because "the emphasis within Protestantism on individual responsibility furthered the emergence of democratic values."[15] In turn, Catholicism, in Lipset's view (1960: 72–3), was antithetical to democracy in pre–World War II Europe and Latin America. Yet even Catholicism is not the worst enemy of democracy: Islam and Confucianism hold the palm (Eisenstadt 1968: 25–7). Thus, Huntington (1993: 15) reported that "no scholarly disagreement exists regarding the proposition that traditional Confucianism was either undemocratic or antidemocratic." Similar views about Islam abound (Gellner 1991: 506; Lewis 1993: 96–8).

According to our analysis, none of those assertions can withstand scrutiny. Indeed, the only effect of religions that emerges from the statistical examination is that democracies are more likely to survive in countries in which there are more Catholics. Neither Protestantism nor Islam seems to have an effect on the emergence or the durability of democracy.

6. A colonial legacy has little effect on regime stability once all the other factors are considered. Democracies are somewhat more likely to survive in countries that were British colonies (BRITCOL), but having been a colony at all (NEWC) has no effect. Note that the rates of democratic failure observed between 1950 and 1990 were much higher among democracies that were established after 1950 (0.0620, with an expected life of 16.8 years) than in the entire set of democracies (0.0237, with an expected life of 42.2). Yet this effect vanishes

---

[15] Lipset does not point to any specific text of Weber. Neither do Almond and Verba (1963: 10), who assert that "the development of Protestantism, and in particular the nonconformist sects, *have been considered* vital to the development of stable political institutions in Britain, the Old Commonwealth, and the United States" (italics added).

in the statistical analysis, indicating that the observed difference was due to the low incomes of these countries, not the timing of independence.

7. The political history of regimes, their past instability, has an important role in affecting the chances that the current regime will survive or die. In countries that experienced more transitions to dictatorship (STRA) in the past, both types of regimes are less stable, and the effect is about three times larger for democracies.

This last finding suggests that political learning is a complex matter. It is frequently argued – Russia is a good example – that the absence of democratic traditions is an impediment to consolidating new democratic institutions and, conversely, that democracy is more stable in the countries that have enjoyed it in the past – here Chile is the paradigmatic case. Yet what that argument misses is that if a country has had a democratic regime in its past, it also has experienced subversion of democracy. Political learning thus cuts both ways. Perhaps democrats find consolidation easier when they can rely on past traditions, but anti-democratic forces also have an experience from which they can draw lessons: People know that an overthrow of democracy is possible, how it happens, and how to bring it about. If the Russian coup of 1991 was more of a coup de theatre than a coup d'état, it was perhaps because the Russian *golpistas* simply did not know how to do it and were justly ridiculed by their experienced Latin American soulmates.

8. Finally, whereas the international political climate (ODWP) has an impact on the stability of democracies, it has no effect whatever on transitions to democracy. The probability that once established a democracy will die is lower when many countries in the world are democratic. But the probability that a democracy will be established does not depend on the proportion of countries in the world that have democratic regimes. This finding casts doubts on the notion that democratization comes in waves, a topic we discussed earlier.

To put these findings in perspective, it is necessary to remember that regime transitions are relatively rare. Although we have seen that some countries experience a fair amount of regime instability, in most countries a single regime will continue for long periods. This heterogeneity appears to be due to the factors that we analyzed earlier, particularly to past history: Once these factors are considered, the sample is no longer heterogeneous in the statistical sense. But inertia remains high: In each year, most countries have the same regimes they had in the preceding year.

Yet regimes do die, and the transitions can be explained. When the impacts of different factors are taken one by one, it again becomes clear that the level of economic development is crucial for the stability of democracies, whereas both regimes are affected by their economic performance and by the frequency of turnover of heads of government. Of all the other variables, past regime instability plays the greatest role. Religious or ethnolinguistic heterogeneity also affects the stability of both regimes. In turn, the colonial heritage and cultural patterns, at least as indicated by the frequency of major religions, play almost no role.

The impact of the level of development, of leadership turnover, and of past regime instability is robust, in the (Leamer) sense that these variables are highly significant regardless which other factors are introduced into the analysis. Economic performance variables always matter, but their statistical significance is somewhat affected by the presence of other variables. The impact of all the other variables is not robust: In some specifications, they appear as statistically significant, but in others they do not. When per capita income is not considered, Protestantism becomes somewhat important, and ethnolinguistic fractionalization dominates religious heterogeneity. In some other specifications, having been a colony appears to have an impact independent of the British colonial heritage. One should not be surprised, therefore, that the determinants of regimes have been the subjects of such extensive debates. Yet we think that the basic patterns are clear and robust: The level of economic development, economic performance, past regime instability, and leadership turnover tell almost all of the story.

Democratic Institutions and the Sustainability of Democracy

Democracies are not all the same. Systems of representation, divisions of powers, legal doctrines, and the bundles of rights and obligations associated with citizenship all differ significantly among regimes that are generally recognized as democratic. And these institutional arrangements may have an impact on the sustainability of democracy. The durability of democracies may not be simply a matter of economic, social, or cultural conditions, because their institutional frameworks may differ in their capacity to process conflicts, particularly when these conditions become so adverse that democratic performance is considered to be inadequate.[16] Democracy is sustainable when its institutional

---

[16] Seminal studies along this line are those by Zimmerman (1987, 1988), who found that the timing and the depth of the recession of 1929–1932 could not predict whether or not a democracy would survive that crisis.

framework promotes normatively desirable and politically desired objectives, but also when these institutions are adept at handling crises that occur when such objectives are not being fulfilled.

The institutional distinction that appears particularly important is that between presidential and parliamentary systems. We discussed this distinction in Chapter 1. Now we must examine whether or not it makes a difference for the durability of democracies.

A glance at the descriptive patterns shows immediately that Linz (1990a,b) was right about the durability of these respective institutional systems. During the period under consideration there were sixteen (28 percent of 57 spells) democracies that died under a parliamentary system and twenty-three (54 percent of 42 spells) that died under a presidential one.[17] Among those democracies that died, parliamentary systems lasted on the average two years less than presidential ones: 7.6 years as opposed to 9.6. But the parliamentary democracies that were still around as of 1990 were much older: on the average about forty-one years, as compared with twenty-four for presidential regimes. The probability that a presidential democracy will die during any particular year is 0.0477, and the probability that a parliamentary democracy will die is 0.0138. Thus, the expected life of democracy under presidentialism is approximately twenty-one years, whereas under parliamentarism it is seventy-three years. The oldest democracy in the world is presidential, but this is a distant exception. Moreover, to dispel the view that instability of presidential democracies is due to the fact that they exist primarily in Latin America, it is worth noting that the completed spells of presidentialism were on the average longer on that continent (10.6 years) than elsewhere (6.5 years), that is, in the Congo (1960–1962), Ghana (1979–1980), Nigeria (1979–1982), Uganda (1980–1984), and the Philippines (1950–1964) (Table 2.19).

We have seen that democracies are more likely to survive in wealthy countries, and parliamentary democracies are found disproportionately often under such conditions: Whereas two-thirds of presidential systems were observed in countries with incomes under $4,000, only 30 percent of parliamentary democracies were in countries below that threshold. Hence, the immediate question is whether or not the durability of the parliamentary systems is due simply to wealth.

---

[17] Note that we lump mixed systems together with parliamentary ones (see Chapter 1). Mainwaring (1993) counted democratic breakdowns since 1945. He found nineteen under parliamentarism, twenty-seven under presidentialism, and four under other types.

Table 2.19. Observed rates of transition to dictatorship, by lagged per capita income (LEVLAG) and lagged rate of economic growth (GLAG), of parliamentary and presidential democracies and the hypothetical numbers of transitions if there had been as many presidential democracies as parliamentary democracies under all circumstances

LEVLAG GLAG	PLA	TLA	TL	PPA	TPA	TP	PPA	HTPA	TL
0–1,000	0.1094	7	64	0.2000	2	10	0.2000	12.8	64
G ≤ 0	0.1667	4	24	0.3333	1	3	0.3333	8	24
G > 0	0.0750	3	40	0.1429	1	7	0.1429	5.7	40
1,001–2,000	0.0467	5	107	0.0621	9	145	0.0621	6.6	107
G ≤ 0	0.0833	3	36	0.0755	4	53	0.0755	2.7	36
G > 0	0.0282	2	71	0.0543	5	92	0.0543	3.9	71
2,001–3,000	0.0233	2	86	0.0594	6	101	0.0594	5.1	86
G ≤ 0	0.1176	2	17	0.0690	2	29	0.0690	1.2	17
G > 0	0	0	69	0.0556	4	72	0.0556	3.8	69
3,001–4,000	0.0250	2	80	0.0313	2	64	0.0313	2.5	80
G ≤ 0	0.0526	1	19	0.0455	1	22	0.0455	0.9	19
G > 0	0.0164	1	61	0.0238	1	42	0.0238	1.5	61
4,001–5,000	0	0	72	0.0556	2	36	0.0556	4	72
G ≤ 0	0	0	13	0.0769	1	13	0.0769	1	13
G > 0	0	0	59	0.0435	1	23	0.0435	2.6	59
5,001–6,000	0	0	100	0.0909	1	11	0.0909	9.1	100
G ≤ 0	0	0	13	0	0	3	0	0	13
G > 0	0	0	87	0.125	1	8	0.1250	10.9	87
6,001–7,000	0	0	108	0.0588	1	17	0.0588	6.4	108
G ≤ 0	0	0	23	0.1667	1	6	0.1667	3.8	23
G > 0	0	0	85	0	0	11	0	0	85
7,001–	0	0	546	0	0	98	0	0	546
G ≤ 0	0	0	94	0	0	23	0	0	94
G > 0	0	0	452	0	0	75	0	0	452
Total	0.0138	16	1,163	0.0477	23	482	0.0400	46.5	1,163
G ≤ 0	0.0418	10	239	0.0658	10	152	0.0736	17.6	239
G > 0	0.0065	9	924	0.0394	13	330	0.0306	28.3	924

Notes: G ≤ 0 means that per capita income declined or remained the same; G > 0 means that per capita income increased. PLA stands for the probability of transition from parliamentarism to authoritarianism; TLA is their number. TL is the total number of annual observations of parliamentarism. PPA stands for the probability of transition from presidentialism to authoritarianism; TPA is their number. TP is the total number of annual observations of presidentialism. HTPA stands for the expected number of transitions from presidentialism if there were exactly as many presidential as parliamentary democracies.

Presidential democracies are more likely to die than parliamentary democracies at any level of development. Indeed, in countries with incomes above $4,000, no parliamentary democracy died during 826 years they enjoyed such incomes, whereas four presidential democracies died during 162 years (one in forty years) under the same conditions. The richest parliamentary democracy that died was Suriname, which had a per capita income of $3,923 in 1980 (see Table 2.6). The second wealthiest was Greece, with income of $3,176 in 1967. In contrast, six transitions from presidential democracies to dictatorships occurred in countries that were wealthier, all the way up to Argentina in 1976, with an income of $6,055. The difference among countries with incomes under $4,000 is much smaller, but still in favor of parliamentarism: Sixteen parliamentary democracies died under such circumstances during 337 years (one in twenty-one years), compared with nineteen presidential democracies during 320 years (one in seventeen years).

To isolate how much of the difference in the durability of democracy under these two systems is due to wealth, we calculated what would have been the rate of transition from presidential democracies to authoritarianism if there had been exactly as many of them as there were parliamentary democracies in each band of $1,000 of per capita income. The answer is that presidential democracies would have died at an only slightly lower rate than under the observed conditions: 0.0400 (one in twenty-five) instead of 0.0477 (one in twenty-one). Hence, the difference in longevity between parliamentary and presidential democracies was not due to the wealth of the countries in which these democracies existed.

How adept are the alternative institutional arrangements in coping with economic crises? One in twenty-four parliamentary democracies dies (at the rate of 0.0418) when the economy experiences negative rates of growth. When the economy grows, only one in 154 parliamentary democracies collapses (0.0065). Hence, parliamentary democracies are sensitive to economic crises. Presidential systems are less sensitive to economic performance. One in fifteen presidential democracies collapses when incomes decline (0.0658), and one in twenty-five (0.0394) when they grow. But note that parliamentary systems are almost as likely to survive when the economy shrinks as presidential systems are likely to survive when it expands.

We already know that parliamentary democracies endure in countries with incomes above $4,000 regardless of their economic performance. Such democracies survived 143 years during which per capita incomes declined, and 683 years when they grew. Presidential democracies, however, died in four instances in such wealthy countries: two in forty-five years when incomes declined (one in 22.5), and two in 117 years when incomes increased (one in 58.5). Moreover, parliamentary democracies survive with incomes below $4,000 if the economy grows – only one in 40 (0.0248) of them died under these conditions – much better than presidential ones, which died at the rate of one in 19.4 (0.0511). Yet the enthusiasm for parliamentary systems should be somewhat mitigated, for it seems that their capacity to cope with economic crises is limited to countries that are wealthy. When they are poor, they are vulnerable to economic crises: One in 9.6 of them (0.1042) dies when incomes decline. This rate is higher than that for presidential systems – one of which in 13.4 (0.0748) dies under such conditions – but this difference is due to the fact that the poor parliamentary democracies were poorer than the poor presidential ones. Had poor presidential democracies occurred at the same income levels as the poor parliamentary systems, they would have died at the rate of 0.1333, one in 7.5. Thus, presidential democracies are just unstable, in wealthy as well as in poor countries, when the economy declines and when it expands. Parliamentary democracies are stable in wealthy countries and survive at high rates when the economy grows in poor countries. But they are vulnerable in poor countries that face economic crises.[18]

Statistical analyses highlight the different impacts of the level of development on the survival of parliamentary and presidential democracies. Whereas parliamentary democracies are much less likely to die in countries in which the per capita income is high, the chances of survival for presidential democracies are independent of per capita income. Moreover, once other factors are considered, presidential democracies appear somewhat more sensitive to their economic performance (Table 2.20).

These two economic factors play their same roles whether or not they are placed in a broader context. But non-economic variables do play a role in determining the chances of survival for the two types of

---

[18] Note that in our standard classification of regimes we count as authoritarian the periods before elected governments overthrow democracy from above ("consolidation rule" of Chapter 1). But if such instances (listed in Appendix 1.3) should prove to be more frequent under parliamentarism, then our results would be an artifact of classification. To test that possibility, we reproduced Table 2.20 reclassifying such periods as democratic and treating such *autogolpes* as transitions. None of the qualitative conclusions was affected.

Table 2.20. Dynamic probit analysis of regime transitions, by type of democracy

Binomial probit model
Maximum-likelihood estimates

Dependent variable	REG
Number of observations	3,927
Iterations completed	10
Log-likelihood function	−337.9800
Restricted log-likelihood	−2,630.362
Chi-squared	4,584.764
Degrees of freedom	17
Significance level	0.0000000

	Transitions to democracy		Transitions to dictatorship			
			From parliamentarism		From presidentialism	
Variable	Coefficient	Pr[|Z| ≥ z]	Coefficient	Pr[|Z| ≥ z]	Coefficient	Pr[|Z| ≥ z]
Constant	−2.4358	0.00000	−1.413	0.00000	−1.867	0.00000
LEVLAG	0.7674E-04	0.04158	−0.4268E-03	0.00401	−0.1261E-03	0.46306
GLAG	−0.1627E-01	0.08018	−0.2897E-01	0.08296	−0.3513E-01	0.01543
TLAG	0.6591	0.00038	0.7195	0.00104	0.5302	0.00144
RELDIF	−0.3177	0.30042	0.6762	0.62051	1.660	0.07734
STRA	0.3759	0.00000	0.3995	0.00363	0.1244	0.00008
SEATS	−0.5318E-02	0.00136	0.3597E-02	0.83106	−0.2993E-02	0.26070
MAJORITY	−0.4399	0.00228	0.1734	0.40417	−0.3708	0.00245
DEADLOCK	0.8453	0.01376	-0.6142E-01	0.08420	0.4827	0.00129
MAJORITY	0.3979	0.00706	0.3592	0.94205	−0.1209	0.12600
DEADLOCK	0.6274	0.07104	0.2415	0.17335	0.3989	0.02739

Notes: The first panel presents results for the five variables considered together. Next, the results for each variable are added to the first five (the values of coefficients and probabilities are almost unaffected by these additions). Finally, the bottom panel shows the results of DEADLOCK and MAJORITY being added simultaneously to the basic five variables. LEVLAG, lagged per capita income; GLAG, lagged rate of growth; TLAG, lagged cumulative rate of leadership turnover; RELDIF, religious fractionalization; STRA, cumulative number of past transitions to authoritarianism; SEATS, share of seats of the largest party; DEADLOCK, dummy variable that equals 1 if 0.33 < SEATS < 0.50; MAJORITY, dummy variable that equals 1 if SEATS > 0.50.

democracies. Religious heterogeneity appears to affect only presidential systems, which are less stable in heterogeneous societies. In turn, past regime instability lowers the chances of survival for democracy under both systems, more so under parliamentarism.

There are good reasons to believe, however, that the functioning of these institutions depends not only on economic or social factors but also on the relationships of the political forces within them. In particular, a claim has been made repeatedly (Mainwaring 1993; Stepan and Skach 1993; Jones 1995; Carey 1997; Mainwaring and Shugart 1997) that presidential systems are particularly unstable when they function under a highly fractionalized party system. One way to examine this hypothesis is to study the effect of the share of the largest party in the lower house of the legislature under the two systems (SEATS). This variable has no impact on the survival of either type of democracy. The absence of a majority party (MAJORITY), however, does have a strong impact on the stability of presidential democracies, which are unstable when no party controls a majority of seats in the lower house. The chances of survival for parliamentary democracies, in turn, are independent of the existence of a majority party (Table 2.21).

The story, however, does not end there. Presidential democracies appear particularly vulnerable in situations in which the largest legislative party controls more than one-third but less than one-half of seats, a situation that we term "DEADLOCK." Note that both the MAJORITY variable and the DEADLOCK variable assume values of zero in situations of extreme fractionalization, when no single party controls more than one-third of seats. Hence, what distinguishes them are situations in which the largest party has more than one-third but less than one-half of seats. And presidential democracies are much less likely to survive under the conditions of such moderate fractionalization.[19]

The reason we refer to these situations as deadlocks is based on the following intuition. Suppose that the plurality party is the same as the president's party, but the opposition parties can muster a majority if they unite against the president. Then the opposition can pass legislation. The president can veto it, and, under typical procedures for overruling the veto, the president will have enough support to make it stand. Hence, a deadlock ensues. Yet we may be barking up the wrong tree, for if legislative deadlocks are what underlie such situations, then such deadlocks should also ensue when a party different from that of the president controls a majority of seats. Hence, we examined the

---

[19] "Deadlocks" occurred in 30.9% of presidential and 45.0% of parliamentary years. Majority parties existed in exactly one-half of presidential and 43.1% of parliamentary years. Finally, situations of extreme fractionalization are not infrequent: In 19.1% of years under presidentialism and 11.9% under parliamentarism, no party controlled more than one-third of seats.

Table 2.21. Hazard rates for parliamentary and presidential democracies, by political conditions

	Total			Parliamentary			Presidential		
Variable	PDA	TDA	TD	PLA	TLA	TL	PPA	TPA	TP
SEATS									
0.0–33.3	0.0220	5	227	0.0147	2	136	0.0330	3	91
33.4–50.0	0.0224	15	668	0.0077	4	519	0.0738	11	149
50.1–66.6	0.0204	11	540	0.0146	5	343	0.0304	6	197
66.7–100	0.0402	8	199	0.0325	5	154	0.0667	3	45
MINORITY	0.0223	20	895	0.0091	6	656	0.0581	14	241
MAJORITY	0.0256	19	741	0.0201	10	498	0.0373	9	241
EFFPARTY									
0–2	0.0261	9	345	0.0240	6	250	0.0316	3	95
2–3	0.0154	9	585	0.0051	2	394	0.0366	7	191
3–4	0.0281	9	320	0.0041	1	246	0.1081	8	74
4–5	0.0272	5	184	0.0149	2	134	0.0600	3	50
5–	0.0126	2	158	0.0097	1	103	0.0182	1	55

Notes: Totals differ because some data for seats and for the number of effective parties are not available. SEATS, share of seats of the largest party; MAJORITY, dummy variable that equals 1 if SEATS > 0.50; EFFPARTY, index of the number of effective parties. PDA stands for the probability of transition from democracy to authoritarianism. TDA is their number. TD is the total number of annual observations of democracy. PLA stands for the probability of transition from parliamentarism to authoritarianism. TLA is their number. TL is the total number of annual observations of parliamentarism. PPA stands for the probability of transition from presidentialism to authoritarianism. TPA is their number. TP is the total number of annual observations of presidentialism.

effect of a version of the DEADLOCK variable in which we added all the instances of divided government (which occurred in seven countries, during forty-nine years) to the previous version. Yet the effect of this new variable on the stability of presidential democracies is much weaker. Hence, it may be not deadlock that weakens presidential democracies, but something about the difficulty of forming legislative coalitions when there are a few parties with similar strengths. And note that the descriptive patterns presented in Table 2.21 show that presidential systems are particularly brittle when the number of effective parties in the legislature is between three and four. The process of forming legislative coalitions in presidential systems has been little

135

studied (but see Figueiredo and Limongi 2000), and we do not know how it works.

Before concluding, however, that instability of democracy is an inherent effect of presidentialism, we need to examine one more rival hypothesis. If presidentialism is a military legacy, then perhaps presidential democracies last for shorter periods simply because they emerge in countries where the military is politically relevant. We thus need to compare separately the hazard rates for parliamentary and presidential democracies distinguished by their origins. It is apparent that a military legacy shortens the life of democracy regardless of its institutional framework. Democracies that emerged from civilian dictatorships died at the rate of 0.0158, with an expected life of 63.4 years; those that succeeded military dictatorships died at the rate of 0.0573, with an expected life of 17.5 years. Parliamentary democracies, however, are still more stable regardless of their origins. Given civilian origins, parliamentary democracies died at the rate of 0.0119 and had an expected life of 83.7 years, and presidential democracies died at the rate of 0.0329, with an expected life of 30.4 years. Given military origins, parliamentary systems died at the rate of 0.0400, with an expected life of 25 years, and presidential systems died at the rate 0.0628 and had an expected life of 16 years. Thus, again, the stability of democracies seems to be an effect of their institutional frameworks, not only of their origins.

Thus, although we remain uncertain about the reasons, it is clear that presidential democracies are less durable than parliamentary ones. This difference is not due to the wealth of the countries in which these institutions were observed, nor to their economic performance. Neither is it due to any of the political conditions under which they functioned. Presidential democracies are simply more brittle under all economic and political conditions.

Conclusion

We began this chapter with the observation that democracies are much more frequent in developed countries, and dictatorships in poor ones. Yet this observation is not very illuminating, and neither are the innumerable cross-sectional analyses of this pattern. The regimes we observe in particular countries at any moment depend on the conditions under which these regimes were born and on the conditions they encountered and produced as time passed. And because our systematic observations begin only in 1950 or when countries first became independent (in some cases when data became available), we took the regimes under which the countries entered the sample as given and studied their subsequent dynamics.

The most important lesson we have learned is that wealthy countries tend to be democratic not because democracies emerge as a consequence of economic development under dictatorships but because, however they emerge, democracies are much more likely to survive in affluent societies. We find it difficult to explain why dictatorships die and democracies emerge. Although we are willing to believe that economic development may open the possibility for transition to democracy, even when the conditions for democracy are ripe, the outcomes of political conflicts are indeterminate. Hence, we failed to detect any thresholds of development that would make the emergence of democracy predictable. In sum, modernization theory appears to have little, if any, explanatory power.

In turn, we found that the survival of democracies is quite easily predictable. Although some other factors play roles, per capita income is by far the best predictor of the survival of democracies. Democracies survive in affluent societies whatever may be happening to them. They are brittle in poor countries. But they are not always sentenced to die: Education helps them to survive independently of income, and a balance among the political forces makes them more stable. Institutions also matter: Presidential democracies are less likely to survive under all circumstances we could observe than are parliamentary ones.

Yet one should not forget that we are dealing only with chances, probabilities, not certainties. And if all we can predict are chances, there must be other factors that matter, some we did not identify. These may be idiosyncratic, impossible to catch in a statistical analysis; but on the other hand, they might be systematic, and we may simply have failed to find them. Whichever they are – this is not a book on the philosophy of history – they remain hidden from our scrutiny. And this is a fact with consequences for what follows.

Appendix 2.1: Dynamic Probit Model

To decide which mechanism generates the relationship between development and democracy, we need to determine how the respective transition probabilities change with the level of development or other exogenous variables. To estimate the impacts of these variables on transition probabilities, we rely on Amemiya (1985, chap. 11).

Our data obey a first-order Markov process,[20] that is, the present regime depends only on the regimes during the preceding year, but not beyond. Such processes are defined by

$$E(R_t = A|R_{t-1}, R_{t-2}, \ldots) = \mathbf{P}(t)R_{t-1},$$

where $R = A$, D stands for regimes, $R = A$ for dictatorship and $R = D$ for democracy, and $\mathbf{P}(t)$ is the matrix of transition probabilities, with elements $p_{jk}(t)$, $j = D$, A, $k = D$, A. Hence, in regression terms,

$$R_t = \mathbf{P}(t)R_{t-1} + u_t.$$

Taking expectations of both sides yields

$$\begin{bmatrix} p(R_t = A) \\ p(R_t = D) \end{bmatrix} = \begin{bmatrix} p_{AA} p_{DA} \\ p_{AD} p_{DD} \end{bmatrix} \begin{bmatrix} p(R_{t-1} = A) \\ p(R_{t-1} = D) \end{bmatrix},$$

where the sum of columns of the transition matrix $\Sigma_j p_{jk} = 1$. Hence

$$\begin{aligned} p(R_t = A|R_{t-1}) &= p_{AA}(t)p(R_{t-1} = A) + p_{DA}(t)p(R_{t-1} = D) \\ &= p_{DA}(t) + [p_{AA}(t) - p_{DA}(t)]p(R_{t-1} = A). \end{aligned}$$

Now let $\mathbf{X}$ be the vector of the exogenous variables. Assume that

$$p_{DA}(t) = F(\mathbf{X}_{t-1}\beta),$$

$$p_{AA}(t) = F[X_{t-1}(\alpha + \beta)],$$

where $F(\cdot)$ is the c.d.f. of the normal distribution, with derivatives

$$\frac{dp_{DA}}{dX} = f(X_{t-1}\beta)\beta \quad \text{and} \quad \frac{dp_{AD}}{dX} = -f[X_{t-1}(\alpha + \beta)](\alpha + \beta).$$

Note that $p_{jk}(t)$ is the probability of transition from being in state j at time $t - 1$ to being in state k at time t. Given that whenever a transition occurs we code the regime as the one that became installed during this year, the probability of transition between $t - 1$ and t depends on the conditions at $t - 1$. Hence, we lag the X's.

Letting $R = 1$ when the regime is authoritarian and $R = 0$ when it is democratic, so that $p(R = A) = p_R$,

---

[20] If the process is of order 1, then all the information about the lagged values of the exogenous variables is summarized by the lagged value of the dependent variable. If the process is of a higher order, then lagged values of the exogenous variables affect the current value of the dependent variable. Our tests indicate that only the contemporaneous values of the exogenous variables matter, that is, the process is of order 1.

$$p(R_t = A|R_{t-1}) = p_{DA}(t) + [p_{AA}(t) - p_{DA}(t)]p_R(t-1)$$
$$= F(X_{t-1}\beta) + \{F[X_{t-1}(\alpha + \beta)] - F(X_{t-1}\beta)\}p_R(t-1)$$
$$= F(X_{t-1}\beta) + F(X_{t-1}\alpha)p_R(t-1) = F(X_{t-1}\beta + X_{t-1}R_{t-1}\alpha).$$

Hence, to estimate α and β, from which one can calculate p_{DA} and p_{AA}, and thus $p_{DD} = 1 - p_{DA}$ and $p_{AD} = 1 - p_{AA}$, all we need is to maximize

$$L = \Pi_{it}F(X_{t-1}\beta + X_{t-1}\alpha R_{t-1})^{R(t)}[1 - F(X_{t-1}\beta + X_{t-1}\alpha R_{t-1})]^{1-R(t)}.$$

This is the model we used to generate the results presented in several tables in the main body of the text, with $R(0)$ as observed.

To study the effect of the type of democracy on the transition probabilities, we estimated the equation

$$p(R_t = A|R_{t-1}) = p_{AA}(t)p(R_{t-1} = A) + p_{LA}(t)p(R_{t-1} = L) + p_{PA}(t)p(R_{t-1} = P),$$

where L stands for parliamentarism and P for presidentialism, using the observed fact that $p_{LP} \approx p_{PL} \approx 0$ to identify $p_{LA} = 1 - p_{LL}$ and $p_{PA} = 1 - p_{PP}$, and letting

$$p_{AA}(t) = F(X_{t-1}\beta),$$

$$p_{LA}(t) = F[X_{t-1}(\alpha + \beta)],$$

$$p_{PA}(t) = F[X_{t-1}(\alpha + \gamma)].$$

Appendix 2.2: Survival Models

Survival models allow a relatively simple test of the hypothesis that the probability of survival is independent of age. To test whether or not democracies become consolidated as a result of the passage of time, that is, whether or not they are more likely to be around the longer they have been around, we estimate, first, models without any right-hand-side variables and then control for per capita income.

The hazard function, that is, the probability that a regime will die at a particular time, $t = 1, \ldots$, given that it has lasted until then, for the Weibull distribution is

$$h(t) = \lambda p(\lambda t)^{p-1}.$$

Assuming that observations are gamma-heterogeneous, the hazard function for the Weibull distribution is

$$h(t) = \lambda p(\lambda t)^{p-1} / [1 + \Theta(\lambda t)^p],$$

where Θ is the parameter of the gamma distribution of survival pro-babilities across observations, with a high Θ indicating that observa-tions are heterogeneous. Finally, for the logistic distribution, the hazard function is

$$h(t) = \lambda p(\lambda t)^{p-1} / \left[1 + (\lambda t)^p\right].$$

The time derivatives of the hazard function for the Weibull distrib-ution are

$dh(t)/dt < 0 \quad$ if $p < 1,$

$dh(t)/dt = 0 \quad$ if $p = 1,$

$dh(t)/dt > 0 \quad$ if $p > 1.$

For the logistic these derivatives are

$dh(t)/dt < 0 \quad$ if $p < 1 + (\lambda t)^p,$

$dh(t)/dt = 0 \quad$ if $p = 1 + (\lambda t)^p,$

$dh(t)/dt > 0 \quad$ if $p > 1 + (\lambda t)^p.$

Fitting the models to data yields the coefficients $\sigma = 1/p$ and an inter-val estimate of p (t statistics in parentheses).

The hypothesis that the Weibull distribution is homogeneous is not rejected [$\Theta = 10.73$, t statistic $= 1.402$, $\Pr(t) = 0.16$], so there is no reason to assume heterogeneity.

Model	σ	min $< p <$ max
Weibull	1.6194	$0.32 < 0.61 < 0.91$
	(4.091)	
Logistic	1.2661	$0.47 < 0.79 < 1.11$
	(4.860)	

The estimates of p are thus safely smaller than 1.00, which indicates that the hazard rates are declining with time, in other words, that democracies become consolidated.

These results are, however, misleading, because as time goes on, countries develop, and as they develop, the probability that democracy will fall declines. Hence, to isolate the effect of time, we need to dis-tinguish it from the effect of development. To do that, we make the lambdas at each time functions of $X = 1$, LEVEL, so that

$$\lambda(X_t) = \exp(-\beta X_t),$$

and substitute these lambdas into the hazard functions.

The distribution is again homogeneous, and the results are

Model	σ	min < p < max	LEVEL
Weibull	0.9854	0.70 < 1.01 < 1.33	0.6729
	(6.282)		(5.178)
Logistic	0.7718	0.94 < 1.29 < 1.65	0.6576
	(7.075)		(5.386)
Exponential	—	—	0.6779
			(6.265)

Because the Weibull p is almost exactly 1.00, the Weibull hazard rate is a constant function of time: Given their level of development, democracies are equally likely to die at any age. Hence, what may appear as "consolidation" is in fact a consequence of development, not merely of the passage of time. The logistic $p = 1.29$ implies that with the average hazard rate of 0.025, this hazard rate declines during the first fifteen to sixteen years and then increases.

The results for dictatorships, however, show that their hazard rates tend to decrease somewhat over time (the Weibull distribution is not heterogeneous).

Model	σ	min < p < max	Θ	LEVEL	LEVSQR
Exponential	—	—	—	−0.7780	0.0552
				(−2.728)	(1.372)
With het	—	—	0.48	−0.9358	0.0637
			(1.757)	(−2.344)	(1.008)
Weibull	1.3005	0.56 < 0.77 < 0.98	—	−1.0372	0.0717
	(7.074)			(−2.601)	(1.340)
Logistic	1.0369	0.71 < 0.97 < 1.23	—	−1.0892	0.0776
	(7.303)			(−2.067)	(0.895)

The Weibull estimates of σ are higher than 1.00, indicating that p is somewhat less than 1.00, and hazard rates tend to fall, even if slowly, over the life of a dictatorship.

Chapter Three

Political Regimes and Economic Growth

Introduction

With the birth of new nations in Asia and Africa, the fear that democracy would undermine economic growth began to be voiced in the United States. The first statements to that effect were perhaps those by Walter Galenson and by Karl de Schweinitz, who argued, both in 1959, that in poor countries democracy unleashes pressures for immediate consumption, which occurs at the cost of investment, hence of growth. Galenson mentioned both the role of unions and that of governments. He thought that unions "must ordinarily appeal to the worker on an all-out consumptionist platform. No matter how much 'responsibility' the union leader exhibits in his understanding of the limited consumption possibilities existing at the outset of industrialization, he cannot afford to moderate his demands." As for governments, he observed that "the more democratic a government is, . . . the greater the diversion of resources from investment to consumption." According to de Schweinitz (1959: 388), if trade unions and labor parties "are successful in securing a larger share of the national income and limiting the freedom for action of entrepreneurs, they may have the effect of restricting investment surplus so much that the rate of economic growth is inhibited." That argument enjoyed widespread acceptance under the influence of Huntington, who claimed that "the interest of the voters generally leads parties to give the expansion of personal consumption a higher priority via-à-vis investment than it would receive in a non-democratic system" (Huntington and Domiguez 1975: 60; Huntington 1968).

Democracy was thus seen as inimical to economic development. Moreover, via a rather dubious inference, proponents of that view concluded that dictatorships were therefore better able to force savings and launch economic growth. To cite a more recent statement: "Economic development is a process for which huge investments in personnel and material are required. Such investment programs imply cuts in current consumption that would be painful at the low levels of living that exist in almost all developing societies. Governments must resort to strong measures and they enforce them with an iron hand in order to marshal the surpluses needed for investment. If such measures were put to a popular vote, they would surely be defeated. No political party can hope to win a democratic election on a platform of current sacrifices for a *bright future*" (Rao 1984: 75).[1]

The reasoning bears reconstruction. First, that argument assumes that poor people have a higher propensity to consume.[2] This is why democracy may be compatible with growth at high but not at low levels of income. Second, the underlying model of growth attributes it to the increase in the stock of physical capital. Finally, democracy is always responsive to pressures for immediate consumption. The chain of reasoning is thus the following: (1) Poor people want to consume immediately. (2) When workers are able to organize, they drive wages up, reduce profits, and reduce investment (by lowering either the rate of return or the volume of profit or both). (3) When people are allowed to vote, governments tend to distribute income away from investment (either they tax and transfer or they undertake less public investment). (4) Lowering investment slows down growth. Note, as well, that this reasoning implies that the impact of mean-preserving inequality on growth is ambivalent: In the Kaldor-Pasinetti models, inequality promotes growth, as it increases the incomes of those who save more, but in the median-voter models it slows down growth to the extent to which the political system responds to demands for redistribution.

Arguments in favor of democracy are not equally sharp, but they all focus in one form or another on allocative efficiency: Democracies can better allocate the available resources to productive uses. One view is that because authoritarian rulers are not accountable to electorates,

---

[1] At least Huntington and his collaborators wrote during a period when many dictatorships, "authoritarian" and "totalitarian," did grow rapidly. But Rao's assertion was made in 1984, after the failure of several Latin American authoritarian regimes and Eastern European communist regimes was already apparent.

[2] Pasinetti (1961) claimed that the propensity to consume is higher for workers than for capitalists, and Kaldor (1956) believed that it is higher for wages than for profits, whereas the scholars discussed here seem to assume that in general the marginal propensity to consume declines with income. Barro and Sala-i-Martin (1995: 77–9) show that in the optimal growth model the savings rate decreases as a result of the substitution effect and increases in income as a consequence of the income effect, the net effect being ambivalent.

they have no incentive to maximize total output, but only their own rents. As a result, democracies better protect property rights, thus allowing a longer-term perspective to investors. There is also a vague sense that by permitting a free flow of information, democracies somehow improve the quality of economic decisions.

According to the first view, the state is always ready to prey on the society (North 1990), and only democratic institutions can constrain it to act in a more general interest. Hence, dictatorships, of any stripe, are sources of inefficiency. Barro (1990), Findlay (1990), Olson (1991), and Przeworski (1990) have constructed models that differ in detail but generate the same conclusion. These models assume that some level of government intervention in the economy is optimal for growth. Then they all show that, depending on the details of each model, dictatorships of various stripes can be expected to undersupply or oversupply government activities. One interesting variant of this approach is by Robinson (1995), who thinks that dictators are afraid, at least under some conditions, that development would give rise to political forces that would overturn them, and thus they deliberately abstain from developmentalist policies.

Perhaps the best-known informational argument is based on the Drèze and Sen (1989) observation that no democracy ever experienced a famine, which they attribute to the alarm role of the press and the opposition. Thus, Sen (1994a: 34) observes that "a free press and an active political opposition constitute the best 'early warning system' that a country threatened by famine can possess." He also cites an unlikely source, Mao, reflecting on the great Chinese famine of 1962, to the effect that "without democracy, you have no understanding of what is happening down below." Yet it is not apparent whether this is an argument strictly about avoiding disasters or about average performance.[3]

This summary makes no pretense to being exhaustive. All we want to highlight is that the arguments in favor of dictatorship and those in favor of democracy are not necessarily incompatible. The arguments against democracy claim that it hinders growth by reducing investment; the arguments in its favor maintain that it fosters growth by promoting allocative efficiency. Both may be true: The rate at which

---

[3] Sah and Stiglitz (1988) compared the quality of the decisions whether or not to undertake a series of economic projects made under different decision rules. Their conclusions are ambivalent: Although majority rule is conducive to good decisions under many conditions, decisions by smaller groups are better when the costs of information are high, whereas decisions by larger groups are superior when the chances of adopting a bad project are high.

productive factors grow may be higher under dictatorship, but the use of resources may be more efficient under democracy. And because these mechanisms work in opposite directions, the net effect may be that there is no difference between the two regimes in the average rates of growth they generate. The patterns of growth may differ, but the average rates of growth may still be the same.

Rates of growth may thus differ between regimes either because the productive inputs increase at different rates or because they are used with different efficiencies. To assess the impact of regimes on growth, we proceed by the following steps:

First, we examine whether or not it is valid to assume that the productive inputs grow at the same rates under the two regimes. This is a test of the validity of the hypothesis that regimes do not affect the rates of growth of productive resources.

Second, we estimate separately for each regime a production-function model, $Y = AF(K, L) = AK^{\alpha}L^{\beta}$, in growth form (suppressing the i, t subscripts):[4]

$$\dot{Y}/Y = \dot{A}/A + \alpha \dot{K}/K + \beta \dot{L}/L + \Theta\lambda + e,$$

where λ is the instrument for the regime variable. The coefficients[5] $\dot{A}/A$, α, and β provide selection-unbiased estimates of, respectively, technical progress and the efficiency with which capital stock and labor force contribute to growth under each regime. This is then a test of the hypothesis that the efficiency with which resources are used is the same under the two regimes.

To calculate the effects of regimes independent of the exogenous conditions under which they were observed, we need to generate the growth rates that would be expected had each country been observed each year under each regime. If the hypothesis that the growth of productive inputs is exogenous with regard to regimes is not rejected, the expected values of the growth rates under the two regimes are obtained by multiplying the coefficients characterizing each regime by the rates of growth of the productive inputs observed for each country during each year. If the growth of productive inputs is endogenous with regard to regimes, the expected growth rates are obtained by multiplying the coefficients characterizing each regime by the average rate of growth

---

[4] A notational explanation for non-economists: The dots over the variables indicate time derivatives, so that for any X, $\dot{X} = dX/dt$, and $\dot{X}/X$ is the rate of growth.

[5] We refer to $\dot{A}/A$ as a coefficient because we treat it as a constant, either for regimes or for countries or for years, depending on estimation methods.

of productive inputs observed under each regime. In either case this procedure generates predicted values of growth for each country during each year under each regime. These values are then averaged over all observations, and the regime averages are compared. The regime effect is the difference between these averages.

Finally, we study whether or not the production function and the rate of growth of productive inputs are stable for each of the regimes. Because the two regimes are observed at different income levels, and because both the production functions and the growth of inputs may depend on the level of development, we need to test whether the observed differences are indeed due to regimes or merely to wealth.

Political Regimes and Economic Growth

The observed rate of growth of total income ($YG = \dot{Y}/Y$) is higher under dictatorships, 4.42, than under democracies, 3.95, implying that income doubles in 15.8 years under dictatorship and in 17.7 years under democracy. Yet we already know that one should not draw inferences from the observed values.

To identify the effect of regimes, we need to distinguish the effects of the conditions under which these regimes were observed from the effect of regimes. We present first the results concerning the effect of regimes on the growth of productive inputs, then those concerning the efficiency with which these inputs are used under each regime, and, finally, the conclusions about the overall effect of regimes on the growth of total income.

Do productive inputs grow at the same rate under the two regimes? The claim that democracy undermines investment, whether in general or only in poor countries, finds no support in the evidence. The observed average share of investment in gross domestic product (GDP), $INV = I/Y$, was in fact much higher in democracies, 20.90 percent, than in dictatorships, 14.25 percent. But because investment shares increase with per capita income, and because, as we already know, dictatorships have generally existed in poorer countries, this could be just an effect of income. Indeed, controlling for income, as well as for a number of other variables in a selection model, shows that regimes have no overall effect on investment.[6] Table 3.1 presents the results of

---

[6] The variables in the investment equation include lagged investment share (given that investment decisions made one year take time to realize, INVLAG), lagged per capita income (an instrument for expected domestic demand, LEVLAG), the average rate of

146

Table 3.1A. Investment share in GDP (INV), by per capita income (LEVEL)

LEVEL	Proportion dictatorships	Investment share		
		All	Dictatorships	Democracies
0–1,000	0.9273	8.89	8.79	10.14
1,001–2,000	0.7472	13.53	13.66	13.17
2,001–3,000	0.6207	17.87	17.83	17.93
3,001–4,000	0.5874	20.04	20.47	19.42
4,001–5,000	0.5424	22.76	23.75	21.57
5,001–6,000	0.4308	24.35	25.48	23.50
6,001–	0.0812	25.40	29.92	25.00
Total ($N = 4,126$)		16.90	14.25	20.90

Note: All cell entries are based on at least 68 observations.

statistical analyses that used different estimation methods.[7] Regardless of the method, the regime difference between the selection-corrected expected investment shares is never larger than 1 percent. Moreover, among poorer countries, those with per capita incomes lower than $3,000, both the observed and the corrected investment shares are slightly higher in democracies. Hence, there is no reason to think that regimes affect investment even in poor countries: Had these regimes

growth in the world (a measure of world demand, WORLD), and the relative price of investment goods (PINV). Alternatively, we estimate a 2SLS model with the predicted growth rate as an instrument for the current demand. For a review of econometric models of investment, see Rama (1993).

[7] Because we present several tables with the same structure, here is a short guide to reading them, first by row, then by column. "Biased" stands for the observed values or ordinary least squares (OLS) regressions in which regime (REG) is a dummy variable. Then follow various selection-corrected average predicted values of the dependent variable under the two regimes. The correction for selection is always based on the dynamic probit described in Appendix 2.1. The performance models depend on the structure of the pooled time series, specifically autocorrelation, homogeneity, and simultaneity. Finally, the last two rows refer to an alternative manner of estimating selection models, due to Heckman (1988): "Unobservable" assumes that selection entails unobserved variables, and "Observable" that it entails only observed ones. The columns "Regime means" give the average values of the dependent variable under the two regimes. "Constant regime effect" assumes that the regime effect is an intercept dummy, and "Individual regime effect" assumes that it is a sum of differences in slopes multiplied by the values of the independent variables. For details, see Appendix I.

Table 3.1B. Selection-corrected estimators of investment share (INV)

Estimator (selection/INV)	Regime means		Regime effect	
	Dictatorships ($N = 2,396$)	Democracies ($N = 1,595$)	Constant	Individual
			($N = 3,991$)	
Biased	14.28	20.98	0.0860	0.0362
	(9.40)	(8.02)	(0.1041)	(0.3340)
MLE	17.19	16.97		
	(9.26)	(9.09)		
1F-HATANAKA	21.61	21.25		
	(6.97)	(6.50)		
1F-AR1	16.69	17.73		
	(7.60)	(7.69)		
2SLS-1F-AR1	16.84	17.69		
	(7.85)	(7.81)		
Unobservable			0.0806	0.0348
			(0.1092)	(0.3437)
Observable			0.0797	0.0042
			(0.1019)	(0.3118)

By per capita income (LEVEL)

	LEVEL < 3,000		LEVEL ≥ $3,000	
	Dictatorships ($N = 1,875$)	Democracies ($N = 469$)	Dictatorships ($N = 478$)	Democracies ($N = 1,104$)
Biased	11.95	14.38	23.41	23.87
	(7.80)	(6.08)	(9.11)	(6.99)
1F-AR1	12.17	13.23	23.68	23.61
	(2.14)	(1.70)	(1.95)	(0.86)
1F-HATANAKA	14.90	12.91	24.07	24.15
	(4.76)	(5.30)	(4.43)	(5.54)

Notes: Probit equations include lagged values of LEVEL, STRA, and RELDIF. The INV equations include INVLAG, LEVEL, PINV, and WORLD. The 2SLS estimation uses fitted values of YG as instrument. Standard errors in parentheses.

Table 3.2A. Rate of growth of capital stock (KSG), by per capita income (LEVEL)

LEVEL	Proportion dictatorships	KSG		
		All	Dictatorships	Democracies
0–1,000	0.9273	5.624	5.440	7.947
1,001–2,000	0.7472	7.627	8.112	6.189
2,001–3,000	0.6207	8.925	9.860	7.390
3,001–4,000	0.5874	7.494	7.621	7.314
4,001–5,000	0.5424	8.074	6.806	9.576
5,001–6,000	0.4308	8.038	9.297	7.085
6,001–	0.0812	6.080	10.650	5.676
Total ($N = 4{,}126$)		7.007	7.310	6.547

Note: All cell entries are based on at least 68 observations.

existed under the same conditions, specifically in countries with the same per capita incomes, facing the same relative prices of investment goods and world demand, and had they been matched for unobservable factors that affect regime selection, their shares of investment in GDP would have been the same.

Hence, even if pressures for immediate consumption are higher in poor countries, democracies do not transform them into lower rates of investment than do dictatorships. Poor countries simply invest little regardless of their regime: Cape Verde between 1977 and 1983, Zambia during 1966–68 and 1970–75, and Romania between 1967 and 1981 are the only countries with per capita incomes under $1,000 that maintained investment rates above 30 percent, whereas many wealthier countries invested at such rates. The share of investment is the same under the two regimes in wealthier countries, those with incomes over $3,000.

Another way to think about investment is in terms of the growth of capital stock.[8] The observed rate of growth of capital stock (KSG = $\dot{K}/K$) is somewhat higher under dictatorships, 7.31, than under democracies, 6.56 (Table 3.2). The observed difference for countries with

[8] Note that the investment share is INV = I/Y, and the rate of growth of capital stock is KSG = $\dot{K}/K = (I - \delta K)/K$. The depreciation rate implied by the Penn World Tables (PWT) data is quite high.

149

Table 3.2B. Selection-corrected estimators of the rate of growth of capital stock (KSG)

Estimator (selection/INV)	Regime means		Regime effect	
	Dictatorships (N = 2,396)	Democracies (N = 1,595)	Constant (N = 3,991)	Individual
Biased	7.24	6.49	0.5420	−0.3571
	(14.00)	(10.78)	(0.5094)	(1.4630)
MLE	7.50	6.99		
	(2.57)	(2.26)		
2SLS-MLE	7.01	7.06		
	(9.99)	(9.57)		
Unobservable			0.5856	−0.3601
			(0.5350)	(1.4642)
Observable			0.6202	0.0056
			(0.5127)	(5.6502)

By per capita income (LEVEL)

	LEVEL < 3,000		LEVEL ≥ 3,000	
	Dictatorships (N = 1,917)	Democracies (N = 487)	Dictatorships (N = 479)	Democracies (N = 1,108)
Biased	7.03	6.71	8.05	6.39
	(14.47)	(13.29)	(11.91)	(8.29)
2SLS-MLE	6.88	7.09	7.94	6.94
	(11.46)	(12.25)	(6.85)	(6.61)

Notes: Probit equations include lagged values of LEVEL, STRA, and RELDIF. The KSG equations include LEVLAG, WORLD, PINV, PRIME, and COMEX. The 2SLS estimation adds YG, with YGLAG as intrument. In 1F PANEL: LEVLAG, WORLD, PINV, and PRIME. Standard errors in parentheses.

incomes below $3,000 is negligible. Above $3,000, capital stock grew faster under dictatorship, at the rate of 8.05, than under democracy, where it increased at the rate of 6.39. Correcting for selection, with the same exogenous variables we used for the investment share, shows again, however, that regimes do not affect the growth of capital stock in the sample as a whole and not among countries with incomes under

Table 3.3A. Rate of growth of labor force (LFG); by per capita income (LEVEL)

LEVEL	Proportion dictatorships	Rate of labor-force growth		
		All	Dictatorships	Democracies
0–1,000	0.9273	2.314	2.338	2.019
1,001–2,000	0.7472	2.320	2.312	2.342
2,001–3,000	0.6207	2.295	2.365	2.181
3,001–4,000	0.5874	2.013	2.254	1.670
4,001–5,000	0.5424	1.561	1.979	1.066
5,001–6,000	0.4308	1.205	1.711	0.822
6,001–	0.0812	1.395	1.711	1.367
Total ($N = 4,128$)		2.006	2.270	1.608

Note: All cell entries are based on at least 68 observations.

$3,000. Above $3,000, the selection-corrected values are somewhat higher under dictatorship, 7.94, as opposed to 6.94 under democracy.

Hence, different regimes affect neither the share of investment in GDP nor the rate of growth of capital stock. Moreover, contrary to all the arguments, poor countries invest little regardless of the regime, and it is in wealthier countries that investment is slightly higher under dictatorships.

In turn, the rate of growth of the labor force (LFG = $\dot{L}/L$) is higher under dictatorships (Table 3.3). The observed values are 2.27 percent per annum under dictatorships and 1.61 under democracies. Note again the observed patterns. The rates of growth of the labor force are about the same under the two regimes in countries with per capita incomes of less than $3,000. But in countries with higher incomes, the difference between them becomes dramatic. Indeed, the labor force grows faster in dictatorships with incomes above $6,000 than in democracies with incomes between $3,000 and $4,000.

Because the labor force grows at a slower rate in wealthier countries, one might suspect again that this difference is due to the distribution of regimes by income. Some of it is, but not enough to eradicate the effect of regimes. Even when the regimes are matched for their income, their colonial heritage, and the frequencies of Catholics,

151

Table 3.3B. Selection-corrected estimators of labor force growth (LFG)

| Estimator (selection/LFG) | Regime means | | Regime effect | |
	Dictatorships (N = 2,396)	Democracies (N = 1,595)	Constant (N = 3,991)	Individual (N = 3,991)
Biased	2.28 (1.94)	1.59 (1.20)	0.2565 (0.0695)	0.0820 (0.3354)
2SLS	2.17 (0.37)	1.72 (0.28)		
AR1	2.17 (0.37)	1.72 (0.28)		
HATANAKA	2.16 (0.53)	1.75 (0.68)		
2F PANEL	2.00 (0.79)	1.81 (0.53)		
Unobservable			0.2795 (0.0728)	0.0870 (0.3353)
Observable			0.2863 (0.0702)	0.0893 (0.3462)

LFPW sample	**N = 2,076**	**N = 1,254**		
Biased	2.39 (1.93)	1.65 (1.19)		
OLS	2.27 (0.41)	1.81 (0.66)		

By per capita income (LEVEL)

| Estimator | LEVEL < 3,000 | | LEVEL ≥ 3,000 | |
	Dictatorships (N = 1,917)	Democracies (N = 487)	Dictatorships (N = 479)	Democracies (N = 1,108)
Biased	2.35 (2.03)	2.22 (1.02)	2.03 (1.54)	1.32 (1.17)
OLS-AR1	2.33 (0.27)	2.35 (0.44)	1.92 (0.50)	1.26 (0.44)

Notes: Probit equations include lagged values of LEVEL, STRA, and RELDIF. The LFG equations include LEVEL, NEWC, BRITCOL, CATH, PROT, and MOSLEM, plus LFPW in the LFPW sample. The 2SLS estimation is based on the same variables plus YG, with YGLAG as instrument. Standard errors in parentheses.

Protestants, and Moslems, even if they are matched for demand (2SLS), or for the lagged rate of population growth (HATANAKA estimator), or for country-specific effects (PANEL estimator), as well as for the factors affecting selection, and, in a smaller sample, for the labor-force participation of women (LFPW), the labor force grows faster under dictatorships. The selection-corrected difference is small in countries with incomes under $3,000, but quite large in those over $3,000.[9]

Hence these findings generate a surprise. Contrary to all the arguments, the kind of regime does not affect the rate of investment and the growth of capital stock. And for reasons to be investigated later, it appears that the regime type does affect the growth of the labor force.

To examine the effect of regimes on the efficiency with which resources are used in production, we need to compare the coefficients of the respective production functions. The constant measures total factor productivity, and the coefficients on capital and labor represent the elasticities of output with regard to these factors.[10]

As shown in the first two columns of Table 3.4, which provide the results for the entire sample, total factor productivity is somewhat higher in democracies. The elasticity with regard to capital is slightly higher in dictatorships, but elasticity with regard to labor is higher in democracies. Hence, one is led to conclude that democracies benefit more from technical progress and use labor more effectively, but dictatorships more efficiently employ the physical capital stock. Yet because there are reasons to suspect that production functions depend on the composition of each regime sample, we shall return to this topic later.

What, then, is the overall effect of regimes on growth? Assuming that the two regimes exist under the same conditions reduces the difference between the expected growth rates almost to zero. Whether one estimates the model by unconstrained OLS or constrains the coefficients of the production function[11] or uses the appropriate panel methods or

---

[9] The results for the split sample should be treated with some skepticism. A labor-force growth series is hard to estimate: It has some simultaneity, it is autocorrelated, and it probably has a cyclical component; given that we need to use country-invariant variables, we cannot use fixed effects, and the random-effects model does not fit well. To see if it makes a difference how the model is estimated, we provide in Table 3.3B several alternative estimators. Fortunately, they all lead to the same conclusion. When the sample is split, however, statistical problems become overwhelming. The best estimator seems to be OLS-AR1, which is what we report.

[10] For comments on estimation methods, see Appendix 3.1.

[11] When selection is estimated by the dynamic probit, the OLS results, constrained or not, are almost identical with the maximum-likelihood estimates.

Table 3.4. Barebones model, by low and high per capita incomes, decomposed by sources of growth, with LFG taken as exogenous

	Entire Sample		Income ≤ $3,000		$3,000 ≤ Income < $8,000		Income > $3,000	
Estimator	Dic	Dem	Dic	Dem	Dic	Dem	Dic	Dem
N	2,396	1,595	1,917	487	594	462	479	1,108
Y/P	1,909	6,210	1,227	1,761	4,469	5,490	4,642	8,165
Biased	4.43	3.92	4.30	4.11	4.83	4.30	4.91	3.83
	(6.94)[a]	(4.82)	(6.97)	(6.20)	(6.75)	(4.51)	(6.81)	(4.07)
Best estimate:								
Method	OLS	2F	OLS	OLS	OLS	2F	OLS	2F
Constant	0.8966	1.0430	0.8680	0.9226	0.9353	1.7785	0.9230	1.3439
	(0.1433)	(0.2078)	(0.1551)	(0.3957)	(0.3902)	(0.3058)	(0.3733)	(0.2058)
α	0.4004	0.3447	0.3937	0.3929	0.4409	0.2643	0.4383	0.2751
	(0.0060)	(0.0086)	(0.0064)	(0.0470)	(0.0178)	(0.0160)	(0.0166)	(0.0119)
β	0.3138	0.3974	0.3173	0.2524	0.2926	0.3838	0.2960	0.5530
	(0.0435)	(0.1132)	(0.0460)	(0.1532)	(0.1332)	(0.1891)	(0.1295)	(0.1286)
Θ	-1.1099	-0.0180	-0.1804	-0.0193	-1.2962	-0.0353	-1.1945	0.0719
	(0.3355)	(0.2461)	(0.3941)	(0.2748)	(0.7035)	(0.4791)	(0.6903)	(0.4288)
YG-HAT	4.30	4.23	4.35	4.23	4.81	4.44	4.40	4.09
	(5.03)	(4.34)	(5.57)	(5.56)	(4.61)	(2.80)	(4.21)	(2.73)
Capital	2.7776	2.3914	2.7430	2.7376	3.3985	2.0373	3.0201	1.8958
Labor	0.6303	0.7983	0.7370	0.5737	0.4784	0.6274	0.4738	0.8479
TFP	0.8966	1.0430	0.8680	0.9226	0.9353	1.7785	0.9230	1.3439

Constrained OLS (α + β = 1)

F for constraint Probability	41.26 (0.0000)	17.19 (0.0001)	37.56 (0.0000)	5.38 (0.0207)	3.90 (0.0489)	5.49 (0.0185)	4.13 (0.0427)	10.06 (0.0017)
Constant	0.1939	0.5796	0.1447	0.1036	0.3323	1.0229	0.3333	0.9053
	(0.0934)	(0.0934)	(0.1016)	(0.1798)	(0.2438)	(0.1713)	(0.2355)	(0.1110)
α	0.4094	0.3619	0.4033	0.3984	0.4466	0.3179	0.4430	0.3199
	(0.0059)	(0.0079)	(0.0063)	(0.0115)	(0.0176)	(0.0143)	(0.0165)	(0.0111)
β	0.5906	0.6381	0.5967	0.6016	0.5534	0.6821	0.5570	0.6801
	(0.0059)	(0.0079)	(0.0063)	(0.0115)	(0.0176)	(0.0143)	(0.0165)	(0.0111)
Θ	−1.0397	0.2609	−1.1933	−0.0029	−1.0751	0.4813	−0.9831	0.3965
	(0.3381)	(0.2133)	(0.3978)	(0.2870)	(0.6967)	(0.4106)	(0.6847)	(0.3665)
YGHAT	4.22	4.37	4.34	4.28	4.68	4.59	4.24	4.15
	(5.17)	(4.60)	(5.73)	(5.66)	(4.71)	(3.43)	(4.30)	(3.19)
Capital	2.8398	2.5104	2.8100	2.7762	3.4424	2.4507	3.0527	2.2045
Labor	1.1864	1.2818	1.3859	1.3972	0.9047	1.1150	0.8540	1.0427
TFP	0.1939	0.5796	0.1447	0.1036	0.3323	1.0229	0.3333	0.9053

[a] Standard errors in parentheses.

applies the Heckman (1988) instrumental-variable approach, the differences between selection-unbiased expected rates of growth are minimal. Introducing human capital, specifically, the rate of growth in the years of education attained by the average member of the labor force (EDTG = $\dot{H}/H$), reduces the size of the sample, but the results are again the same.

Because the labor force grows faster under dictatorship even when the two regimes are matched for exogenous conditions, lines with "LFG endogenous" in Table 3.5 take the rate of growth of the labor force at the mean values observed for each regime. These results are somewhat more favorable to dictatorships. But the difference between regimes is still minuscule. Hence, there is no reason to think that the regime type affects the rate of growth of total income.

Another way to test the effect of regimes is to focus on the countries that experienced regime changes. Here again, however, one should proceed prudently. Countries in which regimes are unstable may be different from those that have had single regimes persisting during the entire period. Yet the observed average rate of growth was the same in those countries that did not experience any regime transitions and in those that underwent one or more regime changes: The rate of growth for the former was 4.23 percent ($N = 2,813$), and for the latter 4.25 ($N = 1,313$). Stable dictatorships grew at the rate of 4.38 percent ($N = 1,709$), whereas dictatorships in the countries that also experienced democracy grew at the rate of 4.51 ($N = 772$). Stable democracies grew at the rate of 3.98 percent ($N = 1,104$), and democracies that rose from or gave way to dictatorships grew at 3.88 percent ($N = 541$). Hence, there is no reason to think that growth in the countries where regimes were stable was different from that in countries where regimes changed.[12]

With this reassurance, we can compare the rates of growth of democracies preceding dictatorships with those of democracies following dictatorchips, and vice versa. The average rate of growth during all the years of democracies preceding dictatorships was 4.49 percent ($N = 290$), and for dictatorships following democracies, 4.37 ($N = 425$). Hence, transitions from democracy to dictatorship did not affect the rate of growth. Growth during all the years of dictatorships preceding democracies was higher, at the average of 4.74 percent ($N = 607$), than the average of 3.64 percent ($N = 371$) during all the democratic years that followed. But because recovery from the crises accompanying transitions to democracy is slow, and the observations are right-hand

---

[12] For a more extensive discussion of the effect of regime stability on growth, see Chapter 5.

Table 3.5. Selection-corrected estimators of the rate of growth of income (YG)

	Regime means		Regime effect	
Estimator	**Dictatorships** (N = 2,396)	**Democracies** (N = 1,595)	**Constant** (N = 3,991)	**Individual**
Biased	4.43	3.92	−0.0227	0.0006
	(6.94)	(4.82)	(0.1252)	(0.4908)
Unconstrained OLS	4.30	4.24		
	(5.02)	(4.48)		
Constrained OLS	4.22	4.37		
(LFG exogenous)	(5.17)	(4.60)		
Constrained OLS	4.38	4.11		
(LFG endogenous)	(5.15)	(4.55)		
PANEL	4.22	4.23		
(LFG exogenous)	(5.17)	(4.34)		
PANEL	4.38	4.07		
(LFG endogenous)	(5.15)	(4.34)		
Unobservable			0.0741	0.0461
			(0.1312)	(0.4871)
Observable			−0.0926	0.0490
			(0.1537)	(0.5061)
EDTG sample	**N = 1,745**	**N = 1,042**		
Biased	4.57	3.91		
	(6.91)	(4.71)		
Unconstrained OLS	4.45	4.34		
(LFG exogenous)	(4.71)	(3.88)		
Constrained OLS	4.36	4.94		
(LFG exogenous)	(4.87)	(4.01)		
2F PANEL	4.45	4.33		
(LFG exogenous)	(4.71)	(3.74)		

Notes: Probit equations include lagged values of LEVEL, STRA, and RELDIF. The "barebones" model includes KSG, LFG, and, in a smaller sample, EDTG. "Constrained" means that the coefficients on the arguments of the production function were constrained to 1.00. PANEL is OLS for dictatorships and 2F for democracies. "LFG exogenous" is based on the assumption that LFG is exogenous; "LFG endogenous" takes LFG at the observed mean of each regime.

censored, the conclusion that transitions to democracy slow down growth would be erroneous. Just note that many of the democratic observations followed transitions from either bureaucratic-authoritarian or communist dictatorships during the 1980s, including the very end of the decade. Because those democracies did not have time to recover by 1990, they weigh down the democratic average.

In sum, neither the selection-corrected values for the entire sample nor the paths of growth associated with regime transitions give any support to the claim that regime types affect the rate of growth of total income. Selection-corrected average rates of growth are the same for the two regimes. And there is no reason to think that steady-state rates of growth would be different under the two regimes when countries experience regime transitions.

The first conclusion, therefore, must be that political regimes have no impact on the rate of growth of total income. The arguments about the superiority of dictatorships in mobilizing savings for investment find no support in the evidence. Indeed, the input that grows faster under dictatorships is not capital but labor. The differences in the efficiency with which productive inputs are utilized are small. And, as a consequence, the selection-corrected average expected values of growth are almost identical. Yet conclusions are premature, for there are still methodological problems to confront.

Poor and Wealthy Countries

We still face the following difficulty: Dictatorships existed predominantly in poor countries: 38.5 percent of annual observations (946 out of 2,481) of dictatorships were in countries with incomes under $1,000, but only 4.5 percent of democracies (75 out of 1,645) were that poor. Democracies flourished in wealthy countries: 46.8 percent of them (769) were observed in countries with incomes above $6,000, whereas only 2.8 percent (68) of dictatorships existed at such income levels. Hence, nearly all our observations of countries with incomes below $1,000, 92.6 percent (946 out of 1,021), are of dictatorships, and nearly all our observations of countries with incomes above $6,000, 91.9 percent (769 out of 837), are of democracies.

Now, examining the rates of growth in countries classified by intervals of $500 of per capita income (Table 3.6) shows that very poor countries (under $1,000) grow slowly, at about 3.5 percent. Growth accelerates in wealthier economies, reaching a peak of 5.1 percent between $2,000 and $3,000. Then it slows down again to about 3.8

Table 3.6. Rate of growth of GDP (YG), by per capita income (LEVEL)

LEVEL	Proportion dictatorships	Rate of growth of GDP[a]		
		All	Dictatorships	Democracies
0–1,000	0.9273	3.519	3.464	4.220
1,001–2,000	0.7472	4.636	4.809	4.123
2,001–3,000	0.6207	5.142	5.633	4.335
3,001–4,000	0.5874	4.740	4.915	4.492
4,001–5,000	0.5424	4.552	4.507	4.606
5,001–6,000	0.4308	4.312	4.772	3.963
6,001–	0.0812	3.770	6.054	3.568
Total (N = 4,128)		4.233	4.424	3.945

[a] All cell entries are based on at least 68 observations.

Moving averages of rates of growth by bands of $500

LEVEL	All	Dictatorships	Democracies
250–750	3.071	3.107	2.380
500–1,000	3.689	3.647	4.164
750–1,250	4.140	4.050	4.724
1,000–1,500	4.505	4.682	3.848
1,250–1,750	4.969	5.381	3.932
1,500–2,000	4.827	5.021	4.396
1,750–2,250	4.972	5.092	4.744
2,000–2,500	5.444	5.664	5.055
2,250–2,750	5.793	6.989	3.993
2,500–3,000	4.827	5.599	3.653
2,750–3,250	4.808	4.955	4.613
3,000–3,500	5.130	5.238	4.977
3,250–3,750	4.594	4.183	5.445
3,500–4,000	4.317	4.565	3.965
3,750–4,250	4.382	5.065	3.491
4,000–4,500	4.984	4.908	5.086
4,250–4,750	4.742	4.771	4.714
4,500–5,000	3.965	3.881	4.050
4,750–5,250	4.558	4.580	4.535
5,000–5,500	4.217	4.360	4.088
5,250–5,750	4.116	4.003	4.194
5,500–6,000	4.418	5.350	3.845
5,750–6,250	3.363	4.479	2.878
6,000–	3.770	6.054	3.568

percent when countries reach incomes above $6,000. Hence, in accordance with Quah (1996), incomes diverge among poor countries, until about $2,500, and they converge among wealthy countries.

If very poor and very rich economies both grow slowly regardless of the regime they have, then this pattern does not present a problem. But if poor countries grow slowly because they are ruled by dictatorships, or rich ones because they are democratic, then we cannot make such an inference, for perhaps if the poor countries had been democratic they would have grown faster. In fact, the 75 democratic years at incomes under $1,000 witnessed growth at the rate of 4.22 percent, but dictatorships grew at the rate of 3.46 percent in equally poor countries. Conversely, if the rich countries had been authoritarian, perhaps they would have grown faster. Again, the 68 authoritarian years at incomes above $6,000 enjoyed growth at the rate of 6.05 percent, whereas democracies had a rate of growth of 3.57 percent at those incomes. Our counterfactual procedure matches the regimes for the conditions under which they existed, specifically for their productive inputs and a variety of other conditions. But to find out how a country observed, say, as a dictatorship would have grown had it been a democracy under the same conditions, we use the information about the way these productive inputs are transformed into outputs under each regime. And this information, about production functions, is derived from the actual observations, which means disproportionately from poor dictatorships and rich democracies. Hence these production functions may be different not because of the impact of regimes but because of the effect of wealth.

Thus, to test whether or not the results depend on the samples, we need to estimate production functions separately for different levels of development, as always measured by per capita income (Table 3.4). First we consider only countries with incomes under $3,000, which we shall call "poor." Their production functions are almost identical, and regimes make no difference for the average growth rates. Then we take countries with incomes above $3,000, "wealthy," where the difference between the observed growth rates is particularly high, 4.91 percent for dictatorships, and 3.83 for democracies. The difference between the average values almost vanishes when corrected for selection, but the production functions are quite different. Finally, given that there are very few dictatorships with incomes above $8,000,[13] we need to

[13] The wealthiest dictatorship we observed was Singapore, with an income of $11,698, and the wealthiest democracy in our sample, the United States, had an income of $18,095. There were 200 democratic years with incomes above that of Singapore.

know if the difference between wealthy dictatorships and wealthy democracies is still due to the composition of the respective samples, so we analyze separately countries within the $3,000–$8,000 income band.

These tests suggest that per capita income of $3,000 is the natural breaking point.[14] The production functions are almost identical in countries with incomes below $3,000, but they differ between regimes in wealthier countries. In particular, the difference between the two regimes becomes visible if we consider only countries within the $3,000–$8,000 income band. Hence, this difference is not due to diminishing returns in wealthy democracies.

Poor Countries

In poor countries, the two regimes are almost identical, with observed rates of growth of 4.34 percent under dictatorship and 4.28 under democracy. The two regimes generate productive inputs at the same rate and use them in identical ways. They invest about 12.5 percent of GDP and increase capital stock at the rate of about 6 percent, and labor force at the rate of about 2.2 percent. An increase of 1 percent in the capital stock raises output by about 0.40 percent under both regimes, and an increase in the labor force by 1 percent augments output by about 0.60 percent.[15] Neither regime benefits much from technical progress, about 0.1 percent per annum; both get 2.8 percent in growth from an increase in capital stock, and 1.4 percent from an increase in labor force. With identical supplies of factors and their identical utilization, they grow at the same rate under the two regimes: The selection-corrected average growth rates are the same.

The idea that democracies in poor countries process pressures for immediate consumption, resulting in lower investment and slower growth, seemed persuasive at the time it was advanced, and it was not implausible. There appear to be good reasons to think that people in poor countries want to consume more immediately: They cannot afford to make intertemporal trade-offs if they cannot expect to live to benefit from their short-term sacrifices. It is also plausible that unions, particularly if they are decentralized, and political parties, competing for

[14] We have investigated several more income bands, beginning with $0–$3,000 and moving the lower and upper cutoffs by $1,000, until $8,000–$11,000.

[15] This is a constrained estimate. Constrained estimates are cited in the rest of this paragraph.

votes, would push forward demands for immediate consumption. Yet, as likely as that view may seem, it simply is not true. Perhaps this only means that democracy is not very effective at processing what people want; perhaps developmental goals are not any more attractive to people under dictatorship than under democracy; perhaps poverty is so constraining that even dictators cannot squeeze savings out of indigent people.

The last explanation is most plausible. One piece of evidence is that very few countries that were very poor when we first observed them ever developed. Of the forty-eight countries that entered our purview with incomes below $1,000, only three made it to above $3,000 by 1990. The two miracles were Taiwan, which had an income of $968 in 1950 and $8,067 in 1990, and South Korea, which went from $814 in 1950 to $6,665 in 1990. Thailand had an income of $815 in 1950 and $3,570 in 1990. Four more countries that began under $1,000 made it to more than $2,000, and eleven more to at least $1,000. But at the end of the period, thirty – out of forty-eight – very poor countries remained within the income band in which they had begun. The experiences of countries that were first observed with incomes between $1,000 and $2,000 were more heterogeneous, but, again, of the forty-five first observed at that level, only five experienced sustained growth: Japan, which went from $1,768 in 1950 to $14,317 in 1990, Singapore from $1,845 in 1965 to 11,698 in 1990, Portugal from $1,314 in 1950 to 7,487 in 1990, Greece from $1,480 in 1950 to $6,768 in 1990, and Malta from $1,377 in 1964 to $6,627 in 1990. Four countries descended to below $1,000, and twelve still had incomes between $1,000 and $2,000 in 1990. In turn, none of the forty-two countries that were first observed with per capita incomes above $2,000 fell below their starting range, and all but seven of them at least doubled their incomes by the end of the period. Because the observation periods were not the same for all countries and typically were shorter for the poorer ones, many of which became independent around 1960, these data are somewhat biased against poor countries. Nevertheless, most countries that we first observed below $2,000 had about thirty years to grow, and yet most remained poor: evidence of a "low-level trap" (Table 3.7).

Thus, poverty constrains. Whatever the regime, the society is too poor to finance an effective state. Collecting total revenues of $127 per capita, as governments do on the average in countries with incomes under $1,000, can pay for little else than collecting these revenues. Government expenditures add up to $167 per person in these

Table 3.7. Per capita income at the beginning and end of the period, by bands of $1,000

Entered	Exited											Total
	0–1	1–2	2–3	3–4	4–5	5–6	6–7	7–8	8–9	9–10	10–	
0–1	30	11	4	1	0	0	1	0	1	0	0	48
1–2	4	12	15	6	2	1	2	1	0	0	2	45
2–3	0	0	1	3	3	1	0	1	0	3	1	13
3–4	0	0	0	2	0	2	0	1	0	0	4	9
4–5	0	0	0	0	2	0	1	0	0	0	5	8
5–	0	0	0	0	0	0	1	1	0	0	10	12
Total	34	23	20	12	7	4	5	4	1	3	22	135

Notes: "Entered" stands for 1950 or the year of independence or the first year data were available, and "Exited" for 1990 or in some cases the last year data were available. Per capita incomes are given in thousands (1985 PPP USD). Cell entries are numbers of countries.

countries, so they run deficits higher than 7 percent of GDP. In countries with incomes between $1,000 and $2,000, governments collect $372 per capita and spend $450, still running deficits over 7 percent. And, like the investment share, government revenue (particularly tax revenue) as a share of GDP increases monotonically in per capita income.[16] Thus already in countries with incomes between $2,000 and $3,000, revenues of the central government add to $668 per capita. Between $3,000 and $4,000 they are $904, and above $6,000 they are $2,608. To put it differently, per capita public expenditures in countries with incomes between $3,000 and $4,000 are larger than total per capita incomes in countries with incomes under $1,000; per capita public expenditures in countries with incomes above $6,000 are about the same as total per capita incomes in countries between $3,000 and $4,000.

Poor countries cannot afford a strong state, and when the state is weak, the kind of regime matters little for everyday life. In a village located three days' travel away from the capital, often the only presence of the state is a teacher and occasionally roving uniformed bandits.[17] Just calculate: If a mile of road costs about a million dollars, in a country with

---

[16] Cheibub (1998) shows that selection-corrected tax revenues are the same for the two regimes.

[17] The best portrayal of life under a weak state is by Alvaro Mutis (1996).

per capita income under $1,000 it would take the total government expenditures per 600,000 persons to build 100 miles of road. There is little room for regimes to make a difference when the state is that poor.

Note that we are not arguing that a fiscally large or otherwise large state is necessarily good for development, but only that if the state is to be able to make a difference for better conditions, it must have resources. The role of the state in economic development is a notoriously controversial issue. Most of the statistical research on this topic has been mindless: Studies that discover that the state is bad for growth simply stick government-consumption expenditures into the equation for growth and discover that its sign is negative. Needless to say, the same would happen if one did that with private-consumption expenditures: We did it and know it to be so. If one thinks that government-consumption expenditures affect growth, the term introduced into the production-function equation should be the change in government consumption, not the share of government consumption in GDP.[18] But the real test of the impact of government is to consider separately the effects of private and public capital stocks. The idea, due to Barro (1990), is that private capital and public capital play different roles in development and that they are complementary, so that even if the production function exhibits diminishing returns in each stock, the joint returns will be constant or even increasing. Moreover, because the ideal combination of private and public capital stocks is one in which their marginal products are equal (with an appropriate correction if public investment is financed by distortionary taxes), for each level of private capital stock (and investment) there is an optimal level of government capital stock (and investment).[19] The state, as measured by the size of the government capital stock, can thus be too small, just right, or too big.

This is a plausible view, but it hurls itself against a practical problem, namely, that standard national accounts do not measure the public capital stock, only current capital expenditures by the central govern-

---

[18] Ram (1986) has shown that the model that introduces the level of government-consumption expenditures into the production-function equation is misspecified. He has developed a specification that allows an assessment of the impact of government on growth without having explicit information about the public capital stock. We (Cheibub and Przeworski 1997) applied Ram's specification to our data set and discovered that the contribution of the state is positive, but for various reasons we have second thoughts about this approach.

[19] It is a different matter whether or not a government, even a benevolent one, would implement it. On the time inconsistency of optimal taxation, see Benhabib and Velasco (1996).

ment. And without such data, estimating the effect of government capital is difficult, if not impossible. What one would want to estimate would be a production function of the form

$$\dot{Y}/Y = \dot{A}/A + \alpha(\dot{P}/P) + \tau(\dot{S}/S) + \beta(\dot{L}/L) + e,$$

but we have no separate information about private and public capital stocks, $P + S = K$. In Appendix 3.2 we perform some heroics that permit us to estimate instead an equation of the form

$$\dot{Y}/Y = \dot{A}/A + \alpha(\dot{K}/K) + \Omega(\dot{S}/Y) + \beta(\dot{L}/L) + e,$$

where Ω can be interpreted as the marginal product of government capital stock when private capital and public capital grow at the same rate.

Note first that whereas government capital expenditures (GXPK-TOTL), $\dot{S}$, account for a relatively large share of public expenditures in poor countries, they add up to almost nothing in absolute terms: $46 per capita in countries with incomes under $1,000, and $109 in those with incomes between $1,000 and $2,000. In countries between $3,000 and $4,000, per capita public capital expenditures already amount to $190; in those with incomes above $6,000, they are $369.

Table A3.1.1, which we put in Appendix 3.1 because interpreting the results requires understanding how they were derived, shows that government capital expenditures have no effect on growth in poor countries, but they do have a sizable positive effect in wealthy countries. Unfortunately, the interpretation of the coefficient Ω is ambivalent: Either the marginal product of public capital increases as total capital per worker (CAPW = K/L) rises or private capital stock grows in the more-developed countries faster than public capital stock. And even if Ω is a valid measure of the marginal product of public capital, it is not clear why it should increase as countries become more developed. One interpretation would be that governments in poor countries simply allocate capital expenditures unwisely, but the almost monotonic relation between Ω and K/L makes that farfetched. The interpretation we find more plausible is that the complementarity between private investment and public investment, the latter largely in infrastructure, increases as the private capital stock increases. A road contributes to development only to the extent that there something to be transported.

Ideally, we would want to see if public capital stock plays different roles under the two regimes. Unfortunately, the sample that contains information about public capital expenditures ($N = 1,366$) is extremely unbalanced: There are very few observations of wealthy dictatorships and equally few of poor democracies. Hence, whereas going through our standard steps, that is, correcting for selection and estimating the production functions separately for the two regimes, shows that public capital plays no role under dictatorships and a positive role under democracies, this is just an effect of sample composition. In turn, splitting the sample between poor and wealthy countries is not feasible given its imbalance. Yet for the purpose of our argument it is sufficient to know that in poor countries the state plays little, if any, productive role, but in wealthy countries it does.

In sum, poor countries are too poor to afford a strong state, and without an effective state there is little difference any regime can make for economic development. Investment is low in poor democracies, but it is not any higher in poor dictatorships. The labor force grows rapidly in both. Development is factor-extensive: Poor countries benefit almost nothing from technical change. Clearly, this does not imply that all poor countries are the same or even that regimes may not make a difference for other aspects of people's lives; indeed, we show later that they do. But not for economic development in poor countries.

Wealthy Countries

Once countries reach some level of development – somewhere between $2,500 and $3,000, that of Algeria in 1977, Mauritius in 1969, Costa Rica in 1966, South Korea in 1976, Czechoslovakia in 1970, or Portugal in 1966 – patterns of economic development under democracy and dictatorship diverge. In countries with incomes above that threshold, regimes do make a difference for how resources are used, for how much people produce and how much they earn. To show that this is true, we have to go through a number of steps, piecing together bits of evidence derived from disparate sources and based on distinct samples. Yet we think that the overall conclusion is overwhelming.

Dictatorships appear not to change their ways whether they are in poor or wealthy countries. Although in more-developed economies they rely somewhat less on growth of the labor force and somewhat more on the growth of capital stock, they use the inputs in almost the same way and get little benefit from productivity growth. Democracies, in turn, exhibit different patterns in poor and wealthy countries. Their capital stock grows somewhat slower, and the labor force much slower, when they are affluent; they use labor more productively and benefit more from productivity growth. As a result, the patterns of growth are different in wealthier dictatorships and democracies.

Note, back in Table 3.4, that the factors that differentiate wealthy dictatorships from wealthy democracies are the patterns, not averages. Corrected for selection, the average rates of growth of income are again almost identical under the two regimes. Although the observed rates of growth are higher under dictatorships, if the two regimes had used the same inputs in production, they would have grown at the same rate. But they would have grown in different ways.

Growth under wealthy dictatorships is labor-extensive. The labor force grows at a much faster pace under dictatorships, at 2.03 percent, than under democracies, where it grows at 1.32 percent. And whereas the elasticity of output with regard to labor is about 0.56 under dictatorship, it is 0.68 under democracy. Wealthier dictatorships benefit little from technical progress, 0.33; they get most of their growth from capital, 3.05, and in spite of employing many more workers, they get less of it from labor, 0.85. Wealthier democracies benefit from technical progress, 0.91, get less growth out of capital, 2.20, and more from the labor input, 1.04, even though they employ fewer additional workers.

Because the labor force grows faster under dictatorships, and the elasticity of output with regard to labor is lower, output per worker (GDPW = Y/L) is also lower. In the entire sample, the observed values are obviously lower: \$5,113 under dictatorships and \$14,554 under democracies. But selection-corrected values, controlled for capital stock and the size of the labor force, are still much lower for dictatorships: An average worker produces \$6,843 under dictatorship versus \$9,054 under democracy. As we would by now have expected, the difference in poor countries is negligible: Output per worker is \$3,519 in dictatorships, and \$3,639 in democracies. But above \$3,000, the difference is large: \$13,410 versus \$17,857. To harp on what may by now be obvious, these are the outputs that would be generated under the two regimes if they had exactly the same capital stock, labor force, and whatever it is that we do not observe that affects both regime selection and output per worker.

Thus, dictatorships in countries with incomes above \$3,000 use labor extensively. Their labor force grows faster, the marginal worker contributes less to output, and the average worker produces less than in democracies. It merits noting that this difference is not due to labor-force participation by women (LFPW), whose values are almost identical under the two regimes at every income level. More women participate in gainful activities in very poor countries, where they work in agriculture,

Table 3.8A. Labor exploitation (labor-share sample, $N = 2,061$)

LEVEL	Average labor shares		
	All	Dictatorships	Democracies
0–1,000	33.04 (308)	32.21 (277)	40.48 (31)
1,001–2,000	32.61 (429)	32.90 (332)	31.61 (97)
2,001–3,000	30.43 (282)	30.70 (158)	30.10 (124)
3,001–4,000	33.44 (218)	34.17 (138)	32.18 (80)
4,001–5,000	35.10 (131)	33.55 (81)	37.63 (50)
5,001–6,000	36.59 (102)	31.08 (48)	41.48 (54)
6,001–	48.94 (693)	36.43 (29)	49.59 (562)
Total	35.53 (2,061)	32.63 (1,063)	42.71 (998)

and in wealthy countries, where they are disproportionately employed in services. Regimes have no effect on their labor-force participation: The observed participation rates are 31.9 under dictatorships and 31.0 under democracies. Once the proportion of the labor force working in agriculture is controlled for, selection-corrected rates are also the same. Dictatorships simply rely on using many additional workers, of whatever sex, even if they produce less on the average and at the margin.

Perhaps the reason is that dictatorships exploit labor.[20] To examine that possibility, we must rely on a different data source and a much smaller sample[21] (Table 3.8). The average labor share of value added

---

[20] This is not to say that workers are not, in some sense, exploited under democracies. We use the term in Roemer's sense (1982): Workers under dictatorship would be better off if they could withdraw, with the same endowments, to democracy.

[21] The labor-share data come from the World Bank (1995), whose 1995 development report (p. 234) describes this series as "derived by dividing total earnings of employees by value added in current prices to show labor's share in income generated in the manufacturing sector." There are 2,061 observations, all for the period 1961–1990. They cover countries that are, on the average, wealthier than the full sample, but in the entire range, from $370 to $18,095. The mean is 35.5 (s.d. = 13.0), with a minimum of 6.1 in Rwanda in 1977 and a maximum of 100.1 in the Bahamas in 1981. Note that the unconstrained labor elasticities in Table 3.4 are 0.27 for dictatorships and 0.39 for democracies; hence, they are close to the competitive labor share. For some developed countries, the numbers are surprisingly small: The 1990 labor share in the United States was 35.6 (48.5 in 1963), and in Sweden 34.8 (56.5 in 1963). For other countries they are closer to what one would expect: The 1989 labor share in France was 58.4 (68.4 in 1980), and the 1990 share in Norway was 59.0 (54.7 in 1963). Altogether, these numbers appear reasonable.

Table 3.8B. Accounting for the difference in wages

	Dictatorships (N = 1,052)		Democracies (N = 994)		
Observed values:					
(1) GDPW = Y/L	6,332	(4,858)	16,665	(8,871)	-10,335
(2) LS = wL/Y	32.5	(11.42)	42.7	(13.78)	-3,671
(3) WAGE = LS*(Y/L)	2,058	(1,873)	7,116	(5,376)	-5,058
Selection-corrected values:					
LS | Y/P	33.5	(1.74)	40.0	(4.19)	-1,387
LS | Y/L, OTHER (2SLS)	33.7	(3.20)	41.2	(9.29)	-3,154
(4) (Y/L) | A,K,L	8,375	(4,895)	11,529	(7,858)	-1,120
(5) WAGE | (Y/L)	3,733	(2,864)	5,057	(4,442)	-1,324
Accounting for difference in wage:					
(6) Actual output/worker (from line 1)	6,332	–	16,665	=	
(7) Wages assuming same labor share (line 6*0.3553)	2,250	–	5,921	=	
(8) Actual wages (from line 3)	2,058	–	7,116	=	
(9) Difference due to labor shares (line 8 minus line 9)	–192	–	1,195	=	
(10) Output/worker assuming same inputs (from line 4)	8,375	–	11,529	=	
(11) Wages assuming same inputs, same labor share (line 10*0.3553)	2,976	–	4,096	=	
(12) Wages assuming same output per worker (from line 5)	3,733	–	5,057	=	
Summary:					
(13) Due to difference in inputs (line 7 minus line 11)	-2,551		-2,551		
(14) Due to difference in productivity (line 11)	-1,120		-1,120		
(15a) Due to difference in labor shares (line 9)					
(15b) Due to difference in labor shares (line 12)	-1,387		-1,324		
(16) Total difference in wages (lines 13 + 14 + 15)	-5,058		-4,995		
(17) Error (line 8 minus line 16)			-63		

in manufacturing (LS) during the 1,052 dictatorial years was 32.5 percent, and the average during the 994 democratic years was 42.7 percent. Only a part of this difference vanishes when controlled for output per worker: Selection-corrected labor shares are still larger for democracies, and the estimates are tight. Hence, even if they had generated the same output per worker, dictatorships would have paid workers a smaller share of value added than would democracies. See also Rodrik (1998).

Although the labor-share data concern only the manufacturing sector, another way to see the same result is to calculate annual wage rates (WAGE), multiplying output per worker by the labor share. The observed wage under dictatorship is $2,058, whereas under democracy it is $7,116, a difference of $5,058 in favor of democracies. If the labor share had been the same under the two regimes, 35.5 percent, their difference in wages would have been $3,671. Hence, $1,387 of the observed difference is due to labor shares.

Because a large part of the observed difference is obviously due to income levels, in Table 3.8 we engage in some accounting. The assumption that dictatorships and democracies have exactly the same productive inputs yields the conclusion that the average output per worker would be $8,375 under dictatorship and $11,529 under democracy, for a difference of $3,154: As in the full sample, workers produce less under dictatorships. If the two regimes had had the same inputs and the same labor share, the difference in wages due only to productivity would have been $1,120. Hence, if labor shares were the same, the difference in inputs would account for $2,551 ($3,671 − $1,120), and the difference in productivity would account for $1,120, of the differences in wages. In turn, assuming that output per worker is the same under the two regimes yields a selection-corrected difference of $1,324.

Hence, of the observed difference in wages (to remind, $5,058), $2,551 is due to the fact that the regimes existed under different conditions and used different productive inputs, $1,120 is due to dictatorships being less productive, and $1,387 is due to differences in labor shares.

Although the number of observations is too small to permit correcting for selection within subsamples, it appears again that the gap between regimes opens up at about $3,000 of per capita income. Whereas the labor share and average wage were much higher in India than in China when both countries had similar per capita incomes, that pattern is not characteristic of other poor countries.[22] Under $3,000, the labor share during 767 dictatorial years was almost identical, at 32.2 percent, with the 32.0 percent during the 252 democratic years. Between $3,000 and $8,000, the labor share under 288 years of dictatorship was 33.7 percent, but under 323 years of democracy it climbed to 39.6 percent. Wages offer a similar picture. Under $3,000, an average worker earned $1,238 under dictatorship and $1,698 under democracy, but this difference is due entirely to the fact that democracies are still somewhat wealthier in this income range. Between $3,000 and $8,000, the average wage was $4,193 under dictatorship, $1,556 less than the $5,649 under democracy. Some of this difference is again due to the fact that democracies have higher output per worker in this range than do dictatorships. But even if workers under wealthy dictatorships had produced the same output as under democracy, they would have earned $4,777, still $872 less.

There are few observations in this sample for which labor-share data are available for both the entry and exit of a regime. But the impact of transitions to dictatorship can be seen: In the eighteen cases we observed, dictatorships immediately reduced labor share by 2.6 per-cent of value added, from 27.4 to 24.8. The "bureaucratic-authoritarian" regimes in Latin America were particularly brutal in redistributing incomes from labor to capital. The Argentine military reduced the labor share from 29.4 in 1975 to 18.1 in 1976 and to 14.2 in 1982, its last year of existence. In Chile, labor share was squeezed from 29.6 in 1972 to 16.3 in 1973 and to 14.8 by the end of dictatorship, in 1989. Transitions to democracy, however, had no immediate effect on income shares.

To get an intuitive sense of these patterns, compare first the neo-liberal miracle, Singapore, with the persistently social-democratic Austria, when the two countries had the same levels of per capita income (Figure 3.1). In 1976 Singapore had per capita income of $5,606, and the average worker produced $13,394. The labor share was 33.1, which meant that the average worker earned $4,433. Austria had almost the same per capita income, $5,672, by 1963, and output per worker was somewhat lower, $12,328. But the Austrian worker took home 48.6 percent of what he or she produced, so that the average wage was $5,991: $1,558 more. By 1990, Singapore had per capita

---

[22] As India reached per capita income of $1,000 in 1984, the labor share was 50.3, and the average wage was $1,313. China reached that level of income a year earlier, with a labor share of 15.9 and a wage of $287.

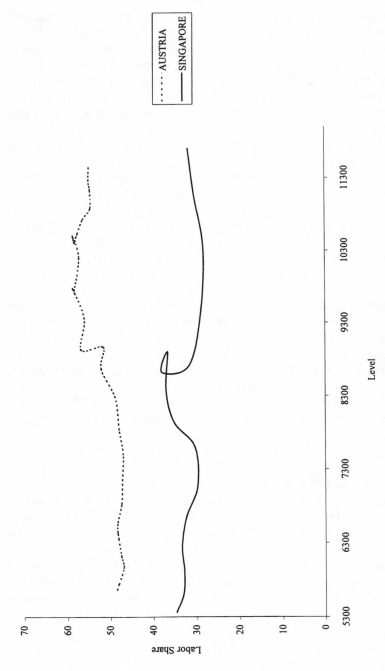

Figure 3.1. Labor shares in Singapore and Austria at similar levels of per capita income from year to year

income of $11,698, and output per worker reached $24,396. The labor share was 31.7, and average wage was $7,725. Austria reached the income of $11,462 by 1987, and the average worker produced $24,366 by that time. The labor share was 54.7, so that the average wage was $13,328: $5,603 more than in Singapore. And this illustration is not tendentious: Among all countries in the same income range, between $5,606 and $11,698, average output per worker was $17,143 under dictatorship ($N = 45$) and $21,004 under democracy ($N = 426$), the average labor shares were, respectively, 34.3 and 48.9, and the average wages were $6,882 and $10,402: a difference of $3,620.

The experience of Mexico and Portugal during the 1980s, when the two countries had incomes in the $4,974–$6,575 range, is similar (Figure 3.2). Mexico's labor share hovered around 20 percent; Portugal's declined from 46.9 to 36.2 during that period. Still, by 1989, an average Mexican worker earned $3,192, and a Portuguese earned $4,917.

Finally, examine the experience of Argentina, where we can observe several regimes: dictatorship until 1972, democracy between 1973 and 1975, another dictatorship between 1976 and 1982, and a new democracy after 1983. The advent of democracy in 1973 increased the labor share by about 4 percent, and the wage went up from $3,942 in 1972 to $4,697 one year later (Figure 3.3). Wage reduction by the military regime of 1976 was drastic: Labor share fell from 29.4 percent in 1975 to 18.1 percent, and average wage tumbled from $4,716 to $2,825. When democracy was reestablished in 1983, labor share increased only slightly, as the Argentine economy was buffeted by crises. By 1990, it stood at 20.5, and average wage was $2,748: higher than the $2,155 during the last year of the military dictatorship, but well below the Argentine historical levels.

Thus, growth under wealthier dictatorships is both labor-extensive and labor-exploitative. The labor force grows faster under dictatorship, the marginal worker produces less, and the average worker much less, than under democracy. Even if they were matched for capital stock and labor force, workers would produce less under dictatorship. And labor earns less under dictatorship. Some of this difference is attributable to lower output, but a large difference remains even when we account for differences in factor endowments and even if we assume away differences in productivity. Democracy entails the freedom for workers to associate independently of their employers and the state. And strikes are three times more frequent under democracy than under dictatorship: 0.2434 per year under the former and 0.0895 under the latter. Because, in addition, under democracy workers also vote, these results

173

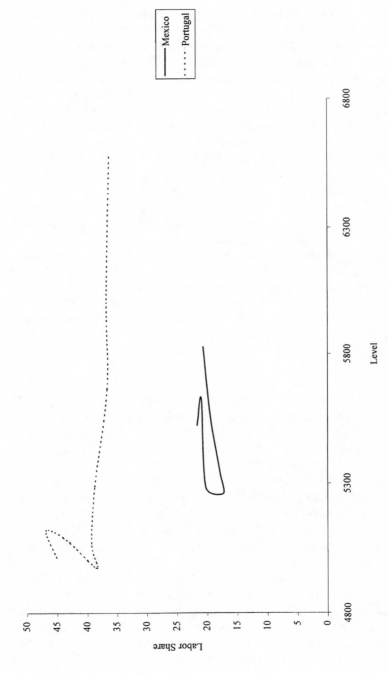

Figure 3.2. Labor shares in Mexico and Portugal at similar levels of per capita income from year to year

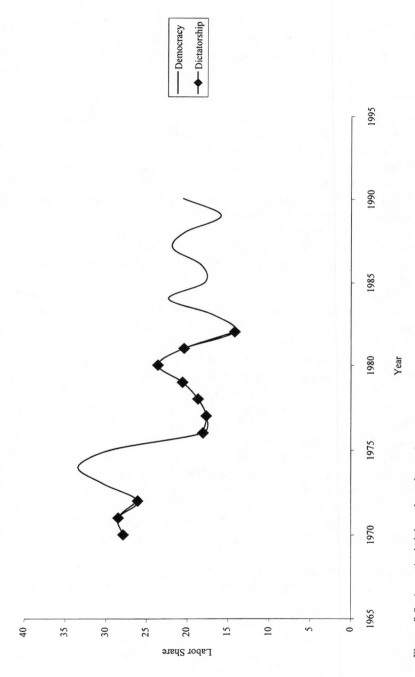

Figure 3.3. Argentina's labor share by regime

are not surprising. Dictatorships repress workers, exploit them, and use them carelessly. Democracies allow workers to fight for their interests, pay them better, and employ them better.

Miracles and Disasters

A list of regimes under which economies grew at the average rate of at least 7 percent per year, thus doubling incomes in ten years, consists almost exclusively of dictatorships. Indeed, the only exception is the somewhat peculiar case of the Bahamas. But the list of countries in which total income declined or grew at less than 1 percent per year during at least seven years looks almost the same: Almost all regimes on that list are also dictatorships.[23] The observed variation of performance is simply much higher for dictatorships (s.d. = 7.04) than for democracies (s.d. = 4.85), and so is the selection-corrected variance. Hence, looking only at best practice leads to dangerously misleading conclusions.

Although some countries, notably Singapore, South Korea, and Taiwan, sustained rapid rates of growth over the entire period, glory is transitory (Table 3.9). Of the countries that grew fastest during the 1950s – Turkey, Costa Rica, West Germany, and the Philippines – none appears on the list of tigers in the successive periods. The next two decades were periods of sustained growth: Gabon, Ivory Coast, Iraq, Jordan, South Korea, Singapore, Malta, and Romania grew at the average rates above 7 percent during the 1960s and 1970s. But growth collapsed during the 1980s, and only four countries maintained their rhythm of the previous decade: South Korea, Singapore, Taiwan, and the Yemen Arab Republic. In turn, some earlier miracles turned into disasters. In Iraq, after two decades of rapid growth, income fell at the rate of 7.04 percent during the eight years in the 1980s for which data are available. The same was true for Ivory Coast, which, having sustained rapid growth between 1960 and 1980, suffered a declining income afterward. Nigeria, having experienced spectacular growth during the 1970s, had income growing at only 0.32 during the next decade. Suriname grew at 8.50 during the 1970s, only to decline to a rate of 2.27 in the 1980s. Yugoslavia grew at 7.40 during the 1970s, and –1.25 during the next decade.

---

[23] Among Temple's ten miracles (1999: 116) between 1960 and 1990 there were two democracies, Japan and Malta, and among his ten disasters there was one democracy, Venezuela, and one country that experienced regime transitions, namely, Ghana.

Table 3.9. Miracles and disasters (fastest- and slowest-growing regimes, over periods of at least ten years)

Country	Number of years	First year	Growth rate	Regime	Comment
Fastest (more than 7%):					
Botswana	24	1966	9.55	Dic	Primary-commodity exporter
Nigeria	13	1966	9.24	Dic	Oil exporter
Yemen A. R.	20	1970	9.19	Dic	
Singapore	26	1965	9.14	Dic	
South Korea	27	1961	8.66	Dic	
Taiwan	39	1952	8.41	Dic	
Ecuador	16	1963	7.82	Dic	Oil exporter
Brazil	15	1964	7.54	Dic	
Turkey	10	1951	7.49	Dic	
Bahamas	10	1978	7.47	Dem	
Cape Verde Islands	16	1975	7.40	Dic	
Syria	30	1961	7.02	Dic	One year of war
Jordan	36	1955	7.01	Dic	Two years of war
Slowest (less than 1%):					
Madagascar	30	1961	0.85	Dic	Primary-commodity exporter
Comoros	16	1975	0.81	Dic	Primary-commodity exporter
Western Samoa	11	1980	0.64	Dic	
Papua New Guinea	16	1975	0.62	Dem	
Chad	30	1961	0.61	Dic	War, primary-commodity exporter
Peru	10	1980	0.48	Dem	War, primary-commodity exporter
Uruguay	12	1973	0.48	Dic	Primary-commodity exporter
Guyana	25	1966	0.33	Dic	Primary-commodity exporter
Angola	15	1975	0.08	Dic	War, oil exporter
Mozambique	16	1975	−0.95	Dic	War

Some of the sharp oscillations in growth were due to wars, about which we say more in the next chapter. Another source of variance in growth rates was reliance on the export of primary commodities (COMEX). Countries that derived at least half of their export revenue from primary commodities grew, in general, at a slower rate, 3.47 (s.d. = 7.42; N = 1,346), than countries that did not, which grew at the rate of 4.60 (s.d. = 5.58; N = 2,780). Note that commodity-exporting countries experienced greater variance in their growth performance. Finally, oil exporters (OIL) grew at a faster rate, 4.78 (s.d. = 7.71; N = 413), than countries that did not export oil, 4.17 (s.d. = 6.09; N = 3,713), but the variance in growth rates was again higher among oil exporters.

Once we eliminate the years of wars and of post-war recoveries and the countries that export oil or other primary commodities, the variance in growth rates is reduced under both regimes. But it is still much larger, s.d. = 6.08, under dictatorships than under democracies, s.d. = 3.87. And the lists of miracles and disasters are still populated almost exclusively by dictatorships. Thus, looking at best practice is misleading: The tigers may be dictatorships, but dictatorships are no tigers.

Conclusion

The main conclusion of this analysis is that there is no trade-off between democracy and development, not even in poor countries. Although not a single study published before 1988 found that democracy promoted growth, and not one published after 1987 concluded in favor of dictatorships (Przeworski and Limongi 1993), there was never solid evidence that democracies were somehow inferior in generating growth – certainly not enough to justify supporting or even condoning dictatorships. We hope to have put the issue to rest. There is little difference in favor of dictatorships in the observed rates of growth. And even that difference vanishes once the conditions under which dictatorships and democracies existed are taken into account. Albeit in omniscient retrospect, the entire controversy seems to have been much ado about nothing.

Poverty appears to leave no room for politics. In countries with incomes below $3,000, the two regimes have almost identical investment shares, almost identical rates of growth of capital stock and of labor force, the same production function, the same contributions of capital, labor, and factor productivity to growth, the same output per worker, the same labor shares, and the same product wages. Poor countries invest little, get little benefit from total factor productivity, and pay low wages. And though a few countries have escaped this bond of poverty, most poor countries, have remained poor. Democracy is highly fragile in such countries, and thus most of them have dictatorial regimes. But regimes make no difference for growth, quantitatively or qualitatively.

Perhaps surprisingly, affluence differentiates regimes. Wealthier dictatorships invest a somewhat larger share of income, experience higher growth of the labor force, have higher capital and lower labor elasticities, derive more growth from capital input and less from labor input and from total factor productivity, have lower output per worker, have a lower labor share, and pay lower wages. Wealthier dictatorships grow by using a lot of labor and paying it little. Because they repress labor, they can pay it little; perhaps because they can pay it little, they care less how it is used. They pay more for capital – the average relative price of investment goods is higher under dictatorships – and they use it well. But because they rely on force to repress workers, they can pay lower wages and use labor inefficiently.

In the end, total output grows at the same rate under the two regimes, both in poor countries and in wealthier countries. But the reasons are different: In poor countries, regimes simply do not matter. In wealthier countries, their average growth rates are the same, but the patterns of growth are different.

Appendix 3.1: Identification, Specification, and Robustness

Regimes can affect growth by influencing either the growth of factors that enter into production or their utilization. But the effect of regimes can be identified only if there are some conditions that are exogenous with regard to regimes. Our general strategy, then, is to test repeatedly whether or not the variables that enter on the right-hand side of a growth equation are exogenous with regard to regimes, and, if they are not, to repeat the procedure with regard to these factors until the right-hand-side variables are all exogenous.

Because our purpose is to examine how political regimes affect economic growth, we need to develop first an understanding of its proximate causes. These causes are economic: Whereas political factors affect the decisions of governments and of private agents (households and firms) concerning the allocation of resources and the distribution of incomes, the performance of an economy results from these decisions. Hence, we look first for proximate causes of growth and then for the factors that in turn affect these proximate causes, both the supply of productive factors and their productivity.

To choose a growth model, we looked first for a specification that would best account for the variations in the observed growth rates in the entire sample, would make economic sense, and would not a priori favor one political regime over another.

There are many such models. The statistical literature explaining the growth of countries, via "growth regressions," is now voluminous, and new variables that matter are discovered almost every week. But it turns out that few are robust. Levine and Renelt (1992) employed virtually every variable that had previously been used in growth models. They also listed 40 cross-sectional growth studies published between 1980 and 1990. Only investment (in physical capital) and the initial level of income were always robust, in the Leamer (1983, 1985) sense. They discovered that the coefficients on other terms were fragile and were particularly sensitive to the factor of education. Because we do not want to prejudice the findings concerning regimes by our specification of the growth model, we are thus led to a minimalist approach, working with only those variables that are robust and testing for robustness by introducing additional variables.[24]

In the end, we use throughout what we call a "barebones" model: a simple production function of the form $Y = AF(K, L)$. To test robustness, we augment this production by some other variables, listed in Table A3.1.1. We do not use the initial level of income among the right-hand-side variables, because that practice strikes us as mindless if the model is estimated in growth form. If the income level affects the rate of growth, it must influence it via the return to factors. Hence, to test the effect of income, we estimate the production function separately for countries within different income bands (see Table 3.4), rather than attempting to "control" for it statistically.

We estimate the model in growth form to avoid problems due to autocorrelation of output levels over time.[25] With an apology to economists, we show how this growth form is derived.

---

[24] This approach is not without problems. See Temple (1999).

[25] An alternative would be to estimate the growth model in the form used by Mankiw, Romer, and Weil (1992), in which the rate of convergence can be inferred from the values of the coefficients. Both practical and theoretical considerations, however, speak against that approach. From the practical point of view, that approach requires averaging growth rates over some periods of time, whether decennia or quintennia, to avoid problems of autocorrelation. From the theoretical point of view, it is not apparent how to interpret the convergence coefficients (Quah 1993).

The theoretical point of departure in analyses of growth is the production function:

$$Y(t) = F(\cdot, \cdot, \cdot). \tag{1}$$

Particular models differ in specifying what productive factors enter into the parentheses and how.

The "barebones" model is (dropping time subscripts)

$$Y = AF(K, L), \tag{2}$$

where K is capital stock, and L is the labor force. Let F be the Cobb-Douglas function of the form

$$Y = AK^{\alpha}L^{\beta}. \tag{3}$$

Then all we need to do is take logarithms of both sides of (3), and then the derivatives of the logs with regard to time, to get

$$\dot{Y}/Y = \dot{A}/A + \alpha(\dot{K}/K) + \beta(\dot{L}/L),$$

where $AF_K(K/Y) = \alpha$ is the marginal elasticity of output with regard to capital, and $AF_L(L/Y) = \beta$ is the elasticity with regard to labor.

Both α and β have, therefore, theoretical interpretations, and we have expectations about the values of these numbers. If F is Cobb-Douglas, then in a competitive economy the elasticities equal the income shares, respectively, of capital and labor. The exact numbers are matters of some controversy. The World Bank (1991: 43) estimated the marginal elasticity of output with regard to capital to be 0.4 between 1960 and 1987. In perhaps the most careful study to date, Islam (1995) arrived at estimates slightly over 0.4 for a sample of 96 non-oil-producing countries. In turn, the World Bank (1991: 43) estimated β to be about 0.45. Our estimates of α and β are extremely robust, not affected by the presence of other variables. In the entire sample, the unconstrained estimate of α is 0.40, and of β a somewhat low 0.33. Constraining the elasticities to sum up to 1 does not change α and brings β to its complement to 1, that is, 0.60. Yet the constraint $\alpha + \beta = 1$ is almost always rejected by the F test. Adding human capital, which we do not introduce into our basic specification because the data are available for only a much smaller sample ($N = 2,787$), brings the values of α and β down somewhat, but the unconstrained elasticity with regard to human capital is very low and not statistically significant. When the sum of the three elasticities is constrained to 1 in OLS, the growth of human capital becomes significant, but it is still very small.

Our data set consists of annual observations. Contrary to frequent practice, we do not average these observations over some longer periods (decades, quintennia), a procedure typically used to smooth business-cycle effects. It may be a matter of dispute whether or not our coefficients on the labor input are always of a reasonable magnitude. But because we have to match economic performance with regime changes, and these occur on an annual basis, we must consider growth on the same basis. Averaging over time may smooth business-cycle effects, but we have seen too many regressions in which political characteristics have been said to have caused economic performance that occurred earlier.

To control for the omitted variables that are constant over time or over countries, whenever possible we have used panel methods. To consider the endogeneity of the right-hand-side variables, we also followed the suggestion of Temple (1999) to use their lagged values as instruments in panel analyses. Those results, however, turned out to yield nonsensical values for coefficients.

One specification issue is to what extent country-specific characteristics, rather than external shocks, determine growth rates. Easterly et al. (1993) observed that country growth rates were highly unstable over time, whereas country characteristics used to explain growth were much more stable. Hence, shocks, especially those to terms of trade, play a large role in explaining growth. Nevertheless, our finding that the entire 1950–1990 sample and various subsamples almost never pass tests for homogeneity goes against the Easterly et al. (1993) argument: We do find country-specific effects, and most of the time the Hausman test indicates that these are fixed effects. Nevertheless, as suggested by Easterly and associates, we modeled external shocks, taking as the independent variables the average rate of growth for the entire world during a particular year (WORLD) and the U.S. prime rate (PRIME). The latter variable never matters once WORLD is present in a specification, and we dropped it. As Table A3.1.1 shows, none of the results is affected by the presence of these additional variables.

Finally, the quality of the PWT data set is very uneven. Hence, one factor that may affect the results is biased reporting of data. We thus test robustness with regard to the rating of data quality, PPPQUAL.

Table A3.1.1 shows the effect of model specification on the selection-corrected values of growth under the two regimes. The results are perfectly robust: Whatever variable one introduces into the speci-

Table A3.1.1. Robustness

Variables: KSG, LFG, and:	Method	Dictatorships		Democracies	
		Mean	YGHAT	Mean	YGHAT
WORLD	2F	2.83	4.30	2.81	4.26
			$(4.87)^a$		(4.40)
OPENC	2F	47.73	4.28	55.17	4.25
			(4.87)		(4.31)
COMEX	OLS	0.40	4.30	0.21	4.24
			(5.02)		(4.48)
CPI	2F	20.80	4.31	46.92	4.22
			(4.46)		(4.08)
XR	2F	83.21	4.28	54.73	4.25
			(4.87)		(4.35)
PPPQUAL	OLS	2.27	4.32	6.60	4.25
			(5.04)		(4.45)

Notes: WORLD is the average rate of growth in the world during the particular year. OPENC is the sum of exports and imports as a proportion of GDP. COMEX is a dummy variable indicating that a country is a primary-commodity exporter. CPI is the rate of change in the consumer price index. XR is the nominal exchange rate (local currency to dollars). PPPQUAL is a rating of data quality (1 = worst, 10 = best).
^{a} Standard errors in parentheses.

fication of the growth equations, regimes do not affect the average growth rates. Note in particular that whereas the data quality (measured on a 1-to-10 scale) is much lower for dictatorships, which also tend to be much poorer, the quality of the data is not correlated with the reported growth rates and does not affect regime results.

The most difficult decision, and perhaps a dubious decision, we made in classifying regimes was to consider as dictatorships those countries that had regular and apparently free elections but in which the incumbents always won the elections (see Chapter 1, the "alternation" rule). Such countries grew at an exceptionally fast pace, 5.11 per annum ($N = 377$), as contrasted with the rate of 4.30 ($N = 2,104$) for other dictatorships, and 3.95 ($N = 1,645$) for democracies. To test the robustness of our conclusions with regard to this classification rule, we reclassified these cases as democracies and replicated our standard analysis. The results, presented in Table A3.1.2, show that this reclas-

Table A3.1.2. Selection-corrected estimators of the rate of growth of income (YG), under modified classification of regimes

Estimator (selection/YG)	Regime means	
	Dictatorships ($N = 2{,}030$)	Democracies ($N = 1{,}961$)
Biased	4.32	4.12
	(7.02)	(5.19)
Unconstrained OLS	4.13	4.30
	(4.97)	(4.73)
Constrained OLS	4.10	4.40
	(5.14)	(4.81)
PANEL	4.17	4.29
	(4.84)	(4.62)

sification does alter the results slightly in favor of democracy, but far from enough to undermine the conclusions.

Appendix 3.2: Estimating the Contribution of Public Investment

Assume now that output is produced in different ways by private capital stock, P, and government capital stock, S, with

$$P + S = K. \tag{1}$$

Let the production function be Cobb-Douglas:

$$Y = AP^{\alpha}S^{\tau}L^{\beta}. \tag{2}$$

Then (2) can be written in growth form as

$$\dot{Y}/Y = \dot{A}/A + \alpha(\dot{P}/P) + \tau(\dot{S}/S) + \beta(\dot{L}/L). \tag{3}$$

Our problem is that we do not know $\dot{P}$, P, and S.

Now let

$$\tau = \alpha X + \delta, \tag{4}$$

where X is such that

Appendix 3.2: Contribution of Public Investment

$$\dot{P}/P + (\dot{S}/S)X = \dot{K}/K = (\dot{P} + \dot{S})/(P + S),$$

or

$$X = (\dot{S}/S)(\dot{K}/K - \dot{P}/P). \tag{5}$$

Substituting (5) into (4) and then into (3) yields

$$\dot{Y}/Y = \dot{A}/A + \alpha(\dot{K}/K) + \tau(\dot{S}/S) + \beta(\dot{L}/L). \tag{6}$$

Because this expression still contains S, we multiply $\dot{S}/S$ by Y/Y to obtain

$$\dot{Y}/Y = \dot{A}/A + \alpha(\dot{K}/K) + \Omega(\dot{S}/Y) + \beta(\dot{L}/L), \tag{7}$$

where $\Omega = \delta(Y/S)$, and α is now the elasticity of output with regard to private capital stock.

We have all the data necessary to estimate (7), but the difficulties with this way of proceeding are that the coefficient Ω need not be a constant, and it does not have an obvious interpretation even if it is. Note from (4) that $\delta = \tau - \alpha X$, so that

$$\Omega = \delta(Y/S) = (\tau - \alpha X)(Y/S). \tag{8}$$

Given (3), τ is the elasticity $(dY/dS)(S/Y)$. Substituting (5) yields, therefore,

$$\Omega = dY/dS - \alpha(\dot{K}/K - \dot{P}/P)(Y/\dot{S}). \tag{9}$$

In a steady state in which $\dot{K}/K = \dot{P}/P = \dot{S}/S$, Ω is then the marginal product of government capital. If public capital stock rises faster than private, then the estimate of the marginal product is downward-biased; if private capital stock increases faster, the bias is upward.

Now, if Ω is a marginal product, then we would expect its value to fall in the stock of public capital. In fact, when we split the 1,366 available observations according to the values of total capital per worker, we observe it to increase (Table A3.2.1). The OLS estimates increase slowly, but the two-way fixed-effects estimates rise sharply. Therefore, either the marginal product of public capital in fact increases with total capital per worker or private capital grows faster than public capital in the more-developed countries.

Table A3.2.1. Coefficients (Ω) on public capital, by capital per worker

K/L	N	Ω OLS	2F	K/L	N	Ω OLS	2F
–1,000	259	4.13 (1.452)	1.12 (0.191)	1,001–	1,107	3.27 (1.113)	16.36 (3.291)
–2,000	347	2.41 (0.856)	1.54 (0.300)	2,001–	1,019	4.85 (1.559)	18.79 (3.569)
–3,000	415	2.83 (0.951)	3.48 (0.584)	3,001–	951	4.46 (1.391)	17.10 (3.227)
–4,000	499	2.76 (1.030)	8.03 (1.627)	4,001–	867	4.40 (1.181)	21.58 (3.311)
–5,000	565	3.19 (1.131)	8.16 (1.608)	5,001–	851	4.03 (1.045)	21.63 (3.267)
–6,000	600	3.09 (1.137)	7.84 (1.629)	6,001–	766	4.10 (0.988)	22.40 (3.260)
–7,000	640	2.42 (0.879)	6.92 (1.440)	7,001–	726	6.27 (1.509)	27.35 (3.721)
–8,000	669	3.17 (1.155)	7.83 (1.647)	8,001–	697	2.75 (0.638)	20.92 (2.783)

Note: All samples under the given values are homogeneous; hence the appropriate estimator is OLS. All samples above the given values are heterogeneous, and random effects are biased; hence the appropriate estimator is two-way (country and year) fixed effects.

Chapter Four

Political Instability and Economic Growth

Introduction

Not everyone will be surprised to learn that political regimes have no effect on average rates of economic growth. One generally held view, made influential by Huntington (1968), is that what matters for economic development is political stability, rather than the particular political institutions. Any system of political institutions promotes development as long as it maintains political order. The danger is "political instability."

We put "instability" in quotation marks because the concept is congenitally muddled. The functionalist sociology that dominated thinking about development during most of the post-war era was constitutionally incapable of conceptualizing social change in other than vaguely evolutionary terms. Under the influence of Parsons (1951), its theoretical program was to search for conditions of the "equilibrium," conceptualized in a *sui generis* way as "functional balance." Anything that disturbed this balance, any abrupt change, was seen as a "breakdown," a limiting category. As such, it could not be conceptualized any further. The conclusion was that things are stable when they do not change: "We may say that the political system is stable when the impact on the system and the environment are neutralized to the extent of keeping them from altering . . . the structure of the political system" (Ake 1967: 100–1).

When combined with an anti-communist ideology, the "structural-functional approach" turned "instability" into the central peril facing the "new nations." Instability became a specter, a harbinger of revolution. That ideological construction permeated even statistical research: The most frequently used index of "instability" blended routine forms of democratic activity (such as alternations in office, strikes, and peaceful demonstrations) with violent acts (such as coups, riots, and political assassinations).[1]

Given that history, we probably would do best to abandon the language of instability altogether. But given the grip of linguistic conventions, perhaps all we can do is to purge this term of its ideological connotations. To do this, we must begin by recognizing that not all political change constitutes "instability." Distinctions, therefore, are needed.

Political upheavals divert resources and energies away from production and thus affect the contemporaneous growth of the economy. War is most prominent among them, but one can expect that other events of historical importance, such as regime transitions, will have immediate economic repercussions. Even less momentous political events, such as changes of heads of governments, may entail short-term economic adjustments. Several studies have found that several other political events, "socio-political unrest," can reduce investment or economic growth.[2]

Whether or not past political upheavals affect the present tempo of development is already a more complex question, for it is by no means obvious how the past would affect the present. One mechanism may be that political disruptions retard the rate of accumulation of productive factors, whether physical or human capital, and thus their current stocks. Public infrastructure may have suffered from neglect due to political upheavals; successive waves of emigration may have driven

---

[1] In one of the first scales of that kind, Feierabend and Feierabend (1966) included resignations of cabinet officials, peaceful demonstrations, political assassinations, mass arrests, coups, and civil wars, assigning increasing weights to those events. Others considered turnovers of chief executives (Russett 1964: 101–4), executive transfers (Root and Ahmed 1979), and political strikes and riots (Schneider and Frey 1985). Cukierman, Edwards, and Tabellini (1992) lumped together riots, political executions, changes in the compositions of governments, unsuccessful coups and changes of governments, and durations of governments. Alesina and Perotti (1997) commingled changes of chief executives, changes in partisan control over governments, and changes of government composition not leading to the replacement of the chief executive, whether or not those changes were constitutional, and coups. For an early critique of such scales, see Hurwitz (1973).

[2] Trying to avoid business-cycle effects, cross-country studies of growth typically have averaged each country's observations over time and then analyzed regressions on the averages. To remove endogeneity, some of those studies have considered the reduced form of a simultaneous-equations model. Alesina and Perotti (1997), for example, have studied a model in which socio-political instability affects investment, which in turn affects instability. We are skeptical that their approach solves the problem of causality, because events that occurred later were still considered as having affected those that transpired earlier: A coup in 1983 entered as an independent variable for investment in 1973.

educated people abroad. Thus stocks of productive inputs may be lower in countries that have experienced frequent political changes in the past. Yet past stability may be a mixed blessing. At least with regard to democracies, Olson (1982) claimed that stable political institutions allow special interests to entrench their influence and to tear the economy apart with their distributional demands. Hence, the effect of past political events on the current rhythm of development is an open question.

Finally, a central claim of economic theory is that the behavior of strategic actors, whoever they may be, is oriented by their expectations. Hence, the question is whether or not anticipations of political changes, whether by the political rulers or by the potential investors, affect current economic outcomes. Faced with the prospect of losing power, those who make political decisions may engage in pillage, rather than pursue developmental policies that would enhance the welfare of their successors. But they may also react differently, trying to increase the welfare of their constituents so as to enhance their chances of surviving in power. Private investors, in turn, may react to prospective political changes by putting off their projects until the uncertainty resolves itself, or, if they can, they may invest elsewhere.

Thus, the present rate of economic growth may be affected by present, past, or anticipated political events. Within the limits of the available data, we examine these effects one by one.

Contemporaneous Political Upheavals

Moments of dramatic political change are economically costly. We examine in turn the effects of wars, regime transitions, changes of chief executives, and different forms of political unrest.

The ultimate form of political upheaval, war, was quite frequent during the period under our scrutiny.[3] In one out of fourteen years, countries suffered from war on their territory. As one would expect, wars hurt growth: Whereas the average rate of growth during peacetime was 4.39 percent (s.d. = 5.84; $N = 3,837$), during war years economies grew at 2.15 percent (s.d. = 10.15; $N = 289$). Wars devastated some economies, notably in Uganda after 1978, El Salvador, Nicaragua, and Peru in the late 1980s, and Iraq after 1978. Yet other wars had little economic effect: The standard deviation of growth rates

---

[3] Our WAR variable includes only the wars occurring on the territory of a country, but, in turn, it counts both foreign and civil wars. Hence, our conceptualization differs from that used in the "democratic peace" literature.

was almost twice as large during the war years. And recovery (RECOV-ERY) from wars was rapid: The average rate of growth during the five years following a war was 5.98 percent (s.d. = 6.63; N = 192), and during other years it was 4.15 (s.d. = 6.23; N = 3,934).[4]

Countries run by dictatorships were more likely to experience wars, which occurred once in twelve years, as contrasted with once in every twenty-one years under democracy. Moreover, wars caused more damage under dictatorships, where the rates of growth were 4.68 (s.d. = 6.66; N = 2,269) during peacetime and 1.68 (N = 212) during wars, than under democracies, where the economies grew at 3.97 (N = 1,568) during peacetime and at 3.46 (N = 77) during wars. In turn, recoveries were also faster under dictatorships than under democracies. Alto-gether, then, whereas under dictatorships wars brought economic disasters, over a longer run wars had little effect on economic growth.

Regime transitions are also economically costly. During the two years surrounding the eighty-nine transitions,[5] the rate of growth was, on the average, as low as 2.03 percent, but in other years it was 4.33 percent. Regime transitions are momentous events that absorb atten-tions and energies, cause some people to drastically change their lives, and often are shrouded by extreme uncertainty. Hence, it is not sur-prising that economies stagnate during the moments of transition. Moreover, the share of investment in GDP was 3 percent lower during the years of transition: 14.01 percent, as contrasted with 17.01 at other times. Capital stock grew at a rate of 6.09 percent during transitions and at 7.04 during other periods.

Although wars and regime transitions are both accompanied by eco-nomic crises, not all political change constitutes "instability." The ide-ological connotations of this concept become most apparent when we think of alternations of heads of governments. Changes of chief ex-ecutives (HEADS) are just part of the normal life of democracy, out-comes of a process that is rule-governed, repeated, and expected. Indeed, we have seen in Chapter 2 that regular alternations in office extend the lives of democratic regimes. In turn, changes of heads of governments under dictatorships are, albeit with some exceptions,[6]

---

[4] Referring to the examples of Japan and Germany in the aftermath of World War II, Barro and Sala-i-Martin (1995: 176) sought to explain the rapid post-war recoveries, arguing that whenever a war destroyed only one productive factor, the rate of return to other factor(s) becomes larger, thus spurring rapid growth.

[5] These two years are the last full year of the previous regime and the year during which the transition occurred.

[6] Principally Mexico, plus brief periods in Bolivia, Brazil, and El Salvador.

sporadic, unruly, and often violent episodes. Death is often the only way out of office for dictators.[7] And any change of the dictator threatens the survival of the dictatorship.

Numbers concerning the frequency of changes of heads of governments are eloquent. The chief executive changed once in about nine years under dictatorship, and once in about four under democracy. The half-life of a dictator was 8.45 years; the half-life of a democratic chief executive was 3.96 years. One-fourth of dictators survived in power at least 16.90 years; three-fourth of democratic rulers were gone after 7.93 years. Indeed, seven dictators in our sample ruled continuously for at least thirty-five years; only two democratic chief executives stayed in office nineteen years, and only one, Tage Erlander in Sweden, twenty-three years.

As we would expect, turnover of democratic chief executives, though much more frequent, has almost no impact on the rate of growth of income nor on the investment share. The democratic economies grew at the rate of 4.03 percent and invested 20.6 percent of GDP during the 1,188 years in which no change in chief executive occurred and grew at 3.92 percent, while investing 21.6 percent, during 345 years when the chief executive changed once. Only when changes of government heads were more frequent (two changes occurred in forty-nine years, three in six years, and four in one year) did the economy slow down to 3.37 percent, even though investment share remained at 21.8 percent. Under dictatorship, in turn, any change of head of government wreaks havoc. Whereas dictatorships grew at the rate of 4.64 and invested 14.2 percent during the 2,198 years when a dictator remained in power, growth fell to 3.29, with investment at 14.4 percent, during the 223 years when just one change occurred, and to 0.95, with investment falling to 12.9 percent, during the years when power changed more than once (twice in forty-two years, thrice in seven years, and five times in one year).[8]

---

[7] Thirty-nine out of 351 dictators, or 11.1 percent, died while in office, as contrasted with 25 out of 441, or 5.7 percent, leaders of democratic governments. Dictators are particularly vulnerable to being airborne: Bartholomy Boganda in the Central African Republic in 1959, Abdel Salam Muhammad Aref in Iraq in 1966, René Barrientos in Bolivia in 1969, Omar Torrijos, who was the *éminence grise* in Panama, in 1981, Samora Machel in Mozambique in 1986, and Muhammed Zia ul-Haq in Pakistan in 1988 all died under such circumstances.

[8] These findings are consistent with the results of Alesina, Özler, Roubini, and Swagel (1996), who distinguished among coups and "major" and "regular" government changes, to discover that growth is affected by the first two, but not by routine government alternations.

Table 4.1. Selection-corrected effects of socio-political unrest on growth

Variable	Dictatorships	Democracies
N	2,341	1,552
Method	OLS	2F
STRIKES		
Mean	0.09	0.24
Coefficient	−0.2308	−0.1182
(Standard error)	(0.1694)	(0.1302)
RIOTS		
Mean	0.51	0.78
Coefficient	−0.1518	−0.0194
(Standard error)	(0.0462)	(0.0349)
DEMONSTRATIONS		
Mean	0.49	0.88
Coefficient	−0.1443	−0.0123
(Standard error)	(0.0500)	(0.0349)
UNREST		
Mean	1.08	1.90
Coefficient	−0.0842	−0.0114
(Standard error)	(0.0248)	(0.0180)
Predicted growth	4.33	4.29
(Standard error)	(5.10)	(4.38)
Cost of unrest	−0.1166	−0.0158
(Standard error)	(0.3600)	(0.0487)

Notes: UNREST is the sum of STRIKES, DEMONSTRATIONS, and RIOTS. *F* tests always indicate OLS for dictatorships and two-way fixed effects for democracies. The selection model is based on lagged per capita income (LEVLAG), lagged sum of past transitions to dictatorship (STRAL), and an index of religious fractionalization (RELDIF). The growth model includes the growth of capital stock (KSG), growth of the labor force (LFG), and the respective UNREST variables.

Finally, "socio-political unrest" (UNREST),[9] though more frequent under democracy, affects growth only under dictatorship (Table 4.1). If strikes, anti-government demonstrations, and riots are considered as constituting "instability," dictatorships are much more "stable" than

---

[9] UNREST is nothing else but what was called MOBILIZATION in Chapter 2, namely, the sum of general strikes (STRIKES), anti-government demonstrations (AGDEMONS), and riots (RIOTS). The very terminology reveals the ideological assumptions: What is seen

democracies: Strikes are almost three times as frequent in the latter, and demonstrations and riots almost twice as frequent. Yet they reduce growth only in dictatorships; democracies somehow live with "unrest" without any economic consequences. When the frequencies of these phenomena are added together, to form an index of "unrest," the effect on growth under dictatorships is almost eight times larger than under democracies, and even though unrest is half as frequent under dictatorships, its cost in terms of growth is more than seven times greater.

Hence, political upheavals affect contemporaneous economic performance, and they are endogenous to the two political regimes and, in turn, affect them differently. Wars are more frequent and more devastating under dictatorships, which also recover faster from the destruction they cause. Regime transitions are accompanied by economic crises that are deep but also short-lived. Although more frequent, alternation in office has little effect on economic performance under democracy, but it throws dictatorships into economic disarray. Finally, again more frequent under democracy, strikes, demonstrations, and even riots have no effect on their economies, whereas they are economically costly under dictatorships.

Past Instability

Past political upheavals may affect present economic performance by slowing the accumulation of stocks of productive inputs. We first examine the impact of the past on the present by studying the effects of the number of past regime transitions (STTR = STRA + STRD)[10] and of the number of changes of chief executives during the life of a regime (ACCHEAD).

Past regime transitions were found to have no visible effect on current growth rates except for the few cases in which a country had experienced more than four regime changes in its past. As Table 4.2 shows, the average growth rate among the 2,884 instances in which a country had experienced no regime transition in the past was more or less the same as in the 1,171 cases in which the number of past

---

as "mobilization" in the literature on transitions to democracy becomes "unrest" in the literature on political instability. We follow these usages to better relate our findings to the respective bodies of literature.

[10] Remember that to discount somewhat the effect of the distant past, we code any number of regime transitions before 1950 as one.

Table 4.2. Growth of income (YG), by the number of past regime transitions (STTR) and the current regime (REG)

| | Average growth rate | | | | | |
| | All | | Dictatorships | | Democracies | |
Number of past Transitions	YG	N	YG	N	YG	N
0	4.20	2,884	4.36	1,858	3.90	1,026
1	4.63	660	4.80	363	4.42	297
2	4.43	321	5.60	117	3.76	204
3	3.86	142	3.84	89	3.90	53
4	4.43	48	3.71	21	4.98	27
5	2.39	30	1.93	18	3.09	12
6	2.14	22	3.69	7	1.42	15
7	2.19	4	−0.54	1	3.10	3
8	0.38	7	0.38	7	—	0
9	−0.45	8	—	0	−0.45	8

transitions ranged from one to four.[11] Only in the seventy-one cases in which the past was exceptionally stormy was growth slower.[12] This pattern holds for both regimes.[13]

Past changes of chief executives during the life of a particular regime again appear to matter only in those cases in which government instability was exceptionally high (Table 4.3). The rate of growth among the regimes that experienced one to five changes of government heads in the past, 4.28 percent, was almost the same as that among those governed by the founding ruler, 4.54. Only when the number of past changes was greater than five did growth slow down, and, again, that effect was more pronounced for the dictatorships. When introduced

[11] Note that studies that average over time and analyze relationships among those averages lump together past and future instability. If we were to proceed in that fashion, we would want to know the average rates of economic growth of countries distinguished by the number of regime transitions during the entire period 1950–1990. The result would be the same: Only extreme instability, six or more regime changes, was associated with lower growth rates.

[12] These cases include two years in Sudan, nine each in Guatemala and Honduras, twenty-three years in Peru, and twenty-eight in Argentina.

[13] When introduced into our basic growth model, past regime transitions have no impact on current growth rates, whether in OLS or in fixed-effects panels.

Table 4.3A. Growth of income (YG), by the number of past changes of chief executives (HEADS) and the current regime (REG)

Number of past changes of heads	All		Dictatorships		Democracies	
	YG	N	YG	N	YG	N
0	4.54	1,473	4.59	1,114	4.38	359
1–5	4.28	2,068	4.44	1,246	4.02	822
>5	3.41	534	3.05	110	3.50	424

Table 4.3B. Growth of income (YG), by the frequency of past changes of chief executives (TURNOVER) and the current regime (REG)

Turnover	Frequency of changes	All		Dictatorships		Democracies	
		YG	N	YG	N	YG	N
≤0.1	>10 years	4.44	2,010	4.46	1,580	4.33	430
0.1–0.33	3–10 years	3.84	1,433	4.19	654	3.54	779
>0.33	<3 years	4.64	632	5.06	236	4.40	396

into (as always, selection-corrected) regression analysis, past changes of heads play no role whatsoever under either regime, regardless how one estimates the model. Even a dummy variable for more changes than five is statistically irrelevant.

Because we are considering the numbers of changes of heads of government during the life of each regime, and because regimes differ in their longevity, another way to consider the past changes is to measure the frequency of such changes relative to the age of the regime (TURNOVER). An eye inspection of the data indicates that growth is slower under both regimes when the accumulated frequency of changes is between 0.1 and 0.33, meaning that heads of government change every ten to three years. Regimes in which chief executives change less or more frequently grow faster. Yet, again, turnover of heads proves to be irrelevant in statistical analyses, even when we introduce a non-linear effect.

All that one can conclude is that past instability, whether of regimes or of heads of governments, has no effect on present rates of growth, perhaps unless the instability is extreme. Although contemporaneous political upheavals do retard, somewhat, accumulation of the physical capital stock (and perhaps also of human capital stock, which we have not studied), these effects must wane as time passes. One plausible explanation is that investment is simply postponed until things quiet down and then implemented at levels that compensate for the waiting. Remember that even the effects of wars do not linger for a long time.

Our findings are thus consistent with those of Londregan and Poole (1990), but go against the results of Alesina and Perotti (1997). The former find that poverty increases the probability of coups and that once a coup occurs, future coups are more likely, and yet coups do not affect growth. Hence, Londregan and Poole speak of a "coup trap." The latter authors also find that past instability propagates instability, but claim that past instability retards growth: Hence Alesina and Perotti find a "poverty trap." We find that past regime transitions and past turnover of chief executives increase the probability that such changes will occur again, but that they do not affect growth. Hence, ours is an "instability" but not a "poverty" trap.

What, then, of the rival hypothesis, due to Olson (1982), namely, that long-lasting democratic regimes ossify interest-group influence, thus increasing pressures for distribution at the cost of development? If that hypothesis is true, then the age of the regime (AGER), a proxy for interest-group influence, should have a negative effect on growth (Table 4.4).

Although several studies, as summarized by Mueller (1989: chap. 16), have contended that older democracies grow slower, we do not find such an effect. When we replicate those studies, considering, as they do, only democracies in the OECD countries, we find that the coefficient on regime age is -0.0095, with a t value of -3.409, highly significant. In the full sample, however, the effect of regime age vanishes. We think that the reason for this discrepancy is the following: It is by now generally accepted that among the developed countries the rate of growth tends to decline in per capita income. In turn, as democracies in these countries become older, they also have higher income levels. Hence, the convergence effect is mistaken for the effect of regime

---

Table 4.4. Effect of regime age (AGER) on the growth of income (YG); selection-corrected panel estimates

---

Dictatorships: OLS estimates

OLS without group dummy variables
Ordinary least-squares regression: weighting variable = ONE; dependent variable Y; mean = 4.42613; s.d. = 6.9409
Model size: observations = 2,396; parameters = 5; degrees of freedom (d.f.) = 2,391
Residuals: sum of squares = 40,480.7; standard deviation = 4.11466
Fit: R^2 = 0.64916; adjusted R^2 = 0.64857
Model test: $F(4, 2,391)$ = 1,106.00; probability value = 0.00000
Diagnostic: log-likelihood = −6,786.5524; restricted (β = 0) log-likelihood = −8,041.3516; Amemiya probability criterion = 16.966; Akaike information criterion = 5.669

Panel data analysis of Y (one-way): unconditional ANOVA (no regressors)

Source	Variation	Degrees of freedom	Mean square
Between	9,728.20	100	97.2820
Residual	105,652	2,295	46.0359
Total	115,381	2,395	48.1757

Variable	Coefficient	Standard error (s.e.)	$z = b$/s.e.	$P[\|Z\| \geq z]$	Mean of X
λ	−1.161860	0.33903	−3.427	0.00061	0.7599E-01
KSG	0.4002971	0.60358E-02	66.320	0.00000	7.236
LFG	0.3113418	0.43562E-01	7.147	0.00000	2.284
AGER	−0.2594649E-02	0.24524E-02	−1.058	0.29006	33.80
Constant	0.9945064	0.17062	5.829	0.00000	

Test statistics for the classical model

Model	Log-likelihood	Sum of squares	R^2
(1) Constant term only	−8,041.35156	0.115381E+06	0.0000000
(2) Group effects only	−7,935.82966	0.105652E+06	0.0843140
(3) X variables only	−6,786.55239	0.404807E+05	0.6491553
(4) X and group effects	−6,755.64571	0.394497E+05	0.6580909
(5) X individual and time effects	−6,723.90605	0.384183E+05	0.6670304

(continued)

Table 4.4 (continued)

	Hypothesis tests						
	Likelihood ratio test			*F* tests			
Comparison	Chi-squared	d.f.	Prob. value	*F*	Num.	Denom.	Prob. value
(2) vs. (1)	211.044	100	0.00000	2.113	100	2,295	0.00000
(3) vs. (1)	2,509.598	4	0.00000	1,105.995	4	2,391	0.00000
(4) vs. (1)	2,571.412	104	0.00000	31.255	104	2,291	0.00000
(4) vs. (2)	2,360.368	4	0.00000	976.139	4	2,291	0.00000
(4) vs. (3)	61.813	100	0.99860	0.599	100	2,291	0.99940
(5) vs. (4)	63.479	38	0.00589	1.592	38	2,253	0.01251
(5) vs. (3)	125.293	139	0.79201	0.870	139	2,253	0.85678

Democracies: two-way (country and year) fixed-effects estimates

Least squares with group dummy variables and period effects

Ordinary least-squares regression: weighting variable = ONE; dependent variable Y; mean = 3.91555; s.d. = 4.8232

Model size: observations = 1,595; parameters = 115; degrees of freedom (d.f.) = 1,480

Residuals: sum of squares = 14,350.0; standard deviation = 3.11383

Fit: R^2 = 0.61276; adjusted R^2 = 0.58293

Model test: $F(114, 1,480)$ = 20.54; probability value = 0.00000

Diagnostic: log-likelihood = $-4,015.2140$; restricted ($\beta = 0$) log-likelihood = $-4,772.3475$; Amemiya probability criterion = 10.395; Akaike information criterion = 5.179

Estimated autocorrelation of $e(i, t)$: 0.059719

Variable	Coefficient	Standard error (s.e.)	$z = b$/s.e.	$P[|Z| \geq z]$	Mean of X
λ	$-0.4256338E-01$	0.24952	-0.171	0.86455	-0.1141
KSG	0.3448888	0.85873E-02	40.162	0.00000	6.489
LFG	0.4015232	0.11343	3.540	0.00040	1.595
AGER	0.9236399E-02	0.15375E-01	0.601	0.54802	36.33
Constant	0.6969873	0.61231	1.138	0.25500	

Test statistics for the classical model

Model	Log-likelihood	Sum of squares	R^2
(1) Constant term only	$-4,772.34752$	0.370820E+05	0.0000000
(2) Group effects only	$-4,686.83567$	0.333116E+05	0.1016764
(3) X variables only	$-4,126.84596$	0.165060E+05	0.5548778
(4) X and group effects	$-4,079.73793$	0.155593E+05	0.5804095
(5) X individual and time effects	$-4,015.75267$	0.143597E+05	0.6127591

(continued)

Table 4.4 (continued)

	Hypothesis tests						
	Likelihood ratio test			F tests			
Comparison	Chi-squared	d.f.	Prob. value	F	Num.	Denom.	Prob.value
(2) vs. (1)	171.024	71	0.00000	2.428	71	1,523	0.00000
(3) vs. (1)	1,291.003	4	0.00000	495.513	4	1,590	0.00000
(4) vs. (1)	1,385.219	75	0.00000	19.459	75	1,519	0.00000
(4) vs. (2)	1,214.195	4	0.00000	462.555	4	1,519	0.00000
(4) vs. (3)	94.216	71	0.03411	1.302	71	1,519	0.04942
(5) vs. (4)	127.971	38	0.00000	3.256	38	1,481	0.00000
(5) vs. (3)	222.187	110	0.00000	2.012	110	1,481	0.00000

Selection-corrected predicted values of YG

Variable	**Mean**	**s.d.**	**Cases**
Dictatorships	4.3283	4.8856	3,991
Democracies	4.2176	4.3353	3,991

age. Once convergence is removed, by including democracies in less-developed countries, the impact of regime age vanishes.[14]

Finally, given what we already know about the effect of past changes of chief executives, unsurprisingly we find that the duration of tenure of a particular head of government (AGEH) has no impact on the current rate of growth under either regime.

To summarize again, past instability, whether of regimes or of governments, does not matter for economic growth one way or another. Although we found some descriptive indications that extremely frequent changes of regimes may reduce growth, statistical analyses lead to the conclusion that growth of the economy is not affected by past regime changes, nor past government changes, nor the age of the current regime, nor the length of tenure of the current chief executive.

---

[14] Our confidence in this interpretation is somewhat mitigated by the finding that once the fixed country and year effects are considered (and they are indicated by the F test), the effect of per capita income on the rate of growth turns out to be positive, even when the sample is limited to countries with incomes above $3,000. Unfortunately, regime age and per capita income are highly correlated (0.76), and we could not find an instrument for LEVEL that would not be correlated with AGER.

Expectations

Unless effects of the past cumulate or unless the past is used to forecast the future, there is no reason that past instability should affect current economic performance. Political and economic actors make decisions looking ahead, not behind. What matters for their decisions are the consequences their actions will generate. And this means that these decisions are based on beliefs about the future, expectations.

But how can we determine what people expect? Note that the fact that past instability does not affect current performance implies that the relevant actors do not extrapolate the past into the future.[15] How, then, do they form expectations? Our strategy is to assume that they know all that we can learn from studying the observable patterns, and probably much more. We have observed, for example, that democracies survive unconditionally in wealthy countries, and we impute the same belief to the protagonists. We have learned through statistical analyses that past turnover of heads of governments makes it less likely that the current chief executive will survive long in office: Again, we impute this belief to the actors. Undoubtedly, agents' expectations are also based on factors we cannot observe, so that they are much more refined than our imputations. Nevertheless, if we can predict with reasonable accuracy whether or not regimes or heads of governments will survive the current year, we have at least some basis on which to impute expectations to the actors.

Because earlier we subjected regime stability to extensive analysis, we can base our imputations of expectations concerning regime survival on those findings. Using the dynamic probit model, described in Chapter 2, we calculate the probability that a regime will not survive the current year, conditional only on variables independent of anyone's actions.[16] The probability that a democracy will not survive the current year is PDA, and that for a dictatorship is PAD.

To construct expectations concerning the survival in power of heads of governments, we proceed in a similar manner. We estimate

---

[15] Clague, Keefer, Knack, and Olson (1997: 102) take the past duration of a regime as the proxy for the expectation of its life. Yet we know from Chapter 2 that, conditioned on per capita income, hazard rates for democracies are constant with regard to regime age, whereas for dictatorships they increase somewhat in duration. Hence, this is not a good proxy.

[16] They are (lagged one year whenever appropriate): the sum of past regime transitions (STTR), the proportion of other democracies in the region (ODRP), the index of religious fractionalization (RELDIF), the proportion of Moslems (MOSLEM), a dummy for post-colonial status (NEWC), and a dummy for the OECD countries.

(fixed-effects panel) regressions in which the dependent variable is the number of changes of chief executives during a particular year (HEADS) and calculate the predicted probability that a change of a chief executive will occur during this year (HEADHAZ). Note again that all the predetermined variables are exogenous with regard to economic performance and that they are all different from those used to determine regime transition probabilities.[17]

To assess the impact of expectations on current economic growth, we study a model in which probabilities predicted for the next year are assumed to affect the behavior of the economy this year. Hence, the statistical model is

$$\dot{Y}(t)/Y(t) = A/A + \alpha \dot{K}(t)/K(t) + \beta \dot{L}(t)/L(t) + \gamma HAZ(t+1) + \Theta\lambda(t) + e(t),$$

where HAZ stands either for the probability of regime transitions (EXPPDA, EXPPAD) or for the probability of changes of chief executives (EXPHAZH), and all other variables are the same as in Chapter 3.[18]

Here is the intuition. Political and economic actors in a particular country make decisions at t anticipating the likelihood that, given the conditions independent of their actions, the regime and/or the current head of government will survive or fall at $t + 1$. Given exogenous conditions at t, rulers – whoever makes public policy – face the choice between engaging in pillage and running away or making every effort to enhance the welfare of the relevant political actors so as to survive in power. When rulers face a high exogenous probability that they will be forced out of power or that the regime will collapse, they will extract all they can: At least that is the general line of the economic analyses of the predatory state (Olson 1993, 1997; McGuire and Olson 1996). In turn, when the exogenous probability of survival is high, rulers may be better off extracting low rents and maximizing their chances of remaining in power. Hence, the empirical hypothesis is that insecure

[17] They include the degree to which the military influences politics (CIVMIL), lagged past turnover of heads of governments (TLAG), and two dummy variables indicating whether or not either legislative or presidential elections took place this year (LEGELEC, PRE-SELEC).

[18] Though adding a correction for regime selection, this approach follows Londregan and Poole (1990, 1992), as well as Cukierman et al. (1992) and Alesina et al. (1996). Note that the PAD and PDA variables measure the probability of a regime dying during the next year given the conditions this year, and the instrument for regime selection, LAMBDA, is the marginal probability that the regime would have been different this year had the present conditions been slightly different. Hence, these variables are independent, and in fact uncorrelated.

rulers, those with a high probability of being forced out of office, will generate bad economic performance. We should thus observe that the higher the hazards facing the regime and the head of government, the lower should be the rate of growth.

Table 4.5 presents results of statistical analyses that include both regime and head hazards (the results are the same when these two threats are considered separately). Threats to regimes have no effect

---

Table 4.5. Effects of expected hazards to regime (EXPHAZR) and to heads of governments (EXPHAZH) on the growth of income (YG); selection-corrected two-way (country and year) fixed-effects estimates

Dictatorships: OLS estimates

OLS without group dummy variables

Ordinary least-squares regression: weighting variable = ONE; dependent variable Y; mean = 4.50829; s.d. = 6.9608

Model size: observations = 2,312; parameters = 6; degrees of freedom (d.f.) = 2,306

Residuals: sum of squares = 39,722.4; standard deviation = 4.15038

Fit: R^2 = 0.64526; adjusted R^2 = 0.64449

Model test: $F(5, 2,306)$ = 838.89; probability value = 0.00000

Diagnostic: log-likelihood = −6,568.0204; restricted (β = 0) log-likelihood = −7,766.0517; Amemiya probability criterion = 17.270; Akaike information criterion = 5.687

Panel data analysis of Y (one-way): unconditional ANOVA (no regressors)

Source	Variation	Degrees of freedom	Mean square
Between	9,672.29	100	96.7229
Residual	102,302	2,211	46.2698
Total	111,975	2,311	48.4530

Variable	Coefficient	Standard error (s.e.)	$z = b$/s.e.	$P[|Z| \geq z]$	Mean of X
λ	−0.9847312	0.36536	−2.695	0.00703	0.7450E-01
KSG	0.3987071	0.61948E-02	64.361	0.00000	7.416
LFG	0.3074352	0.46609E-01	6.596	0.00000	2.267
EXPHAZH	−1.398653	0.53845	−2.598	0.00939	0.1456
EXPPAD	−0.9620452	2.7833	−0.346	0.72961	0.2271E-01
Constant	1.153648	0.16993	6.789	0.00000	

(continued)

Table 4.5 (continued)

Test statistics for the classical model

Model	Log-likelihood	Sum of squares	R^2
(1) Constant term only	−7,766.05163	0.111975E+06	0.0000000
(2) Group effects only	−7,661.61895	0.102302E+06	0.0863792
(3) X variables only	−6,568.02038	0.397224E+05	0.6452561
(4) X and group effects	−6,534.99719	0.386037E+05	0.6552466
(5) X individual and time effects	−6,506.03398	0.376485E+05	0.6637770

	Hypothesis tests						
	Likelihood ratio test			F tests			
Comparison	Chi-squared	d.f.	Prob. value	F	Num.	Denom.	Prob. value
(2) vs. (1)	208.865	100	0.00000	2.090	100	2,211	0.00000
(3) vs. (1)	2,396.063	5	0.00000	838.893	5	2,306	0.00000
(4) vs. (1)	2,462.109	105	0.00000	29.702	105	2,206	0.00000
(4) vs. (2)	2,253.244	5	0.00000	738.928	5	2,206	0.00000
(4) vs. (3)	66.046	100	0.99552	0.639	100	2,206	0.99779
(5) vs. (4)	57.926	37	0.01546	1.487	37	2,169	0.03001
(5) vs. (3)	123.973	138	0.79866	0.866	138	2,169	0.86427

Democracies: two-way (country and year) fixed-effects estimates

Least squares with group dummy variables and period effects

Ordinary least-squares regression: weighting variable = ONE; dependent variable Y; mean = 4.04603; s.d. = 4.7533

Model size: observations = 1,482; parameters = 111; degrees of freedom (d.f.) = 1,371

Residuals: sum of squares = 13,268.4; standard deviation = 3.11093

Fit: R^2 = 0.60318; adjusted R^2 = 0.57134

Model test: $F(110, 1,371)$ = 18.94; probability value = 0.00000

Diagnostic: log-likelihood = −3,727.1336; restricted (β = 0) log-likelihood = −4,412.5516; Amemiya probability criterion = 10.403; Akaike information criterion = 5.180

Estimated autocorrelation of $e(i, t)$: 0.064337

(continued)

Table 4.5 (continued)

Variable	Coefficient	Standard error (s.e.)	$z = b$/s.e.	$P[|Z| \geq z]$	Mean of X
λ	−0.8218807E-02	0.25353	−0.032	0.97414	−0.1162
KSG	0.3407804	0.89056E-02	38.266	0.00000	6.698
LFG	0.4057808	0.12025	3.374	0.00074	1.605
EXPHAZH	0.2288663E-01	0.40964	0.056	0.95545	0.2859
EXPPDA	7.133481	8.7859	0.812	0.41683	0.2423E-01
Constant	0.9317520	0.33272	2.800	0.00510	

Test statistics for the classical model

Model	Log-likelihood	Sum of squares	R^2
(1) Constant term only	−4,412.55157	0.334608E+05	0.0000000
(2) Group effects only	−4,341.49816	0.304014E+05	0.0914347
(3) X variables only	−3,821.90677	0.150787E+05	0.5493623
(4) X and group effects	−3,787.81487	0.144007E+05	0.5696255
(5) X individual and time effects	−3,727.67390	0.132781E+05	0.6031756

	Hypothesis tests						
	Likelihood ratio test			F tests			
Comparison	Chi-squared	d.f.	Prob. value	F	Num.	Denom.	Prob. value
(2) vs. (1)	142.107	67	0.00000	2.124	67	1,414	0.00000
(3) vs. (1)	1,181.290	5	0.00000	359.872	5	1,476	0.00000
(4) vs. (1)	1,249.473	72	0.00000	17.952	72	1,409	0.00000
(4) vs. (2)	1,107.367	5	0.00000	335.077	5	1,409	0.00000
(4) vs. (3)	68.184	67	0.43675	0.990	67	1,409	0.50093
(5) vs. (4)	120.282	37	0.00000	3.135	37	1,372	0.00000
(5) vs. (3)	188.466	105	0.00000	1.772	105	1,372	0.00001

on the rate of growth under either regime. But threats to dictators cause economic performance to deteriorate, whereas similar threats to democratic chief executives have no effect whatsoever. Even though changes of chief executives are relatively infrequent in dictatorships, the average cost of dictators' insecurity is to lower the annual growth rate by 0.20, but under democracies this cost is zero.[19]

We cannot tell whether this difference is due to the institutional constraints or to motivations of rulers. One could think that both dictators and heads of democratic governments would have predatory motivations – they seek to extract rents – but dictators have more influence over the economy than do individual democratic rulers, who are constrained by various checks and balances. Democratic rulers can manipulate the economy somewhat – at least some studies have found evidence for electoral business cycles (for a review, see Alesina 1995) – but the institutional constraints are severe.

Yet it is also conceivable that public officials in democracies are more likely to be public-spirited, motivated to selflessly serve their countries. Motivations of political rulers have an endogenous component as well as an exogenous component. People who want to become wealthy do not seek office under democracy, because holding democratically elected office is not the best way to get rich. A Somoza or a Marcos could not stash billions in Swiss banks under democracy: They would have been thrown out of office or would have ended up in jail or both. Hence, one could expect that the accountability mechanisms characteristic of each regime separate the types of people who seek power. The accountability mechanism is a menu of contracts that specify sanctions (jail, out of office, in office) depending on outcomes (theft, bad but legal performance, good performance). Hence, only people for whom the particular contracts are incentive-compatible will take them. True, as always when information is asymmetric, rents are unavoidable. But some people who would accept a contract "in office whatever" would not accept one saying "in office only if rents are low." Thus, even if the distribution of motivations is the same in all countries, the recruitment of types to power is endogenous with regard to political regimes.

Yet, whatever the source of the difference between regimes, the fact is that institutions matter: Threats to dictators produce the effect that is generally expected, that of "instability," but similar threats to democratic rulers do nothing of the sort.

The effect of expected political changes on investment is a more complicated topic, even if typically awash in banalities.[20] Most students

[19] The average cost of insecurity is the product of the average incidence of unrest and its regression coefficient on growth.

[20] Eager to demonstrate that political instability reduces investment, several studies have proceeded as if only the variance and not the expected return determined the optimal rate of investment. Yet, if investment is reversible or if it cannot be delayed, then the

of political instability believe that it reduces investment. Indeed, the typical chain of reasoning proceeds from political instability (sometimes seeing instability as caused in turn by income inequality) to investment and only then to growth: The effect of instability on growth is seen as being mediated by its effect on investment. The ritualistically repeated claim is that political instability threatens the security of property rights, inducing uncertainty, which in turn reduces investment.

Without additional distinctions, that story makes little sense. Consider expectations that the political leader may change. Investors may expect that when the head of government changes, so may policy: Hence, expectations of a change of chief executive would induce uncertainty among investors. They may also expect that insecure rulers are more likely to engage in pillage. If investment entails fixed costs, uncertainty may cause investors to postpone their projects until it resolves itself or, if they can, to reallocate them elsewhere. But the fear of increased rent extraction by the ruler is more likely to affect the utilization of the already installed capacity than to affect investment: A ruler who is about to grab all he can and run away will not take with him a newly constructed building or a newly purchased machine, but rather the output from the already installed factories. Hence, the fear of pillage by an outgoing ruler should lead private actors to reduce production, not investment. Indeed, diverting resources to investment may be a way of protecting one's liquid resources. This is why we find that where rulers can pillage – and this is true only of dictatorships – the rate of growth of output does fall. But because uncertainty and fear of confiscation may work in opposite directions, the effect on investment of expectations that dictators will change cannot be foretold. And, indeed, we learn that threats to chief executives have no effect on investment under either regime (Table 4.6).

Threats to regimes are different matters. What one would expect about their effect on investment would depend on what one thinks of the impact of political regimes on the security of property rights: a topic shrouded in ideologically motivated confusion. One recently popular argument is that democracies safeguard property rights. North was

amount of optimal investment will depend only on the expected rates of return. If investment is irreversible (i.e., assets can be sold only at a price different from that at which they were purchased) and if it can be postponed, the amount of optimal investment will decline as the value of waiting (which in turn increases in uncertainty) becomes greater. Yet even if optimal investment declines under most circumstances as uncertainty increases, it still does increase in the expected return. See Pindyck (1991).

Table 4.6. Effects of expected hazards to regime (EXPHAZR) and to heads of governments (EXPHAZH) on the share of investent in GDP (INV); selection-corrected, AR1, one-way (country) fixed-effects estimates

Dictatorships

Least squares with group dummy variables
Ordinary least-squares regression: weighting variable = ONE; dependent variable Y; mean = 4.53340; s.d. = 3.7121
Model size: observations = 2,211; parameters = 108; degrees of freedom (d.f.) = 2,103
Residuals: sum of squares = 15,023.2; standard deviation = 2.67277
Fit: R^2 = 0.50667; adjusted R^2 = 0.48157
Model test: $F(107, 2,103)$ = 20.19; probability value = 0.00000
Diagnostic: log-likelihood = −5,255.5781; restricted (β = 0) log-likelihood = −6,036.6940; Amemiya probability criterion = 7.493; Akaike information criterion = 4.852
Estimated autocorrelation of $e(i, t)$: 0.683293

Variable	Coefficient	Standard error (s.e.)	$z = b$/s.e.	$P[|Z| \geq z]$	Mean of X
λ	−0.3571177E-01	0.26036	−0.137	0.89090	0.9196E-02
LEVEL	1.397619	0.22572	6.192	0.00000	0.6364
PINV	−0.3100040E-02	0.17128E-02	−1.810	0.07030	34.24
WORLD	−0.1149058	0.41293E-01	−2.783	0.00539	0.8947
PRIME	0.1120425	0.29213E-01	3.835	0.00013	2.899
EXPHAZH	−0.1277436	0.48291	−0.265	0.79137	0.5240E-01
EXPPAD	−23.36819	8.8062	−2.654	0.00796	0.7952E-02

Test statistics for the classical model

Model	Log-likelihood	Sum of squares	R^2
(1) Constant term only	−6,036.69400	0.304525E+05	0.0000000
(2) Group effects only	−5,297.85375	0.156088E+05	0.4874368
(3) X variables only	−5,708.17003	0.226237E+05	0.2570840
(4) X and group effects	−5,255.57810	0.150232E+05	0.5066678

Hypothesis tests

Comparison	Likelihood ratio test Chi-squared	d.f.	Prob. value	F tests F	Num.	Denom.	Prob. value
(2) vs. (1)	1,477.681	100	0.00000	20.066	100	2,110	0.00000
(3) vs. (1)	657.048	7	0.00000	108.906	7	2,203	0.00000
(4) vs. (1)	1,562.232	107	0.00000	20.185	107	2,103	0.00000
(4) vs. (2)	84.551	7	0.00000	11.711	7	2,103	0.00000
(4) vs. (3)	905.184	100	0.00000	10.639	100	2,103	0.00000

(continued)

Table 4.6 (continued)

Democracies

Least squares with group dummy variables
Ordinary least-squares regression: weighting variable = ONE; dependent variable Y;
  mean = 6.00054; s.d. = 2.9618
Model size: observations = 1,413; parameters = 73; degrees of freedom (d.f.) =
  1,340
Residuals: sum of squares = 6,409.38; standard deviation = 2.18704
Fit: R^2 = 0.48253; adjusted R^2 = 0.45473
Model test: $F(72, 1,340)$ = 17.35; probability value = 0.00000
Diagnostic: log-likelihood = −3,073.2221; restricted (β = 0) log-likelihood =
  −3,538.6734; Amemiya probability criterion = 5.030; Akaike information
  criterion = 4.453
Estimated autocorrelation of $e(i, t)$: 0.717687

Variable	Coefficient	Standard error (s.e.)	$z = b$/s.e.	$P[|Z| \geq z]$	Mean of X
λ	0.2002355E-01	0.17690	0.113	0.90988	−0.3422E-02
LEVEL	0.2083183	0.10095	2.064	0.03905	1.856
PINV	−0.7306690E-02	0.23773E-02	−3.074	0.00212	23.77
WORLD	0.1191477	0.40349E-01	2.953	0.00315	0.8116
PRIME	0.5693934E-01	0.33139E-01	1.718	0.08576	2.393
EXPHAZH	0.1648749	0.20816	0.792	0.42832	0.8292E-01
EXPPDA	13.30201	10.248	1.298	0.19429	0.6666E-02

Test statistics for the classical model

Model	Log-likelihood	Sum of squares	R^2
(1) Constant term only	−3,538.67337	0.123861E+05	0.0000000
(2) Group effects only	−3,088.31220	0.654775E+04	0.4713633
(3) X variables only	−3,365.31538	0.969103E+04	0.2175895
(4) X and group effects	−3,073.22208	0.640938E+04	0.4825347

Hypothesis tests

	Likelihood ratio test			F tests			
Comparison	Chi-squared	d.f.	Prob. value	F	Num.	Denom.	Prob. value
(2) vs. (1)	900.722	65	0.00000	18.478	65	1,347	0.00000
(3) vs. (1)	346.716	7	0.00000	55.819	7	1,405	0.00000
(4) vs. (1)	930.903	72	0.00000	17.355	72	1,340	0.00000
(4) vs. (2)	30.180	7	0.00009	4.133	7	1,340	0.00019
(4) vs. (3)	584.187	65	0.00000	10.555	65	1,340	0.00000

Notes: LEVEL is per capita income; PINV is the relative price of investment goods; WORLD is
the average rate of growth (of per capita income) in the world during the year; PRIME is the U.S.
interest rate.

perhaps the first to argue that security of property rights is critical for growth (North and Thomas 1973; North 1990). According to North and Weingast (1989: 803): "The more likely it is that the sovereign will alter property rights for his or her own benefit, the lower the expected returns from investment and the lower in turn the incentive to invest. For economic growth to occur the sovereign or government must not merely establish the relevant set of rights, but make a credible commitment to them" [21] Yet North was never explicit about the institutions that would embody that commitment: We could find only one passage in his book on institutions in which he explicitly identified those institutions as democratic (1990: 109). This connection was postulated by Olson (1991: 153), who claimed that a dictator ("autocrat") cannot credibly commit himself: "If he runs the society, there is no one who can force him to keep his commitments." But Olson as well fails to explain how democratic institutions could provide such a credible commitment. His followers merely observe that "for democracies, new leaders are constrained in their ability to alter the property and contract rights established in previous administrations. Consequently, investors are concerned with the expected longevity of democracy more than with the expected tenure of a leader. Autocrats, on the other hand, are relatively unconstrained in their ability to disregard previously established rights" (Clague et al. 1997: 102).

The property-rights literature treats the state as the only source of potential threat. But property rights can be threatened by private actors: Capitalist property is threatened by organized workers, landlords' property by landless peasants. It is by no means clear that the villain is necessarily "the ruler." Indeed, one liberal dilemma is that a strong state may be a potential threat to property, but a strong state is required to protect property from private encroachments.

Democracy in the political realm exacerbates the threat to property from the propertyless by equalizing the right to influence the allocation of resources. Distributions of consumption caused by the market and those voted on by citizens must differ, because democracy offers those who are poor, oppressed, or otherwise miserable as a consequence of the initial distribution of endowments an opportunity to find redress via the state. Endowed with political power in the form of universal suffrage, those who suffer as a consequence of private property will attempt to use that power to expropriate the riches.

---

[21] North and Weingast discovered that in seventeenth-century England, democracy did secure property rights – a finding not particularly surprising given that only the propertied enjoyed political rights.

The economic consequences of democracy were at the center of debates concerning the rights to vote and to organize during the first half of the nineteenth century. Conservatives agreed with socialists that democracy, specifically universal suffrage and the freedom to form unions, must threaten property. The Scottish philosopher James Mackintosh predicted in 1818 that if the "laborious classes" gained franchise, "a permanent animosity between opinion and property must be the consequence" (cited in Collini, Winch, and Burrow 1983: 98). David Ricardo was prepared to extend suffrage only "to that part of them [the people] which cannot be supposed to have an interest in overturning the right to property" (Collini et al. 1983: 107). Thomas Macaulay, in his speech on the Chartists in 1842 (1900: 263), pictured universal suffrage as "the end of property and thus of all civilization." Eight years later, Karl Marx expressed the same conviction that private property and universal suffrage are incompatible (1952: 62). According to his analysis, democracy inevitably "unchains the class struggle": The poor would use democracy to expropriate the riches; the rich would be threatened and would subvert democracy, typically by "abdicating" political power to the permanently organized armed forces. As a result, either capitalism or democracy would crumble. The combination of democracy and capitalism was thus seen as an inherently unstable form of organization of society, "only the political form of revolution of bourgeois society and not its conservative form of life" (1934: 18), "only a spasmodic, exceptional state of things ... impossible as the normal form of society" (1971: 198). Hence, in that view it is democracy, not dictatorship, that imperils property.

Our findings offer a surprisingly resounding resolution of that controversy. A 10 percent increase in the expected probability that a dictatorship will fall (EXPPAD) causes the investment share to decline by 1.37 to 2.55.[22] In turn, whereas the coefficients on the threats to democracies are not significant unless one considers that growth and investment are simultaneously determined by some exogenous variables (SURE estimator), they are invariably positive and also quite large. Hence, it is clear what investors think about the security of their property under each regime. If our measure of investors' expectations

---

[22] Different estimators yield different values for this effect, but they are always negative and large. See Appendix 4.1. As one would expect, when we exclude the 147 (out of 2,163) observations of communist regimes and thus consider only those economies in which there existed private property to be threatened and in which investment was to a large extent a result of private decisions, the effect of threats to dictatorships is even stronger.

is accurate – we should not ignore the caveat, because this analysis entails several assumptions – they will reduce investment when dictatorships are likely to fall, and most likely will increase their stakes when democracies are about to die.

The association of democracy with secure property rights is so widespread that economists routinely use the former as a proxy for the latter. Indeed, Barro (1989: 22) could find in the entire world only three dictatorships – Chile, South Korea, and Singapore – that were not hostile to private property. Yet most dictatorships repress labor and keep wages down (see Chapter 3). On the average, dictatorships tax at rates no higher than those under democracy: Observed tax rates are lower under dictatorships, and selection-corrected rates are almost the same under the two regimes (Cheibub 1998). On the average, dictatorships are less likely to nationalize private firms: Between 1960 and 1979, there were 85 acts of nationalization in 326 democratic years, one in every 3.83 years, and 406 acts of nationalization in 1,255 authoritarian years, or one in every 3.09 years (Kobrin 1980).[23]

Thus, whereas some dictatorships are hostile to capital – the MNR in Bolivia in the 1950s, the Peruvian military regime of 1968, the Sandinista regime in Nicaragua, "socialist" dictatorships in Africa, and the short-lived military regime in Portugal come to mind – most non-communist dictatorships have been and continue to be resolutely committed to defending private property from encroachment by those without it. Hence, investors seem to know what they are doing. It is not "instability" they fear, but democracy.

Conclusion

Although much more frequent under democracies, political instability affects economic performance only under dictatorships.

Only wars are more frequent in dictatorships, and they cause more short-term damage to the economy. Changes of chief executives, though much less frequent in dictatorships, are economically costly only in these regimes. The same is true of various forms of "socio-political unrest": Strikes, anti-government demonstrations, and riots occur more often in democracies, but they retard growth only in dictatorships.

Effects of the past are generally short-lived, so that past instability has almost no effect on current economic performance. Unless the instability is extreme, economies catch up quickly, so that effects of the past wane.

---

[23] We thank Stephen Kobrin for sharing his data.

Whether because of institutional constraints or because of the motivations of those who govern democracies, expected changes in the heads of governments have no economic consequences under democracies. But under dictatorships, economic growth slows down significantly when the tenure of rulers is threatened. Finally, the effect of threats to the stability of regimes on investment shows that investors fear democracy and hope to find a safe haven in many dictatorships: The prospective demise of a dictatorship causes investors to flee, but its advent makes them flock.

Thus, we find that political instability retards growth exclusively under dictatorships. Huntington and other "realists" got it all wrong. Studies of political instability have been guided by the hypothesis that, to state it in the words of Alesina and Perotti (1997: 21), "what influences growth is not so much the type of regime (dictatorship or democracy) but regime instability, that is, the propensity to coups and major changes of government." That hypothesis is logically incoherent, for "political instability" cannot even be defined independently of political institutions. The notion that alternation in office or other manifestations of popular opposition, whether strikes or anti-government demonstrations, constitute "instability" under democracy is just ludicrous. Such phenomena are frequent in democracies precisely because democracy is a system in which people are free to express their dissatisfaction with governments. And they are rare in dictatorships because it is to prevent such forms of expression that dictatorships are established and maintained. Democracies are inherently "unstable": The phenomena that constitute anomalies, breakdowns of rule, under dictatorship are just essential, definitional features of democracy. Changes of chief executives in democracies occur consequent to elections or other regularized procedures, but under most dictatorships the only way that a ruler can be changed is by a coup. To discover, as Alesina at al. (1996) do, that coups reduce growth, but regular alternations in office do not, is not to find that some forms of "political instability" affect development, but only that some political events that constitute instability under dictatorship do not under democracy.

Once it is understood that the same political phenomena have different meanings under different systems of political institutions, it is not surprising that economic actors react to them differently. Under dictatorships, whenever the regime is threatened, whenever rulers in fact change or are expected to change, whenever workers muster the courage to strike or masses of people to demonstrate their opposition to the government, the economy suffers. Under democracy, everyone knows that the government will change from time to time, that workers may strike, and people may express their dissatisfaction with the government in a variety of ways. Hence, when such phenomena do transpire, they evoke at most an economic yawn.

Appendix 4.1: Estimating the Impact of Expectations on Economic Performance

Although the qualitative results are surprisingly robust, estimates of the impact of expectations on growth and investment are somewhat sensitive to the estimating methods. Indeed, we are surprised that the results are so stable, because (1) growth and investment share may be interdependent in different ways, (2) except for growth under dictatorships, both series have fixed effects, and (3) the investment series is highly autocorrelated. Because simultaneity, fixed effects, and autocorrelation can be treated in different ways, we provide the results of applying different estimators:

1. Panel for growth, YG, only. These are the same results as in Table 4.5 in the text. F tests indicate that the dictatorial sample is homogeneous, but the democratic sample has strong country and year effects.

2. Panel for investment, INV, only. Same as Table 4.6. Because both series have fixed effects and because both are autocorrelated, we estimate one-way (country) fixed effects with first-order autocorrelation, 1F-AR1.

3. Because investment is autoregressive, as an alternative to AR1 estimates, we lag investment and correct for autocorrelation using one-way fixed effects and the Hatanaka estimator, 1F-HAT.

4. One way to consider interdependence between growth and investment is by estimating two-stage least squares, with predicted investment and predicted growth as instruments. Given the fixed effects, we estimate a 1F model with AR1 for investment. Hence, the model is 2SLS-1F-AR1.

5. Finally, instead of thinking of growth and investment as reciprocally influencing each other, we can consider them as jointly determined by the predetermined variables, a SURE regression model. We allow for different values of the autocorrelation (LIMDEP Model 1). Because this model cannot be estimated with country effects, we use regional dummies. Hence, the model is SURE-AR1, with regional dummy variables.

Table A4.1.1. Alternative estimators of the effects of hazards on growth and investment

Model	N	Rate of Growth (YG)		Investment (INV)	
		EXPHAZH	EXPPJK	EXPHAZH	EXPPJK
PANEL					
Dictatorship (OLS)	2,312	−1.3987	−0.9620		
		(0.5385)	(2.7831)		
Democracy (2F)	1,482	0.0229	7.1334		
		(0.4096)	(8.7850)		
1F-AR1					
Dictatorship	2,211			−0.1277	−23.3682
				(0.4829)	(8.8062)
Democracy	1,413			0.1649	13.3020
				(0.2082)	(10.2480)
1F-HATANAKA					
Dictatorship	2,211			−0.1892	−25.5281
				(0.4887)	(8.3104)
Democracy	1,413			0.2826	10.1023
				(0.2948)	(6.8620)
2SLS-1F-AR1					
Dictatorship	2,211	−1.9042	−10.3226	−0.1712	−19.8435
		(0.6721)	(6.2826)	(0.4889)	(8.6305)
Democracy	1,413	0.0180	2.1543	0.1748	14.2092
		(0.4177)	(8.3964)	(0.2087)	(10.1490)
SURE-AR1					
Dictatorship	2,312	−1.2968	−4.5280	−0.4194	−13.6541
		(0.5655)	(4.0328)	(0.5038)	(5.6299)
Democracy	1,482	0.0403	1.8544	0.3668	24.1056
		(0.3891)	(4.6827)	(0.2359)	(6.3859)

The results in Table A4.1.1 show that all of the qualitative results are robust, except for the impact of threats to democracy on investment. All models show that whenever dictators expect to be thrown out, growth declines sharply, but threats to democratic chief executives do not affect growth. Threats to either regime have no impact on growth. All the models agree, again, that threats to chief executives have no consequences for investment and that the higher probabilities of dictatorships falling strongly reduce investment. The impact of threats to the survival of democracy is always to increase investment, but the coefficients are significant only in the SURE model. Otherwise, the probability that these effects will be positive ranges between 10 and 19 percent.

The growth and investment models in Table A4.1.1 are the same as in Tables 4.5 and 4.6, respectively. We show only the coefficients on the expected hazards to heads and to regimes. All the estimates are selection-corrected. Standard errors are in parentheses.

Chapter Five

Political Regimes and Population

Total Income, Population, and Per Capita Income

Although total income grew faster under dictatorships (at the rate of 4.42) than under democracies (3.95), the observed average rate of growth of per capita income was higher under democracy: Per capita income grew at the rate of 2.46 under democracy and at the rate of 2.00 under dictatorship. The same is true of consumption. Whereas total consumption increased at the rate of 4.24 under dictatorship and 3.92 under democracy, per capita consumption grew faster under the latter, at 2.43 per year as opposed to 1.82 under dictatorship.

Because what matters for individual well-being is the growth of each person's income and consumption, rather than the development of the aggregate economy, the impact of regimes on the growth of per capita income and consumption is what we ultimately care about. Indeed, Lucas (1988: 3) saw the problem of economic development as "simply the problem of accounting for the observed pattern, across countries and across time, in levels and rates of growth of per capita income."

That is why most studies take the growth of income per capita as the variable to be explained. Yet even if per capita income is the correct focus, treating it as the single explanandum confounds the effects of two social processes that are to some extent independent: the growth of total output and the dynamics of population.[1] Note that the rate of growth of per capita income $[G = (\dot{Y/P})/(Y/P)]$ is the difference between

---

[1] To see the econometric problems entailed in taking per capita income as the dependent variable, substitute the production-function formulation in place of $\dot{Y}/Y$: $(\dot{Y/P})/(Y/P) = \dot{A}/A + \alpha\dot{K}/K + \beta\dot{L}/L - \dot{P}/P$. To estimate this equation, one either (1) must assume that the labor force and the population grow at the same rate (as did Przeworski and Limongi 1997), so that $(\dot{Y/P})/(Y/P) = \dot{A}/A + \alpha\dot{K}/K + (\beta - 1)\dot{L}/L$, with an obvious bias if the assumption

the rate of growth of total income (YG = $\dot{Y}/Y$) and the rate of growth of population (POPG = $\dot{P}/P$):

$$(Y/P)(Y/P) = \dot{Y}/Y - \dot{P}/P.$$

Yet growth economists tend either to relegate population growth to the status of an exogenous datum or to ignore it altogether. As Barro and Sala-i-Martin (1995: 308) observed, "most modern theories of growth have assumed that the rate of population growth is an exogenous constant." Even textbooks on endogenous growth theory rarely discuss population growth, with some notable exceptions cited later.

Because the effects of political regimes, as well as of other factors, on the growth of the economy and on the growth of population need not be the same, taking the growth of per capita income as the dependent variable obscures the autonomous contributions of these two processes. Indeed, the most surprising finding in our entire study is that regimes matter more for the growth of population than for the growth of income. In the end, regimes have more to do with demography than with economics.

Consider some basic facts: Under dictatorships, population grew at the rate of 2.42 percent per annum, and under democracies at the rate of 1.49: At those rates the population will double in thirty-four years under dictatorship, but only in forty-seven years under democracy. Decomposing the observed rates of growth of per capita income yields

Regime	G	= YG	– POPG
Dictatorships	2.00	= 4.42	– 2.42
Democracies	2.46	= 3.95	– 1.49
Difference	–0.46	= 0.47	– 0.93

Correcting for regime selection attenuates these differences. As we saw in Chapter 4, our best selection-corrected estimates of the rate of growth of GDP were 4.30 for dictatorships and 4.24 for democracies. Our best estimates of selection-corrected rates of population growth (Table 5.1B, Hatanaka estimator) are 2.18 for dictatorships and 1.59 for democracies. Using these estimates gives

$\dot{L}/L = \dot{P}/P$ does not hold, or (2) must assume that the population grows at a constant exogenous rate (as did Mankiw et al. 1992; Helliwell 1994), or omit labor force and population from the specification altogether (as did Barro 1997).

Regime	G	= YG	– POPG
Dictatorships	2.12	= 4.30	– 2.18
Democracies	2.65	= 4.24	– 1.59
Difference	–0.53	= 0.06	– 0.59

If the regimes had been matched for the exogenous factors that determine selection as well as for those that drive the growth of total income and of population, per capita incomes would have grown at a faster rate under democracies: They would have doubled in about thirty-five years under dictatorship and in about twenty-six years under democracy. And note that almost all of this difference is due to differences in the growth of population, rather than of total income.

Population, therefore, deserves to be studied even if all one wants to explain is the dynamic of per capita income. Yet the demographic patterns that cause population to grow slowly or quickly – birth and death rates, fertility, infant mortality – have profound consequences for well-being in their own right. They are sources of joys and sorrows; they represent the quality and the length of lives; they shape the life prospects of children. They particularly affect women: their choices, their status within the household, and within the society at large.

The dynamic of population is a complex process. The rate of population growth is the difference between birth rates and death rates, and again regimes may affect these rates differently. Hence, having established that population grows faster under dictatorships, we decompose population growth and examine the effect of regimes on various aspects of demographic behavior. We then return to the impact of demography on the growth of per capita incomes.

Political Regimes and Population Growth

Population was found to grow faster under dictatorships than under democracies. We were bewildered by this fact, and the remainder of this chapter seeks to explain it. But first we need to establish that it is a fact.

Table 5.1A shows the observed rates of population growth by levels of per capita income.[2] In countries with per capita incomes under

---

[2] Average income is not the best measure of the wealth of a country for the purposes of analysis of demographic patterns, because it obscures patterns of distribution. Two countries may have the same average income, but have different proportions of the population under some particular income levels. If what matters for demographic patterns

Table 5.1A. Observed rates of population growth (POPG), by per capita income (LEVEL)

LEVEL	Proportion dictatorships	Rate of population growth		
		All	Dictatorships	Democracies
0–1,000	0.9273	2.641	2.645	2.583
1,001–2,000	0.7472	2.581	2.582	2.578
2,001–3,000	0.6207	2.165	2.290	2.960
3,001–4,000	0.5874	1.906	2.038	1.719
4,001–5,000	0.5424	1.581	1.880	1.228
5,001–6,000	0.4308	1.176	1.526	0.911
6,001–	0.0812	1.022	1.463	0.983
Total (N = 4,126)		2.049	2.423	1.486

Note: All cell entries are based on at least 68 observations.

$2,000, population grows at almost exactly the same rate under the two regimes. As incomes become larger, population growth slows down. But the rates at which it falls are sharply different under the two regimes. Below $2,500, population grew at the rate of 2.58 under dictatorship (N = 1,851) and 2.47 under democracy (N = 417). Between $2,500 and $5,000, the gap opened up: The rate of population growth under dictatorship was 2.10 (N = 478), and 1.61 (N = 348) under democracy. Above $5,000, population grew at the rate of 1.50 (N = 152) under the former, and 0.97 (N = 880) under the latter.

With caveats concerning regime selection, this finding is reinforced by a diachronic analysis. In the countries that were ruled by dictatorships during the entire period of our study, population grew at the rate of 2.43 per annum. In the countries that were observed only as democracies, population increased at the rate of 1.12. This difference is enormous, but it is largely due to the levels of per capita income at which those regimes were stable. To assess the diachronic impact of regimes,

are absolute income levels, then the country with a more skewed distribution will exhibit behavior characteristic of a poorer country with a less skewed distribution. When a data set was sufficiently large, we added a measure of skewness, simply the share of the median quintile, to all the other variables: This measure always matters, and always in expected directions. In most cases, however, the overlap between income distribution and other data is too small to permit statistical analyses.

Table 5.1B. Selection-corrected estimators of population growth (POPG)

| | Regime means | | Regime effect | |
| | Dictatorships | Democracies | Constant | Individual |
Estimator	(N = 2,396)	(N = 1,595)	(N = 3,991)	
Biased	2.42	1.46	0.2238	0.0460
	(1.57)	(1.11)	(0.0745)	(0.2964)
OLS-AR1	2.12	1.70		
	(0.64)	(0.52)		
HATANAKA	2.18	1.59		
	(0.59)	(0.63)		
PANEL 1F/2F	2.43	1.51		
	(0.85)	(0.33)		
Unobservable			0.2458	0.0500
			(0.0806)	(0.2957)
Observable			0.2182	0.0462
			(0.0759)	(0.3297)
LFPW sample	N = 2,076	N = 1,254		
Biased	2.49	1.40		
	(1.50)	(1.10)		
PANEL 1F/2F	2.50	1.22		
	(0.80)	(0.62)		
EDT sample	N = 1,745	N = 1,042		
Biased	2.45	1.42		
	(1.38)	(1.07)		
PANEL 2F/2F	2.37	1.32		
	(0.19)	(0.31)		
LFPW and EDT sample	N = 1,692	N = 1,015		
Biased	2.48	1.42		
	(1.38)	(1.07)		
PANEL 2F/2F	2.66	1.28		
	(0.71)	(0.52)		

(continued)

Table 5.1B (continued)

FEMSEC sample	$N = 1,002$	$N = 648$
Biased	2.49	1.23
	(1.24)	(1.09)
OLS-AR1	2.17	1.67
	(0.67)	(0.71)
LFPW, EDT, FEMSEC	$N = 770$	$N = 459$
Biased	2.51	1.28
	(0.87)	(1.05)
OLS-AR1	2.35	1.53
	(0.41)	(0.55)

Notes: Probit equations include the lagged values of LEVEL, STRA, and RELDIF plus the exogenous variables in the LFG equations. These are LEVEL, NEWC, BRITCOL, CATH, PROT, MOSLEM, COMEX, plus LFGLAG in the Hatanaka estimator, plus the variables defined under each sample. Standard errors in parentheses.

we examine the countries that experienced regime transitions, thus controlling the fixed-effects characteristics of particular countries. Examine the columns in Table 5.2 that exclude the communist dictatorships, which had exceptionally slow population growth, as discussed later. In dictatorships that were to give way to democracies, population grew at the rate of 2.33, and the democracies that followed those dictatorships had a rate of 2.27. In turn, in democracies that were to be followed by dictatorships, population grew at the rate of 2.36, but once those regimes became dictatorships, population grew at the rate of 2.40. These differences are not large, but the fact that population grows faster in dictatorships that follow democracies is astonishing, given the general trend for population growth to slow down with time. Hence, except for the communist regimes, the effect of regimes is diachronic, not just cross-sectional.

As always, given that dictatorships and democracies exist under different conditions, not only at different levels of development, one must test whether it is indeed regimes and not those conditions that account for the difference. Table 5.1B presents several estimates of the population growth expected under the two regimes matched for per capita

Table 5.2. Observed diachronic effects of regimes on population growth

Regime	Entire sample		Excluding communist	
	N	POPG	*N*	POPG
Stable dictatorship	1,709	2.52	1,603	2.63
		(1.57)		(1.55)
Stable democracies	1,104	1.12	1,104	1.12
		(0.98)		(0.98)
Dic preceding Dem	607	2.10	532	2.33
		(1.42)		(1.35)
Dem following Dic	371	2.24	366	2.27
		(1.03)		(1.01)
Dem preceding Dic	290	2.36	290	2.36
		(2.05)		(2.05)
Dic following Dem	425	2.40	425	2.40
		(1.63)		(1.63)

income (LEVEL), the extent of reliance on exports of primary commodities (COMEX), colonial legacy (NEWC, BRITCOL), frequencies of Catholics (CATH), Protestants (PROT), and Moslems (MOSLEM), level of education (EDT), labor-force participation of women (LFPW), rates of female enrollment in secondary education (FEMSEC), and in some analyses the lagged rate of population growth. Whatever statistical model one uses – correcting for autocorrelation, with or without a lagged dependent variable, a fixed-effect panel model, or Heckman's (1988) instrumental variables with constant effects – a difference remains.

In sum, all the evidence indicates that regimes affect the rate of population growth. The observed rates of growth of population are higher under dictatorship at each level of per capita income, and much higher in countries with incomes above about $2,500. Correcting for other exogenous variables does not erase this difference. Finally, even though the diachronic effects are small, regime transitions affect population growth regardless of their direction. Thus, the finding is robust. We find it surprising.

The rate of growth of population (POPG) is itself a composite of three rates: rate of births (BIRTHS), rate of deaths (DEATHS), and rate of net

Table 5.3A. Observed rates of population growth under dictatorship and democracy (small sample)

	Rate of population growth					
LEVEL	All		Dictatorships		Democracies	
267–500	2.47	(2.28)	2.47	(2.28)	—	
501–1,000	2.54	(2.46)	2.54	(2.47)	2.47	(2.35)
1,001–1,500	2.59	(2.22)	2.63	(2.21)	2.48	(2.28)
1,501–2,000	2.52	(2.25)	2.49	(2.21)	2.65	(2.40)
267–2,000	2.54	(2.33)	2.54	(2.33)	2.54	(2.33)
267–2,500	2.52	(2.31)	2.52	(2.31)	2.52	(2.33)
267–3,000	2.49	(2.28)	2.51	(2.30)	2.43	(2.16)
267–1,000	2.52	(2.43)	2.53	(2.43)	2.47	(2.35)
1,001–2,000	2.56	(2.23)	2.57	(2.21)	2.55	(2.33)
2,001–3,000	2.33	(2.05)	2.34	(2.12)	2.31	(1.94)
3,001–4,000	1.93	(1.76)	2.03	(1.85)	1.82	(1.66)
4,001–5,000	1.21	(1.33)	1.27	(1.34)	1.13	(1.32)
5,001–6,000	0.83	(0.82)	0.80	(0.86)	0.85	(0.81)
6,001–18,095	0.68	(0.86)	1.01	(1.45)	0.66	(0.82)
Total ($N = 1,493$)	1.54	(1.52)	2.22	(2.08)	1.00	(1.08)

Note: The rate of population growth is calculated as the difference between birth and death rates. The rates of population growth for the same observations in the original data file (POPG) are in parentheses.

migration. Population may grow slower in democracies because their birth rates are lower, because their death rates are higher, or because people migrate to dictatorships. Hence, we need to do some more decomposing.

The data concerning birth and death rates are available only for a much smaller sample and come from a different source (World Bank). In Table 5.3A we show the "domestic" rates of population growth, derived as the difference between birth and death rates. These domestic rates differ from the rates of population growth shown in Table 5.1A (and in parentheses in Table 5.3A for the same sample) by net migration. It is apparent that migration occurs from poor to rich countries: Regardless of their regimes, in countries with per capita incomes under $4,000 the rates of domestic population growth are higher than the rates including migration. Wealthier countries tend to attract migrants, again regardless of their regimes. Nevertheless, the overall structure of this sample preserves most patterns of the larger one: Population grows faster under dictatorships in all but one income band, poor countries differ little regardless of regimes, and the rate of domestic population growth falls faster as income increases in wealthier democracies than in wealthier dictatorships.

To assess the impact of regimes, we must be careful that they are not observed at different stages of the demographic transition from high birth and death rates to low birth and death rates. In Western Europe, this process moved from annual death rates in the range of 20 to 50 per thousand and birth rates in a very similar range, with population growing at under 1 percent per annum, during the eighteenth century, to death rates under 10 per thousand and birth rates again only slightly higher, with population growing at rates under 0.5 percent during recent years. Because death rates fell first and at a steeper rate than birth rates, during the transition the population grew at much higher rates. That process was slow and long in Western Europe, and rates of growth of population rarely exceeded 2 percent. Fertility rates did not decline immediately when death rates fell, exhibiting varying degrees of "inertia." Moreover, crude birth rates continued to increase well after fertility decline because of the increase in the proportion of women of childbearing age – a phenomenon referred to as "demographic momentum" (Merrick 1994: 90).[3] The result of the combined effects of inertia and momentum was that total population increased by a factor ranging from 1.62 in France between 1785 and 1970 to 3.83 in Sweden between 1810 and 1960. (This summary is based on Livi-Baci 1997: chap. 4).

Figure 5.1 shows a stylized picture of the demographic transition that combines assumptions about the period preceding our observations (in this case, pre-1960) with data derived from our demographic sample. An income of $250 per capita (as always, 1985 PPP USD) is generally considered to be the absolute subsistence minimum. The picture is drawn assuming that during the earlier period, before advances in medicine and the development of artificial methods of birth control, death rates in countries at that minimum hovered around 30 per thousand, and birth rates around 45, yielding a population growth

---

[3] Note that birth rates (BIRTHS) are numbers of births per thousand people, and fertility rates (FERTIL) are numbers of children per woman during her lifetime.

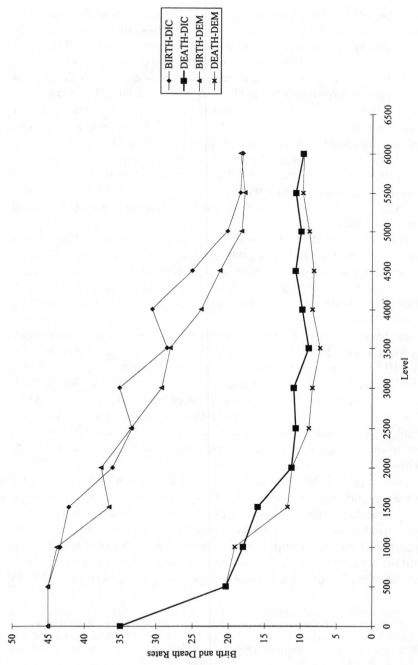

Figure 5.1. Demographic transitions by per capita income and regime

of 1.5 percent.[4] The lowest income observed in our sample was $267, the highest death rate was 32.4, and the highest birth rate 57.2. The 50 annual observations of countries with incomes below $500 show an average death rate of 20.3 and an average birth rate of 45.0. During the period of our scrutiny, poor countries were already in the grip of transition: Death rates fell sharply with income, followed by somewhat lagging birth rates. As a result, the poor countries we observed had very high rates of population growth, over 2.5 percent. Death rates become stationary in countries with incomes over $2,000, but both fertility inertia and demographic momentum (discussed later) continue to operate, so that birth rates fall less rapidly. They decline slowly as countries get richer. In countries with incomes above $5,000, the transition appears to be completed, and the population grows at less than 1 percent per year.

The notable feature in Figure 5.1 is that democracies have lower death rates and lower birth rates at almost all income levels. Hence, the reason the population grows at a slower rate under democracies is not that they have higher death rates. In fact, they have lower death rates, but also lower birth rates, sufficiently lower for their population to grow slower.

Examine Table 5.3B. The observed birth rate (BIRTHS) under dictatorships was 36.2 per thousand people, and under democracies it was 19.5. And, except for democracies with incomes under $1,000, for which there are only eleven observations (six from India alone), birth rates are higher under dictatorship at every income level. Hence, while birth rates decline with per capita income, the difference between regimes is not due solely to their incomes. More children are born under dictatorships, even when they are matched for income with democracies.

Death rates (DEATHS) were also higher under dictatorships, 14.1 per thousand, as contrasted with 9.4 under democracies. The death rate in dictatorships with incomes under $2,000 was 15.9, and in democracies with such incomes it was 12.9. The death rate was also higher under dictatorships with incomes between $2,000 and $5,000. Only in countries with incomes above $5,000 were these rates about the same under the two regimes: 9.54 under dictatorships and 9.36

---

[4] Estimates of pre-transition birth and death rates vary. It is generally thought that they were about equal, at the rate of 45 per thousand, until the eighteenth century. Recent research, however, has emphasized that they were more variable over time and less homogeneous than previously thought. The estimates we use are consistent with the findings of Livi-Baci as well as Crook (1997: 60).

Table 5.3B. Observed birth and death rates under dictatorship and democracy

LEVEL	All				Dictatorships				Democracies			
	Births		Deaths		Births		Deaths		Births		Deaths	
0–1,000	43.7	(246)	18.5	(246)	43.7	(235)	18.5	(235)	43.8	(11)	19.1	(11)
1,001–2,000	39.1	(229)	13.4	(229)	39.6	(179)	14.0	(179)	37.0	(50)	11.5	(50)
2,001–3,000	33.0	(132)	9.9	(129)	33.9	(81)	10.8	(79)	31.7	(51)	8.6	(50)
3,001–4,000	27.9	(112)	8.5	(110)	29.5	(61)	9.3	(57)	26.0	(51)	7.6	(53)
4,001–5,000	21.6	(88)	9.5	(88)	23.1	(50)	10.4	(50)	19.7	(38)	8.4	(38)
5,001–6,000	18.1	(90)	9.8	(90)	18.2	(30)	10.3	(30)	18.1	(60)	9.6	(60)
6,001–	16.1	(606)	9.3	(603)	19.0	(34)	8.9	(33)	15.9	(572)	9.3	(570)
Total	26.9	(1,503)	11.5	(1,495)	36.2	(670)	14.1	(663)	19.5	(833)	9.4	(832)

Note: Birth and death rates are per 1,000; numbers of observations in parentheses.

under democracies. Hence, except for relatively wealthy countries, more people die under dictatorship at every income level.[5]

The lower death rates under democracy are to some extent due to lower infant mortality (INFMORT), lower again at every income level. Table 5.3C shows that the difference between regimes is large: Except for very poor countries, for each 1,000 children born, between seven and twenty more die under dictatorship. But decomposing the mortality rates (Table 5.3D) shows that adults also die at higher rates under dictatorship: Of the average deaths under dictatorships, 14.1 per thousand, 3.4 deaths were of infants, and 10.7 of adults, whereas under democracy, of the 9.4 deaths per thousand, infants accounted for 0.5, and adults for 8.9. Infant mortality constitutes a large share of total mortality in poor countries, but as both birth rates and mortality of infants fall with income, it is a small source of total mortality in richer ones. Yet infant mortality rates persist at high levels even in wealthy dictatorships: They are as high in dictatorships with incomes above $6,000 as in democracies with incomes between $4,000 and $5,000.

The effect of these patterns on life expectancy (LIVES) is startling.[6] People live longer under democracy. And the difference is large, very large: about four years longer within each band of per capita income. In democracies with incomes between $3,000 and $4,000, people live almost as long as those in dictatorships which have twice that income. Moreover, regime differences in life expectancy are similar for males and females: Men live 66.2 years under democracy and 50.8 under dictatorship, and women 71.5 years under democracy and 54.2 under dictatorship. Hence, there is no reason to think people live shorter lives under dictatorships because they send young boys to die in wars. Lives are simply shorter under dictatorship.

Thus, there is no doubt that regimes affect birth rates, death rates, and life expectancy. Observed population growth is lower under democracies because they experience both fewer births and fewer deaths: With the birth rate at 1.95 per hundred and the death rate at 0.94, democracies in this sample had populations growing at an average rate

[5] Democracies with incomes above $6,000 are, on the average, wealthier ($Y/P = \$14,429$) than dictatorships in this income range ($Y/P = \$7,322$). They also have more people over age 65, as discussed later. This explains the higher death rates in wealthy democracies.

[6] It may appear strange to speak of life expectancy under a particular regime when individuals outlive regimes. But life expectancy is only a summary statistic for the current age-specific death rates.

Table 5.3C. Observed infant mortality (INFMORT) and life expectancy (LIVES) under dictatorship and democracy

LEVEL	All		Dictatorships		Democracies	
	INFMORT	LIVES	INFMORT	LIVES	INFMORT	LIVES
0–1,000	131.1 (239)	46.5 (226)	130.5 (228)	46.4 (215)	142.9 (11)	47.2 (11)
1,001–2,000	97.4 (207)	53.1 (183)	101.7 (162)	52.2 (144)	81.6 (45)	56.3 (39)
2,001–3,000	69.3 (120)	60.8 (93)	75.4 (70)	59.2 (59)	60.9 (50)	63.6 (34)
3,001–4,000	45.6 (101)	65.5 (74)	52.1 (50)	64.2 (44)	39.3 (51)	67.3 (30)
4,001–5,000	34.2 (82)	67.3 (44)	39.9 (48)	65.0 (25)	26.1 (34)	70.2 (19)
5,001–6,000	25.4 (82)	70.1 (41)	29.6 (31)	68.6 (18)	22.8 (51)	71.3 (23)
6,001–	14.9 (586)	72.9 (255)	26.0 (27)	67.6 (18)	14.4 (559)	73.2 (239)
Total	55.1 (1,417)	60.2 (916)	93.6 (616)	53.3 (521)	25.4 (801)	69.3 (395)

Note: Infant mortality per 1,000; numbers of observations in parentheses.

Table 5.3D. A decomposition of death rates under dictatorship and democracy

	All		Dictatorships		Democracies	
LEVEL	INFMORT	Rest	INFMORT	Rest	INFMORT	Rest
0–1,000	5.7	12.8	5.7	12.8	6.3	12.8
1,001–2,000	3.8	9.6	4.0	9.9	3.0	8.5
2,001–3,000	2.3	7.6	2.6	8.2	1.9	6.7
3,001–4,000	1.3	7.2	1.5	7.8	1.0	6.6
4,001–5,000	0.7	8.8	0.9	9.5	0.5	7.9
5,001–6,000	0.5	9.3	0.5	9.8	0.4	9.2
6,001–	0.2	9.1	0.5	8.4	0.2	9.1
Total	1.4	10.0	3.4	10.7	0.5	8.9

Notes: Deaths due to infant mortality are calculated by multiplying birth rates by rates of infant mortality. "Rest" is the remainder from death rates.

of 1.00 percent, but dictatorships, with the birth rate at 3.62 and the death rate at 1.41, had populations increasing at 2.22 percent.

Note that although the rates of growth of population implied by these birth and death rates are exactly the same for the two regimes in countries with incomes under $2,500, 2.52 percent, regimes make a difference even in poor countries. Both birth and death rates are higher under dictatorships: Aggregating all observations under $2,500 yields birth rates (per hundred) of 4.11 for dictatorships and 3.67 for democracies, and death rates of 1.60 for dictatorships and 1.15 for democracies. In countries with incomes above $2,500, the difference in death rates almost vanishes: 0.99 for dictatorships and 0.92 for democracies. But the difference in birth rates increases: 2.57 for dictatorships and 1.73 for democracies. The gap in rates of population growth among wealthier countries – 1.57 for dictatorships and 0.82 for democracies – is thus due almost entirely to the difference in birth rates.

These facts do not cease to amaze us, but one must be careful not to attribute to regimes effects that are in fact caused by the conditions under which they exist. We have already seen that these differences are not due to per capita income; they occur at almost every income level. They are also not due to the timing of regimes: Because birth rates and death rates decline in time, and life expectancy increases, the observed patterns would have been biased against dictatorships if they had been more frequent during the earlier periods. But that is not the case: The distribution of regimes over time is almost the same in this sample.[7] Hence, timing does not bias the observed patterns.

Controlling for selection statistically is difficult with these data. First, as Figure 5.1 shows, they are highly non-linear: The changes in all the variables are extremely rapid at low income levels, but at higher levels there is almost no change. At least with regard to death rates, a logarithmic transformation does not linearize all the convexity, so that even log-linear regressions generate errors that are correlated with per capita income, biasing the results somewhat in favor of democracy. Second, the observations are highly autocorrelated. Third, there are strong country and period effects. Finally, the effects of selection are strong, so that selection-corrected values are sensitive to the specification of selection mechanisms.

Yet, though the exact magnitudes may be off, regimes affect births, deaths, and durations of lives independently of the conditions under which they exist. We provide the details of selection-based analyses later, when we try to explain these patterns. Taking only per capita income and year (or fixed time effects) confirms that if the two regimes had had the same income levels and had existed at the same time, dictatorships would have had higher birth rates, higher death rates, and shorter lives. Corrected for selection, the differences between regimes with regard to birth rates are in the range of 5.5 to 11.8 per thousand; the differences with regard to death rates range from 1.2 to 4.4; and the differences in life expectancy range from 5.8 to 18.7 years in favor of democracy (Table 5.4).

Perhaps even more persuasive are the diachronic effects of regime transitions. As Table 5.5 shows, transitions from dictatorship to democracy were associated with birth rates falling from 29.2 to 26.3. One might think that because birth rates have generally fallen over time, that decline was simply due to the timing of the regimes. But transitions from democracy to dictatorship were associated with an increase of birth rates from 34.6 to 36.3, even though those dictatorships followed democracies in time. Fertility exhibits the same pattern. Whereas in dictatorships that were to give way to democracies an average woman had 4.1 children, in the democracies that succeeded

---

[7] Between 1960 and 1974, dictatorships constituted 0.42 of regimes; between 1975 and 1990, they made up 0.47 of regimes. Hence, if anything, dictatorships made up a larger proportion of observations during the latter period.

Table 5.4. Selection-corrected rates of births and deaths and of life expectancy

Regime	Biased BIRTHS	Selection-corrected predicted		
		BIRTHS (OLS-AR1)	Log-BIRTHS (OLS-AR1)	Log-BIRTHS (2F PANEL)
Dictatorship	35.44	27.04	26.19	29.00
N = 589	(12.60)	(11.16)	(9.00)	(4.75)
Democracy	18.69	21.50	20.05	17.23
N = 781	(7.89)	(4.73)	(3.77)	(0.18)

Regime	Biased DEATHS	Selection-corrected predicted		
		DEATHS (OLS-AR1)	Log-DEATHS (OLS-AR1)	Log-DEATHS (2F PANEL)
Dictatorship	13.52	11.03	10.39	12.61
N = 582	(5.90)	(3.97)	(3.02)	(0.42)
Democracy	9.28	9.39	9.17	8.24
N = 780	(2.19)	(0.56)	(0.51)	(1.54)

Regime	Biased LIVES	Selection-corrected predicted				
		LIVES (OLS-AR1)	Log-LIVES (OLS-AR1)	Log-LIVES (2F PANEL)	Log-Gap (OLS-AR1)	Log-Gap (2F PANEL)
Dictatorship	53.99	60.95	61.24	53.01	60.99	58.77
N = 440	(10.17)	(11.94)	(14.33)	(0.03)	(9.34)	(4.73)
Democracy	70.28	67.34	67.06	71.70	67.95	70.66
N = 343	(6.64)	(4.09)	(4.28)	(2.18)	(3.95)	(0.94)

Notes: The selection equation is estimated by dynamic probit, with STRA, RELDIF, and LEVEL. The exogenous variables for the demographic variables are LEVEL and YEAR in OLS and LEVEL in the two-way fixed-effects (2F) panel. Log columns indicate that the dependent variable was estimated in logs, and the predicted values were exponentiated. Gap = (85 − LIVES)/85, where LIVES stands for life expectancy.

them the fertility fell to 3.7. In turn, whereas fertility in democracies that preceded dictatorships was 5.0, in the dictatorships that followed them the fertility increased to 5.3. Transitions from dictatorships to democracies were accompanied by death rates falling from 11.8 to 9.9, and the transitions from democracies to dictatorships again contradict temporal patterns: Death rates rose from 12.0 to 12.5. Finally, life

Table 5.5. Observed diachronic effects of regimes on births, fertility, deaths, and life expectancy[a]

Regime	N	BIRTHS	N	FERTIL	N	DEATHS	N	LIVES
Stable dictatorships	441	38.9	408	5.6	434	15.0	361	51.3
Stable democracies	681	17.7	572	2.4	682	9.3	291	71.7
Dic preceding Dem	185	29.2	177	4.1	185	11.8	124	59.6
Dem following Dic	112	26.3	114	3.7	110	9.9	82	64.1
Dem preceding Dic	61	34.6	52	5.0	61	12.0	43	55.8
Dic following Dem	115	36.3	103	5.3	115	12.5	99	55.9

[a] Because some regimes both preceded and followed alternative regimes, they are double-counted in this table.

expectancy increased in democracies that followed dictatorships, rising to 64.1 from 59.6, and it remained stagnant in dictatorships that followed democracies, at 55.9. As a result of those changes in birth and death rates, the rate of (domestic) population growth declined from 1.74 in dictatorships preceding democracies to 1.65 in the democracies that succeeded them, but it increased from 2.26 in democracies that did not survive to 2.38 in the dictatorships that followed them. The effects in dictatorships that followed democracies are astounding, because they hurl themselves against the general trends for birth rates and death rates to decline and for life expectancy to increase with time. And on the demographic scale, these are huge differences.

Explanations

A Methodological Digression

The causes of these differences between regimes are not easy to determine. Before proceeding with explanations, we need to pause and consider what it means to "explain" differences between regimes.

We have observed that the two kinds of regimes differ in their demographic patterns. Moreover, this difference does not disappear when we match regimes for per capita income and timing. Suppose that we find that when the regimes are matched for some other exogenous conditions, then the difference vanishes, as it does with regard to the rate of growth of total income. That would mean that the difference is caused not by regimes, but rather by the conditions under which they exist, something we previously failed to detect. We then would have explained the observed difference.

Suppose, however, that the list of plausible and available exogenous variables is exhausted, and the difference persists. We then would conclude that the observed difference is not due to exogenous conditions but is an effect of regimes. But how can this difference be explained?

Matching regimes for the observed exogenous conditions will not eliminate the difference between them when the effects of those conditions are not the same under the two regimes. Regimes may process exogenous conditions in distinct ways. An example that is now classic concerns nascent famines (Sen 1981): When lives are threatened, the free press and other voices raise alarms in democracies, putting pressure on the government to act, whereas in dictatorships the calamity remains obscured from public scrutiny and takes its toll. In regression terms, the coefficients on the exogenous variables are different: The effect of the proportion of the labor force in agriculture on the death rate should not be different from zero in democracies, but positive in dictatorships. If the share of the labor force employed in agriculture is exogenous with regard to regimes, the counterfactual matching of regimes is valid, but the difference in death rates persists because of the distinct ways in which regimes respond to a large agricultural sector.

Still, the coefficients on all the exogenous variables may be the same under the two regimes, and the difference between them may remain when they are matched for the values of these variables. Algebraically, this means that the regression constants must differ. This may indicate that we have omitted some additional exogenous variable(s). Such omission will bias the coefficients on the included variables if the omitted variable is correlated with them in the sample, or it will bias the intercept estimator (unless the mean of the observations of the omitted variable is zero). Although statistical tests are available, even if the model passes these tests, the possibility that it is misspecified should always be kept in mind as the rival hypothesis. Yet if the model does pass these tests, there is a strong presumption that there is something about regimes that, on the average, makes them different.

Sometimes the constants have a theoretical interpretation that can provide a handle for an explanation. For example, we interpreted the intercepts of the production function as the rate of technical progress, and we told a story in which wealthy dictatorships pay little attention to it because they compete by repressing workers and keeping wages down. Often, however, such interpretations are far from obvious. For all we know, for example, life under dictatorships may be so grim that what kills people may be despair: Despair can kill. Clearly, chagrin is not something we can systematically observe. In the end, then, explaining regime differences may inevitably entail simply telling intuitively plausible stories, as always subject to rival interpretations.

Deaths, Infant Mortality, and Life Expectancy

Mortality began to decline in Europe in the second half of the eighteenth century, as a result of the reduced frequencies of epidemics and of famines and because of practices that reduced the spread of infectious diseases (Livi-Baci 1997: chap. 4). Sustained and substantial reductions in mortality, however, date only to the second half of the nineteenth century (Easterlin 1998: 8). Such gains accelerated until the middle of the twentieth century. Notwithstanding the war, the period of maximum progress, due to pharmacological discoveries, was between 1930 and 1950. The reduction in mortality extended during that period to twenty-one developing countries (Coale and Hoover 1958; Ray 1998: 312).[8] Subsequently, mortality declined and life expectancy increased in almost all countries. Indeed, whereas per capita incomes tended to diverge during the post-war era, mortality rates differ much less now than they did some fifty years ago.

Although life expectancy increased for all age brackets, the reduction in mortality and the corresponding gains in life expectancy were concentrated among young people. Livi-Baci (1997: 122–3) cites studies according to which about two-thirds of the gains in life expectancy have resulted from a decline in mortality during the first fifteen years of life.

Easterlin (1998: chap. 6) emphasizes that reductions in mortality were largely due to independent technological innovations in medicine and public health, rather than being merely consequences of improved standards of living. Nevertheless, as Figure 5.1 shows, during the period under our scrutiny, reductions in mortality were extremely rapid as incomes increased from very low levels, whereas in countries with per capita incomes over $2,000, further increases in incomes had almost no effect.

Because the demographic data sample contains few poor democracies (only 61 observations under $2,000) and equally few wealthy dictatorships (63 observations over $5,000), the functions relating

---

[8] According to Crook (1997: chap. 6), the decline in mortality in colonies was largely due to health measures undertaken by the colonial powers in order to protect their soldiers.

mortality to per capita income are very different for the two regimes. Hence, to correct for effects of selection, we use a method, due to Heckman (1988), that allows us to analyze all the observations together and examine regime effects as intercept and slope dummies. Conceptually, this method is equivalent to what we have done with regard to the growth of output, where we also cited some Heckman (1988) estimators along with Heckman (1976, 1979) methods.

Mortality rates differ between regimes even when we assume that their populations have the same age structure. Note that in the modern (post-demographic-transition) order of things, people are more likely to die as they get older. Hence, regimes in countries with relatively more people over age 65 (OVER65) should be expected to have higher mortality rates. In fact, democracies have a larger proportion of old people, 8.31 percent ($N = 1,299$), than dictatorships, where old people constitute 3.77 percent ($N = 1,984$) of the population. Hence, the bias in the observed world goes against democracies, which nevertheless have lower observed mortality. Yet the ordering of deaths by age is a new phenomenon: In the pre-modern era, the probability that children would die before their parents was very high (Livi-Baci 1997: 118). Hence, in very poor countries one should expect that mortality will be higher if there is a higher proportion of people under age 15 (UNDER15). Indeed, mortality is positively correlated with the proportion of old people under democracy, and with the proportion of young people under dictatorship. And the population is younger in dictatorships, where young people constitute 42.35 percent of the population, compared with 31.32 in democracies. Hence, in this respect, the sample is biased against dictatorships, which have higher observed mortality.

Correcting for the age structure of the population and for per capita income – assuming they are the same under the two regimes – does not eliminate the difference in mortality rates. But this correction may be insufficient if large numbers of deaths are associated with childbirth. According to the World Health Organization, as cited by Lloyd (1994: 208), half a million women die in childbirth each year. And when we use our birth and infant mortality rates, we arrive at about another half a million infants who die during the first year of life, with higher rates in poor countries and under dictatorship. Finally, a rough calculation shows that about 45 million people die, on the average, each year in the world as a whole. Hence, the 1 million deaths associated with childbirth account for approximately 2.2 percent of all deaths: a significant share.

Introducing fertility rates into the analysis shows that they are important in determining mortality under both regimes, somewhat more under dictatorships. As Table 5.6A shows, mortality falls sharply with income and with time, and in both cases faster in dictatorships. A higher fertility rate is an important cause of mortality under both regimes, only slightly higher under dictatorship. The results concerning the structure of the population should be viewed with caution, because the age variables are highly collinear. Yet even when regimes are matched for age structure, per capita income, and fertility, mortality rates under dictatorship remain higher, by 1.86 per thousand.

Mortality rates depend on various conditions that are subject to government policies. We broach this subject separately because there are good reasons to think that social expenditures are endogenous with regard to regimes,[9] something we cannot test given the paucity of the data. The proportion of GDP spent on social expenditures by the central government – a sum of central-government spending on education, social security and welfare, health, housing, and recreation and culture – is much higher in democracies, 18.9 percent ($N = 569$), than the 9.2 percent ($N = 549$) in dictatorships. Almost the entire difference is due to expenditures on social security and welfare, which consume 10.4 percent of GDP in democracies and 2.1 percent in dictatorships. The expenditures on education are almost the same, respectively 3.9 and 4.1 percent of GDP, but expenditures on health are twice as large in democracies, 3.3 percent, as compared with 1.7 percent in dictatorships. Expenditures on housing and culture are small and are the same under the two regimes, and we ignore them in what follows. And note that if government expenditures are exogenous with regard to regimes, then we can treat the situation as ceteris paribus, but if they are not, we should not correct for them.

How does government spending on various aspects of social policy affect mortality? The combined sample that contains data for demographic variables and government spending is even smaller, but the results appear quite robust. Statistical analysis shows that government social expenditures reduce mortality, approximately equally under the two regimes. When expenditures are disaggregated, it turns out that expenditures on social security and welfare have no effect on death rates under democracy, but reduce them somewhat under dictatorship. Educational expenditures sharply decrease mortality under both regimes, confirming the claim of Livi-Baci (1997: 172) that "improved

[9] Moreover, the overlap between data sets that contain mortality, fertility, and government expenditures is too small to use these variables together.

Table 5.6A. Effect of regimes on the logarithm of death rates[a]

AR1 model: $e(t) = \rho e(t - 1) + u(t)$
Initial value of $\rho = 0.73515$
Maximum iterations = 20
Iterations = 4; sum of squares = 15.614; log-likelihood = 933.177909
Final value of $\rho = 0.85452$
Durbin-Watson: $e(t) = 0.29096$
Standard deviation: $e(t) = 0.21852$
Standard deviation: $u(t) = 0.11350$
Durbin-Watson: $u(t) = 2.07924$
Autocorrelation: $u(t) = -0.03962$
$N(0, 1)$ used for significance levels

Variable	Coefficient	Standard error (s.e.)	$z = b$/s.e.	$P[|Z| \geq z]$	Mean of X
Constant	5.510743	1.6478	3.344	0.00083	
LEVEL	−0.1274850E-04	0.37101E-05	−3.436	0.00059	5,648
YEAR	−0.1818836E-02	0.84144E-03	−2.162	0.03065	1,976
UNDER15	−2.043796	0.40408	−5.058	0.00000	0.3266
OVER65	3.507457	0.70420	4.981	0.00000	0.7853E-01
FERTIL	0.2121669	0.12648E-01	16.775	0.00000	3.787
Dictatorship (compared with democracy)					
REG	15.32860	2.2074	6.944	0.00000	0.4359
LEVEL	−0.4565579E-04	0.81470E-05	−5.604	0.00000	895.6
YEAR	−0.7053947E-02	0.11352E-02	−6.214	0.00000	861.1
UNDER15	−2.381716	0.52383	−4.547	0.00001	0.1749
OVER65	−4.366002	1.0122	−4.314	0.00002	0.1972E-01
FERTIL	0.2924777E-01	0.15896E-01	1.840	0.06577	2.308
Control for regime selection					
EBAR	−0.2715914	0.57594E-01	−4.716	0.00000	−0.4390E-02

Regime differences in log-DEATHS[b]

Variable	Mean	Standard deviation	Minimum	Maximum	Cases
Democracy	9.7404	1.9504	5.2084	16.5867	1,225
Dictatorship	11.5973	4.3235	3.7727	23.7727	1,225

Note: The variables for dictatorship are intercept and slope dummies, $X * \text{REG}$, where REG = 1 if the regime is a dictatorship. Hence, the coefficients indicate differences from democracy.
[a] Selection on unobservables; individual regime effect; Heckman (1988) estimator.
[b] Expected values of death rates if regimes had been matched for all independent variables.

education . . . appears to be a necessary prerequisite to improved sanitary conditions." Health expenditures have the same effect, independently of education, again in accordance with Livi-Baci's observation that "those countries which have had particular success in combating death are those in which government policy has allocated sufficient human and economic resources to the health sector."

As Table 5.6B shows, if social expenditures are assumed to be endogenous with regard to regimes, the expected mortality under dictatorship will be 10.95, and under democracy 9.20: a difference of about two deaths per thousand. If these expenditures are in fact an effect of regimes, we should stop here. But we can also ask whether or not dictatorships still would have had higher mortality rates had they spent as much on each social policy as democracies. It turns out that had the regimes been matched for all the exogenous factors listed earlier (except fertility), and had they spent exactly the same amounts on various social policies, the mortality rates would have been identical: 8.83 per thousand.

In sum, exposed to the same exogenous conditions, dictatorships would have had much higher mortality rates. If we assume public expenditures to have been endogenous, mortality would have been still higher under dictatorship. Only when public expenditures are treated as exogenous with regard to regimes does the difference in mortality vanish.[10]

We will not retrace all the steps with regard to infant mortality. The effect of regimes on infant mortality is much more pronounced. Regardless of the specification of the model and the method of estimation, selection-corrected average infant mortality is much higher under dictatorships. Perhaps surprisingly, educational expenditures have little, if any, impact on infant mortality. Health expenditures, in turn, do reduce it sharply under both regimes, and their effect is greater than on gross mortality.[11] When regimes are matched for all the exogenous

---

[10] One set of variables that may have been omitted comprises the environmental conditions. Communist dictatorships have been particularly notorious for environmental catastrophes. Yet democracies, from the United States to Italy to India, have also had their share of environmental disasters. Without systematic data, we hesitate to go further.

[11] When absolute amounts of per capita expenditures are used, health expenditures do not matter under democracy, and they reduce mortality somewhat under dictatorship. This finding may indicate threshold effects. One prenatal visit and a vaccination may be sufficient to increase rates of survival, and because an average dictatorship spends only $33 on health, the statistical analysis may be showing the difference between those dictatorships that are below and above some threshold. But if that were all, we would not have observed the statistical relationship between expenditures as shares and mortality among democracies, which spend, on the average, $291. Because our concern is to assess the impact of regimes, rather explain infant mortality, we leave it at that.

Table 5.6B. Effect of regimes on the logarithm of death rates[a]

AR1 model: $e(t) = \rho e(t-1) + u(t)$
Initial value of ρ = 0.70035
Maximum iterations = 20
Iterations = 4; sum of squares = 8.792; log-likelihood = 421.977027
Final value of ρ = 0.88048
Durbin-Watson: $e(t)$ = 0.23904
Standard deviation: $e(t)$ = 0.25772
Standard deviation: $u(t)$ = 0.12218
Durbin-Watson: $u(t)$ = 2.17600
Autocorrelation: $u(t)$ = −0.08800
$N(0, 1)$ used for significance levels

Variable	Coefficient	Standard error (s.e.)	$z = b$/s.e.	$P[\|Z\| \geq z]$	Mean of X
Constant	7.201781	3.1244	2.305	0.02117	
LEVEL	−0.9422765E-05	0.49916E-05	−1.888	0.05906	7,798
YEAR	−0.3432290E-02	0.15599E-02	−2.200	0.02779	1,980
UNDER15	3.481486	0.43837	7.942	0.00000	0.2949
OVER65	10.73364	0.92944	11.548	0.00000	0.9101E-01
GXPDSSEC	−0.8482766E-03	0.35967E-02	−0.236	0.81355	9.668
GXPDEDUC	−0.2733571E-01	0.73131E-02	−3.738	0.00019	4.027
GXPDHLTH	−0.1931424E-01	0.71485E-02	−2.702	0.00690	3.050
Dictatorship (compared with democracy)					
REG	12.87115	4.4377	2.900	0.00373	0.3003
LEVEL	−0.7954322E-04	0.11181E-04	−7.114	0.00000	768.4
YEAR	−0.5620413E-02	0.22293E-02	−2.521	0.01170	594.5
UNDER15	−2.692637	0.58188	−4.627	0.00000	0.1205
OVER65	−2.698238	1.6588	−1.627	0.10382	0.1201E-01
GXPDSSEC	−0.1186252E-01	0.64192E-02	−1.848	0.06460	0.7222
GXPDEDUC	−0.4307885E-02	0.98115E-02	−0.439	0.66061	1.229
GXPDHLTH	0.9076060E-02	0.15080E-01	0.602	0.54726	0.4987
Control for regime selection					
EBAR	−0.2131209	0.69873E-01	−3.050	0.00229	−0.6662E-03

(continued)

Table 5.6B (continued)

Regime differences in log-DEATHS[b]

Variable	Mean	Standard deviation	Minimum	Maximum	Cases
Expenditures endogenous					
Democracy	9.1993	1.7295	5.1996	15.5567	606
Dictatorship	10.9521	2.6055	4.8773	19.0811	606
Expenditures exogenous					
Democracy	8.8305	1.8020	4.6046	15.5567	606
Dictatorship	8.8300	2.5699	3.7642	15.8390	606

Note: The variables for dictatorship are intercept and slope dummies, $X * $ REG, where REG = 1 if the regime is a dictatorship. Hence, the coefficients indicate differences from democracy.
[a] Selection on unobservables; individual regime effect; Heckman (1988) estimator.
[b] Inner product of exogenous variables and dictatorship dummies.

conditions, including fertility and social spending, the predicted rate of infant mortality is 41.5 under dictatorships and 31.2 under democracies: a difference of 10.3.

Finally, given what we have learned about gross and infant mortality, we would expect that differences in life expectancy would not disappear when regimes are matched for different conditions and even for social spending. When regimes are matched for their per capita income, time, and age structure, the expected difference in life expectancy is 5.0 years. When they are also matched, in a smaller sample, for the proportion of the labor force in agriculture, the difference is 4.9 years. Agriculture shortens life under both regimes, but its effect is low when controlled for income and other factors. Finally, when we assume, perhaps invalidly, that regimes have the same social spending, the difference is still 3.4 years. The effects of social spending on life expectancy are positive and identical under the two regimes: Both educational and health expenditures lengthen lives. Given that the effects of exogenous conditions and of social spending are the same, we are left with an unexplained difference.

Fertility and Births

Prior to demographic transition, European birth rates ranged from a low of about 30 to a high above 45 per thousand. The poor countries in our sample were close to the upper limit. According to Livi-Baci (1997: 176), "this is due primarily to higher levels of nuptiality: poor country age at marriage (or the age at which reproductive union is established) has traditionally been low, with almost no one remaining unmarried, unlike the situation in the West."[12] The average birth rate in the "more developed countries" between 1990 and 1995 was 12.6 (Livi-Baci 1997: table 5.2).

Birth rates depend on the proportion of women of childbearing age in the population and on their individual fertility. The first factor is a cumulative effect of demographic history; the second is a decision or, as the case may be, a non-decision. If dictatorships are experiencing the second phase of demographic transition, in which fertility is falling or already has fallen to a stable level, but the population is young as a result of high fertility in the past, then they will have high birth rates because of conditions they inherited. Hence, to see if birth rates are an effect of regimes, we must isolate the effect of fertility from that of age structure.

Because the birth rate is the product of the proportion of women of fertile age and their fertility (per year), we can decompose the regime-specific birth rates into the part due to demographic momentum and the part due to fertility. This is easier said than done, because the age category in our data set includes all people between ages 15 and 65, and because fertility rates are per lifetime rather than per year. Hence, we must make some assumptions: Appendix 5.1 explains how we arrived at the relevant estimates. But the conclusion is clear: Regimes differ in their fertility rates, not in their age structure. The proportion of women of childbearing age in the population we estimate to be 19 percent for democracies and 21.5 percent for dictatorships. Observed fertility differences, in turn, are large: 2.7 per woman under democracy, and 5.2 under dictatorship. If we assume the reproductive age to last 25 years, between ages 15 and 40, then birth rates per woman per year are 0.089 under democracy and 0.142 under dictatorship. Combining these estimated age distributions with the annual fertility rates yields birth rates higher under dictatorship by 13.6 per thousand. Thus, we calculate that if the age structure were the same under the two regimes, the dictatorial birth rate would be between 10 and 11 (per thousand) higher than under democracy. Hence, the difference in birth rates is not due to "momentum" but to "inertia."

---

[12] But see Dasgupta (1995: 1,890) for evidence that social mechanisms of fertility control have been used in some parts of Africa.

Even though the relationship between birth rates, on the one hand, and fertility and age structure, on the other hand, is purely algebraic, we also tested the conclusions of these calculations by regressing the logarithm of birth rates on the logarithms of fertility and of the proportion of the population between ages 15 and 65, which is the bracket for which we have data. If birth rates are due to momentum, then age structure should matter. It does not: The coefficients on fertility are high and significant under both regimes, and the coefficients on the age structure have high errors. Birth rates are higher under dictatorships because of higher fertility, not because of age structure.

To explain the regime differences in the birth rates, we must therefore explain the differences in fertility. Note that because death is something that, except for suicide or euthanasia, happens regardless of one's will, it is a rare province to have escaped the attention of microeconomists. Fertility, however, became a subject of the "new economic demography" (Schultz 1974).

Before we review economic theories of fertility decisions, some background information will be useful. Fertility depends on the age at which women establish reproductive unions, on the proportion of women who ever enter such unions, and on the duration of postpartum sexual abstinence: These are social mechanisms that regulate it. Fertility can be also regulated by traditional methods of birth control, coitus interruptus and abortion. Finally, it can be regulated by contraceptive devices. A total fertility rate (TFR) of seven children per woman is generally considered to be the norm of "natural fertility," that is, the number of children a woman would bear in her lifetime if fertility were not regulated by any methods. The highest known fertility rate for a human population is that of French Canadians born before 1860, 11.4 per woman (Livi-Baci 1997: 61–6). Social mechanisms of regulation reduce fertility to five per woman, but to cite Livi-Baci again (1997: 126), voluntary fertility control was the decisive factor in fertility decline. Fertility rates in Europe during the first half of the twentieth century fell to three per woman; in several present-day European countries, they are one per woman.

Thus, different mechanisms cause fertility reduction from different levels. Dasgupta (1995: 1,880) observed that "the factors that would influence the drop in the total fertility rate in a society from, say, 7 to 5 should be expected to be different from those that would influence the drop from 5 to 3 in that same society." Whether or not fertility is a matter of decision depends on the availability of the technology for regulating it. This technology, which according to Livi-Baci (1997: 183) consisted of traditional methods, appeared in the rural areas of France in the late eighteenth century and spread to other European countries during the second half of the nineteenth century. Artificial methods of birth control were illegal in the West until World War II.

Although the data are sparse, Table 5.7 shows that the use of contraception is much higher under democracy. More than 50 percent of women use contraception in democratic countries; only one in four in dictatorships. Moreover, the frequency of contraception is again higher under democracy at each level of income, and the differences are large. According to Sen (1994b, 1995), consensual methods of family planning are more effective than coercive ones, and dictatorships are more likely to rely on the latter. Yet we suspect that the use of coercive methods is rare (Livi-Baci 1997: 183–4). Most dictatorships either oppose all methods of population control or rely on consensual methods. This was certainly true of Eastern Europe, where the most prevalent method of population control seems to have been abortion. Hence, even if Sen's comparison of Kerala with China does show that consensual methods are more effective, we see no reason to think that regimes differ systematically in the methods of family planning they use.

Moreover, there is strong evidence that the mere availability of contraception seems to have little effect on fertility (Pritchett 1994). Although the use of contraception is strongly related to fertility, a prior question is why people do or do not use contraceptive methods. And there is a fair degree of consensus that what drives fertility decisions is the demand for children. Contraception is a technology that enables people to make choices, but people may decide against using it even when it is available.[13]

People want to have children for many reasons. They are sources of pleasure and of self-confirmation. Yet viewing children as an autonomous value does not explain why fertility should vary across populations and across conditions. If we want to have as many children as possible, then why does fertility decline as incomes increase?[14] If we

---

[13] This is not to say that access to contraception is universal. It is estimated that more than 100 million couples (about 15% of couples in which the wife is of reproductive age) would wish to limit their fertility but do not have access to contraception (Cassen 1994: 6). According to Lloyd (1994: 191), 16% of births are unwanted in countries where fertility rates average above 6, 30% in countries where fertility rates average between 4 and 6, and 25% where fertility falls below 4.

[14] In the classic model of Becker and Lewis (1973), as rendered by Razin and Sadka (1995: chap. 3), parents care about their own consumption, c, but also about the number, n, and the "quality," z, of children, maximizing $u(c, z, n)$, with all partial derivatives

Table 5.7A. Observed patterns of contraception and fertility, by per capita income and regime[a]

LEVEL	All CONTRACEPTION	All FERTILITY	Dictatorships CONTRACEPTION	Dictatorships FERTILITY	Democracies CONTRACEPTION	Democracies FERTILITY
0–1,000	10.4 (73)	6.1 (239)	8.3 (60)	6.1 (228)	19.9 (13)	6.2 (11)
1,001–2,000	23.0 (85)	5.7 (208)	21.9 (65)	5.8 (164)	26.3 (20)	5.5 (44)
2,001–3,000	36.9 (59)	4.7 (112)	31.3 (35)	5.1 (69)	45.1 (24)	4.1 (43)
3,001–4,000	51.8 (31)	3.8 (92)	48.8 (15)	4.0 (53)	54.6 (16)	3.5 (39)
4,001–5,000	53.7 (20)	3.0 (76)	44.6 (9)	3.2 (50)	61.1 (11)	2.6 (26)
5,001–6,000	51.3 (13)	2.6 (82)	48.2 (11)	2.5 (30)	68.5 (2)	2.7 (52)
6,001–	68.4 (48)	2.2 (526)	60.5 (4)	2.6 (27)	69.1 (44)	2.1 (499)
Total	35.0 (329)	3.8 (1,335)	24.8 (199)	5.2 (621)	50.7 (130)	2.7 (714)

[a] Proportion of women practicing contraception, fertility per woman. Numbers of observations in parentheses.

want to have some fixed number of children, then why doesn't fertility respond immediately to declines in infant mortality? If we want to have as many children as other people do, why do some couples suddenly begin to reduce fertility?

In light of recent economic theory, as excellently summarized by Ray (1998: chap. 9), demand for children depends on three factors: (1) their insurance value, (2) externalities in child-rearing, and (3) the costs, including opportunity costs, of child-rearing.

Dasgupta (1995: 1,894) cited a simulation by May and Heer (1968) according to which an average Indian couple in the 1960s who wanted to be 95 percent sure of having a son surviving when the father reached the age of 65 had to bear 6.3 children. Several features of that example merit attention. First, parents derive support from children during their old age.[15] Let the probability that any one child will support the parents when they are old be p. This probability depends on the chance that the newborn child will survive until the parents are old (most importantly, child mortality), on the chance that the child will earn enough income to support himself and the parents, and on social norms that make children responsible for their aged parents. Second, how many children people will want will also depend on the alternatives other than children's support: parents' assets, but also non-contributory old-age insurance schemes. Let the probability of deriving support from sources other than one's offspring be q. The total number of children a couple will then want so as to be 95 percent sure of support in old age is the n that solves $(1 - q)(1 - p)^n = 0.05$.[16] Note that as q gets larger, the number of children required for insurance declines. Assuming $p = 0.3$, the requisite number of children is 6.5 when $q = 0.1$, and it is 1.9 when $q = 0.7$.[17]

---

positive, subject to the non-linear budget constraint $c + zn \leq y$, where y is income. The effect of income on fertility is not clear in this model, depending on various elasticities of substitution in the parents' utility function.

[15] According to the World Bank (1984: 52), 80–90% of parents interviewed in Korea, the Philippines, Thailand, and Turkey counted on receiving economic assistance from their children in old age.

[16] This reasoning is based on the work of Ray (1998: 311), with some modifications. The equation is derived as follows: Because p is the probability of being supported by any one child, $(1 - p)^n$ is the probability that no child will support the parents; hence $s = [1 - (1 - p)^n]$ is the probability that at least one child will. The probability of being supported either by the state or by one's own assets is q. Hence, the probability of being supported by one source or another is $qs + q(1 - s) + (1 - q)s$. Simplifying and setting the right-hand side to 0.95 yields $1 - (1 - q)(1 - p)^n = 0.95$ or $(1 - q)(1 + p)^n = 0.05$.

[17] The insurance or "old-age security" hypothesis states that if parents care about children only as sources of support in old age, then the availability of other sources of

The number of children required for insurance against old age also declines as the probability of being supported by any single one of them increases. When $q = 0.1$, the requisite number of children is 6.5 with $p = 0.3$, but it is 2.9 with $p = 0.6$. This example introduces the issue of gender bias (Dasgupta 1995; Ray 1998). We used the masculine gender in the preceding paragraph deliberately: In many societies, only sons are educated, and only sons acquire the capacity to earn income. Hence, if insurance were to be derived equally from sons and daughters, p would be doubled, increasing, say, from 0.3 to 0.6, and with almost no outside sources of insurance ($q = 0.1$), optimal fertility would decline from 6.5 to 2.9.

Looking ahead to statistical analyses, we will thus expect that fertility will be low when infant mortality (INFMORT) is low and when government spending on health (GXPDHLTH) and female school enrollments (FEMSEC) are high, all increasing p, and when government spending on social security (GXPDSSEC) is high, thus increasing q. Clearly, these are not the only considerations implied by this theory, but these are the only insurance-related factors we can systematically observe.

The second set of factors affecting fertility encompasses various kinds of externalities. Some occur within the household or, in cultures where the term "household" does not have much meaning (Dasgupta 1995), within a broader and looser unit. Even within a household, the costs and benefits of children need not be the same for all household members. The woman of reproductive age may bear all the costs, but the man or his mother (Sen 1995: 6) may reap some of the benefits. Hence, if the power within the household rests with people other than the childbearing woman, the decision may be to have more children than the woman might desire. Basu, as cited by Sen (1995: 6), argues that "the real pity is often not that men wield so much domestic power," but that it is "during the prime reproductive years that female power

support will lower the number of children they (or the society on the average) will have, where other sources include (1) investment (lending at a positive rate of return) or (2) a social security scheme whereby the current productive generation is taxed to subsidize the subsistence of the beyond-the-productive-age generation. As the assumptions indicate, this hypothesis is not very robust. The relationship between the availability of alternative sources of support and a reduction of fertility does not or need not hold if (1) parents care about the quantity and quality of children per se, (2) they can borrow and not only lend, and (3) the social security scheme includes lump-sum transfers to children – analysis based on Razin and Sadka (1995). Hence, on prior grounds the validity of this hypothesis appears doubtful, and it is surprising that it holds as well as it does in democracies, as discussed later.

is at its lowest." Moreover, both Dasgupta (1993, 1995) and Ray (1998) emphasize that externalities may extend beyond the narrow reproductive unit. If grandparents or other kin bear some of the costs of rearing children, fertility will be higher. According to Ray (1998: 319), some public services – public education, but also subsidized housing and health services – may also lower the private costs of having children and lead to higher fertility rates.

Unfortunately, we do not have systematic information about family structure. What we know are the public expenditures on education (GXPDEDUC) and the frequencies of three religions, namely, Catholics (CATH), Protestants (PROT), and Moslems (MOSLEM). Clearly, cultural factors that shape the family structure are not limited to religions, but one would expect that religions would affect fertility and that some of that impact would assume the form of division of labor within the reproductive units.

Finally, fertility should depend on the cost of having children, including opportunity costs. As a result of capital accumulation and technical progress, the cost of producing market goods and service falls relative to the cost of raising children (Barro and Sala-i-Martin 1995: 313). Hence, the costs of children rise with income, wages, or other measures of opportunity costs. Because women bear most of the burden of child-rearing, the opportunity costs are higher if they engage in gainful activities and if they are educated. Galor and Weil (1996) argued that increases in capital per worker raise women's relative wages and that, in turn, this reduces fertility by raising the costs of children more than it raises the household income.[18]

Hence, with costs in mind, fertility should depend again on labor-force participation of women (LFPW), on income (LEVEL), on the level of educational attainment (EDT), and, if Galor and Weil are correct, on capital per worker (CAPW).

Notwithstanding Dasgupta's observation that "a general theory of fertility behavior is not currently available" (1995: 1881), this economic model goes a long way toward explaining the observed patterns. When we apply it to study the entire set of observations, regardless of

[18] In their model, an increase in the income of the male will increase the demand for children, whereas an increase in the income of the female will have both an income effect and a substitution effect, so that equal increases of both will have an ambiguous effect. But if women's wages increase by more than men's, then the cost of raising children will grow faster than household income, and fertility will decline.

regimes, all the variables have the signs predicted by the theory, and they are almost always statistically significant.[19] Moreover, in various specifications and the corresponding subsamples, they invariably account for at least 86 percent of variance. This is strong performance for any theory.

Capital per worker, which is supposed to raise women's relative wages and thus opportunity costs, according to Galor and Weil (1996), is negatively associated with fertility. It is also, however, highly correlated with per capita income, so one cannot distinguish the effect of average income from the effect of women's relative wages. When used together with income, the coefficient on capital per worker flips signs from one specification to another, whereas the coefficient on income remains robustly negative. Given this collinearity, we do not use capital per worker in the analysis of regimes.

Given the paucity of data, we cannot organize the analysis of regimes by theoretical considerations – insurance value, externalities, and opportunity costs – but only by sample size. We use two samples: without (sample A; $N = 552$) and with (sample B; $N = 276$) social expenditures. Table 5.7B shows the observed patterns of fertility by income levels and summarizes the results of regression analyses, with variables ordered by theoretical considerations.

The insurance variables are much more robust for democracies, where infant mortality (INFMORT), female secondary-school enrollment rates (FEMSEC), social security expenditures (GXPDSSEC), and expenditures on health (GXPDHLTH) have robust signs. Female enrollment rates negatively affect fertility under dictatorship. Infant mortality increases fertility under dictatorships only when public expenditures are not considered. And expenditures on social security and on health have no effect on fertility under dictatorship. Hence, insurance considerations are much more powerful under democracy. Later we discuss why this may be so.

Externalities play the same role under the two regimes. Public educational expenditures behave in the way postulated by Ray (1998: 319), that is, higher expenditures are associated with higher fertility. Hence, it seems that public education is a source of externality in child-rearing. To the extent to which the three religions for which we have data (and implicitly the fourth category, namely, all others) affect the household structure, one could also think that they indicate externalities in

---

[19] We could not use female illiteracy because the overlap between data on fertility and on illiteracy consists of only 12 observations.

Table 5.7B. Summary of selection-corrected regressions of fertility, by regime

Variable	Sample A			Sample B		
	All	**Dic**	**Dem**	**All**	**Dic**	**Dem**
Constant	−5.78	−5.84	2.66	−5.60	−16.97	10.99
Insurance:						
INFMORT	+++	+++	+++	+++	0	+++
FEMSEC	–––	–––	–––	–––	––	–––
GXPDSSEC				–––	0	–––
GXPDHLTH				––	0	–––
Externalities:						
GXPDEDUC				++	++	+++
CATH	0	++	+	+++	++	++
PROT	+++	++	+++	+++	++	++
MOSLEM	0	0	0	++	++	–
Opportunity costs:						
LFPW	–––	–––	–––	–––	0	0
LEVEL	–––	0	––	–––	–	0
EDT	––	0	–	–	––	0
YEAR	+++	++	0	++	+++	—
N	552	246	306	276	94	182
R^2	0.86	0.79	0.74	0.91	0.87	0.84
FERTILITY:						
Observed	3.67	5.21	2.44	3.13	5.18	2.07
Predicted		3.89	3.48		2.77	2.31

Notes: Pluses and minuses indicate signs of coefficients. Three signs indicate significance at the 0.01 level, two at the 0.05 level, and one at the 0.10 level; a zero means the coefficients are not statistically significant. Selection equation includes STRA, RELDIF, ODWP, NEWC, and BRITCOL. The estimators are OLS-AR1, separately for each regime.

child-rearing. The coefficients, however, make little sense and, except for a positive impact of Protestantism, are unstable.

Finally, opportunity costs are important under both regimes. Labor-force participation of women matters under both regimes, but only when social expenditures are not considered, suggesting that the opportunity costs of women working outside the household are lower when the state picks up educational and health expenditures. High per capita income is associated with lower fertility in the entire sample, but its impact is much weaker when the regimes are distinguished. Finally, the level of education of an average member of the labor force seems to have a weak negative effect on fertility, although this result is not robust.[20]

The effect of labor-force participation by women (LFPW) requires a separate comment. The relationship between female participation and fertility is non-linear under both regimes, but in different ways: Under dictatorships, it is U-shaped, but under democracy it is strictly convex to the origin. To put it in words, under dictatorship, fertility is high when the labor force contains either few or many women; under democracy, it is high when fewer women are in the labor force. Because female participation is itself U-shaped with regard to the proportion of the labor force in agriculture, what this must mean is that fertility declines in both regimes as the role of agriculture declines, and female participation with it, but as the society becomes more services-oriented and more women again enter into the labor force, fertility increases under dictatorship, but it continues to decline under democracy. And what this, in turn, implies is that women in wealthy dictatorships are doubly exploited: As workers, they receive lower wages than under democracy (see Chapter 3); as mothers, they continue to work outside the household while bringing up children. Indeed, according to Lloyd (1994: 193), "time devoted to children is largely responsible for differences in total work time between the sexes."

Female secondary-school enrollment rates increase with income under both regimes, but here the picture is more nuanced.[21] As Table 5.8 shows, both male and female secondary enrollments are higher in democracies with incomes up to $3,000 and above $5,000 than in dictatorships with such incomes. But between $3,000 and $5,000 both male and female enrollment rates are higher in dictatorships. In part, this is due to communist dictatorships: Enrollments in Eastern Europe were high and equal across genders. Yet removing communist countries from the sample does not quite obviate this pattern, because Latin

---

[20] The general evidence about the impact of female educational attainment on fertility is overwhelming (Sen 1995: 17). If we are not getting strong results, it is probably because our educational-attainment variable (EDT) does not distinguish sexes.

[21] The rates of primary-school enrollment are higher under democracy, for females and males, but many of them are above 100 percent, meaning that the school population is larger than the relevant age bracket, which implies in turn that there is a lot of recidivism. Hence, these rates cannot be unambiguously interpreted.

Table 5.8. Observed enrollment ratios, by gender, under dictatorship and democracy

LEVEL	All			Dictatorships			Democracies		
	Females	Males	N	Females	Males	N	Females	Males	N
Primary school									
0–1,000	52.8	72.0	(453)	52.8	71.7	(228)	52.8	77.9	(24)
1,001–2,000	76.2	89.7	(361)	75.4	89.7	(287)	79.3	89.6	(74)
2,001–3,000	95.3	103.0	(184)	92.6	102.7	(124)	109.0	103.6	(60)
3,001–4,000	103.1	104.8	(142)	101.7	103.7	(87)	105.3	108.6	(55)
4,001–5,000	99.7	102.9	(90)	96.0	100.2	(58)	106.4	107.9	(32)
5,001–6,000	105.1	106.2	(94)	102.8	104.1	(48)	107.5	108.4	(46)
6,001–	102.2	101.4	(405)	103.8	109.2	(29)	102.1	102.0	(376)
Total	83.2	92.0	(1,729)	73.6	86.8	(1,062)	98.5	100.3	(667)
Secondary school									
0–1,000	9.0	17.2	(420)	8.7	16.5	(396)	13.7	29.2	(24)
1,001–2,000	22.8	30.2	(340)	22.0	30.0	(269)	26.0	30.7	(71)
2,001–3,000	37.0	41.6	(176)	34.5	41.1	(122)	42.5	42.9	(54)
3,001–4,000	49.1	52.8	(141)	51.7	55.8	(87)	45.1	47.5	(53)
4,001–5,000	56.4	62.0	(82)	57.8	65.9	(53)	53.9	54.0	(28)

(continued)

5,001–6,000	65.8	67.5	(91)	61.9	65.4	(47)	70.0	69.6	(43)
6,001–	82.2	80.8	(413)	64.2	69.3	(39)	84.1	82.0	(373)
Total	41.8	46.2	(1,663)	26.2	33.3	(1,013)	66.1	66.3	(650)

Secondary-school enrollment ratios by region

Region	Females	Males	N
Africa	11.4	19.0	522
South Asia	22.0	35.9	79
East Asia	54.8	66.9	32
Southeast Asia	40.8	44.3	82
Oceania	31.3	34.7	21
Middle East and North Africa	36.3	50.4	167
Latin America	39.4	37.1	241
Caribbean	55.5	52.7	79
Eastern Europe	77.3	78.1	65
Industrialized	83.1	82.8	375

Note: Enrollment ratios are ratios of population enrolled to the relevant age categories.

American countries, which are frequent in this income range, have somewhat higher enrollments for females than for males. Hence, it is not necessarily true that dictatorships educate fewer women: They do so in some parts of the world, but not in others.

Note that education enters into the determination of fertility in three ways. Public expenditures on education encourage fertility by lowering the cost of raising children, but female enrollment in secondary schools lowers fertility. A higher educational level of the labor force seems to reduce fertility, but these results are weaker because we cannot distinguish genders.

What, then, is the impact of regimes on fertility? We have seen that, to some extent, regimes have different ways of processing the conditions under which they operate. Specifically, insurance incentives operate more strongly under democracy, but externalities and opportunity costs seem to have the same effect under the two regimes. Assessing the net impact of regimes is difficult, because several of the variables that shape fertility may or may not be exogenous with regard to regimes. We have seen that infant mortality is higher under dictatorships matched for exogenous conditions. We may also suspect that public expenditures are shaped by regimes. Nevertheless, even if we assume that all these factors are exogenous, fertility appears to be higher under dictatorships: 3.89 versus 3.48 when social expenditures are not considered, and 2.77 versus 2.31 when they are included.

Why, then, would regimes affect fertility even when they face the same conditions? The most plausible explanation for this finding is policy stability.[22] At least with regard to social security expenditures, under democracy people know that it is unlikely that these could be drastically reduced: Citizens know that they can vote politicians out of office if the latter curtail these expenditures, and they can expect that, knowing this, elected politicians will not curtail them. Hence, even if governments come and go, this is one budget item that is close to sacrosanct. In turn, when dictators change, fiscal policy can take any turn, and even when dictators remain in place, policy directions can change.

This argument can be generalized. Fertility is something intimate, a matter for private decisions. As Drèze (1992: 158) observed, "for most of us, 'adding a new person to the world' is first and foremost adding a

---

[22] We owe this suggestion to James Vreeland.

new person to the *family*."[23] Except for outright coercion, such as involuntary sterilization, governments affect fertility decisions only by changing the incentives for the individual reproductive units. This system of incentives, as we have seen, consists of two sets of components: those that affect the likelihood that the members of the current reproductive cohort will be able to sustain themselves in old age without the aid of their children, and those that affect the prospects that their offspring will be able and willing to support them. Reproductive decisions are made with a very long time horizon, about forty years. Hence, the uncertainty they entail is very high: It is difficult to plan for forty years from now. Moreover, the decision not to have the next child becomes irreversible long before the uncertainty resolves itself: The lag between the end of the reproductive age and that of the productive age is also large. And what is at stake is vital. Hence, there are good reasons for people to exhibit a high degree of risk aversion, perhaps to the point of using maximin as the criterion.

This structure of reproductive decisions implies that people will desist from having the next child only if they are very sure that they will be supported in the distant future by their already living children or by their private assets or by the government. Any threat to stability, economic or political, will lead reproductive units to hoard children: to have as many as possible, given the costs. And planning for a distant future is much more risky under dictatorship; we have cited the evidence throughout this book. As regimes, dictatorships are much less durable than democracies. Once we distinguish successive dictatorships, say ayatollahs replacing a shah, we find that the expected lives of dictatorships are much shorter than those of democracies. Just looking at the incidences of closings and reopenings of legislatures within authoritarian regimes shows that the expected life for regimes we call "autocracies," those without legislatures, is shorter than ten years, and the expected life for dictatorships with legislatures is about twenty-five years, whereas the expected life for democracies is about forty years (see Tables 1.5 and 1.6 in Chapter 1). Any change of the chief executive threatens the current authoritarian regime, but under democracy such changes are a part of everyday life (Chapter 2). And, as a result, economic performance under dictatorships is much more volatile than under democracies: The average duration-weighted

---

[23] The private nature of fertility decisions has been a persistent theme for Sen (e.g., 1995).

standard deviation of the rate of growth of total income is 6.94 during the spells of dictatorship, and 4.82 during the spells of democracy (Chapter 3).[24]

Hence, even if during a particular year under dictatorship the economy is booming, old people are receiving pensions, and younger people's daughters are receiving secondary education, there is little assurance that growth will be sustained forty years hence, that one will receive a pension, or that one's daughters will find employment. And because children are the least risky asset that people can accumulate, parents hoard children, rather than target their optimal number. For the effect of uncertainty on hoarding versus targeting, see Ray (1998: 314).[25]

Human Capital, Fertility, and Economic Growth

Societies can accumulate children, human capital, or physical capital. But at any particular moment they cannot accumulate everything: People are constrained by their resources. Hence, people must choose what to accumulate. If children, human capital, and physical capital are produced with different technologies and at different costs, and if they combine differently in production, the decisions people make will depend on the value they attach to each outcome and the relative rates of return to their eventual investments. These rates of return will depend on the relative magnitudes of the stocks: how many children people already have, how educated the labor force is, and how many machines there are.

At this level of abstraction, no more can be said. One might think that if a society confronted a situation in which there were machines that could not be operated because people did not have the necessary skills, then people would invest in education, and, vice versa, when people could not use their skills because there were not enough machines, they would invest in physical assets. But the situation is complicated by the fact that people have a third alternative, namely, to have many children, not educate them, and not invest in physical assets. Moreover, when people are poor and cannot borrow to educate

[24] A question arises at this point as to why investments in physical capital stock do not differ between regimes and yet investment in children is motivated by uncertainty.

[25] Note that this explanation illuminates the reasons that fertility was very low under communism. Those regimes did offer income security, mainly through full employment, and they educated women on par with men. And they were expected by everyone, eminent U.S. political scientists included, to last forever.

their children, they may have no choice but to have many children. Hence, entire societies may find themselves in a trap, a low-level equilibrium. In this trap, people are poor; because they are poor, they have more children rather than educate them or accumulate physical assets; because they do not accumulate either human or physical capital, they remain poor, and so forth.

What exactly entraps societies in poverty is far from clear. But we find evidence in favor of one story, told by Becker, Murphy, and Tamura (1990). Theirs is a complicated model. They have to make so many assumptions that listing them would require us to summarize half of their article. The key idea is that human capital is accumulated with increasing returns, so that when human capital is abundant, investing in the education of the children one already has ("quality") is more beneficial than having additional children ("quantity"). As a result, societies with a low stock of human capital tend to have higher fertility. The low-level trap arises when countries do not have enough human capital to operate the available stock of physical capital.

If a country is caught in this trap, either (1) both human and capital stocks will decline or (2) human capital will decline but physical capital will be accumulated.[26] The story is in some ways counterintuitive. The reason the stock of physical capital will decline when it is high relative to human capital is intuitively clear: Machines cannot be fully exploited when there are no skills to operate them, so that the return to physical investment is low. But whether or not the stock of human capital will decline will depend on whether a higher physical capital stock will raise the cost of the time spent investing in human capital more than it will increase the utility of future consumption, which will be true only under some conditions that we cannot observe directly (Figure 5.2).

If Becker, Murphy, and Tamura (B-M-T) are correct, then one should observe the following: With each point in the space constituted by H (on the horizontal axis) and K (on the vertical axis), both observed when the country entered our sample, one can associate the average rate of growth of per capita income during the period the country was observed. A B-M-T trap exists if one can draw through this space an appropriately sloped (convex, passing through the origin) line, $M(H)$, that represents the largest physical capital stock that can be fully

[26] In our data set, which includes the level of education of an average member of the labor force (EDT), which we take as the measure of human capital, H, there are 40 annual observations (out of 2,900) in which both K and H decline, and 222 observations in which K increases and H declines.

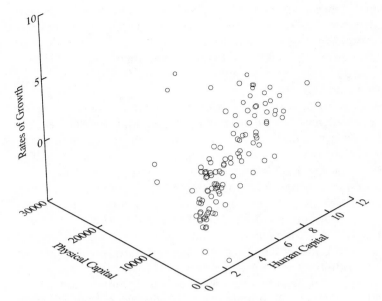

Figure 5.2. Growth of countries in and out of the trap

exploited given the level of human capital. Points above this line, that is, points for which $K(H) > M(H)$, should then be characterized by poor economic performance, and points below it by good performance. Note that if long-term economic growth were random with regard to combinations $\{H, K\}$, then for every line drawn through this space, the difference in performance associated with points above and below it would be zero. Hence, if we can draw a line such that performance above it is poorer than below it, then the conclusions of the B-M-T model are supported. Indeed, if economic performance depended only on the stocks of human and physical capital, then only instances of failure would be above this line, and only instances of success below it.

The evidence strongly supports the existence of such a trap. Drawing the line $M(H)$ that maximizes the difference in average performance between countries above and below it,[27] we find that in the twenty-one countries in the trap, per capita incomes grew in the long run at the average rate of 0.62 percent, while the ninety-two countries below it

[27] We used brute force, taking a quadratic function that passes through the origin, iterating over the two parameters, and calculating averages above and below the line.

had the rate of 2.58, a difference of –1.96. Among the twenty-one countries initially observed in the trap region, seven ended up with per capita incomes lower than those with which they began, and five more had incomes growing at less than 1 percent per year. Among the ninety-two countries that began below the trap region, only six declined over the period, two of them (Burundi and Mozambique) ravaged by civil wars. Moreover, in accordance with the theory, the average fertility at the end of the period, some twenty to thirty years later, was 5.96 among the countries that were originally in the trap, and 3.81 among the countries that were not.

Comparing some trajectories of countries in the H, K space is most telling. Figure 5.3A shows the time paths of H and K for some countries that began in the trap, and Figure 5.3B portrays some paths for countries that started outside of the trap. Whereas human capital was accumulated by all countries, the stock of physical capital remained stagnant or declined over time in Benin, the Central African Republic, Gabon, Madagascar, Colombia, and Iran – countries that started with educational levels insufficient to operate their physical capital. Gabon, with its heavy reliance on oil, experienced a rapid accumulation of physical capital, but it turned out to be transitory even as the stock of human capital increased. In turn, except for India, countries that started with levels of education high relatively to their stocks of physical capital increased both stocks. Brazil, which started with a relatively low level of education but also of physical capital, accumulated physical capital very rapidly, but then experienced a sharp drop. Most startling, however, are the experiences of South Korea and Taiwan, two countries that in the early 1960s had extremely low levels of physical capital and high levels of education. In both countries, the accumulation of physical capital was simply explosive.

What causes what is less apparent. But, contrary to Barro (1989), we find that in our data set increased fertility has a clear impact of reducing the growth of per capita income (Table 5.9). In the model that includes on the right-hand side the growth of productive inputs, each additional child reduces the growth of per capita income by 0.43. Given that the average fertility is about four, and the average rate of growth of per capita incomes is 2.46, this means that, ceteris paribus, in countries in which women have two children, per capita incomes double in about twenty-one years, and in countries in which fertility is six, they double in about forty-three years, almost a generation later.

Most of the observations in the trap are of poor countries, some with extremely low levels of education, almost none. Democracies, as we

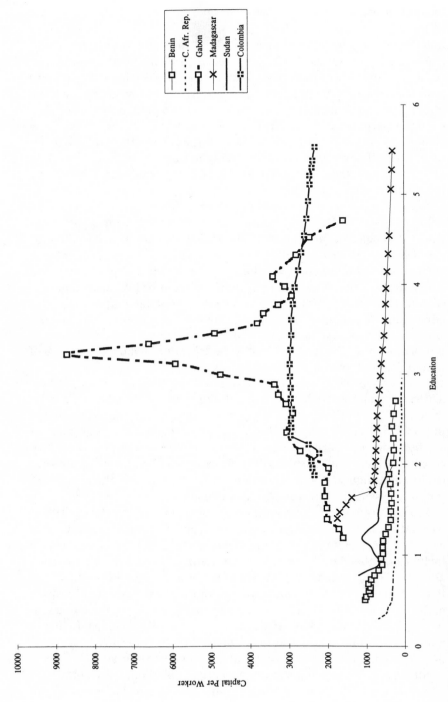

Figure 5.3A. Countries in the trap

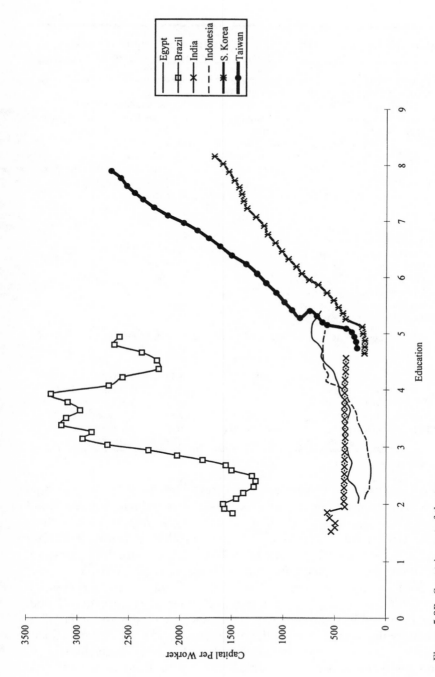

Figure 5.3B. Countries out of the trap

Table 5.9. Impact of fertility on the growth of per capita income

Ordinary least-squares regression: weighting variable = ONE; dependent variable is G;
  mean = 2.46091; standard deviation = 5.2782
Model size: observations = 1,087; parameters = 5; degrees of freedom = 1,082
Residuals: sum of squares = 14,630.4; standard deviation = 3.67718
Fit: R^2 = 0.51643; adjusted R^2 = 0.51464
Model test: $F(4, 1,082)$ = 288.88; probability value = 0.00000
Diagnostic: log-likelihood = −2,955.3139; restricted (β = 0) log-likelihood =
  −3,350.2010; Amemiya probability criterion = 13.584; Akaike information criterion =
  5.447
Autocorrelation: Durbin-Watson statistic = 2.24911; ρ = −0.12456

AR1 model: $e(t) = \rho e(t - 1) + u(t)$
Initial value of ρ = −0.12456
Maximum iterations = 20
Final value of ρ = −0.12562
Durbin-Watson: $e(t)$ = 2.25124
Standard deviation: $e(t)$ = 3.67738
Standard deviation: $u(t)$ = 3.64825
Durbin-Watson: $u(t)$ = 2.00264
Autocorrelation: $u(t)$ = −0.00132

Variable	Coefficient	Standard error (s.e.)	$z = b$/s.e.	$P[|Z| \geq z]$	Mean of X
Constant	1.133814	0.23336	4.859	0.00000	
KSG	0.3855428	0.11020E-01	34.986	0.00000	6.894
LFG	0.5458592E-01	0.86468E-01	0.631	0.52786	1.826
EDTG	0.9638270E-01	0.22294E-01	4.323	0.00002	2.879
FERTIL	−0.4310592	0.60930E-01	−7.075	0.00000	3.962
ρ	−0.1256196	0.30104E-01	−4.173	0.00003	

know, are rare among such countries. Yet it is striking that only a single observation of a poor democracy, Papua New Guinea, is to be found among the trap cases, which consist of several African dictatorships with very low education, Nepal, three oil-producing dictatorships with higher educational levels, namely, Gabon, Iran, and Iraq, and two wealthier democracies, Colombia and Venezuela (Table 5.10).

Because countries caught in the trap were almost exclusively ruled by dictatorships, the impact of regimes on fertility can be questioned: The observed difference between regimes may be due to the fact that dictatorships were caught in the demographic trap, while democracies enjoyed levels of human capital that allowed them to escape it. Because only three democracies were initially in the trap, and two of them were

Table 5.10. Countries in the trap and their long-term growth

Country	Year	K/L	H	G	FERTIL	REG
Angola	1975	379	0.514	−2.733893	6.4	Dic
Benin	1960	539	0.515	−0.058952	6.5	Dic
Burkina Faso	1960	88	0.075	0.133211	7.0	Dic
Central African Republic	1961	210	0.305	−0.561102	5.8	Dic
Ethiopia	1960	43	0.095	0.823698	7.0	Dic
Gabon	1961	1,917	1.190	2.939512	5.5	Dic
Gambia	1965	284	0.320	1.571987	6.5	Dic
Guinea	1966	128	0.030	1.600147	6.5	Dic
Ivory Coast	1961	242	0.220	1.409908	6.8	Dic
Madagascar	1961	2,462	1.400	−1.787089	6.5	Dic
Mali	1961	320	0.155	0.150148	7.0	Dic
Mauritania	1961	784	0.065	0.357157	6.8	Dic
Senegal	1961	688	0.315	0.457079	6.5	Dic
Sudan	1971	940	0.780	−0.201483	6.4	Dic
Tunisia	1961	1,109	0.610	3.480121	4.3	Dic
Colombia	1960	4,414	1.875	2.376248	2.9	Dem
Venezuela	1960	14,994	2.520	−0.064273	3.5	Dem
Iran	1960	3,348	0.800	1.400212	6.3	Dic
Iraq	1960	8,529	0.240	1.255016	6.2	Dic
Nepal	1961	183	0.090	1.826954	6.3	Dic
Papua New Guinea	1975	1,750	1.170	−1.422171	5.3	Dem

Notes: "Year" is the first year for which education data were available. *K/L* is capital per worker. *H* is EDT: years of education completed by an average member of the labor force. G is the average rate of growth of per capita income between the initial year and 1990 or the closest year for which data were available. FERTIL is fertility per woman during the last year data were available. REG is regime during the period.

relatively wealthy, even the fact that the twenty dictatorships caught in the trap ended with an average fertility of 6.33, and the three democracies with 3.87, is not very telling. But the trajectories of countries that were initially not in the trap testify again to the effect of regimes: The forty-three dictatorships ended with an average fertility of 5.13, and the forty-eight democracies with a fertility of 2.64.[28] And even if

---

[28] These numbers do not add up to the total of countries, because in two cases fertility data were not available.

those democracies initially had much higher stocks of both human and physical capital, the B-M-T theory asserts that the dictatorships, even though poorer, would have reduced their fertility and grown over the long run. Yet we find that although this theory finds strong support in the data, regimes still have a profound impact on demographic behavior.

Note that we now have seen two distinct explanations for fertility. In the insurance model, parents want to have children only because they offer a potential source of future support. In the B-M-T model, parents want to have children because they derive satisfaction from having children. These models are not rivals; both motives can play a role. Moreover, they both imply that fertility should be higher in poor countries. And both models are strongly supported by the data. Hence, we are willing to believe that both insurance and altruistic considerations lead people in poor countries to have more children. Nevertheless, even in poor countries political regimes affect fertility. And this difference, we believe, is due to the insecurity inherent in dictatorships. It is this insecurity that leads people to invest in the least risky asset, namely, children. Hence, political regimes do make a difference even when countries are matched for the exogenous conditions that drive fertility in both models.

Conclusion

The overall picture of life and death under the two political regimes is startling. Even if we assume that regimes face the same conditions, democracies have lower birth rates and lower death rates. Women in democracies have fewer children. More children survive to adulthood. As adults, they live longer, years longer.

It is useful to look at these findings in reverse order. Birth rates are higher under dictatorship because they have higher fertility, not because of different age structures. And they would have higher fertility even if they faced the same conditions as democracies, most likely because policy uncertainty leads parents to hoard children rather than to target their number.

The regime difference in death rates is lower than that between birth rates. The observed differences in infant mortality are larger, and so are differences corrected for selection. And the effect of regimes on life expectancy is astonishing: The observed difference is enormous at each income level, and this difference again does not vanish when regimes are matched for exogenous conditions.

Regardless of regime, poverty forces women to procreate, it exposes them to the tragedy of seeing their infants die, and it exposes all people to disease and premature death. The effects of poverty are overwhelming: People in very poor countries, with incomes below $1,000, live 46.5 years on the average, but in countries with incomes above $6,000, they live 72.9 years. Poor people have many more children, much higher infant mortality, and much higher death rates. But political regimes matter, and they matter even in poor countries: For several aspects we have considered, their effect is equivalent to a difference of $1,000 in per capita income.

The effect of political regimes on the lives of women is glaring. Remember that the rates of labor-force participation do not differ between regimes. What this means is that under dictatorship women engage in gainful activities outside the household as frequently as under democracy. But in addition they bear many more children, see more of them die, and are themselves more likely to die. And, as Sen (1995: 16) observed,[29] "one of the most important facts about fertility and family size is that the lives that are most battered by over-frequent child birth are those of the women who bear these children. . . . It is not only the case that at least half a million women die every year from maternity-related causes through afflictions that are entirely preventable, but also hundreds of millions of women are shackled involuntarily to a life of much drudgery and little freedom because of incessant child bearing and rearing."

Because the difference in birth rates is larger than that in death rates, population grows slower under democracies, again matched with dictatorships for exogenous conditions. And because the difference between regimes in population growth is larger than the difference in the growth of total output, per capita incomes grow faster under democracy.

Appendix 5.1: Calculating Age Structure

For the sample that contains data on age distribution and birth rates, we know that the age distribution is

---

[29] See also Cassen's overview of the literature: "The clearest evidence of negative effects of population growth under high fertility [is seen] at the individual and household levels. Mothers exposed to large numbers of pregnancies have a high risk of dying; many of these deaths are from unsafe abortions. Children with large [numbers] of brothers and sisters will be more likely to be deprived in various ways. Girls suffer in particular; and once they fail to be educated, the scene is set for intergenerational transmission of poverty and high fertility" (1994: 4).

	Democracy	Dictatorship
N	816	569
0–15	0.27	0.40
15–65	0.63	0.55
65–	0.10	0.05
Birth rate (per hundred)	1.92	3.69

We want to know the proportion of the population of childbearing age, which we take to be between ages 15 and 40.

Inspecting the annual data shows that this age structure is almost invariant over time. Hence, to standardize everything to 100, suppose that during each year the population of each of the two regimes consists of 100 persons distributed in the foregoing proportions.

Now, we also know that 1.92 persons are born each year under democracy, and 3.69 under dictatorship. Because 15 years later there will be 27 persons under age 15 in democracy, and 40 persons in dictatorship, it must be true that

$$15(1-i)B = P_1,$$

where $(1-i)$ is the survival rate for people under age 15, B stands for births (per hundred), and P_1 is the number of people under age 15. Solving this equation yields

	$1 - i$	i
Democracy	0.94	0.06
Dictatorship	0.73	0.27

This may appear to be an enormous difference, but note that infant mortality (i.e., mortality during the first year of life) is 2.54 per hundred under democracy, and 9.36 under dictatorship. This implies that of the 1.92 children born each year under democracy, 0.0488 will die during the first year, 0.0664 will die during the next fourteen years, and 1.8048 will survive beyond the age of 15 and enter into the 15–65 cohort. Under dictatorship, in turn, of the 3.69 children born each year, 0.3388 will die in the first year, 0.6386 will die during the next fourteen years, and 2.6937 will enter into the 15–65 cohort.

If the number entering each year into the 15–65 cohort is E, then it must be true in turn that

$$50(1 - d)E = P_2,$$

where P_2 is the number of persons in this cohort. Solving this equation for each regime yields

	1 – d	**d**
Democracy	0.70	0.30
Dictatorship	0.41	0.59

Again, the difference in these survival rates is huge. But note that the observed life expectancy is 69.3 years under democracy and 53.3 under dictatorship.

Now, if the chance of reaching the age of 65 conditional on having survived until 15 is 0.70 for democracy and 0.41 for dictatorship, the chance of surviving any next year within this age cohort is 0.993 under democracy and 0.982 under dictatorship. This in turn implies that the chance of reaching the age of 40, having reached 15, is 0.84 under democracy and 0.64 under dictatorship. Because under democracy 1.8048 persons will enter this age cohort, which consists of 25 years, the total population at risk is 45, and under dictatorship, where 2.6937 will enter, the population at risk is 67. Multiplying the populations at risk by the survival probabilities yields an estimate of 38 persons between ages 15 and 40 under democracy, and 43 under dictatorship. Hence, the age structure is

	Democracy	**Dictatorship**
0–15	0.27	0.40
15–40	0.38	0.43
41–65	0.25	0.12
65–	0.10	0.05

Note that these estimates of the 15–40 bracket are biased toward low numbers, because we assume that the death rate is uniform in the entire 15–65 bracket. But the bias goes in the same direction under the two regimes, and the shares of the population of childbearing age are very similar under the two regimes.

To see what these numbers imply, examine their consequences for birth rates. Given the observed rates of fertility per woman, and assuming, as we do, that the reproductive period lasts 25 years, the birth rates per woman per year are 0.089 under democracy and 0.142 under dictatorship. Because women of reproductive age are about half of the population that age, the birth rate (per hundred) implied by the estimated age distribution is 1.69 for democracies, as compared with 1.92 observed, and 3.05 for dictatorships, as compared with 3.69 observed. Hence, we are underestimating birth rates because we have underestimated the populations in the childbearing cohorts. But we see that the differences in birth rates between regimes are due to different fertility rates, not to the age structure of the population. If the proportion of women of childbearing age in the entire population had been the same under democracy as under dictatorship, 21.5 percent, the estimated birth rate under democracy would have been 1.91, as compared with 3.05 under dictatorships with the same age structure. If the age distribution under dictatorship had been that estimated for democracy, the birth rate under dictatorship would have been 2.70, as compared with 1.69 under democracy. Hence, what differentiates regimes is fertility, not age structure, "inertia" rather than "momentum."

Conclusion

To make sense of the forest of numbers that populate these pages, we first need a summary of the central findings. And although our question concerns the impact of political regimes, one would be blind not to note first the grip on people's lives of sheer poverty. Although regimes do make a difference for material welfare, their effect pales in comparison with that of scarcity.

In every aspect we have examined, the differences between poor and rich countries have been enormous. For one, even if democracies do occasionally spring up in poor countries, they are extremely fragile when facing poverty, whereas in wealthy countries they are impregnable. Hence, poor people are much more likely to be ruled by dictators. Obviously, poverty means that people consume less. They also live shorter lives, have more children, see more of them die and fewer of them become educated, and are more likely to suffer from collective violence. However one thinks of well-being, people with low incomes lead poor lives.

Moreover, while with regard to mortality rates and life expectancies the gap between poor and rich countries has been closing, the disparities of incomes and of fertility rates have increased. The coefficient of variation (the ratio of the standard deviation to the mean) of death rates fell from 0.44 when the countries were first observed ("entry" year) to 0.40 during the last year each country was observed ("exit" year). The coefficient of variation of life expectancy declined from 0.23 to 0.17. But the coefficient of variation of fertility increased from 0.33 to 0.46, and the coefficient of variation of per capita income rose from an already enormous 0.89 to 1.05. Whereas the multiple of per capita income of the richest to the poorest country when they were first observed was 40.4, at the end of the period it was 57.9.

These disparities of income and fertility increased because countries that were richer to begin with developed further, while many countries that were poor remained poor. Of the eighty-three countries with per capita incomes under $2,000 when first observed, fifty-seven had remained equally poor or had become even poorer some thirty or forty years later. Of the fifty-two countries that began with higher incomes, all but seven at least doubled their income, and none declined over the long run.

Hence, poverty can trap societies in its grip. One way poverty binds is that when a society is poor, so is the state, and when the state is poor it cannot extract resources and provide public services required for development. Another trap occurs when the initial stock of human capital is low relative to the physical capital stock; people tend to have more children, and high fertility sharply reduces the growth of per capita income.

Yet the bonds of poverty are not inexorable. Some countries, notably Taiwan, South Korea, Thailand, Japan, Singapore, Portugal, Greece, and Malta, grew spectacularly, at least quadrupling their per capita incomes, with all the benefits that development brings. Of this list, two (Taiwan and Singapore) were ruled by dictators during the entire period and one (South Korea) during most of it, two were democracies throughout (Japan and Malta), and the remaining three (Thailand, Portugal, and Greece) experienced both regimes. Thus, although such spectacular successes are rare to begin with, there is nothing to indicate that it takes one regime or the other to generate them. But, in any case, to evaluate the impact of regimes, one must look at their entire record, not just their best record.

Political regimes have no impact on the growth of total income when countries are observed across the entire spectrum of conditions. Contrary to widespread concerns, democracies do not reduce the rate of investment even in poor countries. Indeed, it appears that when countries are poor there is little that governments can do, so that it makes little difference for economic growth whether rulers are elected or hold power by force. In wealthier countries, the patterns of growth are not the same. Dictatorships rely on growth of the labor force and on keeping wages low, whereas democracies pay higher wages, use labor more effectively, and benefit more from technical progress. But though growth under wealthier dictatorships is more labor-extensive and labor-exploitative than growth under wealthier democracies, so that the functional distributions of income are different, the average rates of growth of total income are about the same.

The economic effects of political instability differ across regimes.

Indeed, the concept of political stability is not transportable across regime types. The same phenomena that constitute instability in dictatorships – changes of rulers, strikes, demonstrations – are just part of everyday life in democracies. In dictatorships, any change or expectation of change of leaders, any manifestation of political opposition, is economically costly. But though such phenomena are much more frequent in democracies, they are so routine that they do not affect the economy.

Thus, we did not find a shred of evidence that democracy need be sacrificed on the altar of development. The few countries that developed spectacularly during the past fifty years were as likely to achieve that feat under democracy as under dictatorship. On the average, total incomes grew at almost identical rates under the two regimes. The only difference is that wealthier dictatorships have a more unequal functional distribution of income: They pay lower wages. But these findings also imply that the recently heralded economic virtues of democracy are yet another figment of the ideological imagination. Democracy has other virtues, but, at least with regard to the growth of total economies, political regimes are not what matters.

Yet per capita incomes grow faster in democracies. The reason is that democracies have lower rates of population growth. In spite of rapid diffusion of medical advances, death rates remain somewhat higher under dictatorship, and life expectancies are much shorter. But the main reason population grows faster under dictatorships is that they have higher birth rates, and the difference in birth rates is due to higher fertility, not to the age structure of the population. We are not certain why fertility is higher in dictatorships, but there are indications that it is the policy instability inherent in dictatorships that induces families to procreate.

Women are particularly affected by dictatorships. They participate in gainful activities at the same rates as they do in democracies, and, as workers, they get lower wages. But they also have more children, see more of them die, and are themselves more likely to die in childbirth.

These findings add up to a bleak picture of dictatorships. Although democracies are far from perfect, lives under dictatorships are grim and short. Dictatorships are regimes in which political rulers accede to power and maintain themselves in power by force. They use force to prevent people from expressing their opposition and to repress workers. Because they rule by force, they are highly vulnerable to any visible signs of dissent. They are successful economically only if they are "stable," that is, if no one expects that the dictator will be changed or the dictatorship will be abolished. Because in dictatorships the policies depend on the will, and sometimes whim, of a dictator, they exhibit high variance of economic performance: Some generate miracles, some disasters, and many generate both. Because their policies and their performances are so unpredictable, they do not allow people to plan their lives over a longer horizon, and thus they induce households to hoard the least risky asset, namely, children. In the end, per capita incomes grow slower and people live shorter lives in dictatorships. Thus, whereas scarcity makes lives destitute, regimes do make some difference, not only for political liberty but also for material well-being.

Many of our aggregate numbers reveal political repression, material destitution, and mass violence. Yet, in spite of the persistence of occasional massacres, in spite of poverty increasing in large parts of the globe, in spite of widespread dissatisfaction with the functioning of democracy even in wealthy countries, there is no doubt that the past five decades have witnessed historically unprecedented political and material progress. When we first observed these countries, 41 percent of the world's population lived under democracy; when we last observed them, 48 percent did, and even more since then. Per capita income of an average inhabitant of the globe was $1,878 when first observed, and $4,292 around 1990: 2.3 times higher. Of each one thousand people, 15.3 died during the entry year, but only 9.7 died during the exit year. An average person could expect to live 52.3 years when first observed, and 64.7 when last observed, 12 years longer. True, as countries developed they did not necessarily become similar: Wages in authoritarian Singapore were still much lower than in democratic Austria when they became equally wealthy. But both political progress and material progress are evident.

Because China and India add up to one-half of all of us, they deserve special attention. China still remains under authoritarian rule, and India has maintained a democratic regime against all odds. Per capita income in China rose from $470 in 1961 to $1,324 in 1990, and in India per capita income increased from $559 in 1951 to $1,262 in 1990. Death rates fell in China from 14.2 per thousand in 1961 to 6.6 in 1987; in India they declined from 22.2 in 1962 to 11.4 in 1987. Life expectancy in China was 40.5 years in 1961, and 68.7 in 1987, whereas in India it was 45.5 in 1962 and 57.8 in 1987. Finally, fertility tumbled in China from 4.7 in 1961 to 2.1 in 1990, and in India it went down from 6.5 in 1962 to 4.2 in 1987. Hence, progress was not limited to countries that were already wealthy.

Africa is a source of mitigation in any account such as ours. A recent study shows that a dummy variable for this continent is negative and significant in all growth regressions. Africa has experienced slower growth of incomes, slower social development, more corruption and bureaucracy, and more frequent civil wars than the rest of the less-developed countries (Collier and Gunning 1999). Yet even this continent shows some progress, albeit slow and spotty. The average African country had a per capita income of $747 when first observed, and $966 when last observed. Death rates have fallen from 22.1 to 15.8 per thousand, and life expectancy has increased from 41.8 to 50.6 years. In turn, fertility has remained almost unchanged, 6.4 for the first and 6.2 for the last observations. And only 2 percent of Africans lived under democracy as of our last observation, in or before 1990.

Ours has been a strange century, one in which mass murder has repeatedly punctuated the progress of democracy and of material welfare. About 160 million people, roughly 10 percent of the world's population in 1900, were killed in wars in the same hundred years during which democracy became an almost universal value of mankind and technical innovations multiplied incomes and extended lives. Thus, what the future may bring is far from clear. The tools of social science give us little with which to look ahead. Certainly, extrapolating trends is a risky, if not dubious, undertaking. Yet, writing at the eve of a millennium, one cannot but wonder what the future may bring.

Let us first put together all that we learned and then peek ahead. Here are the pieces we have:

1. The probability that a dictatorship will die and a democracy will be established is pretty much random with regard to per capita incomes, about 2 percent each year. But the probability that, once established, a democracy will survive increases steeply and monotonically as per capita incomes get larger. Indeed, democracy is almost certain to survive in countries with per capita incomes above $4,000.

2. Total national incomes grew at an average rate of 4.23 percent per annum. Incomes grew slowly in poor countries; growth rates were highest at income levels between $2,000 and $3,000, declining again at higher incomes. The observed rates of growth were 4.42 under dictatorships and 3.95 under democracies, but when countries were matched for exogenous conditions, the growth rates under the two regimes were almost the same.

3. Rates of population growth were much lower in wealthier countries. But at every income level, population grew faster under dictator-

ships. As a result, the observed rates of population growth were 2.42 percent per annum for dictatorships and 1.46 percent for democracies. When the regimes were matched for exogenous conditions, a large part of that difference remained: Our best guess is that population would have increased at a rate of 2.18 under dictatorships and at 1.59 under democracies had they faced the same conditions.

4. Finally, the incidence of war on the territory of a country was much lower in wealthier countries. We also know independently that democracies do not war with each other. Although wars not only kill but also impede growth, the recovery from wars is rapid, so that they do not have long-term economic effects.

Given what we know about the past forty years or so, we can do two things. First, we can see if this schematic description is sufficient to reconstruct the patterns we observed. And then we can venture into speculations, by using these patterns to look ahead. What we want to know is how many countries will be ruled by democracies in the year 2030, what will be their incomes and their populations, and how many will suffer from wars.

Let us first see how well can we reproduce the patterns we observed. Starting with per capita incomes, population, and regimes observed during the entry years, we can use the dynamic patterns summarized earlier to predict values for the same variables for the exit years (see Appendix C.1). Because the dynamic of regime transitions is probabilistic, we will not get unique answers. Thus, the expected values are based on repeated runs (Table C.1).

Note that the fit between simulated and observed values is very close, except for the incidence of war. The average per capita income observed at the exit year was $4,292, and the average predicted value is $4,300. The proportion of world population living under democracy is slightly underpredicted by simulation, and the predicted number of dictatorships is just one more than observed. The predicted rate of growth of population is a slight overestimate, so that the total world population at the exit year is predicted as 5,101 million, just slightly above the observed value. In turn, the number of countries experiencing wars on their territories is grossly underpredicted by the simulation. The reason is that the 1980s were exceptionally war-ridden, so that the probabilities of war were much higher at the end of the period. But, except for war, this simple simulation seems sufficient to reconstruct the observed patterns (Table C.2).

Given that our predictions for the year 2030 are based on a

Table C.1. Average values of selected indicators observed or predicted during various years

Year Source	Per capita income	Proportion democratic	Number of dictatorships	Population growth	Total population	Countries in war
Entry						
Observed	1,878	0.41	84	1.63	2,764	6
Exit						
Predicted	4,300	0.44	75	1.75	5,101	8.4
Observed	4,292	0.48	74	1.70	5,068	16
2030						
Predicted	11,199	0.67	45	1.23	9,376	5.3

Notes: All the numbers refer only to the 135 countries in our data set. Predicted numbers are based on simulation. "Proportion democratic" is the proportion of the world population living under democracy. "Population growth" is the rate of growth of the world population. "Total population" is the population of the world, in millions. "Countries in war" is the number of countries experiencing wars on their territories.

Table C.2. Distribution of countries in entry year, exit year, and 2030

LEVEL	Entry year			Exit year			2030		
	Number	Wars	Dic	Number	Wars	Dic	Number	Wars	Dic
0–1,000	48	5	41	34	7	34	12	3	11
1,001–2,000	45	1	30	23	4	13	15	2	13
2,001–3,000	13	0	8	20	3	13	8	1	6
3,001–4,000	9	0	2	12	2	6	10	1	6
4,001–5,000	8	0	2	7	0	2	4	0	3
5,001–6,000	5	0	1	4	0	2	3	0	1
6,001–7,000	4	0	0	5	0	0	4	0	1
7,001–10,000	3	0	0	8	0	2	17	0	0
10,001–20,000				22	0	2	26	0	1
20,001–30,000							11	0	1
30,001–40,000							5	0	1
40,001–50,000							4	0	0
50,001–							16	0	0
Total	135	6	84	135	16	74	135	7	44
Minimum level	226			312			523		
Maximum level	9,121			18,073			71,211		
Multiple	40.4			57.9			136.2		

Notes: Numbers for year 2030 are based on one simulation, closest to the average predicted values. LEVEL is income per capita. "Number" is the number of countries in each range of per capita income. "Wars" is the number of countries experiencing wars on their territories. "Dic" is the number of dictatorships.

mechanical extrapolation, caveats would be redundant. But one caveat could invalidate all our optimistic forecasts: depletion of non-renewable resources or severe degradation of the environment. Unfortunately, systematic data concerning environmental degradation are not available. But there are good grounds to fear that if these past trends were also mechanically extrapolated, our future would appear much less rosy. So, with this one caveat, foolishly but valiantly, we present the results:

1. Average world per capita income will be much higher – our guess is about 2.5 times higher – than the 1990 level. Incomes will grow faster than in the past, because there will be fewer poor countries that will grow exceptionally slowly. Some per capita incomes we predict to be extremely high. Obviously, if rates of growth decline as high incomes get even larger, our prediction is grossly overopti-

mistic. But income convergence among the developed countries is just a description of the past. Whether or not increasing returns will set in at the level of entire economies, as distinct from particular firms or sectors, is still an open question.

2. Given that dictatorships will be disappearing, for various reasons, and that per capita incomes will be higher, more democracies will survive, so that most of humanity will live under democracy. But quite a few dictatorships will be left, mostly in poor countries and mostly in Africa. Because India has remained a democracy against all odds, we repeatedly predict it as a dictatorship.

3. Given that population growth declines as incomes become larger and that it is lower in democracies, population growth will slow down. The population of the 135 countries in our sample will be about 9.4 billion in 2030, which is not far from more sophisticated predictions: The United Nations forecast for the entire world in 2025 is 8.5 billion (Livi-Baci 1997: 222).

4. Even though more countries will be rich and more will be democracies, we still predict quite a few wars, all in poor countries – in fact, all in Africa. Given that we did not anticipate that violent conflicts would surge in the 1980s, this is not even an extrapolation: just a *memento mori*.

5. Finally, consistently with other projections (Quah 1996), we believe that if the past patterns continue, income disparities among countries will continue to increase. Because total income grows slowly in very poor countries and population grows rapidly, per capita income increases very slowly. Countries that already have medium income levels grow rapidly, and their population growth slows down sharply as they become richer. In turn, already wealthy countries grow somewhat slower, but they begin at high levels and have low population growth. Hence, distribution of per capita incomes flattens with time, and disparities increase.

Hence, if the patterns we have observed persist, the world will be better, much better. More people will be living in democracies; they will be wealthier; and they will be enjoying all the benefits that wealth brings, probably including great improvements in public health and medical technology. But not all of us will enjoy this progress: Poverty will still be widespread, dictators will still repress, and wars will still ruin lives.

Hence, optimism does not entail quiescence. We have learned that the bonds of poverty are difficult to break, that poverty breeds dictatorships, and that dictatorships make lives miserable. We also know that if we allow the patterns of the past to persist, most people will be much better off, but many will remain within the double grip of poverty and dictatorship – if we allow the patterns of the past to persist.

Appendix C.1: Simulation

This simulation is based on the rates of growth of total income presented in Table 3.6, the probabilities of regime transition by regime from Table 2.3, the rates of population growth by regime from Table 5.1A (modified, see later), and the probabilities of war by per capita income and regime, not shown in the text.

Two simulations were conducted. The purpose of the first was to validate the model. Entry-year values were taken as observed, and the variables were iterated until the exit year. Thus the exit-year values are based on the number of years each country was observed.

The second simulation was used to generate extrapolated values. Observed exit values were used to start, and each country was iterated 40 times, to generate predictions for the year 2030 or close to it (the earliest exit year was 1987).

The two random elements in the simulation are regime transitions and wars. Because the predicted values have very low variance, the averages reported in the text are based in both cases on ten runs.

Observed rates of population growth persistently overpredicted the total population observed by the exit year and underpredicted the average per capita income. To calibrate these rates, we uniformly subtracted 0.004 from all the growth rates presented in Table 5.1A. This was sufficient to generate results very close to observed values.

The program for the simulation, in BASIC, is available on request.

Selection as a Problem of Identification

The problem raised by non-random selection is how to make inferences from what we observe to what we do not.[1]

What we want to know is the probability that some outcome variable Y will assume the specific value y_i for observations $i = 1, \ldots, N$, each characterized by a vector of exogenous factors x_i. Hence, the probability of interest is $\Pr\{Y = y_i | X = x_i\}$, which, to simplify the notation, we will write most of the time as $P(y|x)$.

Now, think of the entire sample as consisting of cases observed in states $d = 0, 1$. Let the probability that $d_i = 1$ depend on some factors $z_i = \{x_i, v_i\}$, where v are those features of i that affect only its states but not the outcomes under each state, and x are the variables that affect the outcome and, perhaps, selection into states. In our context, $d_i = 1$ if country i is observed under a dictatorship, and $d_i = 0$ if it is observed as a democracy.[2] The dependent variable Y is any among those examined earlier. We will use economic growth as the example.

Because the problem is symmetric, let us work with Y_1, which we observe only if $d = 1$, so that

$$y_{i1} = \begin{array}{l} y_{i1} \quad \text{if } d_i = 1 \\ \text{unobserved if } d_i = 0. \end{array} \tag{1}$$

---

[1] This entire section follows Manski (1995). A note on our terminology is needed: Statisticians tend to speak of *endogenous sampling* rather than of non-random selection as the source of selection bias. We depart from this terminology for two reasons: (1) We want to emphasize that selection is not a matter of the sample frame chosen by the researcher but of the mechanisms by which the entire set of observations is produced by "nature." (2) We reserve the terms "endogenous" and "exogenous" *selection* for the mechanisms by which these observations are produced.

[2] Note that in order to lighten the notation, we ignore time.

The probability distribution of y_1 in the entire sample is

$$P(y_{i1}|x_i) = P(y_{i1}|x_i, d_i = 1)P(d_i = 1|z_i) + P(y_{i1}|x_i, d_i = 0)P(d_i = 0|z_i). \qquad (2)$$

What do we know? We observe the selection probability $P(d = 1|z)$, the censoring probability $P(d = 0|z)$, and the distribution $P(y_1|x, d = 1)$ of y_1 conditional on selection. We do not observe, however, the distribution of y_1 for cases observed as $d = 0$, $P(y_1|x, d = 0)$. This last probability concerns counterfactual observations: It is the probability that an observation with $X = x_i$, observed under $d = 1$, would have had a particular value of Y_1, $Y_1 = y_i$, had it been observed under $d = 0$. To put it in terms of our example, $P(y_1|x, d = 0)$ is the probability that a country observed as a democracy would have had a particular rate of growth had it been a dictatorship. And because we do not observe counterfactuals, we do not know what this distribution is.

Given that we cannot observe $P(y_1|x, d = 0)$, the probability $P(y_1|x)$ in (1) is not identified. Moreover, the same is true of the expected value of y given x:

$$E(y_1|x) = E(y_1|x, d = 1)P(d = 1|z) + E(y_1|x, d = 0)P(d = 0|z), \qquad (3)$$

and, again, we do not know $E(y_1|x, d = 0)$.

Manski (1995: 25) shows that even without making any assumptions, the $P(y|x)$ is bounded. Suppose that we want to know the probability that $Y_1 \le y_i$, $P(Y_1 \le y|x)$. Then, setting $P(Y_1 \le y|x, d = 0)$ as alternately zero and one, we can set the bounds on $P(Y_1 \le y|x)$ as

$$P(Y_1 \le y|x, d = 1)P(d = 1|z) \le P(Y_1 \le y|x) \le$$
$$P(Y_1 \le y|x, d = 1)\, P(d = 1|z) + P(d = 0|z). \qquad (4)$$

Hence, the upper bound on the probability of interest, of Y_1 being less than or equal to y, is then equal to the censoring probability, $P(d = 0|z)$. Because the mean of a random variable is not a continuous function of its distribution function, however, no bounds can be established with regard to the expected value (Manski 1995: 26).

Because the same is true for y_0, the observational structure is

$$y_i = \begin{array}{ll} y_{i1} & \text{if } d_i = 1, \text{ unobserved otherwise,} \\ y_{i0} & \text{if } d_i = 0, \text{ unobserved otherwise.} \end{array} \qquad (5)$$

We want to know two distributions, $P(y_1|x)$ and $P(y_0|x)$, and their expected values. The first is the distribution of y *in the entire sample* if all cases are observed as $d = 1$; the second is the distribution of y *in the entire sample* if all cases are observed as $d = 0$. In terms of our example, y_1 is growth under dictatorship, and y_0 under democracy. Obviously, if we want to know the impact on y of being in states d, we want to determine the difference between these two distributions, conditional on x. For example, we may want to estimate the difference of the expected values, $E(y_1|x) - E(y_0|x)$, or the probability that growth under democracy would have been higher than that observed under dictatorship, $P(y_0 > y_1|x)$, or the difference between the probabilities that an economy would decay under either regime, $P(y_0 < 0|x) - P(y_1 < 0|x)$. The question about the impact of regimes on growth concerns such differences.

We already know that we cannot identify $P(y_j|x)$: For each $d = j$, $j = 0, 1$, we observe only the cases with $d = j$, but not those with $d \neq j$. We observe $P(d|x)$, $P(y_1|x, d = 1)$, and $P(y_0|x, d = 0)$, but not $P(y_1|x, d = 0)$ and $P(y_0|x, d = 1)$. Hence, we face underidentification. The same is true of the expected values $E(y_1|x)$ and $E(y_0|x)$.

To see that underidentification is caused by non-random selection, assume that being under $d = j$ has nothing to do with the outcome y_j. Then the conditional probability of each outcome is the same whether the cases are observed under either of the two states $j = 0, 1$, so that $P(y_j|x) = P(y_j|x, d = j)$, and the model is fully identified. This is what experimentalists assume and quasi-experimentalists try to emulate.

To conclude, in the presence of non-random selection we face the problem of how to identify the distribution of cases we do not observe. As always, identification requires additional assumptions. And, as always, stronger assumptions impose narrower bounds on the distribution, but require more theory, or faith, as the case may be. Manski's (1995) general recommendation is that we should use weaker identifying assumptions and be satisfied with interval estimates. Because he discusses various identifying assumptions that arise naturally in the context of selection, we will not pursue this route further.

Statistical Models of Selection

To approach issues entailed in estimating the distributions $P(y_j|x)$, assume that selection into $j = 0, 1$ is governed by some unobserved random variable d^*, such that the observed state is $d = 1$ when $d^* > 0$, and $d = 0$ otherwise, so that $P(d = 1) = P(d^* > 0)$ and $P(d = 0) = 1 - P(d = 1)$.

The joint density of (y_j, d) in the sample is, for any i,

$$f(y_j, d) = P(d \neq j)f(y_j|x, d = j)P(d = j), \qquad j = 0, 1, \tag{6}$$

281

that is, the probability that y_j is not observed, times the density of y_j given that it is observed, times the probability that it is observed.

The density $f(y_1|x, d = 1)$ is the joint density of $(y_1, d^*|z)$ given that $d = 1$ or $d^* > 0$:

$$f(y_1|x, d = 1) = f(y_1, d^* |z, d^* > 0) = f_1(y_1|x)P(d^* > 0|y_1)/P(d^* > 0), \quad (7)$$

with $-\infty \leq y_1 \leq \infty$, $0 \leq d^* \leq \infty$, where $f_1(y_1|x)$ is the marginal density of y_1, and $P(d^* > 0|y_1)$ is the conditional probability of being in the state $d = 1$ given y_1 (Pudney 1989). Substituting into (6) yields

$$f(y_1 \, d) = P(d = 0)^* f_1(y_1|x)P(d = 1|y_1). \quad (8)$$

Similarly for y_0.

The likelihood of y_{i1}, y_{i0}, d_i, z_i in the sample is thus

$$L = \prod_{i=1}^{i=N} L_{i1}^{d_i} L_{i0}^{1-d_i}, \quad (9)$$

where $L_{ij} = f(y_{ij}, d_i)$ is given by (8).

To determine this likelihood, we must determine the probabilities $P(d_i = j)$ and the marginal densities $f_{ij}(y_{ij}|x_i)$, $j = 0, 1$. In other words, we need to identify the mechanisms of selection and of performance conditional on selection. This is what follows.

Selection is a mechanism that allocates observations $i = 1, \ldots, N$ to states $j = 0, 1, \ldots, J - 1$, in our case $J = 2$. Selection can be a consequence of a deliberate decision of the researcher: This is what the arguments about research design are all about. It may result from some irredeemable defect of the sampling process: One cannot phone people who have no phones. Or it may be generated by the world around, independently of any operations by the researcher. Only the last situation is of interest here.

Consider the effect of political regimes on economic growth. If a country has an authoritarian regime, we observe growth under dictatorship; if it is a democracy, we observe growth under democracy. In none of such situations do we observe the consequences of states that were not realized. Hence, we do not observe the entire population, but only a sample.

It may seem strange to refer to the "population" as including unobserved cases. But if we are to compare the effects of states j on the performance of an individual characterized by an x_i, we must allow this individual to be potentially observable under the full range of $j = 0, 1, \ldots, J - 1$. That is, even if in fact we observe the case i only in state

$d_i = j$, we must conjure the possibility of this case having been observed as $d_i \neq j$, and vice versa. We must thus think in terms of a "super-population, consisting of a continuum of 'potential' individuals." The actual sample is then regarded as having been drawn by "nature" from this super-population (Pudney 1989: 45).

If the actual population is a random sample of the potential one, any multivariate combination (x_i, d_i) can be drawn with a positive probability. This property of random sampling is what allows us to isolate the effect of d on y given x, that is, to "control" for x the effect of d on y. If the sample is random, we can "match" pairs $(x_i, d_i = 0)$ and $(x_i, d_i = 1)$. But if sampling is not random, there will be some observations without a "match": Some of the x_i's will not have support. And increasing the sample size will not increase the probability of finding a match. In the presence of non-random selection, quasi-experimental comparisons fail regardless of the number of observations. As a result, we will be unable to tell whether or not democracies would have grown as fast had they faced the same conditions as the observed dictatorships.

How, then, does "nature" do its work? Let us first describe the selection mechanisms generically and then distinguish some types. Assume that each case can be characterized by some proclivity to be in the state $j = 0, 1$, conditional on $z = \{v, x\}$. Let the proclivity to be in state $d = 1$ be d^*. Then, thinking in regression terms, we can write

$$d^* = Z\alpha + u, \tag{10}$$

where Z are the factors observed by the investigator, and u are those that are not observed. Suppose further that we standardize the distribution in such a way that the observed state d is related to the unobserved proclivity by

$$d = \begin{matrix} 1 & \text{if } d^* > 0 \Rightarrow z\alpha > -u \Rightarrow -z\alpha < u, \\ 0 & \text{otherwise.} \end{matrix} \tag{11}$$

The probability that $d = 1$ is then given by

$$P(d = 1) = P(d^* > 0) = \int_{-\infty}^{-z\alpha} u \, du = F(-z\alpha), \tag{12a}$$

where F is some distribution that satisfies the axioms of probability theory, and

$$P(d = 0) = 1 - F(-z\alpha). \tag{12b}$$

Selection is endogenous if an individual chooses d to maximize the utility associated with the outcomes of the choice, that is, solves the problem $\max_j U(y|x)$. The solution to this maximizing problem is to choose

$$d = \begin{matrix} 1 & \text{if } U(y_1|x) > U(y_0|x), \\ 0 & \text{if } U(y_1|x) \le U(y_0|x). \end{matrix}$$

Hence the probability that an individual will choose $d = 1$ is the probability that $U(y_1|x) > U(y_0|x)$.[3] Assuming that each utility depends on factors observable by the investigator, as well as some that are not, the utility of being in state j is $U(y_j|x) = X\beta_j + u_j$. Then $P[U(y_1|x) > U(y_0|x)] = P[U(y_1|x) - U(y_0|x) > 0] = P[(x\beta_1 - x\beta_0) > (u_0 - u_1)] = P[x(\beta_1 - \beta_0) > u_0 - u_1] = P(x\beta > -u)$, where $\beta = \beta_1 - \beta_0$ and $u = u_1 - u_0$. This is the same as (12), except that the only variables that enter into purely endogenous selection are those that determine the eventual outcomes, that is, x.

Selection is exogenous if state d occurs not because of the consequences associated with the choice but because of some features v_i. Then the probability that an individual will behave in the way $d = 1$ will depend on the characteristics v, so that

$$P(d = 1) = P(v\alpha + u > 0) = P(-v\alpha < u),$$

which is again the same as (12), except that the variables that affect the outcome do not enter this model. To use the language of Gambetta (1987), selection is driven by "push" rather than "pull" factors.

To evaluate the relative strengths of these competing explanations, we first need to construct a general model in which both explanations might play roles. The state under which a particular country is observed depends, then, on the strength of the factors V that push the country toward $d = 1$ or the utility that the country derives from the outcomes in state $d = 1$. Hence,

$$d^* = v\gamma + [U(y_1 - y_0)]\delta + u \quad and \quad P(d = 1) = P(d^* > 0), \tag{13}$$

where γ and δ indicate the respective forces of the "push" and the "pull" factors.[4]

---

[3] Or, in the multinomial case, that $U(y_j|x) > \max_{k \ne j} U(y_k|x)$.

[4] For an early example of such a model, see Lee (1978). In some cases, this model can be interpreted in an alternative manner, namely, $V\gamma$ can be viewed as the "transition cost" of moving from state $d = 0$ to $d = 1$. For example, if Y stands for the time needed to commute to work by bus or by car, and V stands for family income, an individual will move from bus to car if the income given up to buy the car is worth less than the utility of the time saved. Hence, the interpretation of the model depends on the substantive meaning attached to the V variables. Yet if V becomes simply "psychic cost," the economic hypothesis becomes tautological.

Thus, if countries are democratic or authoritarian because of their exogenous characteristics, such as level of economic development, education, or urbanization (Lipset 1960), selection is exogenous. If countries have regimes under which they grow faster economically, selection is endogenous. Our analyses invariably show that the factors that enter on the right-hand side of the performance equation are not statistically significant in the selection equation. Hence, throughout the book, we treat selection as exogenous.

Statistical Models of Performance

Assume now that y is a function of x, with the population density $f(y|x)$. Write the regression equations as

$$y_{i0} = x_i\beta_0 + u_{i0},\tag{14a}$$

$$y_{i1} = x_i\beta_1 + u_{i1}.\tag{14b}$$

The expected value of y_1 for the selected sample is, for any i,

$$E(y_1|x, Y_1 \text{ is observed}) = E(y_1|x, d = 1) = E(y|x, d^* > 0)$$
$$= E(y|x, -z\alpha < u) = x\beta_1 + E(u_1|d^* > 0),\tag{15}$$

where $E(u_1|x, d^* > 0)$ is the conditional expectation of u_1 given that y_1 is observed. The expected value for the population is

$$E(y_1|x) = x\beta_1.\tag{16}$$

Similarly for y_0.

Hence, the values expected in the sample differ from the population values by the conditional expectations of errors given that the values are observed. If selection is not random, then u_j, $j = 0, 1$, are correlated with u in the selection equation (10), so that $\text{cov}(uu_j) \neq 0$.

The expected value for the selected samples can be derived as follows. Note first that if the u_j's are correlated with u, then

$$E(u_j|d) = \sigma_{ju}E(u|d),\tag{17}$$

where σ_{ju} is a regression coefficient of u_j on u. In turn, to estimate the expected values $E(u|d^* > 0)$ and $E(u|d^* \leq 0)$, we can use the fact that the expected value of the truncated normal distribution is

$$E(u|d^* > 0) = E(u|-z\alpha < u) = f(-z\alpha)/[1 - F(-z\alpha)] = f(z\alpha)/F(z\alpha) = \lambda_1.\tag{18a}$$

In turn,

$$E(u|d^* < 0) = E(u|{-z\alpha} > u) = -f(-z\alpha)/F(-z\alpha) = -f(z\alpha)/[1 - F(z\alpha)] = \lambda_0, \tag{18b}$$

where the λ_j's are the inverse Mill ratios or the hazard rates.

From (12) we know that Y_1 is observed when $-z\alpha < u$, so we can write the expected values in the observed sample as

$$E(y_1|d = 1) = x\beta_1 + \sigma_{1u}\lambda_1, \tag{19a}$$

and, similarly for y_0,

$$E(y_0|d = 0) = x\beta_0 + \sigma_{0u}\lambda_0. \tag{19b}$$

Note that if (14) is estimated on the basis of the observed sample, the variable λ_j is omitted from the specification. Hence, selection is a source of omitted-variable bias (Heckman 1979).

We can now also understand why controlling ("matching") for the variables that enter into both the selection and outcome equations may in fact exacerbate, rather than attenuate, the selection bias (Achen 1986). Following Heckman (1988), let us distinguish first between selection on observables and on unobservables. Selection on observables occurs when the expected covariance $E(u_j u) \neq 0$, but once the observed variables Z are controlled, it vanishes, so that $E(u_j u|z) = 0$. Selection is on unobservables when $E(u_j u) \neq 0$ and $E(u_j u|z) \neq 0$, so that controlling the factors observed by the investigator does not remove the covariance between the errors in the outcome equations and the selection equations. Now, note that the regression coefficient $\sigma_{ju} = \text{cov}(u_j u)/\text{var}(u_j)$. If selection is on unobservables, controlling for some variable x in the outcome equation may reduce the error variance u_j without equally reducing the covariance $u_j u$. Hence, the coefficient on the omitted variable will be larger, and the bias will be exacerbated. Suppose that countries are more likely to have dictatorial regimes when they are poor or when their leaders are unenlightened and that the rate of growth is lower when per capita income is lower or leaders are unenlightened. The researcher can observe per capita incomes, but not enlightenment. Then controlling for per capita income in the outcome equation will reduce the error variance, but not the covariance due to enlightenment. The observations will be matched for per capita income, but not for enlightenment: There will be no democracies with unenlightened leaders at low levels. Hence, the observed difference in growth will be due purely to the unobserved difference in enlightenment, not to regimes.

This completes the development of the model. We have learned that the expected values for the observed cases are biased because they covary with the variable that determines which cases are observed. If selection is exclusively on observables, this bias can be corrected by traditional controlling techniques. But if it is on unobservables, such controls would only exacerbate the bias.

Estimating Selection-Corrected Models of Performance

Correcting for selection bias is not uncontroversial. Several researchers have found that corrections for selection are not robust, but are highly sensitive to relatively minor changes in assumptions about distributions (Goldberger 1983). Others have found that some estimation methods fail to correct for this bias and may even exacerbate it (Stolzenberg and Relles 1990). We seem to be in the quandary that was spelled out by Heckman (1988: 7): "Different selection methods will produce similar estimates of program or institution impacts *only if there is no problem of selection bias*. The variability in estimates across selection models indicates that selection is a problem." So if there is no selection bias, different methods for correcting it will be robust; if there is a bias, they need not be. The alternative ways out of this dilemma are to rely solely on experiments – a solution that, regardless of its merits, is not feasible in the context of comparative research – or to ignore the problem altogether, or to struggle with the problem by using a variety of approaches. As Heckman (1988: 6) emphasized, "there is no single 'correct' way to eliminate selection bias." But there are alternative approaches, and the differences among them are instructive.

There are two basic approaches to parametric estimation of selection models, plus a number of variations. The first is maximum likelihood; the second is Heckman's (1976) two-step method.

To be able to use maximum likelihood, we must assume joint distributions of (y_j, d^*, z) and derive the respective marginal distributions, $f_j(y_j|x)$, as well as the conditional distributions $P(d = j|y_j)$, $j = 0, 1, \ldots,$ $J - 1$. As long as $J = 2$ and the observations are independent, identically distributed (i.i.d.), and normally distributed, this is not problematic. The marginal distribution is

$$f_{ij}(y_{ij}|x_i) = \sigma_j^{-1}\Phi[(y_{ij} - x_i\beta_j)/\sigma_j], \tag{20a}$$

the probability $P(d_i = j|y_{ij})$ is

$$P(d_i = j|y_{ij}, z_i) = \Phi\left\{[z_i\alpha + \rho_{ju}(y_{ij} - x_i\beta_j)/\sigma_j]/[1-\rho]^{\frac{1}{2}}\right\}, \tag{20b}$$

and the probability $P(d_i \neq j)$ is

$$P(d_i \neq j|z_i) = 1 - \Phi(z_i\alpha). \tag{20c}$$

To get maximum-likelihood estimates (MLEs), all we need to do is to substitute (20) into (8) and maximize the likelihood given by (9), each j at a time. The MLE is consistent and efficient, although sensitive to departures from normality.

Yet under several conditions maximum-likelihood estimation is difficult. This is true when $J > 2$,[5] when the performance series is autocorrelated, or when it exhibits fixed or random effects: problems we often encountered in this study. The main problem is that $P(d = j|y_j, z)$ may be intractable. In those situations, we rely on Heckman's two-step method, which is consistent but not fully efficient.

The advantage of Heckman's method is that its consistency does not require y_j, d^* to be jointly normal, provided that d^* is normally distributed and the errors in equation (22) are distributed independently of d^*, but not that they are normal (Amemiya 1984: 33). Heckman's method is to estimate by maximum likelihood the selection part of the model

$$L = \prod_i^k P(d_i = j), \tag{21}$$

where k is a $(J - 1)$ vector of dummy variables that assume the value $k = 1$ when $d = j$, and $k = 0$ otherwise. Estimating (17) will yield $\hat{\alpha}$, $F_{ij} = F_j(z_i\hat{\alpha})$, and λ_{ij}'s. Equations (15) can then be written as linear regressions:

$$y_{ij} = x_i\beta_j + \sigma_{ju}\lambda_{ij} + \varepsilon_{ij}, \tag{22}$$

where $\varepsilon_{ij} = y_{ij} - E(y_{ij}|d_i = j)$, so that $E(\varepsilon) = 0$.

Discussions of variance and of the properties of this estimator can be found in the work of Amemiya (1985) and Greene (1990).

Heckman (1988) discussed alternative estimators, based on a control-function approach. Although we used those estimators in Chapter 5, we refer the reader to the original source.

---

[5] Lee (1983) assumes that the variables u_{ij} and ε_i, which is a transformation of u_i, have well-defined marginal distributions and that they also have an i.i.d. joint distribution, which will be true in case of multinomial logit. Yet it turns out that this assumption is highly restrictive, because it implies that all the regression coefficients σ_{ju} in (18) must have the same sign (Schmertmann 1994).

Any method for correcting selection effects yields unbiased estimates of the coefficients in the outcome (performance) equations (15). With these coefficients, we can generate the unbiased values, observed and counterfactual, of the y_{ij}'s for each individual i in each state j. All we need to do is to estimate

$$y_{ij}|x_i = x_i\hat{\beta}_j. \tag{23}$$

These are the values of y_i expected in each state j for an individual characterized by x_i. Because for each $i = 1, \ldots, N$ the exogenous conditions x_i are the same across the states, these expected values indicate the effect of being in state j on the outcome y_{ij}, which is what we wanted to know all along. Now we have matched cases: For each x_i, we observe the outcome or performance y_i under each j. We can therefore calculate what would have been the difference between regimes if the entire sample had been observed under both regimes.

Finally, one last complication. In the entire foregoing analysis, we have matched cases by creating the observations we were missing, that is, by constructing counterfactuals. Each of the $y_{-j}|x$ values tells us what the value of the outcome y_i *would have been* had the case i, observed with a particular set of features or under a particular combination of conditions x_i, been observed under each of the states in which it was not. But this procedure entails the assumption that the variables x are exogenous with regard to the states j. If they are endogenous, then the counterfactuals are no longer in the *modus potentialis* but in the *modus irrealis*: If j affects x, then the counterfactual premise "had x_i been the same under a different j" is no longer possible. Suppose that political regimes affect the rate of growth of the labor force – which they in fact do – which in turn enters into the list of the variables explaining growth. Then we cannot conjure a counterfactual in which the labor force would grow at the same rate under the two regimes. Hence, when we calculate the values corrected for selection, but not when we generate unbiased estimators, we should correct only for those x variables that are exogenous with regard to j. But this, in turn, calls for testing the exogeneity of each x, and may lead to a regress.

All of the variables used in this study are listed here in alphabetical order. Information about sources is given in brackets. Variables with no citation of source may be (1) coded by the authors, (2) derived from existing variables, or (3) matters of common knowledge. The names for all variables are in capital letters.

ACCHEAD: Number of changes of chief executives (HEADS) accumulated during the life of a particular political regime as defined by REG.

AGEA: Age in years of the current regime as classified by AUT.

AGEH: Number of years chief executive has been in power. The year the chief executive comes to power is coded 1. In cases in which the chief executive changed more than once during one year (HEADS > 1), AGEH = 1. Also, AGEH = 1 for the first year in countries that became independent after 1950 (even in cases where the chief executive served as a prime minister or governor general of the colony). AGEH is missing for Switzerland, Uruguay (1951–1966), and Yugoslavia after 1980 because of their collective executives. [Banks, Day, and Muller 1997; da Graça 1985; Bienen and Van de Walle 1991]

AGEI: Age in years of the current regime as classified by INST.

AGER: Age in years of the current regime as classified by REG. The year in which the regime comes into existence is coded as 1. When applicable, ages were extended back as far as 1870.

AGETOGO: Number of years before a regime transition (as classified by REG). The transition year is coded as 0. Countries that never experienced a transition during the 1950–1990 period, and the last regime in each country, are coded as missing.

ASPELL: Number of successive spells of political regimes as classified by AUT. A spell is defined as years of continuous rule under the same regime.

AUT: Classification of political regimes in which dictatorships are distinguished by the existence of a legislature (elected or appointed): coded 0 if democracy; 1 if bureaucracy (dictatorship with a legislature); 2 if autocracy (dictatorship without a legislature). Coding adjusted for transitional regimes. A transition year is coded as the regime that emerges in that year.

BIRTHS: Crude birth rate per 1,000 people. [World Bank 1994, series 374]

BRITCOL: Dummy variable coded 1 for every year in countries that were British colonies at any time after 1918, and coded 0 otherwise.

CAPW: Capital per worker, defined as KS/LF.

CATH: Percentage of Catholics in the population. [LPS 1993/94]

CIVMIL: Civil–military relations: coded 1 if a government was controlled by a non-military component of the nation's population; 2 if an outwardly civilian government was effectively controlled by a military elite; 3 if there was direct rule by the military, usually (but not necessarily) following a military coup d'état; 4 if other (all regimes not falling into one or another of the foregoing categories, including instances in which a country, save for reasons of exogenous influence, lacked an effective national government). [Banks 1996]

COMEX: Dummy variable coded 1 for countries that are primary-commodity exporters, as defined by the International Monetary Fund (IMF), and coded 0 otherwise. [IMF 1994]

CONTRACEPTION: Percentage of female population using contraception. [World Bank 1994, series 369]

CPI: Rate of inflation: annual rate of growth of the consumer price index. [IMF 1994]

DEADLOCK: Dummy variable coded 1 for the cases in which the largest legislative party controls more than one-third but less than one-half of seats (33.3 < SEATS ≤ 50), and coded 0 otherwise.

DEATHS: Crude death rate per 1,000 people. [World Bank 1994, series 375]

DEMADIC: Dummy variable coded 1 for all the years of a democracy that follows a dictatorship (as defined by REG), and coded 0 otherwise.

DEMBDIC: Dummy variable coded 1 for all the years of a democracy that precedes a dictatorship (as defined by REG), and coded 0 otherwise.

DEMONSTRATIONS: Any peaceful public gathering of at least 100 people for the primary purpose of displaying or voicing their opposition to government policies or authority, excluding demonstrations of a distinctly anti-foreign nature. [Banks 1996]

DICADEM: Dummy variable coded 1 for all the years of a dictatorship that follows a democracy (as defined by REG), and coded 0 otherwise.

DICBDEM: Dummy variable coded 1 for all the years of a dictatorship that precedes a democracy (as defined by REG), and coded 0 otherwise.

DIVIDED: Classification of political regimes in which dictatorships are distinguished by the number of formal powers: coded 0 if democracy; 1 if dictatorship with a legislature or at least one political party; 2 if dictatorship with executive only. A transition year is coded as the regime that emerges in that year.

EDT: Cumulative years of education of the average member of the labor force (Bhalla-Lau-Louat series). [Bhalla 1994]

EDTG: Percentage annual rate of growth of EDT.

EFFPARTY: Number of effective parties, defined as $1/(1 - F)$, where F = party fractionalization index. [Banks 1996]

ELF60: Index of ethnolinguistic fractionalization, 1960. [Easterly and Levine 1997]

EXPHAZH: HEADHAZ led one year.

EXPPAD: PAD led one year.

EXPPDA: PDA led one year.

EXSELEC: Mode of effective executive selection: coded 1 if direct election (election of the effective executive by popular vote or election of committed delegates for the purpose of executive selection); 2 if indirect election (selection of the effective executive by an elected assembly or by an elected but uncommitted electoral college); 3 if non-elected (any means of executive selection not involving a direct or indirect mandate from an electorate). [Banks 1996, but modified and completed where appropriate]

FEMSEC: Gross enrollment ratio, secondary, female. [World Bank 1994, series 301]

FERTIL: Total fertility rate (births per woman). [World Bank 1994, series 373]

FLAGC: Dummy variable coded 1 for the first year each country is observed, and coded 0 otherwise.

FLAGE: Dummy variable coded 1 for the last year each country is observed, and coded 0 otherwise.

FLAGR: Dummy variable coded 1 in the first year of each regime spell (as classified by REG),and coded 0 otherwise.

G: Annual rate of growth of per capita income (LEVEL).

GDPW: Real GDP per worker, 1985 international prices. [Heston and Summers 1993; hereafter, PWT 5.6]

GINI: Gini index of income distribution. [Deininger and Squire 1996]

GLAG: G lagged one year.

GXPDEDUC: Central-government expenditure on education as a share of GDP (both at factor cost, current national currency). [World Bank 1994, series 450/series 9]

GXPDHLTH: Central-government expenditure on health as a share of GDP (both at factor cost, current national currency). [World Bank 1994, series 451/series 9]

GXPDSSEC: Central-government expenditure on social security and welfare as a share of GDP (both at factor cost, current national currency). [World Bank 1994, series 452/series 9]

GXPKTOTL: Central-government total capital expenditure as a share of GDP (both at factor cost, current national currency). [World Bank 1994, series 462/ series S9]

HEADHAZ: Predicted probability that a change of chief executive will occur during the current year, given CIVMIL, TLAG, LEGELEC, and PRESELEC.

HEADS: Number of changes of the chief executive in each year. Chief executives are presidents in presidential democracies, prime ministers in parliamentary and mixed democracies, and whoever are the effective rulers in dictatorships (designated explicitly as "dictators," or as "heads of military juntas," "presidents," "leaders of the ruling party," "executors of the state of emergency," or "kings"). Contrary to Bienen and Van de Walle (1991), we did not exclude acting or provisional governments, on the assumption that one cannot distinguish between cases in which heads attempted to consolidate power and failed and cases in which heads did not try to do so. HEADS is coded as missing for Switzerland, Uruguay from 1951 to 1966, and Yugoslavia after 1980, cases of a collective executive with specific rules for rotation of the chief executive. For Portugal, the president was considered to be the chief executive between 1976 and 1982, and the prime minister between 1983 and 1990. [da Graça 1985; Bienen and Van de Walle 1991; Banks 1996]

INCUMB: Consolidation of incument advantage. Dummy variable coded 1 if (1) the regime year qualifies as a democratic regime *and* (2) at some time during their current tenure in office the incumbents (person, party, military hierarchy) unconstitutionally closed the lower house of the national legislature and rewrote the rules in their favor.

INEQ: Ratio of income shares of the top quintile to the bottom quintile of income recipients. [Deininger and Squire 1996]

INFMORT: Infant mortality rate per 1,000 live births. [World Bank 1994, series 379]

INST: Classification of political regimes in which democracies are distinguished by the type of executive: coded 0 if dictatorship; 1 if parliamentary democracy; 2 if mixed democracy; 3 if presidential democracy. A transition year is coded as the regime that emerges in that year.

INST2: Identical to INST except for the cases that resulted in a transition from above (by the incumbent). In those cases the incumbent rule (INCUMB) for classification of democracies and dictatorships was not applied, and the regime was classified as parliamentary, mixed, or presidential. [Carlson 1998]

INV: Real gross domestic investment (private and public) as a percentage of GDP (both in 1985 international prices). [PWT 5.6]

INVLAG: INV lagged one year.

KS: Capital stock per capita. Capital-stock data come from PWT 5.6 for 1,578 observations in 62 countries. The remaining cases are generated according to the following procedure: (1) Regress (in logs) output on capital stock and labor force for the observations for which data are available, using a fixed-effects model. (2) Regress the country-specific fixed effects on initial LEVEL and regional dummy variables, and fill for the remaining 73 countries. (3) Use the estimated coefficients from (1) and the predicted fixed effects from (2) to fill both for the missing years in countries for which some data are available and for all years in countries for which they are not. Retain the original observations whenever available, and fill with the estimates when they are not.

KSG: Growth of KS.

LAGREG: Lagged REG. In this case, transition years are coded as the regime that dies. For instance, there was a transition from democracy to dictatorship in Argentina in 1955. In that year, LAGREG = 0.

LEGELEC: Number of elections held for the national lower chamber in a given year. [Mostly taken from Banks 1996, complemented by *Keesing's Contemporary Archives*]

LEGSELEC: Legislative selection: coded 0 if no legislature exists (includes cases in which there is a constituent assembly without ordinary legislative powers); 1 if there is a non-elected legislature (examples include the selection of legislators by the effective executive, or on the basis of heredity or ascription); 2 if there is an elected legislature (legislators, or members of the lower house in a bicameral system, are selected by means of either direct or indirect popular election). [Banks 1996, but modified and completed where appropriate]

LEVEL: Real GDP per capita, 1985 international prices, chain index. [PWT 5.6]

LEVLAG: LEVEL lagged one year.

LEVSQR: LEVEL squared.

LF: Labor force, derived from PWT 5.6.

LFAGRIC: Labor in agriculture (% of total labor force). [World Bank 1994, series 309]

LFG: Labor-force growth; annual rate of growth of LF.

LFGLAG: LFG lagged one year.

LFLAG: LF lagged one year.

LFPW: Labor force, female (% of total). [World Bank 1994, series 308]

LIVES: Life expectancy at birth, total (in years). [World Bank 1994, series 387]

LS: Labor share of value added in manufacturing. [World Bank 1994, series UM VAD WAGE ZS]

MA2GL: Two-year moving average of G, lagged one year.

MA3GL: Three-year moving average of G, lagged one year.

MAJORITY: Dummy variable coded 1 for the cases in which the largest legislative party controls more than one-half of seats (SEATS > 50), and coded 0 otherwise.

MINORITY: Dummy variable coded 1 for the cases in which the largest legislative party controls up to one-half of seats (SEATS ≤ 50), and coded 0 otherwise.

MOBILIZATION: Sum of STRIKES, DEMONSTRATIONS, and RIOTS.

MOBILIZE: Classification of political regimes in which dictatorships are distinguished by the presence of political parties: coded 0 if democracy; 1 if mobilizing dictatorship (with parties); 2 if exclusionary dictatorship (without parties). A transition year is coded as the regime that emerges in that year.

MOSLEM: Percentage of Moslems in the population. [LPS 1993/94]

NEWC: Dummy variable coded 1 for every year in countries that became independent after 1945, and coded 0 otherwise.

ODRP: Other democracies in the regions, percentage. Percentage of democratic regimes (as defined by REG) in the current year (other than the regime under consideration) in the REGION to which the country belongs. For example, in 1980 Kenya had an authoritarian regime. The number of democracies in the region equaled 4, and the total number of regimes in the region equaled 44. ODRP for Kenya 1980 then equaled 4/44. In turn, Austria had a democratic regime in 1980. The number of other democracies in the region was 24, and the total number of regimes in the region was 25. ODRP for Austria in 1980 then equaled 24/25.

ODWP: Other democracies in the world, percentage. Percentage of democratic regimes (as defined by REG) in the current year (other than the regime under consideration) in the world. Constructed in the same way as ODRP.

OIL: Dummy variable coded 1 if the average ratio of fuel exports to total exports in 1984–1986 exceeded 50%, and coded 0 otherwise. [IMF 1994]

OPENC: Exports and imports as a share of GDP (both in 1985 international dollars). [PWT 5.6]

OVER65: Proportion of people over 65 years of age. [World Bank 1994, series 356–8, 364–9]

PAD: Probability that a dictatorship will not survive in the current year, given STTR, ODRP, RELDIF, MOSLEM, NEWC, and a dummy variable for OECD countries.

PARTY: Number of political parties in a given year: coded 0 if no parties (political parties were banned, or elections were held on a non-partisan basis, or incumbents used their electoral victory to establish non-party rule by banning all parties, or the current term in office ended up in a later year in the establishment of non-party rule); 1 if one party (the share of seats in the lower house of the national legislature held by the largest party was 100%, or there was only one party list presented to voters, or incumbents used the electoral victory to establish one-party rule by banning all opposition parties or forcing them to merge with the ruling party, or the current term in office ended up in a later year in the establishment of one-party rule); 2 if more than one party. [Banks 1996, but modified and completed where appropriate]

PDA: Probability that a democracy will not survive in the current year, given STTR, ODRP, RELDIF, MOSLEM, NEWC, and a dummy variable for OECD countries.

PINV: Price level of investment. [PWT 5.6]

POP: Population, in thousands. [PWT 5.6]

POPG: Annual rate of growth of population. [PWT 5.6]

PPPQUAL: Data quality (ranging from 0 = worst to 10 = best) of Penn World Tables, version 5.5, by country. [Appendix A:2 in Summers and Heston 1991]

PRESELEC: Number of presidential elections held in a given year. [Mostly taken from Banks 1996, complemented by *Keesing's Contemporary Archives*]

PRIME: US prime rate. [IMF 1994]

PROT: Percentage of Protestants in the populaton. [LPS 1993/94]

RECOVERY: Dummy variable coded 1 for the first five years after the end of a war (WAR).

REG: Dummy variable coded 1 for dictatorships and 0 for democracies.

A transition year is coded as the regime that emerges in that year. For instance, there was a transition from democracy to dictatorship in Argentina in 1955. In that year, REG = 1.

REGION: Region of the world, coded 1 if Latin America and Caribbean; 2 if Middle East; 3 if Eastern Europe; 4 if Africa; 5 if South Asia; 6 if East Asia; 7 if OECD. [World Bank 1994]

REGION2: Region of the world, coded 1 if sub-Saharan Africa; 2 if South Asia; 3 if East Asia; 4 if Southeast Asia; 5 if Pacific islands/Oceania; 6 if Middle East/North Africa; 7 if Latin America; 8 if Caribbean and non-Iberic America; 9 if Eastern Europe/Soviet Union; 10 if industrial countries.

RELDIF: Index of religious fractionalization, based on CATH, PROT, MOSLEM, and other religions.

RIOTS: Number of violent demonstrations or clashes of more than 100 citizens involving the use of physical force. [Banks 1996]

RSPELL: Number of successive spells of political regimes as classified by REG. A spell is defined as years of continuous rule under the same regime.

SEATS: Percentage of seats in the lower house of the national legislature that are held by the largest political party or party list. [Based on Banks 1996, but modified and completed where appropriate]

SIZE: POP * LEVEL of each country.

STRA: The sum of past transitions to authoritarianism (as defined by REG) in a country. If a country experienced one or more transitions to authoritarianism before 1950, STRA was coded 1 in 1950.

STRAL: STRA lagged one year.

STRD: The sum of past transitions to democracy (as defined by REG) in a country. If a country experienced one or more transitions to democracy before 1950, STRD was coded 1 in 1950.

STRIKES: Number of strikes of 1,000 or more industrial or service workers that involved more than one employer and were aimed at national-government policies or authority. [Banks 1996]

STTR: Sum of STRA and STRD.

T: Cumulative years of life of a regime from the first observation.

TINC: Regime transitions (including transitions by incumbents), as coded by INST2: coded 0 for years in which there was no transition; 1 for years in which TTI = 1; and 2 for years in which there was a regime transition led by the current incumbent. TINC includes all the transitions in TTI (except transitions from one type of democracy to another, two of them in Brazil and one in France), although five cases in which TTI = 1 were recoded as TTI = 2.

TLAG: TURNOVER lagged one year.

TTI: Dummy variable coded 1 if a regime transition (as classified by INST) occurred at any time during the current year, and the regime at the end of the year was different from the regime at the beginning of the year, and coded 0 otherwise.

TTR: Dummy variable coded 1 if a regime transition (as classified by REG) occurred at any time during the current year and the regime at the end of the year was different from the regime at the beginning of the year, and coded 0 otherwise.

TTRLAG: TTR lagged one year.

TTRLEAD: TTR led one year.

TURNOVER: Rate of turnover of chief executives per year of life of a regime. Defined as ACCHEAD/T, where T is the cumulative years of life of the regime from the first observation.

TYPEII: Dummy variable coded 1 if the "alternation" rule for classifying regimes as democracies or dictatorships applies, and coded 0 otherwise.

UNDER15: Proportion of people under 15 years of age. [World Bank 1994, series 356–8, 364–9]

UNREST: The same as MOBILIZATION.

UNSTABLE: Dummy variable coded 1 for all the years in a country that experienced at least one regime transition (as defined by REG) between 1950 and 1990.

WAGE: Annual wage rate, defined as GDPW $*$ LS.

WAR: Dummy variable coded 1 when there was a war of any type (international or civil) on the territory of a country, and coded 0 otherwise. [Singer and Small 1994]

WORLD: Average annual rate of growth of LEVEL for all the countries in the world, weighted by SIZE.

XR: Exchange rate (national currency relative to the U.S. dollar). [PWT 5.6]

YEAR: Calendar year.

YG: Annual rate of growth of real GDP (LEVEL), defined as G + POPG.

YGLAG: YG lagged one year.

References

Achen, Christopher H. 1986. *The Statistical Analysis of Quasi-Experiments*. Berkeley: University of California Press.

Ahmad, Zakaria Haji. 1988. Malaysia: Quasi Democracy in a Divided Society. In *Democracy in Developing Countries: Asia*, edited by L. Diamond, J. J. Linz, and S. M. Lipset, pp. 347–83. Boulder, CO: Lynne Rienner Publishers.

Ake, Claude. 1967. *A Theory of Political Integration*. Homewood, IL: Dorsey Press.

Alesina, Alberto. 1995. Elections, Party Structure, and the Economy. In *Modern Political Economy*, edited by J. S. Banks and E. A. Hanushek, pp. 145–70. Cambridge University Press.

Alesina, Alberto, Sule Özler, Nouriel Roubini, and Phillip Swagel. 1996. Political Instability and Economic Growth. *Journal of Economic Growth* 1(June):189–211.

Alesina, Alberto, and Roberto Perotti. 1996. Income Distribution, Political Instability, and Investment. *European Economic Review* 40:1203–28.

1997. The Politics of Growth: A Survey. In *Government and Growth*, edited by V. Bergström, pp. 11–60. Oxford University Press.

Almond, Gabriel A., and Sidney Verba. 1963. *The Civic Culture: Political Attitudes and Democracy in Five Nations*. Princeton, NJ: Princeton University Press.

Alvarez, Michael. 1997. Presidentialism and Parliamentarism: Which Works? Which Lasts? Ph.D. dissertation, Department of Political Science, University of Chicago.

Amemiya, Takeshi. 1984. Tobit Models: A Survey. *Journal of Econometrics* 24:3–61.

1985. *Advanced Econometrics*. Cambridge, MA: Harvard University Press.

Arat, Zehra F. 1988. Democracy and Economic Development: Modernization Theory Revisited. *Comparative Politics* 21(1):21–36.

Arndt, Heinz Wolfgang. 1987. *Economic Development: The History of an Idea*. University of Chicago Press.

Atkinson, A. B. 1970. On the Measurement of Economic Inequality. *Journal of Economic Theory* 2:244–63.

Banks, Arthur S. 1996. *Cross-National Time-Series Data Archive* (magnetic tape). Binghamton, NY: Center for Social Analysis, State University of New York at Binghamton.

Banks, Arthur S., Alan J. Day, and Thomas C. Muller (eds.). 1997. *Political Handbook of the World, 1997*. Binghamton, NY: CSA Publications.

Barro, Robert J. 1989. Economic Growth in a Cross Section of Countries. In *NBER Working Paper no. 3120*. Cambridge, MA: National Bureau of Economic Research.

1990. Government Spending in a Simple Model of Economic Growth. *Journal of Political Economy* 98(5):103–25.

1997. *Determinants of Economic Growth*. Cambridge, MA: MIT Press.

Barro, Robert J., and Xavier Sala-i-Martin. 1995. *Economic Growth*. New York: McGraw-Hill.

Becker, Gary S., and Gregg H. Lewis. 1973. On the Interaction between the Quantity and Quality of Children. *Journal of Political Economy* 81:279–88.

Becker, Gary S., Kevin M. Murphy, and Robert Tamura. 1990. Human Capital, Fertility, and Economic Growth. *Journal of Political Economy* 98(5):12–37.

Benhabib, Jess, and Andres Velasco. 1996. On the Optimal and Best Sustainable Taxes in an Open Economy. *European Economic Review* 40(1):134–54.

Bhalla, Surjit S. 1994. Freedom and Economic Growth: A Virtuous Cycle? Paper presented at the Nobel Symposium Democracy's Victory and Crisis. Uppsala University, August 27–30.

Bienen, Henry, and Nicolas Van de Walle. 1991. *Of Time and Power: Leadership Duration in the Modern World*. Stanford, CA: Stanford University Press.

Bobbio, Norberto. 1989. *Democracy and Dictatorship*. Minneapolis: University of Minnesota Press.

Bollen, Kenneth A. 1980. Issues in the Comparative Measurement of Political Democracy. *American Sociological Review* 45:370–90.

1993. Liberal Democracy: Validity and Method Factors in Cross-National Measures. *American Journal of Political Science* 37:1207–30.

Bollen, Kenneth A., and Robert W. Jackman. 1989. Democracy, Stability, and Dichotomies. *American Sociological Review* 54:438–57.

Burkhart, Ross E., and Michael S. Lewis-Beck. 1994. Comparative Democracy: The Economic Development Thesis. *American Political Science Review* 88(4):903–10.

Burns, J. H. 1969. J. S. Mill and Democracy, 1829–61. In *Mill*, edited by J. B. Schneewind. London: Macmillan.

Cardoso, Fernando Henrique. 1979. On the Characterization of Authoritarian Regimes in Latin America. In *The New Authoritarianism in Latin America*, edited by David Collier, pp. 33–60. Princeton, NJ: Princeton University Press.

Carey, John M. 1997. Institutional Design and Party Systems. In *Consolidating the Third Wave Democracies: Themes and Perspectives*, edited by L. Diamond, M. F. Platter, Y.-H. Chu, and H.-M. Tien, pp. 67–92. Baltimore: Johns Hopkins University Press.

Carlson, Rolf Eric. 1998. Presidentialism in Africa: Explaining Institutional Choice. Ph.D. dissertation, Department of Political Science, University of Chicago.

Cassen, Robert. 1994. Overview: Population and Development: Old Debates and New Conclusions. In *Population and Development: Old Debates, New Conclusions*, edited by R. A. C. Cassen, pp. 1–28. Washington, DC: Overseas Development Council.

Cheibub, José Antonio. 1998. Political Regimes and the Extractive Capacity of Governments: Taxation in Democracies and Dictatorships. *World Politics* 50(3): 349–76.

Cheibub, José Antonio, and Adam Przeworski. 1997. Government Spending and Economic Growth under Democracy and Dictatorship. In *Understanding Democracy: Economic and Political Perspectives*, edited by A. Breton, G. Galeotti, P. Salmon, and R. Wintrobe, pp. 107–24. Cambridge University Press.

Clague, Christopher, Philip Keefer, Stephen Knack, and Mancur Olson. 1997. Institutions and Economic Performance: Property Rights and Contract Enforcement. In *Institutions and Economic Development: Growth and Governance in Less-*

Developed and Post-Socialist Countries, edited by C. Clague, pp. 67–90. Baltimore: Johns Hopkins University Press.

Coale, Ansley J., and Edgard M. Hoover. 1958. *Population Growth and Economic Development in Low Income Countries: A Case Study of India's Prospects.* Princeton, NJ: Princeton University Press.

Collier, Paul, and Jan Willem Gunning. 1999. Explaining African Economic Performance. *Journal of Economic Literature* 37(1):64–111.

Collini, Stefan, Donald Winch, and John Burrow. 1983. *That Noble Science of Politics.* Cambridge University Press.

Coppedge, Michael. 1992. (De)institutionalization of Latin American Party Systems. Paper read at the XVII International Congress of the Latin American Studies Association, 24–27 September, 1992, Los Angeles.

Coppedge, Michael, and Wolfgang H. Reinicke. 1990. Measuring Polyarchy. *Studies in Comparative International Development* 25:51–72.

Cosslett, Stephen R. 1991. Semiparametric Estimation of a Regression Model with Sampling Selectivity. In *Nonparametric and Semiparametric Methods in Econometrics and Statistics*, edited by W. A. Barnett, J. Powell, and G. Tauchen, pp. 175–98. Cambridge University Press.

Coulon, Christian. 1988. Senegal: The Development and Fragility of Semidemocracy. In *Democracy in Developing Countries: Africa*, edited by L. Diamond, J. J. Linz, and S. M. Lipset, pp. 141–78. Boulder, CO: Lynne Rienner Publishers.

da Graça, John V. 1985. *Heads of State and Government.* New York University Press.

Cramer, J. S. 1986. *Econometric Applications of Maximum Likelihood Methods.* Cambridge University Press.

Crook, Nigel. 1997. *Principles of Population and Development.* Oxford University Press.

Cukierman, Alex, Sebastian Edwards, and Guido Tabellini. 1992. Seigniorage and Political Instability. *American Economic Review* 82(3):537–55.

Dahl, Robert A. 1971. *Polyarchy.* New Haven, CT: Yale University Press.

1990. Transitions to Democracy. Paper read at the symposium Voices of Democracy, March 16–17, University of Dayton Center for International Studies.

Dasgupta, Partha. 1993. *An Inquiry into Well-being and Destitution.* Oxford University Press.

1995. The Population Problem: Theory and Evidence. *Journal of Economic Literature* 33(December):1879–902.

Deininger, Klaus, and Lyn Squire. 1996. A New Data Set Measuring Income Inequality. *World Bank Economic Review* 10(3):565–91.

de Schweinitz, Karl, Jr. 1959. Industrialization, Labor Controls, and Democracy. *Economic Development and Cultural Change* 7(4):385–404.

Diamond, Larry. 1992. Economic Development and Democracy Reconsidered. In *Reexamining Democracy: Essays in Honor of Seymour Martin Lipset*, edited by G. Marks and L. Diamond, pp. 93–139. Newbury Park, CA: Sage Publications.

Diamond, Larry, and Juan J. Linz. 1989. Introduction: Politics, Society, and Democracy in Latin America. In *Democracy in Developing Countries: Latin America*, edited by L. Diamond, J. J. Linz, and S. M. Lipset, pp. 1–58. Bouder, CO: Lynne Rienner Publishers.

Drèze, Jean. 1992. From the "Value of Life" to the Economics and Ethics of Population: The Path Is Purely Methodological. *Recherches Economiques de Louvain* 58.

Drèze, Jean, and Amartya Sen. 1989. *Hunger and Public Action.* Oxford University Press.

Easterlin, Richard A. 1998. *Growth Triumphant: The Twenty-First Century in Historical Perspective*. Ann Arbor: University of Michigan Press.

Easterly, William, Michael Kremer, Lant Pritchett, and Lawrence H. Summers. 1993. Good Policy or Good Luck? Country Growth Performance and Temporary Shocks. *Journal of Monetary Economics* 32(3):459–83.

Easterly, William, and Ross Levine. 1997. Africa's Growth Tragedy: Policies and Ethnic Divisions. *Quarterly Journal of Economics* 112(November):1203–50.

Eisenstadt, S. N. 1968. The Protestant Ethic Theses in the Framework of Sociological Theory and Weber's Work. In *The Protestant Ethic and Modernization: A Comparative View*, edited by S. N. Eisenstadt, pp. 3–45. New York: Basic Books.

Fearon, James D. 1991. Counterfactuals and Hypothesis Testing in Political Science. *World Politics* 43:169–95.

Feierabend, Ivo K., and Rosalind L. Feierabend. 1966. Aggressive Behaviors Within Polities, 1948–1962: A Cross-National Study. *Journal of Conflict Resolution* 10(September):249–71.

Figueiredo, Argelina Cheibub, and Fernando Limongi. 2000. Presidential Power, Legislative Organization, and Party Behavior in Brazil. *Comparative Politics* 32(2):151–70.

Findlay, Ronald. 1990. The New Political Economy: Its Explanatory Power for LDCs. *Economics and Politics* 2(2):193–221.

Frank, Robert H. 1997. The Frame of Reference as a Public Good. *The Economic Journal* 107(November):1832–47.

Freedom House. 1992. *Freedom in the World: Political Rights and Civil Liberties*. New York: Freedom House.

Galenson, Walter. 1959. *Labor and Economic Development*. New York: Wiley.

Galor, Oded, and David N. Weil. 1996. The Gender Gap, Fertility, and Growth. *American Economic Review* 86:374–87.

Gambetta, Diego. 1987. *Were They Pushed or Did They Jump?* Cambridge University Press.

Gastil, Raymond D. 1980. *Freedom in the World: Political Rights and Civil Liberties*. New York: Freedom House.

——— 1990. *Freedom in the World: Political Rights and Civil Liberties*. New York: Freedom House.

Gellner, Ernest. 1991. Civil Society in Historical Context. *International Social Science Journal* 129:495–510.

Goldberger, Arthur. 1983. Abnormal Selection Bias. In *Studies in Econometrics, Time Series, and Multivariate Statistics*, edited by S. Karlin, T. Amemiya, and L. Goodman, pp. 67–84. Stamford, CT: Academic Press.

Goodman, Nelson. 1979. *Fact, Fiction, and Forecast*. Cambridge, MA: Harvard University Press.

Greene, William H. 1990. *Econometric Analysis*. New York: Macmillan.

Gurr, Ted Robert. 1990. *Polity II: Political Structures and Regime Change, 1800–1986*. Ann Arbor, MI: Inter-University Consortium for Political and Social Research.

Han, Sung-Joo. 1988. South Korea: Politics in Transition. In *Democracy in Developing Countries: Asia*, edited by L. Diamond, J. J. Linz, and S. M. Lipset, pp. 267–304. Boulder, CO: Lynne Rienner Publishers.

Hausman, Daniel M. n.d. Causation and Counterfactual Dependence Reconsidered. Unpublished paper, University of Wisconsin, Madison.

Heckman, James J. 1976. The Common Structure of Statistical Models of Truncation, Sample Selection, and Limited Dependent Variables and a Simple

Estimator for Such Models. *Annals of Economic and Social Measurement* 5:475–92.

1978. Dummy Endogenous Variables in a Simultaneous Equation System. *Econometrica* 46:931–59.

1979. Sample Selection Bias as a Specification Error. *Econometrica* 47:153–61.

1988. The Microeconomic Evaluation of Social Programs and Economic Institutions. In *Chung-Hua Series of Lectures by Invited Eminent Economists, no. 14.* Taipei: The Institute of Economics, Academia Sinica.

1990. Selection Bias and Self-selection. In *The New Palgrave: Econometrics*, edited by J. Eatwell, M. Milgate, and P. Newman, pp. 201–24. New York: Norton.

Helliwell, John. 1994. Empirical Linkages Between Democracy and Economic Growth. *British Journal of Political Science* 24(December):225–48.

Heston, Alan, and Robert Summers. 1993. Penn World Tables 5.6. Available on diskette from the National Bureau of Economic Research, Cambridge, MA.

Hirschman, Albert O. 1981. The Social and Political Matrix of Inflation: Elaborations on the Latin American Experience. In *Essays in Trespassing: Economics to Politics and Beyond*, edited by Albert O. Hirschman, pp. 177–207. Cambridge University Press.

Holm, John D. 1988. Botswana: A Paternalistic Democracy. In *Democracy in Developing Countries: Africa*, edited by L. Diamond, J. J. Linz, and S. M. Lipset, pp. 179–216. Boulder, CO: Lynne Rienner Publishers.

Huber, Evelyne, Dietrich Rueschemeyer, and John D. Stephens. 1993. The Impact of Economic Development on Democracy. *Journal of Economic Perspectives* 7(3):71–86.

Huntington, Samuel P. 1968. *Political Order in Changing Societies*. New Haven, CT: Yale University Press.

1991. *The Third Wave: Democratization in the Late Twentieth Century*. Norman: University of Oklahoma Press.

1993. The Clash of Civilizations? *Foreign Affairs* 72(3):22–49.

Huntington, Samuel P., and Jorge I. Dominguez. 1975. Political Development. In *Macropolitical Theory*, edited by F. I. Greenstein and N. W. Polsby, pp. 1–114. Reading, MA: Addison-Wesley.

Huntington, Samuel P., and Joan M. Nelson. 1976. *No Easy Choice: Political Participation in Developing Countries*. Cambridge, MA: Harvard University Press.

Hurwitz, Leon. 1973. Contemporary Approaches to Political Stability. *Comparative Politics* 5(3):449–63.

IMF. 1994. *International Financial Statistics*. Washington, DC: International Monetary Fund.

Inkeles, Alex. 1990. Introduction. *Studies in Comparative International Development* 25:1–16.

Islam, Nazrul. 1995. Growth Empirics: A Panel Data Approach. *Quarterly Journal of Economics* 110(4):1127–70.

Jackman, Robert W. 1973. On the Relation of Economic Development to Democratic Performance. *American Journal of Political Science* 17:611–21.

1974. Political Democracy and Social Equality: A Comparative Analysis. *American Sociological Review* 39:29–45.

Jackson, Karl D. 1988. The Philippines: The Search for a Suitable Democratic Solution, 1946–1986. In *Democracy in Developing Countries: Asia*, edited by L. Diamond, J. J. Linz, and S. M. Lipset, pp. 231–68. Boulder, CO: Lynne Rienner Publishers.

Johnson, Norman Lloyd, and Samuel Kotz. 1970. *Distribution in Statistics: Continuous Univariate Distributions*, 2 vols. Boston: Houghton Mifflin.

Jones, Mark P. 1995a. *Electoral Laws and the Survival of Presidential Democracies.* Notre Dame, IN: Notre Dame University Press.

1995b. A Guide to the Electoral Systems of the Americas. *Electoral Studies* 14(1):5–21.

Kaldor, Nicolas. 1956. Alternative Theories of Distribution. *Review of Economic Studies* 23:83–100.

Kamiński, Marek. 1997. Jak komuniści mogli zachować wโadzę w 1989 roku. Rzecz o (nie)kontrolowalnej odwilży, sondażach opinii publicznej i ordynacji wyborczej. *Studia Socjologiczne* 2:5–35.

Kavka, Gregory S. 1986. *Hobbesian Moral and Political Theory.* Princeton, NJ: Princeton University Press.

Keesing's Contemporary Archives. Several years. London: Keesing's Limited.

Kelsen, Hans. 1945. *General Theory of Law and State.* Cambridge, MA: Harvard University Press.

King, Gary. 1989. *Unifying Political Methodology: The Likelihood Theory of Statistical Inference.* Cambridge University Press.

Kobrin, Stephen J. 1980. Foreign Enterprise and Forced Divestment in LDCs. *International Organization* 34(1):65–88.

La Palombara, Joseph. 1963. *Bureaucracy and Political Development.* Princeton, NJ: Princeton University Press.

Leamer, Edward E. 1983. Let's Take the Con Out of Econometrics. *American Economic Review* 73(1):31–43.

1985. Sensitivity Analyses Would Help. *American Economic Review* 75(3):308–13.

Lee, L. F. 1978. Unionism and Wage Rates: A Simultaneous Equations Model With Qualitative and Limited Dependent Variables. *International Economic Review* 19:415–33.

1982. Some Approaches to the Correction of Selectivity Bias. *Review of Economic Studies* 49:355–72.

1983. Generalized Econometric Models with Selectivity. *Econometrica* 51:507–12.

Levine, Ross, and David Renelt. 1992. A Sensitivity Analysis of Cross-Country Growth Regressions. *American Economic Review* 82(4):942–63.

Lewis, Bernard. 1993. Islam and Liberal Democracy. *Atlantic Monthly* 271(2):89–98.

Lewis, David. 1973. Conterfactuals and Comparative Possibility. *Journal of Philosophical Logic* 2:418–46.

Lijphart, Arend (ed.). 1992. *Parliamentary versus Presidential Government.* Oxford University Press.

Linz, Juan J. 1975. Totalitarian and Authoritarian Regimes. In *Handbook of Political Science: Macropolitical Theory*, edited by F. I. Greenstein and N. W. Polsby, pp. 175–373. Reading, MA: Addison-Wesley.

1984. Democracy: Presidential or Parliamentary. Does It Make a Difference? Manuscript, Department of Political Science, Yale University.

1990a. The Perils of Presidentialism. *Journal of Democracy* 1(1):51–69.

1990b. The Virtues of Parliamentarism. *Journal of Democracy* 1(4):84–91.

Lipset, Seymour Martin. 1959. Some Social Requisites of Democracy: Economic Development and Political Legitimacy. *American Political Science Review* 53(1):69–105.

1960. *Political Man: The Social Bases of Politics.* Garden City, NY: Double day.

1981. *Political Man: The Social Bases of Politics*, expanded edition. Baltimore: Johns Hopkins University Press.

References

Livi-Baci, Massimo. 1997. *A Concise History of World Population*, 2nd ed. Oxford: Blackwell.

Lloyd, Cynthia B. 1994. Investing in the Next Generation: The Implications of High Fertility at the Level of the Family. In *Population and Development: Old Debates, New Conclusions*, edited by R. A. C. Cassen, pp. 181–202. Washington, DC: Overseas Development Council.

Londregan, John B., and Keith T. Poole. 1990. Poverty, the Coup Trap, and the Seizure of Executive Power. *World Politics* 42:151–83.

——— 1992. The Seizure of Executive Power and Economic Growth: Some Additional Evidence. In *The Political Economy of Business Cycles and Growth*, edited by A. Cukierman, Z. Hercovitz, and L. Leiderman, pp. 51–79. Cambridge, MA: MIT Press.

LPS. *Leksykon Państw Swiata 1993/94*. Warszawa: Real Press.

Lucas, Robert E. 1988. On the Mechanics of Economic Development. *Journal of Monetary Economics* 22:3–42.

Macaulay, Thomas B. 1900. *Complete Writings*, vol. 17. Boston: Houghton Mifflin. (Originally published 1:42.)

McDonald, Ronald H., and J. Mark Ruhl. 1989. *Party Politics and Elections in Latin America*. Boulder, CO: Westview Press.

McGuire, Martin C., and Mancur Olson. 1996. The Economics of Autocracy and Majority Rule. *Journal of Economic Literature* 34:72–97.

Macpherson, C. B. 1966. *The Real World of Democracy*. Oxford: Clarendon Press.

Maddala, G. S. 1983. *Limited-Dependent and Qualitative Variables in Econometrics*. Cambridge University Press.

Maddison, Angus. 1995. *Monitoring the World Economy, 1820–1992*. Paris: Organization for Economic Co-operation and Development.

Mainwaring, Scott. 1993. Presidentialism, Multipartism, and Democracy: The Difficult Combination. *Comparative Political Studies* 26(2):198–228.

Mainwaring, Scott, and Matthew Soberg Shugart. 1997. Conclusion: Presidentialism and the Party System. In *Presidentialism and Democracy in Latin America*, edited by S. Mainwaring and M. S. Shugart, pp. 394–439. Cambridge University Press.

Mankiw, N. G., P. Romer, and D. Weil. 1992. A Contribution to the Empirics of Economic Growth. *Quarterly Journal of Economics* 107:407–38.

Manski, Charles F. 1995. *Identification Problems in the Social Sciences*. Cambridge, MA: Harvard University Press.

Marks, Gary, and Larry Diamond (eds.). 1992. *Reexamining Democracy: Essays in Honor of Seymour Martin Lipset*. Newbury Park, CA: Sage Publications.

Marx, Karl. 1934. *The Eighteenth Brumaire of Louis Bonaparte*. Moscow: Progress Publishers.

——— 1952. *The Class Struggle in France, 1848 to 1850*. Moscow: Progress Publishers.

——— 1971. *Writings on the Paris Commune*, edited by H. Draper. New York: International Publishers.

May, D. A., and D. M. Heer. 1968. Son Survivorship Motivation and Family Size in India: A Computer Simulation. *Population Studies* 22:199–210.

Merrick, Thomas W. 1994. Population Dynamics in Developing Countries. In *Population and Development: Old Debates, New Conclusions*, edited by R. A. C. Cassen, pp. 79–105. Washington, DC: Overseas Development Council.

Mill, John Stuart. 1991. *Representations on Representative Government*. Buffalo, NY: Prometheus. (Originally published 1861.)

Montesquieu. 1995. *The Spirit of the Laws*, translated by Thomas Nugent. New York: Hafner Press. (Originally published 1748.)

Moore, Barrington, Jr. 1966. *Social Origins of Dictatorship and Democracy: Lord and Peasant in the Making of the Modern World*. Boston: Beacon Press.

Mueller, Dennis C. 1989. *Public Choice II: A Revised Edition of Public Choice*. Cambridge University Press.

Mueller, John. 1992. Democracy and Ralph's Pretty Good Grocery: Elections, Equality, and the Minimal Human Being. *American Journal of Political Science* 36:983–1003.

Muller, Edward N. 1988. Democracy, Economic Development, and Income Inequality. *American Sociological Review* 53:50–68.

Mutis, Alvaro. 1996. *Adventures of Maqroll: Four Novellas*. New York: Horper-Collins.

North, Douglass. 1990. *Institutions, Institutional Change, and Economic Performance*. Cambridge University Press.

North, Douglass C., and Robert P. Thomas. 1973. *The Rise of the Western World: A New Economic History*. Cambridge University Press.

North, Douglass C., and Barry W. Weingast. 1989. The Evolution of Institutions Governing Public Choice in 17th Century England. *Journal of Economic History* 49:803–32.

O'Donnell, Guillermo. 1973. *Modernization and Bureaucratic-Authoritarianism: Studies in South American Politics*. Berkeley: Institute of International Studies, University of California.

1979. Postscript: 1979. In *Modernization and Bureaucratic-Authoritarianism: Studies in South American Politics*. Berkeley: Institute of International Studies, University of California.

O'Donnell, Guillermo, and Philippe C. Schmitter. 1986. *Transitions from Authoritarian Rule: Tentative Conclusions about Uncertain Democracies*. Baltimore: Johns Hopkins University Press.

Olson, Mancur, Jr. 1963. Rapid Growth as a Destabilizing Force. *Journal of Economic History* 23(December):529–52.

Olson, Mancur. 1982. *The Rise and Decline of Nations: Economic Growth, Stagflation, and Social Rigidities*. New Haven, CT: Yale University Press.

1991. Autocracy, Democracy, and Prosperity. In *Strategy and Choice*, edited by R. J. Zeckhauser, pp. 131–57. Cambridge, MA: MIT Press.

1993. Dictatorship, Democracy, and Development. *American Political Science Review* 87(3):567–76.

1997. The New Institutional Economics: The Collective Choice Approach to Economic Development. In *Institutions and Economic Development: Growth and Governance in Less-Developed and Post-Socialist Countries*, edited by C. Clague, pp. 37–64. Baltimore: Johns Hopkins University Press.

Ozbudun, Ergun. 1988. Turkey: Crises, Interruptions, and Reequilibration. In *Democracy in Developing Countries: Asia*, edited by L. Diamond, J. J. Linz, and S. M. Lipset, pp. 187–230. Boulder, CO: Lynne Rienner Publishers.

Parsons, Talcott. 1951. *The Social System*. Glencoe, IL: Free Press.

Pasinetti, Luigi. 1961. Rate of Profit and Income Distribution in Relation to the Rate of Economic Growth. *Review of Economic Studies* 29(October):267–79.

Pindyck, Robert S. 1991. Irreversibility, Uncertainty, and Investment. *Journal of Economic Literature* 29(3):1110–48.

Pritchett, Lant H. 1994. Desired Fertility and the Impact of Population Policies. *Population and Development Review* 20:1–55.

References

Przeworski, Adam. 1975. Institutionalization of Voting Patterns, or Is Mobilization the Source of Decay? *American Political Science Review* 69:49–67.

—— 1990. *The State and the Economy under Capitalism.* Chur, Switzerland: Harwood Academic Publishers.

—— 1991. *Democracy and the Market.* Cambridge University Press.

—— 1997. Błędy: Informacja a przejście do demokracji. *Studia Socjologiczne* 2:51–66.

Przeworski, Adam, José Antonio Cheibub, and Fernando Limongi. 1997. Culture and Democracy. In *World Culture Report*, pp. 157–87. Paris: UNESCO.

Przeworski, Adam, and Fernando Limongi. 1993. Political Regimes and Economic Growth. *Journal of Economic Perspectives* 7(3):51–70.

—— 1997. Development and Democracy. In *Democracy's Victory and Crisis*, edited by A. Hadenious. Cambridge University Press.

Przeworski, Adam, Bernard Manin, and Susan C. Stokes (eds.). 1999. *Democracy and Accountability.* Cambridge University Press.

Pudney, Stephen. 1989. *Modelling Individual Choice: The Econometrics of Corners, Kinks, and Holes.* Cambridge University Press.

Quah, Danny T. 1993. Galton's Fallacy and Tests of the Convergence Hypothesis. In *Endogenous Growth*, edited by T. M. Andersen and K. O. Moene, pp. 37–54. Oxford: Blackwell.

—— 1996. Twin Peaks: Growth and Convergence in Models of Distribution Dynamics. *The Economic Journal* 106:1045–55.

Ram, Rati. 1986. Government Size and Economic Growth: A New Framework and Some Evidence from Cross-Section and Time-Series Data. *American Economic Review* 76:191–203.

Rama, Martin. 1993. Empirical Investment Equations for Developing Countries. In *Striving for Growth after Adjustment: The Role of Capital Formation, Regional and Sectoral Studies*, edited by Luis Serven and Andres Solimano, pp. 107–43. Washington, DC: World Bank.

Rao, Vaman. 1984. Democracy and Economic Development. *Studies in Comparative International Development* 19(4):67–81.

Ray, Debraj. 1998. *Development Economics.* Princeton, NJ: Princeton University Press.

Razin, Assaf, and Efraim Sadka. 1995. *Population Economics.* Cambridge, MA: MIT Press.

Riker, William. 1965. *Democracy in America*, 2nd ed. New York: Macmillan.

Robinson, James. 1995. Theories of "Bad Policy". *Policy Reform* 1:1–17.

Rodrik, Dani. 1998. Democracies Pay Higher Wages. In *NBER Working Paper no. 6364.* Cambridge, MA: National Bureau of Economic Research.

Roemer, John E. 1982. *A General Theory of Exploitation and Class.* Cambridge, MA: Harvard University Press.

Root, F. R., and A. Ahmed. 1979. Empirical Determinants of Manufacturing Direct Investment in Developing Countries. *Economic Development and Cultural Change* 27(4):751–7.

Rose, Leo E. 1988. Pakistan: Experiments with Democracy. In *Democracy in Developing Countries: Asia*, edited by L. Diamond, J. J. Linz, and S. M. Lipset, pp. 105–42. Boulder, CO: Lynne Rienner Publishers.

Roy, A. D. 1951. Some Thoughts on the Distribution of Earnings. *Oxford Economic Papers* 3:135–46.

Russett, Bruce. 1964. Deaths from Domestic Group Violence per 1,000,000 Population, 1950–1962. In *World Handbook of Political and Social Indicators*, edited by B. E. A. Russett. New Haven, CT: Yale University Press.

Rustow, Dankwart A. 1970. Transitions to Democracy: Toward a Dynamic Model. *Comparative Politics* 2(3):337–64.

Sah, Raaj K., and Joseph Stiglitz. 1988. Committees, Hierarchies and Polyarchies. *The Economic Journal* 98(June):451–70.

Schmertmann, Carl P. 1994. Selectivity Bias Correction Models in Polychotomous Sample Selection Models. *Journal of Econometrics* 60:101–32.

Schmitter, Philippe C. 1991. The International Context for Contemporary Democratization: Constraints and Opportunities upon the Choice of National Institutions and Policies. In *East-South System Transformations*, working paper no. 8, University of Chicago.

Schneider, F., and B. S. Frey. 1985. Economic and Political Determinants of Foreign Direct Investment. *World Development* 13:161–75.

Schultz, T. W. (ed.). 1974. *Economics of the Family: Marriage, Children and Human Capital*. Chicago: National Bureau of Economic Research.

Schumpeter, Joseph A. 1942. *Capitalism, Socialism, and Democracy*. London: George Allen & Unwin.

Sen, Amartya. 1981. *Poverty and Famines: An Essay on Entitlement and Deprivation*. Oxford University Press.

1988. The Concept of Development. In *Handbook of Development Economics*, edited by T. N. Srinivasan. Amsterdam: Elsevier Science.

1993. The Economics of Life and Death. *Scientific American* May, 40–7.

1994a. Freedoms and Needs. *The New Republic*, January 10–7, 31–7.

1994b. Population: Delusion and Reality. *The New York Review of Books* 41(15):1–8.

1995. *Population Policy: Authoritarianism versus Cooperation, International Lecture Series on Population Issues*. New Delhi, India: The John D. and Catherine T. MacArthur Foundation.

Shugart, Matthew Soberg, and John M. Carey. 1992. *Presidents and Assemblies: Constitutional Design and Electoral Dynamics*. Cambridge University Press.

Singer, J. David, and Melvin Small. 1994. Correlates of War Project: International and Civil War Data, 1816–1992 [computer file]. Ann Arbor, MI: J. David Singer and Melvin Small [producers], 1993. Ann Arbor, MI: Interuniversity Consortium for Political and Social Research [distributor], 1994.

Starr, Harvey. 1991. Democratic Dominoes: Diffusion Approaches to the Spread of Democracy in International System. *Journal of Conflict Resolution* 35:356–81.

Stepan, Alfred, and Cindy Skach. 1993. Consitutional Frameworks and Democratic Consolidation: Parliamentarism Versus Presidentialism. *World Politics* 46(1):1–22.

Stolzenberg, Ross M., and Daniel A. Relles. 1990. Theory Testing in a World of Constrained Research Design. *Sociological Methods and Research* 18:395–415.

Summers, Robert, and Alan Heston. 1991. The Penn World Table (Mark 5): an Expanded Set of International Comparisons, 1950–1988. *Quarterly Journal of Economics* May:327–68.

Temple, Jonathan. 1999. The New Growth Evidence. *Journal of Economic Literature* 37(1):112–56.

Tetlock, Philip E., and Aaron Belkin. 1996. Counterfactual Thought Experiments in World Politics: Logical, Methodological, and Psychological Perspectives. In *Counterfactual Thought Experiments in World Politics: Logical, Methodological, and Psychological Perspectives*, edited by P. E. Tetlock and A. Belkin, pp. 1–38. Princeton, NJ: Princeton University Press.

References

Therborn, Goran. 1977. The Rule of Capital and the Rise of Democracy. *New Left Review* 103(May–June):3–41.

Vanhanen, Tatu. 1992. *The Process of Democratization.* New York: Crane, Russak.

Wantchekon, Leonard. 1996. Political Coordination and Democratic Instability. Unpublished manuscript, Yale University.

Weber, Max. 1958. *The Protestant Ethic and the Spirit of Capitalism.* New York: Scribner. (Originally published 1904.)

Weffort, Francisco. 1992. *Qual Democracia?* São Paulo: Companhia das Letras.

Whitehead, Laurence. 1991. The International Dimension of Democratization: A Survey of the Alternatives. Paper read at the XV congress of the International Political Science Association, Buenos Aires, Argentina.

World Bank. 1984. *World Development Report 1984.* Washington, DC: World Bank.

1991. *World Development Report 1991.* Washington, DC: World Bank.

1994. *World Data 1994. World Bank Indicators on CD-ROM.* Washington, DC: World Bank.

1995. *World Development Indicators 1995.* Washington, DC: World Bank. CD-ROM.

1997. *World Development Indicators 1997.* Washington, DC: World Bank. CD-ROM.

Zavoina, R., and W. McKelvey. 1975. A Statistical Model for the Analysis of Ordinal Level Dependent Variables. *Journal of Mathematical Sociology* 4(Summer): 103–20.

Zielinski, Jakub. 1997. The Polish Transition to Democracy: A Game-Theoretic Approach. *European Archives of Sociology* 36:135–58.

Zimmerman, Ekkart. 1987. Government Stability in Six European Countries During the World Economic Crisis of the 1930s: Some Preliminary Considerations. *European Journal of Political Research* 15:23–52.

1988. Economic and Political Reactions to the World Economic Crisis of the 1930s in Six European Countries. *International Studies Quarterly* 32:305–34.

Author Index

Country Index

Subject Index